The Creationist Debate

The Encounter between the Bible and the Historical Mind

Arthur McCalla

T&T CLARK INTERNATIONAL
A Continuum imprint
LONDON • NEW YORK

The Continuum International Publishing Group
The Tower Building, 11 York Road, London SE1 7NX
80 Maiden Lane, Suite 704, New York, NY 10038

www.continuumbooks.com

A catalogue record for this book is available from the British Library.

Typeset by CA Typesetting, www.sheffieldtypesetting.com
Printed on acid-free paper in Great Britain by MPG Books Ltd., Bodmin, Cornwall

ISBN 0-82646-447-5 (hardback)
      0-82648-002-0 (paperback)

To my students at the Religion Department at Reed College, 1999–2004

CONTENTS

Contents

ACKNOWLEDGEMENTS

It is perhaps appropriate that I should say something about the origin and development of a book that examines so many other accounts of origin and development. Its beginnings date from my determination as a newly hired Visiting Professor at Reed College, in Portland, Oregon, to develop a course that would allow me to read Giambattista Vico's *New Science* with my students. I came up with 'Deep Time and the Biblical Narrative', which placed Vico within a sequence of seventeenth- to twentieth-century encounters between biblical accounts of the history of the Earth and of humanity and various emerging historical sciences. The first edition of the course touched only lightly on the creationism controversy. Subsequent editions of the course steadily expanded the section on creationism in response to student interest. I am tremendously grateful to Reed College both for the opportunity to have taught in an academic environment in which students are fully engaged in the life of the mind, and for library and other institutional support, including Stillman-Drake research funding, which permitted, *inter alia*, a visit to the Museum of Science and Earth History in May 2002.

Janet Joyce, then Editorial Director of Continuum Publishing, warmly supported my idea of turning the course into a book aimed at an educated general readership. Although Janet left Continuum shortly thereafter in order to establish Equinox Publishing, this book would not exist without her encouragement and advice.

I, too, relocated during the preparation of the book, returning to Canada for a tenure-track position at Mount Saint Vincent University in Halifax, Nova Scotia. I am grateful to my new colleagues, and especially to Randi Warne, for their warm welcome, and to the MSVU library staff and to Sharon Baker for their assistance during the late stages of this project.

The production of the book has been ably overseen by Georgina Brindley, Joanna Taylor and Haaris Naqvi at Continuum Publishing's London Office. I am particularly indebted to my copy-editor, T. W. Bartel, for his careful reading, apposite suggestions and learned queries.

Special thanks to Annette Cantu, Deborah Strickland, Lisa McKenzie, Jalene Lumb, Brad Tucker, Wally Englert, Jackie Dirks, Tony Iaccarino, Mike Foat, Ken Brashier, Steve Wasserstrom, Kambiz Ghanea-Bassiri, Hugh Hochman, Ben David, Barbara Forrest, my parents, Dennis and Kathleen McCalla, and lastly – but only to prove that every ending is a new beginning – Áine Humble.

'Where are the baby dinosaurs we can pet?' When staff members at the Royal Tyrrell Museum in Drumheller, Alberta, are asked this question – and they often are – they patiently reply that dinosaurs have been extinct for 65 million years.[1] Some visitors refuse to accept this answer; they concede that dinosaurs may no longer be alive today but firmly believe – along with 52 per cent of Americans, according to a 2001 National Science Foundation survey – that dinosaurs and humans lived together on the Earth within the last few centuries.[2] Dinosaurs and humans do, in fact, live together on the outskirts of San Diego at the Museum of Creation and Earth History. Displays inform visitors that God created the dinosaurs along with all other life a few thousand years ago, that most dinosaur fossils are the remains of animals that perished in the Flood, that some dinosaurs (small ones!) were aboard Noah's Ark, and that dinosaurs became completely extinct (if they truly are extinct) only recently. These claims are backed up by proof-texts from chapters 40 and 41 of the book of Job testifying to the existence after the Flood of, respectively, terrestrial and marine dinosaurs.

The two museums are institutional embodiments of competing worldviews: the Royal Tyrrell is one of the leading palaeontological research institutions in the world; the Museum of Creation and Earth History is a showcase for the young-Earth creationist organization, the Institute for Creation Research. Their disagreement over whether dinosaurs co-existed with human beings is a sign of a foundational disagreement over the nature of intellectual, but also social and political, authority in the modern world. This book is about the origin and nature of the conflict between the competing worldviews represented by evolutionary science and creationism. Its thesis is that the critical issue is not the content of evolutionary science itself but rather historical-mindedness in relation to the status of the Bible. In order to make this argument we must go farther afield than the present-day controversy; this book, therefore, traces the successive emergence of various historical sciences (geology, chronology and civil history, biblical criticism, palaeontology, evolutionary biology, anthropology) and examines theological responses to these sciences, paying particular attention to their implications for the status of the Bible. A study of this scope must necessarily be a work of synthesis; this book is heavily – and gratefully – indebted to the work of many scholars (although they are, of course, in no way responsible for the use I have made of their insights).

The book begins with the sixteenth-century shift from symbolic to plain-sense readings of the Book of Scripture and the Book of Nature. The leading figures of the scientific revolution understood themselves to be discovering the blueprint for God's contingent yet providential order of creation. Natural theology, or the attempt to demonstrate the existence, wisdom and benevolence of the Creator by evidences of design and providence in nature, was closely allied with the seventeenth-century understanding of natural philosophy. In this context the earliest attempts to recognize nature as a realm of becoming and radical change raised problems for natural theology, but did not question the content or chronology of sacred history.

Two categories of knowledge, however, did threaten the Bible's status as a uniquely authoritative text. First, the massive expansion of knowledge about human cultures produced by humanist scholarship and voyages of exploration caused difficulties for the biblical account of the world. Second, the textual scholarship of biblical critics demonstrated that the Bible was a book with a human history. By the end of the seventeenth century the claims of biblical exceptionalism had been seriously undermined by evidence that the history of the world exceeds in length and scope the limits of sacred history and that the Bible is a book with a history.

The genre of universal history, which flourished in the seventeenth and eighteenth centuries, attempted to reconcile Gentile historical records with biblical chronology, either by identifying the various rival histories as derived from the biblical narrative itself or by denying them any historical truth. Universal histories occupy an intellectual space midway between the theological meta-narratives, which were once unquestioned, and the secular disciplines of archaeology, prehistory and anthropology, which had not yet been born.

The accumulating evidence in the eighteenth century from rock strata and extinct volcanoes pointed to a history in which the present Earth has come into being out of former worlds massively unlike it. The technique of stratigraphy, which integrated palaeontology with geology, provided the interpretive key that made geology into a historical science by transforming the record of the rocks into reliable historical evidence for radical change and immense duration. Nineteenth-century historical geology challenged the literal truth of the Mosaic creation narrative and cast doubt on the reality of design and providence.

The eighteenth-century concept of progressive revelation, which reinterpreted revelation from being a miraculous communication at a particular moment in time of absolute truth to the development over time of the religious consciousness of humanity as a whole, was the bridge from the earlier textual criticism of the Bible to the historical or higher criticism of the nineteenth century. The fundamental insight achieved by the higher criticism is that the biblical stories reflect the political and social realities of the time and place in which they were written, and that these referents as uncovered by scholars, rather than their surface content, are the true indicators of their date and authorship. The higher criticism set Western culture before a crossroads by separating knowledge about the Bible from the claims made by the Bible itself. But the emergence of a thoroughly secular approach to the Bible was delayed by biblical theology, which located the religious meaning of the Bible in the historical development of the religious consciousness of the biblical writers themselves.

In his *Origin of Species* Charles Darwin both provided evidence that new species come into being through the transmutation of existing species and offered the mechanism of natural selection to explain the operation of the evolutionary process. Because it is not the transmutation of species itself that opposed design and providence but Darwin's mechanism of natural selection, theologians and pious naturalists attempted to reconcile the transmutability of species with Christianity, or at least theism, by affirming that the operation of evolution is providentially guided. The result was a proliferation in the late nineteenth century of non-Darwinian models of evolution that replaced natural selection as the mechanism of evolution with an external guide or designer. Liberal-minded Christians found little difficulty in assimilating a theistic model of evolution into their faith. Few in the nineteenth century grasped that Darwin's radically historical model of evolution subverts any ideology of development or progress.

The naturalization of humanity within an organic evolutionary process posed two separate, though intertwined, problems for Western culture. First, it contradicted the biblical account of humanity, thereby calling into question the theological content of sacred history; second, it denied the traditional view that our mental and moral faculties derive from the soul, or a spiritual agency added to the physical body, and therefore seemed to deny our status as spiritual beings. Theological responses to the mounting evidence for human evolution followed one of three strategies: deny it and identify cavemen as degenerate descendants of Adam; isolate our soul and mind from our physical frame; or radically reinterpret the traditional doctrines.

By the first years of the twentieth century the cumulative effect of the various historical disciplines posed a formidable challenge to the status of the Bible by offering powerful alternatives to sacred history in understanding the world and humanity's place in it. The three possible responses – to reject anything that seemed to compromise the authority of the Bible, to attempt to reconcile science and scholarship with the Bible, or to abandon the Bible altogether as an authoritative source for knowledge about the world – correspond to reactionary biblicism, liberal Protestantism and secular modernism.

Reactionary biblicism had flourished in nineteenth-century America owing to a unique synthesis of evangelical Protestantism, political republicanism and common-sense moral philosophy. Biblical inerrancy, or the idea that the Bible contains no errors whatsoever, was defended by a group of Princeton theologians and was spread throughout the country by Bible and prophecy conferences. Reactionary biblicism crystallized into Fundamentalism early in the twentieth century as a reaction against the influence of the higher criticism on mainstream Protestant denominations. Fundamentalists foundationally held that to admit the Bible contains even the slightest error initiates a chain of questions that ultimately throws into question its testimony to the redemptive work of Christ. Fundamentalists soon linked the higher criticism to biological evolution, and began to organize campaigns to ban the teaching of evolution in public schools. The Scopes trial of 1925 marked the high point of this anti-evolutionary activity, and from the early 1930s Fundamentalists withdrew from mainstream denominations and secular institutions and set to work building a separate network of churches and schools characterized by an absolute commitment to the inerrancy of the Bible.

Early Fundamentalists attacked the higher criticism and evolution but were able to accept an ancient Earth because they interpreted the Genesis 'days' of creation in one or another figurative sense. A new phase in Fundamentalist opposition to evolution opened with the publication in 1961 of *The Genesis Flood*, the founding text of young-Earth creationism. Young-Earth creationists insist on a literal interpretation of the Genesis creation narrative, and therefore deny not only the higher criticism and evolution but also the immense age of the Earth established by geology.

Young-Earth creationists developed the concept of 'creation science' in order to argue that their creationism is something other than mere biblical testimony. Creation science purports to evaluate the physical evidence relating to creation without referring to the Bible or other religious authorities. It presents the 'evolution model' and the 'creation model' as alternative models of origins that can be compared as to their respective capacities for correlating scientific data. Creationist attempts to introduce creationism into public schools have been defeated because the courts have recognized that creation science is not, in fact, an attempt to explain the natural world but rather a defence of a particular interpretation of the Bible. The Intelligent Design movement has responded to these defeats by publicly avoiding overt references to the biblical framework of creation science in an attempt to elude constitutional objections to introducing creationism into public schools and other areas of public life. And yet, despite its apparently ecumenical definition of creationism, Intelligent Design is a strategy to bring people back to the Bible rather than a genuine attempt to advance scientific knowledge.

The creationism–evolution controversy is at bottom a conflict over the status of the Bible in the modern world. Its elucidation, therefore, may benefit from the contributions of scholars of religion as well as scientists and philosophers of science.

Chapter 1

The Two Books

The Museum of Creation and Earth History celebrates Francis Bacon and Isaac Newton as examples of the proper relationship between science and the Bible. In order to understand this relationship we must look the historical context of the seventeenth-century scientific revolution, and particularly the metaphor of the 'Two Books': the Book of Scripture and the Book of Nature.

The first millennium of Christianity knew only one Book. The Bible, as the Word of God, was the authoritative source of religious knowledge and indeed of all knowledge on the matters of which it spoke. And yet, Christians of these centuries viewed the literal sense of the Bible as merely the first of several layers of meanings. The deeper, spiritual senses of the text consisted of the allegorical, or spiritual truths we should believe; the tropological, or teaching on how we should act; and the anagogical, or the divine promises on which our hope rests. Allegory, tropology, anagogy, plus the literal sense constituted the *quadriga*, or fourfold method of interpretation. Applied to Jerusalem, for example, the literal meaning points to the historical city itself, the allegorical refers to the Church of Christ, the tropological to the human soul, and the anagogical to the heavenly New Jerusalem of Revelation. The interpretive principle implicit in the *quadriga* is that while all that Scripture narrates really did happen, Scripture is truly understood only when spiritual readings supplement its literal meaning. Closely related to the *quadriga* is the practice of typology. A typological interpretation identifies a person or an event from the Old Testament as pointing to one in the New Testament. For example, the crossing of the Red Sea prefigures Christ's baptism, while the drawing up to heaven of Elijah prefigures Christ's ascension. The *quadriga* and typology together allowed the Christian Church to claim that it alone truly understood the Old Testament. A merely literal interpretation, or a Jewish interpretation that refuses to see Jesus as its hidden content, remains at the level of the letter; only those with the experience of Christ can read its spiritual meanings.[1] Armed with the *quadriga* and typology, Christian interpreters transformed the Hebrew Bible into the Old Testament and subordinated historically specific elements of the Bible to eternal spiritual truths applicable to Christian readers of later centuries.

Christians of the patristic and early medieval periods did not have a Book of Nature because nature could not be read. That is, prior to the twelfth century the natural world was regarded as a catalogue of objects that possess no intrinsic meaning of their own and that are not discernibly related to each other in any systematic way. Investigating the natural world for its own sake would therefore be at best pointless and at worst idolatrous because its objects are meaningless in themselves.[2] The idea of a Book of Nature emerged in the twelfth and thirteenth centuries as nature came to be seen as a coherent entity whose objects are systematically related to each other as well as to transcendent spiritual truths. The theological argument of scholastic theologians such as Thomas Aquinas and Bonaventure that knowledge of nature provides rationally persuasive knowledge of the divine attributes independently of revelation contributed importantly to the new view of the natural world as a coherent entity. Now possessed of both intelligibility (internal coherence) and meaning (as symbols of spiritual truths), the natural world could be figured as readable; as, that is, a book. In this way the Book of Nature took its place as a locus of divine revelation alongside and as a supplement to the Book of Scripture. The study of the natural world – or exegesis of the Book of Nature – was no longer pointless or impious, but, as with exegesis of the Book of Scripture, both a means of religious knowledge and a pious act in itself.[3]

Renaissance symbolic exegesis

The concept of the Book of Nature, in which natural things are at once symbols and intelligible objects in their own right, blossomed in the Renaissance into an entire worldview. Renaissance philosophers, mages and poets such as Marsilio Ficino, Pico della Mirandola, Paracelsus, John Dee, Edmund Spenser and Sir Philip Sidney interpreted the biblical creation story to mean that God had created the cosmos by instantiating in corporeal substances ideas or forms pre-existing in the divine mind. These ideas in the divine mind served as archetypes for created things, which in turn mirror not only their archetype but also the divine mind itself since ideas in God's mind participate in the divine essence. The divine author having in this way stamped some fragment of his image on created things in the form of traces or signatures, natural objects are linked to other natural objects and to spiritual forces by means of correspondences (or similitudes or sympathies) among physical creation and the spiritual hierarchies. The doubleness of natural things – they are at once truly existing things in themselves and signs of a higher spiritual reality – calls for a symbolic exegesis: in order to understand fully a natural object one must grasp its place in the system of correspondences that underlies and unifies the divinely imprinted Book of Nature. Just as the *quadriga* and typology interpreted the Book of Scripture symbolically, so deciphering the Book of Nature also required a symbolic interpretation.[4]

Adam had been able to name the creatures in the Garden of Eden according to their true essences because the language spoken before the Fall mirrored the nature of things themselves. The possibility of recovering Adam's true knowledge of the Book of Nature therefore depended on the Adamic language having survived the Fall and the confusion of tongues at the Tower of Babel in some corrupted or veiled but still recoverable form. Renaissance natural philosophers thought that the Adamic language now existed only in the symbolic language of things, or the objects on which God had stamped traces of his essence. They sought to recover the Adamic knowledge by reading the Book of Nature by means of a symbolic exegesis of the double nature of natural things.[5]

Various Renaissance practices, notably Ficino's *magia* and Paracelsan medicine, are practical applications of symbolic exegesis of the Book of Nature. In Ficino's spiritual magic the operator reads nature by recognizing the correspondences that link things to each other and to entities at higher levels of the cosmos. He then manipulates these correspondences in order to ward off melancholy or execute some other beneficial end.[6] In the sixteenth century Paracelsus similarly exploited the hidden correspondences among things in his art of reading signs – the *ars signata* – which links fallen humanity with Adam in the Garden. Every natural object – that is, every page in the Book of Nature – carries a 'signature', or the divine imprint that marks its essential nature. Adam could give all creatures their proper names because as an adept of the *ars signata* he could see beneath the mere appearances of natural things and grasp their real natures. The art of reading signs, however, was not an immediate intuition or direct spiritual understanding; it was a technique for reading the true names of things from those signs that God had imprinted on each natural thing at creation, a technique that, given his unfallen nature as *imago dei*, Adam was able to use correctly. Paracelsus was confident that it remains possible for us, even after the Fall, to practise the *ars signata* because a divinely implanted light of nature (*lumen naturae*) enables us to overcome our corrupt state and correctly interpret the signs that God stamped on things. Paracelsian medicine is a particular application of the *ars signata* in which the sage identifies hidden correspondences between afflicted organs of the patient and the specific minerals, plants, animals and planets that correspond to them by reading the divine signatures of things. He then prescribes an appropriate remedy such as healing a kidney ailment by drinking a brew made from the kidney-shaped leaves of a plant whose signature marks it as being in occult sympathy with the kidney.[7]

Renaissance readers of the Book of Nature endeavoured to place a given plant or animal within the complex web of correspondences that God had established for it. This accounts for the striking difference between a Renaissance herbal or bestiary and a modern botany or zoology textbook. Taxonomic or morphological description (corresponding to the literal level of biblical interpretation) was only a minor aspect of the symbolic exegesis of a plant or animal. For example, Conrad Gesner's account of the peacock in his *History of Animals* (1551–58) includes, in addition to its appearance and habits, the network of correspondences linking it with stars, planets, minerals, plants and coins, the sympathies and affinities that link it with other birds and animals, the meaning of its name in various languages, its proverbial associations, and what it symbolizes to pagans and to Christians.[8] This same Renaissance conception of animals as symbols in the divine language of nature permitted Edward Topsell to justify his *Historie of Four-Footed Beastes* (1607) with the claim that a history of animals is superior to an account of human actions because it reveals that Chronicle which was made by God himselfe, every living beast being a word, every kind being a sentence, and al of them togither a large history, containing admirable knowledge & larning, which was, which is, and which shall continue, (if not for ever) yet to the worlds end.[9]

The turn to 'plain sense'

Symbolic exegesis of both the Book of Nature and the Book of Scripture was challenged and largely overthrown by a new approach to the interpretation of texts developed by humanists and Protestant Reformers. Humanist scholars, themselves part of the Renaissance, recovered and studied ancient texts in the hope of returning to the pristine origins of ancient learning and eloquence. Their criterion in seeking to establish accurate texts of classical writers was the intention of the original author. Through attention to changes in the meaning and usage of words over time and across cultures and through the patient collation and comparison of manuscripts, they laboured to disentangle the original words of Plato, Livy and others from textual corruptions and the opinions of generations of editors and commentators. Erasmus, the greatest of the humanist scholars, applied these philological techniques to the text of the Bible in the hope of recovering the pristine text that the Latin translation often distorted. Whether applied to the classical texts or to the Bible itself, humanist scholarship discouraged allegorical interpretation as likely to distort the intention of the original author.[10]

The Protestant Reformers followed the humanists in rejecting the allegorical interpretation of the one text that mattered to them – the Bible. From Martin Luther onwards the Reformers insisted that the Bible alone should be the source of Christian beliefs, morality and even social and political order. No other authority, such as that of Catholic tradition or the Pope, would be tolerated. For a thousand years the Catholic Church had fused the authority of the Bible with the authority of its own interpretative tradition by surrounding the text of the Old and New Testaments in the standard Bible of the medieval Church, the *Glossa Ordinaria*, with the notes and commentaries of the Church Fathers that guided how one was to understand the biblical texts. Luther printed Bibles in which the biblical text appeared alone, liberated from the interpretive framework laid over it by the Fathers.[11] By means of this revolutionary act the Protestant Reformers truly thought they were recovering the pristine text of the Bible after centuries of accretion and distortion. But more fundamental than the recovered text was the interpretive principle they applied to it. If the Bible alone was to be the sole authority for Christian belief and life, then every sentence in it must have a single, clear meaning intended by the apostles and prophets that is understandable to every reader without the aid of a special class of privileged interpreters. Consequently, the Reformers abandoned the *quadriga* with its multiple levels of meaning in favour of a single plain, literal reading of Scripture.[12]

We must not exaggerate the literal-mindedness of the Protestant Reformers. They rejected allegorical interpretation but retained typology, believing every bit as much as Catholics that the Old Testament points to Christ. Furthermore, the New Testament itself offers examples of non-literal interpretation: Jesus spoke in parables, the Gospels present Jesus as the fulfilment of Old Testament prophecies, and Paul himself interpreted the Old Testament figuratively, as in his allegorical reading of Sarah and Hagar in the fourth chapter of the Galatians. The Reformers, then, rejected what they considered fanciful allegorizing, rather than all spiritual interpretation whatsoever. Protestant literalism is better thought of as asserting that biblical passages have a single, clear, fixed meaning that is usually but not always the literal one. The Reformers sought the 'plain sense' of Scripture.[13]

Protestant plain-sense interpretation of the Bible meant that only passages which at a common-sense level contain moral or theological teachings could be read for a moral or theological message. All other biblical passages must have some other primary referent. As a result, many biblical passages, and above all the narrative sections of Genesis and Exodus, were now construed as conveying cosmological or historical knowledge. The narratives of the Flood or of the forty years in the wilderness, which for patristic and medieval interpreters contained spiritual meanings in addition to their literal sense, now were to be understood as, and only as, true accounts of things that had happened in the distant past. Moses himself, from having been a character in the narrative of the Exodus and a type prefiguring Christian truth, became 'the sacred historian', the historical author of a factual account of the first ages of the Earth.[14]

The starkness of Protestant plain-sense interpretation was mitigated by the theory of accommodation. According to this theory, which went back to Augustine's *On the Literal Interpretation of Genesis*, the authors of Scripture had adapted, or accommodated, their words to the intelligence and experience of their original audience. Accommodationism allowed Protestants, to whom allegorical interpretation was forbidden, to reconcile truths discovered by reason with the Bible. In the account of the Flood, for example, Moses was thought to have accurately described what had happened, but in place of a true explanation of the physical mechanisms that had produced it he offered only a simple story that could be understood by his unlearned audience.[15] Science, to anticipate, will 'unaccommodate' the biblical language. John Calvin himself, discussing the Mosaic account of creation in his *Commentaries on the First Book of Moses, called Genesis*, explicitly linked the plain sense of Scripture, accommodationism, and science:

> Moses wrote in a popular style things which, without instruction, all ordinary persons, endued with common sense, are able to understand; but astronomers investigate with great labour whatever the sagacity of the human mind can comprehend. Nevertheless, this study is not to be reprobated, nor this science to be condemned, because some frantic persons are wont boldly to reject whatever is unknown to them. For astronomy is not only pleasant, but also very useful to be known: it cannot be denied that this art unfolds the admirable wisdom of God ... Nor did Moses truly wish to withdraw us from this pursuit in omitting such things as are peculiar to the art; but because he was ordained a teacher as well of the unlearned and rude as of the learned, he could not otherwise fulfil his office than by descending to this grosser method of instruction.[16]

The plain-sense interpretive principle transformed the reading not only of the Book of Scripture but also of the Book of Nature. A new generation of naturalists denied the doubleness of natural objects. Animals, plants, stones, celestial bodies were physical objects rather than veiled symbols whose true meaning lay beyond themselves. God was still the author of the Book of Nature, but now the language in which he had inscribed the Book of Nature was thought to be a language of discrete things linked by physical connections rather than symbols linked by correspondences. The Book of Nature displays order and regularity, but it is an arbitrary order contingent on God's will rather than the necessary imprinting of his essence. To read the Book of Nature was now to reconstruct the physical relationships God had established among discrete things by scrutinizing natural objects, paying as much attention to differences as to similitudes, for clues to their internal order. The non-symbolic text of nature thus required a non-symbolic hermeneutic capable of *de-in-scribing* nature, that is, of *describing* its divinely established order and regularity. The study of nature remains a pious activity because it discloses some part of the wisdom and benevolence of the Creator. But now it tells us nothing about the divine nature or God's intentions for humanity or what we need to know or do in order to be saved; for these we must turn to the other book, Scripture. God's scriptural promises, above all his covenant with Noah, encouraged the search for an order to nature by assuring natural philosophers that God would not arbitrarily overthrow the laws of nature, but for the most part the rejection of a symbolic exegesis of the Book of Nature served to separate the content of the Two Books. The Book of Nature tells us something of the attributes of the divine Creator, while the Book of Scripture reveals the saving truths.[17]

The scientific revolution of the seventeenth century – for the shift from symbolic exegesis to plain-sense description of nature was nothing less – was not a matter of science liberating itself from theology. It followed directly, if largely unwittingly, from the revolution in biblical interpretation effected by humanists and Protestant Reformers. The scientific revolution was a revolution within, not against, Western biblical culture.[18]

Galileo, Kepler, Bacon

The turn to a descriptive hermeneutics of nature was carried out by the great figures of the scientific revolution. Galileo, Johannes Kepler and Francis Bacon figured nature as a text written in a coded but non-symbolic language. There is an important distinction between decoding a language and interpreting a symbol. One can know a language but still not understand a passage written in it because its meaning is veiled in symbols. This is the Renaissance understanding of nature. In the other case, if one does not know the language then even the simplest literal statement will be unintelligible, but once one learns it then intelligibility is simply a matter of decoding fixed and plain signs. For Galileo, as for Kepler, the literal, non-symbolic language of nature is mathematics:

> Philosophy is written in this grand book, the universe, which stands continually open
> to our gaze. But the book cannot be understood unless one first learns to comprehend
> the language and read the letters in which it is composed. It is written in the language
> of mathematics, and its characters are triangles, circles, and other geometric figures
> without which it is humanly impossible to understand a single word of it; without
> these, one wanders about in a dark labyrinth.[19]

'Labyrinth' is a word that recurs frequently in early modern scientific writing. The natural world is a labyrinth for those who have thrown away the symbolic key of resemblances and not yet found the new descriptive key to the order and harmony of nature and indirectly the wisdom and benevolence of its Creator. Galileo insisted that those who wish to read the Book of Nature must work hard in order to master the foreign, mathematical language in which it is written. The language of nature, in other words, is not accommodated to humanity. Galileo's famous assertion that 'nature takes no delight in poetry' should be understood as a repudiation of the application of symbolic exegesis to the Book of Nature.[20]

Galileo's recourse, in his letter to the Grand Duchess Christina of Lorraine, to biblical criticism in order to defend the Copernican heliocentric theory depends on this distinction between the unaccommodated language of the Book of Nature and the accommodated language of the Book of Scripture. Opponents of the Copernican theory pointed out that Scripture states that the Sun moves and that the Earth is stationary (for example, Joshua 10:12–13). Since on this point the Copernican theory contradicts Scripture, which everyone agrees is untouched by error, the theory must necessarily be wrong and impious. Galileo countered by arguing that while Scripture is indeed free from error it is only the true meaning of Scripture that is free from error, and this true meaning is not always identical with its actual language since the biblical writers often accommodated their words to the capacities of their original audience. So far, this is standard exegetical procedure (although he prudently cited Augustine rather than Calvin as his authority). But Galileo took the further, audacious step of asserting that since the authors of Scripture practised accommodation when they wrote about nature, the language of the Bible on such matters should be subordinated to the new scientific knowledge. Science, that is, should guide biblical interpretation. Daring as it seems, it was not this interpretive principle that got Galileo in trouble with the Church, but rather his specific use of it to render heliocentrism compatible with Scripture. The Catholic Church had recently (at the Council of Trent) forbidden interpretations of Scripture that contravene the common sense of the Fathers of the Church (the plain-sense revolution made subservient to Catholic tradition!), and while the Fathers had endorsed accommodationism their cosmology was unquestionably geocentric. Galileo was condemned not for upholding the heliocentric theory but for improper interpretation of Scripture.[21]

Kepler, too, identified mathematics as the language of the Book of Nature. He believed that his Copernican science had decoded the logic of geometrical proportion that had guided the Creator's hand, and he proclaimed in his *New Astronomy* that the study of physics, not Scripture, will teach us the true order of nature and thereby reveal the wisdom and greatness of the Creator. And he too fell back on the principle of accommodation in order to elude the charge that advocating the Copernican system means declaring Scripture to be false. His great advantage over Galileo was that as a Lutheran living in a Lutheran state he did not have to answer to the interpretive traditions of the Catholic Church.[22]

These early modern natural philosophers regarded the Bible as containing genuine scientific knowledge. Francis Bacon, for example, found in the book of Job the plain teaching of the roundness of the Earth, that it hangs in space, and that the stars are fixed. But most often they thought that Moses and the other sacred authors had veiled their cosmological knowledge by accommodating their language to the ignorance of their audience. In arguing that the new knowledge now makes it possible to lift the veil of accommodationist language and recover the cosmological knowledge contained in the Bible, they effected an epochal hermeneutical reversal: whereas formerly the Bible provided the key to the hidden spiritual meanings of the natural world, now scientific discoveries illuminate the hitherto misunderstood cosmological passages of the Bible.[23]

Bacon was every bit as adamant as Galileo and Kepler in his rejection of a symbolic exegesis of the Book of Nature. He regarded the attempt by Renaissance sages and their successors in his own day, such as John Dee, to read the image of God stamped on nature as resting on a prideful refusal to acknowledge the epistemological consequences of the Fall. The corruption of our mental faculties bars recovery of Adam's direct access to nature as surely as the angel with the fiery sword barred re-entry into the Garden of Eden:

> For the mind of man is far from the nature of a clear and equal glass, wherein the beams of things should reflect according to their true incidence; nay, it is rather like an enchanted glass, full of superstition and imposture, if it be not delivered and reduced.[24]

For Bacon the proper approach to knowledge of nature begins, after humble acknowledgement of the gap that exists between the mind and reality, with things – the only uncorrupted 'sound and language' accessible to all mankind. Since one must master the language of creation through the laborious recording of the things of the natural world, Bacon's key to the labyrinth of nature was empirical rather than mathematical. Empirical research is another aspect of the curse on Adam: 'by the sweat of your brow…' Further, since our senses are apt to deceive us, we must test and refine them through constructing experiments; we must, that is, place nature under constraint and 'vex' her in order to decipher her code. It is this empirical, experimental method, necessitated by our fallen nature, that Bacon called his *novum organum*. Not only is this 'new organ or instrument' the key to reading the Book of Nature, but, by restoring to us the true knowledge of nature enjoyed effortlessly by Adam in the Garden, it promises to repair our fallen nature. Baconian science is both an innovation against Renaissance symbolic readings of the Book of Nature and the restoration – a Great Instauration – of Adamic knowledge.[25]

The laborious empiricism of this conception of science is summed up in the motto from the Book of Daniel that Bacon placed on the title-page of *The Great Instauration*: *Multi pertransibunt & augebitur scientia* (Many will run to and fro and knowledge will be increased). Bacon understood his method, which came to be known as the Baconian theory of induction, as a repudiation of theory in science:

> For God forbid that we should give out a dream of our own imagination for a pattern of the world; rather may he graciously grant us to write an apocalypse [revelation of hidden things] of true vision of the footsteps of the Creator imprinted on his creatures.[26]

Bacon's target here was the Renaissance symbolic exegesis, which he condemned as a prideful and illegitimate anticipation of nature. His inductive view of science, according to which true science is the patient accumulation of facts about the way nature behaves followed by the infering of laws of nature from them, should be understood as a polemic against symbolic exegesis of nature rather than as an accurate account of early modern science. The combination of mathematical theorizing and experimental testing of Galileo and Kepler, which was equally opposed to Renaissance presumption, more truly epitomizes the foundations of modern science than Bacon's anti-theoretical induction.[27]

Newton

Isaac Newton (1642–1727), like Galileo and Kepler, held mathematics to be the language in which God had written the Book of Nature. The very structure of his *Mathematical Principles of Natural Philosophy* (1687) – volumes 1 and 2 set out a theory of gravitational forces derived from mathematical deduction while volume 3 verifies the theory with experimentally derived empirical evidence – subverts his famous claim that 'I do not make hypotheses'. Newton's actual practice of science places him with Galileo and Kepler rather than Bacon. More generally, Newton shares with all three the model of science as a description, or decoding, of the blueprint for creation that demonstrates the wisdom and benevolence of its divine draughtsman. *Mathematical Principles* is celebrated retrospectively as a triumph of the mechanical philosophy that eliminated spirit from the operations of nature and explained those operations solely by the mechanical necessity of particles of matter in motion. Yet, Newton himself thought that while the mechanical philosophy did truly describe the operations of inert matter, there was more to nature than inert matter. He believed that a full decoding of the Book of Nature required a second natural philosophy complementary to the mechanical philosophy in order to reach the active, vital, spiritual principles behind particles in motion. It is this conviction that explains his devotion to alchemy, a chemical-spiritual art that posited the activating agency of Spirit as the ultimate explanation of natural phenomena.[28] While there was a fundamental tension between Newton's two models of science, the mechanical and the alchemical, his quest for the Philosopher's Stone should not be seen as a relapse into a Renaissance symbolic exegesis of the Book of Nature. It rather signifies Newton's refusal to accept the epistemological limitations of descriptive science. We are left with the curious spectacle of a man deeply imprinted with the Puritan sense of the fallenness of humanity refusing to accept in his science what Bacon insisted was one of the principal consequences of the Fall: our loss of the ability to understand spiritual truths through unaided reason.

Newton's alchemical supplement to the mechanical philosophy was one of two points on which he diverged from Galileo, Kepler and Bacon. The other, which I shall discuss at greater length, is his passionate engagement with the Book of Scripture. Galileo and Kepler had both been trained in biblical interpretation – Galileo while a novice at the monastery of Vallombrosa and Kepler as a theology student at Tübingen University – before turning to the study of the other Book. Both men considered scriptural exegesis a pedestrian activity, in contrast to which their ability to decode the Book of Nature was a rare and special gift from God.[29] Newton, who over the course of his life produced many thousands of pages of biblical commentary, regarded himself as a privileged decoder of both Books. Further, he was singular in his conviction that the present text of the Bible is defective.

Newton arrived at his conviction that the text of the Bible as we have it is corrupt as a result of pushing the Protestant plain-sense interpretation of the Bible further than all but a very few Protestants would permit. Newton, like the Protestant Reformers themselves, held that the plain sense of the text is the correct one, otherwise there can be no certainty in religion. Worse, any other reading places human imagination or authority above the Word of God (Newton could be as scathing as Bacon on the subject of other interpreters' prideful presumption). When Newton put the plain-sense interpretive principle into practice, he found that not only could he not find in the biblical text the various Catholic traditions that all Reformers agreed were illicit corruptions of primitive Christianity, but he could not find central Christian doctrines such as the Trinity and the uncreatedness of Christ. Placing plain sense ahead of tradition, Newton denied the offending doctrines, and thereby became an Arian. This term, from early Christian heresiology, means that he recognized Christ as a divine mediator between God and man but insisted that Christ was subordinate to the Father who created him. (It is misleading to call him, as is often done, a Unitarian. This slightly later designation for ultra-liberal Protestants carries the sense that Jesus is fully and solely human.) Newton considered those who worship Christ as God (that is, virtually all Christian churches) to be guilty of the fundamental sin of idolatry.[30]

Newton concluded that the doctrine of the Trinity, which asserts that Christ is one of the three persons of the one God, is a massive fraud perpetrated on the Church. His indefatigable historical researches revealed two stages to the fraud. First, sometime in the early centuries of Christianity the false doctrine of the Trinity was invented by people lacking apostolic or prophetic authority. This human invention was then imposed on the Church, thereby corrupting true doctrine, with Athanasius' triumph over Arius and its doctrinal formalization at the Council of Nicaea in 325. Once the Trinitarians had succeeded in corrupting Church doctrine they compounded their wickedness by corrupting the text of the Bible itself so as to provide scriptural support for their counterfeit doctrine.

Displaying an Erasmian devotion to philology, if carried out in a very un-Erasmian spirit of polemic, Newton pored over polyglot Bibles and compared every known printed and manuscript version in order to expose the interpolated and fraudulent nature of those verses such as 1 John 5:7 and 1 Timothy 3:16 that have Trinitarian implications.[31] The consequences of the Trinitarians' corruption of Christianity have been dire. In his private writings Newton denounced, in intemperate language that would have drawn the envy of the most frenzied Puritan anti-Papist, the monstrosity of power and wealth that had usurped the place of the true Church. Here Newton's fulminations joined the English national chorus vilifying the Roman Catholic Church, although Newton in no way thought that the Protestant Reformation, especially in its Anglican version, had undone the corruption.[32] Indeed, the Anglican Church retained so much of corrupt Catholicism, including the doctrine of the Trinity, that Newton refused to take the holy orders normally required for an academic position. Only a special dispensation from King Charles II himself allowed his academic career to continue.

Trinitarian corruptions had turned the Bible into a labyrinth. How, then, could Newton be sure that his anti-Trinitarian reading of it was the correct one? Just as mathematics had provided the key to decoding the labyrinth of the Book of Nature, so Newton seized on prophecy as the key to decoding the Book of Scripture. By 'prophecy' Newton meant above all the books of Daniel and the Apocalypse of Saint John, or Revelation (his comparative biblical studies had persuaded him that these two books had escaped corruption).[33] Prophecy may seem like an unpromising choice for a key to Scripture in as much as the prophetic books – and especially Daniel and Revelation – are written in a non-literal language of symbols. Newton, of course, rejected allegorical interpretation in favour of a plain-sense hermeneutic. His solution was to assign one and only one interpretation to each symbol. In place of allegorical interpretation, in which a given symbol may receive various meanings in various texts or even within a single verse, Newton followed the model of mathematics. Just as pi is always a fixed value, so the prophetic character of 'beast', for example, always signifies 'kingdom' or 'royalty'. Theological conviction underlay Newton's confidence in plain-sense simplicity. His famous assertion that 'It is the perfection of God's works that they are all done with the greatest simplicity. He is the God of order and not of confusion' was intended to justify his method of interpreting prophecy by means of the parallel of the Two Books: 'And therefore as they that would understand the frame of the world must indeavour to reduce their knowledge to all possible simplicity, so it must be in seeking to understand these visions.'[34] Newton compared all the occurrences of a particular symbol in the prophetic books and thereby, with immense labour, worked out a prophetic lexicon. Having thus, in his phrase, 'methodized the Apocalypse', Newton had at his command a divine algebra by which the Book of Scripture could be read as surely as the Book of Nature by mathematics. Just as with the Book of Nature, prophecy is obscure and veiled for those who have not learned the language in which it is written, but there is nothing obscure or veiled (that is, symbolic) about its meaning once one has learned its language:

He that would understand a book written in a strange language must first learn ye language & if he would understand it well must learn the language perfectly. Such a language was that wherein the Prophets wrote, & the want of sufficient skill in that language is the main reason why they are so little understood … they all wrote in one & the same mystical language, as well known without doubt to ye sons of ye Prophets as ye Hieroglyphic language of ye Egyptians to their priests, and this language, as far as I can find, was as certain & definite in its signification as is the vulgar language of any nation whatsoever.[35]

Newton convinced himself that, properly decoded, the books of Daniel and Revelation prove to be compendia of historical prophecies about the early history of the Church and the principal monarchies of Europe and the East. His *Observations upon the Prophecies of Daniel and the Apocalypse of St. John* (1730) offered copious support that they had been fully and exactly fulfilled by subsequent history. Further, since the Old and New Testaments had to harmonize with each other, Newton satisfied himself that the prophecies of Revelation recapitulate exactly those of Daniel.[36]

Newton linked both his spectacular accomplishments in natural philosophy and his ability to decode biblical prophecy to his sense of himself as having been specially chosen by God. He pointed to the penultimate verses of Daniel:

He said, 'Go your own way, Daniel, for the words are to remain secret and sealed until the time of the end. Many shall be purified, cleansed, and refined, but the wicked shall continue to act wickedly. None of the wicked shall understand, but those who are wise shall understand.'[37]

Since God, the text is telling us, uncovers the structure of creation only for his chosen ones, Newton's scientific accomplishments leave no doubt that he is one of them. This special relationship further explains his ability to interpret the prophetic literature. Finally, the fact that God has begun to permit the decoding of his Two Books is, as Daniel indicates, a sure sign that the end-times are approaching.[38] Newton shared this apocalyptic dimension with the many millenarian Puritan expositors of prophecy, such as the Cambridge don Joseph Mede, who searched the prophetic books for clues as to the date, surely very soon, of the Second Coming of Christ. Newton, however, while believing fervently that the Second Coming was imminent, never predicted a date. His caution is tied to his conviction that while the books of prophecy are history, and not all of the history therein prophesied has yet to come to pass, their content cannot be truly understood until after the events prophesied have actually happened.[39] In his *Observations upon the Prophecies*, Newton warned that God gives the gift of interpreting prophecy not in order to cater to human curiosity but to demonstrate his providence:

He gave this and the Prophecies of the Old Testament, not to gratify men's curiosities by enabling them to foreknow things, but that after they were fulfilled they might be interpreted by the event, and his own Providence, not the Interpreters, be then manifested thereby to the world. For the events of things predicted many ages before, will then be a convincing argument that the world is governed by providence.[40]

Newton's fundamental faith in the unity of truth of the Two Books underlay and unified his diverse researches – mechanical philosophy, alchemy, biblical criticism, interpretation of prophecy. Whatever knowledge God has revealed in the (uncorrupted) Book of Scripture is harmonious with what he has inscribed in the Book of Nature. Newton's scientific work, above all his *Mathematical Principles of Natural Philosophy*, demonstrated the providential order governing the phenomena of the natural world, just as his interpretations of prophecy demonstrated the same providential order governing the history of the world. The discovery and display of this order reveals the majesty, power and benevolence of God.[41]

Chapter 2

MACHINE OR RUIN?

That the great figures of the scientific revolution understood themselves to be
discovering the divine blueprint for the contingent but providential order of creation gave their work a theological dimension. Accordingly, the seventeenth and
eighteenth centuries became the great age of natural theology.

Natural theology

Natural theology, or physico-theology as it is sometimes called, is the branch of
theology that deduces knowledge about God from the study of nature. The design
argument, as part of natural theology, asserts that the existence and something of
the attributes of God can be deduced from the evidence of design in the world.
Natural theology predates Christianity and was known to the Church Fathers.
It declined in the Middle Ages, but was revived in the seventeenth century as
astronomers concluded that the universe was the work of a mind that had devised
the motions of celestial bodies on mathematical principles, and naturalists
pointed to examples of contrivance, or the matching of the form of an organ, for
example, to its function, as attesting to a superhuman designer. The chemist and
devout Christian Robert Boyle (1627–1691), himself a highly influential advocate of harmony between the Two Books, summed up the prevailing opinion: 'It
is rational, from the manifest fitness of some things to cosmical or animal ends or
uses, to infer, that they were framed or ordained in reference thereunto by an
intelligent and designing agent.' Natural theology harmonized the Book of
Nature and the Book of Scripture, in a manner appropriate to the plain-sense
interpretive practice of the post-Reformation era.[1]

Natural theology was particularly influential in England, where the Anglican
Church sought in reason and empirical evidence a means of confirming the truth
of revelation independently of both Catholic tradition and Puritan biblicism.[2]
This triple alliance of Bible, Church tradition and reason, enshrined in book 3,
chapter 8 of Richard Hooker's *Of the Laws of Ecclesiastical Polity* (1594–97), is
the context in which Boyle established by his will an annual series of eight
lectures to be directed against unbelievers. The 'Boyle Lectures', delivered in
London churches, spawned such notable works of natural theology as Richard
Bentley's *The Folly and Unreasonableness of Atheism* (1692), Samuel Clarke's
*Demonstration of the Being and Attributes of God and Discourse concerning the
Unchangeable Obligations of Natural Religion and the Truth and Certainty of*

the Christian Revelation (1704–05), and William Derham's *Physico-Theology: or a Demonstration of the Being and Attributes of God from the Works of Creation* (1711–12). John Ray's *The Wisdom of God Manifested in the Works of Creation* (1691), although not originating in a Boyle lectureship, carried particular authority because it was written by an Anglican clergyman who was also England's foremost naturalist.[3] Based on his collections of botanical and zoological specimens gathered from all over Europe, Ray (1628–1705) had written a series of books that laid the foundations of systematic natural history, among them his *History of Plants*, *History of Fishes*, and *Synopsis of Quadruped Animals and of Serpents*. Here and there in these works of analysis and description Ray had paused to note examples of evident contrivance in the matching of form to function, such as webbed feet to swimming, and to praise the wise design of the Creator in giving, for example, webbed feet to geese and not to giraffes. *The Wisdom of God Manifested in the Works of the Creation*, on the other hand, was entirely devoted to demonstrating the wisdom and benevolence of God from evidence of design in nature.[4]

In identifying examples of design in nature as contrivances that were doing precisely what they had been designed to do, Ray, like Newton, Boyle and all the natural theologians of his day, regarded nature as both a completed mechanism and fundamentally unchanged since the creation. The origin or purpose of natural phenomena posed no scientific problem; stars, mountains, oceans, animal species had been created by God in the beginning for the purposes that God had intended them to serve.[5] The sun is hot because its purpose is to provide us with light and warmth. Invariably, the divine purpose was correlated with benevolence, as in Ray's enumeration of the many uses of the wind:

> To ventilate and break the Air, and dissipate noisom and contagious Vapors, which otherwise stagnating might occasion many Diseases in Animals …: To transfer the Clouds from place to place, for the more commodious watering of the Earth. To temper the excesses of the Heat, as they find, who in Brazil, New Spain, the Neighbouring Islands, and other the like Countries near the Equator reap the Benefit of the Breezes. To fill the Sails of Ships, and carry them on their Voyages to remote Countries; which of what eminent advantage it is to Mankind, for the procuring and continuing of Trade and mutual Commerce between the most distant Nations, the illustrating every corner of the Earth, and the perfecting Geography and natural History, is apparent to every Man. To this may be added the driving about of Windmills for grinding of Corn, making of Oyl, draining of Pools, etc. That it should seldom or never be so violent and boisterous, as to overturn Houses; yea whole Cities; to tear up Trees by the Roots, and prostrate Woods; to drive the Sea over the lower Countries; as were it the effect of Chance, or meer natural Causes not moderated by a superior Power, it would in all likelihood often do. All these things declare the Wisdom and Goodness of Him *who bringeth the Winds out of his Treasures*.[6]

The matching of form to function in nature under the guidance of divine wisdom permits no superfluity in Creation. Every being and every part of every being serves a purpose and has been created expressly for that end. There can be no exceptions. What purpose, then, do nipples serve in a man, a malicious caviller might ask? Ray answers, 'partly for Ornament, partly for a kind of conformity between the Sexes, and partly to defend and cherish the Heart'.[7] Just to be sure, however, he adds that it does not follow that 'they or any other parts of the Body are useless because we are ignorant'.

The perfect equilibrium of nature further implies the subservience of lower forms of existence to higher forms. Matter exists to provide a theatre for life; plants and animals to serve the uses of intelligent, moral beings; the lower social orders to serve the higher; and the whole to manifest the Creator's wisdom, power and benevolence. The extent to which natural theologians could go in demonstrating the benevolent wisdom of God's design may be seen in the account of 'the great variety throughout the world of men's faces, voices, and handwriting' in Derham's popular *Physico-Theology*:

> Had Man's body been made according to any of the Atheistical Schemes, or any other Method other than that of the infinite Lord of the World, this wise Variety would never have been: but Men's Faces would have been cast in the same, or not a very different Mould, their Organs of Speech would have sounded the same, or not so great a Variety of Notes; and the same Structure of Muscles and Nerves would have given the Hand the same direction in Writing. And in this Case, what Confusion, what Disturbance, what Mischiefs would the world eternally have lain under! No Security could have been to our persons; no Certainty, no Enjoyment of our Possessions; no Justice between Man and Man; no distinction between Good and Bad, between Friends and Foes, between Father and Child, Husband and Wife, Male or Female, but all would have been turned topsy-turvy, by being exposed to the Malice of the Envious and ill-Natured, to the Fraud and Violence of Knaves and Robbers, to the Forgeries of the crafty Cheat, to the Lusts of the Effeminate and Debauched, and what not! Our Courts of Justice can abundantly testify the dire Effects of Mistaking Men's Faces, of counterfeiting their Hands, and forging Writings. But now as the infinitely wise Creator and Ruler hath ordered the Matter, every man's Face can distinguish him in the Light, and his Voice in the Dark; his Hand-writing can speak for him though absent, and be his Witness, and secure his Contracts in future Generations. A manifest as well as admirable Indication of the divine Superintendence and Management.

As William James, from whom I have taken this passage, remarks: 'A God so careful as to make provision even for the unmistakable signing of bank checks and deeds was a deity truly after the heart of eighteenth-century Anglicanism'.[8]

Their perception of the perfect equilibrium of nature did not mean that Ray and the other natural theologians denied the reality of chance and change. They were real, but subordinate to order and stability in the economy of nature. Change in the form of the cyclical motion of the planets or chance in the form of the random variation in the pattern of dogs' coats adds variety to the spectacle of nature but can never alter its fundamental order. Here, the general providentialism of natural theology, according to which nothing existing could be destroyed and nothing new come into being, joined with and gave extended life to the Neoplatonic principle of plentitude. The result was that the natural order formed a great chain of being in which every being that could exist does exist, and the whole testifies to the perfection of the divine plan of creation. In this view the extinction of an existing species or the coming into being of a new one is inconceivable because it implies a lack of perfection in the original divine plan.[9]

This conception of an intricately constructed world without radical change was expressed in the metaphor of a machine designed and set in motion by a Master Craftsman. And yet, even as Ray and the other natural theologians celebrated the wise and benevolent design of the world-machine, they faced an unsettling challenge from the new Cartesian philosophy. In Descartes' physics every action involving matter is purely mechanistic. This includes the motions of animals, since all animals, not excluding human bodies, are mere machines. Humans possess souls, it is true, but there is no connection between our spiritual and our physico-mental selves (this segregated cohabitation of spirit and matter in human beings is what is meant by Cartesian dualism). God's role in this mechanistic model was solely to endow the universe with motion at the beginning of time. Since, once put into motion, the world-machine runs in accordance with the divine will but otherwise independently of its Creator, the Cartesian philosophy effectively demoted the benevolent and providential God of the Bible to an abstract First Cause. And while his system would seem to permit a minimal argument from design, Descartes himself had forbidden teleological reasoning in natural philosophy: 'when dealing with natural things, we will, then, never derive any explanations from the purposes which God or nature may have had in view when creating them and we shall entirely banish from our philosophy the search for final causes'.[10]

The Cartesians appear in Ray's *The Wisdom of God Manifested in the Works of Creation* as 'Mechanick Atheists'. They are atheists not in that they deny God absolutely but in that their First Cause is not the personal, caring God of the Bible. In order to refute them Ray denied that the world-machine operates perfectly. The mechanical laws governing physical phenomena operate in combinations that require some sort of coordinating oversight; even more strikingly, organic life is inexplicable without some sort of vital principle to supplement the laws governing matter in motion. All this (which closely echoes Newton's belief in a vital, spiritual principle discoverable through alchemy) reinscribes the natural world under the ever-present guidance of divine providence.[11] Ray's universe is still the world-machine, but in order to defend divine providence and the design argument from the Mechanick Atheists he had to detract somewhat from the flawlessness of its operation and, therefore, from the perfection of its original design. An appropriate analogy might be the early steam engines, which required constant oversight and intervention on the part of their engineers.

Fossils

If Mechanick Atheists pushed the world-machine metaphor in a dangerously heterodox direction, the metaphor itself came under attack from another area of early modern scientific enquiry: fossils. The word 'fossil' originally meant 'things dug out of the earth'; until the early eighteenth century, any natural curiosity found underground was called a fossil, including gems and metallic ores, as well as what we now mean by a fossil – the petrified remains of a once-living organism. The objects we now call fossils also belonged to a second category of

Renaissance natural philosophy: 'jokes of nature'. This class of natural objects included all examples of an object mimicking the form of another object: stones in the shape of shells, shells in the shape of human ears, mountains in the shape of human faces, or plant leaves in the shape of a bodily organ. Jokes of nature exist, Renaissance sages taught, because Nature is playful, plastic and creative; they are signs of the correspondences that link things horizontally to other things and vertically to spiritual hierarchies. As such, the study of fossils, according to a symbolic reading of the Book of Nature, included, as in Gesner's *On Fossil Objects* (1565), their potential use in medicine and natural magic.[12]

The origin and nature of 'fossils' resembling plants and animals did not pose a scientific problem for the Renaissance. Fifteenth- and sixteenth-century naturalists had not one but two rational explanations for both their stony matter and their form. Those operating within a Neoplatonic framework, and who thereby lacked a clear-cut distinction between living and non-living natural phenomena, thought that stones grow in the womb of the Earth just as organic life does elsewhere. And the playful, creative moulding force, or *vis plastica*, that explains all similitudes in nature easily accounted for the resemblance between fossils and organic forms. Similarly, a reformed Aristotelianism, associated above all with the University of Padua, separated logically the form of an object from its matter. The form of a thing derives from its formative 'seed'; the seed of a fish, for example, under normal circumstances imposes the form of a fish onto organic matter, producing a fish. But sometimes the seed of a fish percolates deep underground and there produces by spontaneous generation a fish-like object out of rock. The resulting object would have the form of a fish without being, or ever having been, an actual fish. Nor was the location of fossils deep within rock or at high altitude a problem for either Neoplatonic or Aristotelian naturalists, because in either case they could have been produced naturally in such locations. Both Neoplatonism and Aristotelianism adequately explained the stoniness, form and location of those 'fossils' that resembled animals and plants, as long as the presuppositions of their worldviews were accepted.[13] The hypothesis that fossils resembling animals and plants are in fact the petrified remains of once-living animals and plants emerged in the seventeenth century as a consequence of the shift from a symbolic exegesis of the Book of Nature to a descriptive reading of it as God's contingent order of creation.

Renaissance naturalists had identified the function of fossils as signalling the spiritual correspondences among things and thereby indicating their medicinal or magical efficacies. The plain-sense revolution's reading of the Book of Nature brought about the extinction of 'jokes of nature'. The impact of this extinction threw up a scientific and theological problem in regard to fossils: what were these curious objects if not the whimsies of playful nature and what could the function of their resemblances be if not to signal correspondences? That such resemblances had a function could not be doubted, since the manifest function of everything in nature was now the principal means by which the contingent order God had imposed on nature testified to his wisdom and benevolence (the basis of natural theology). A possible answer was that the form of a fossil shell, for example, had the same function as the shell of the living mollusc that it resembles; that is, it had served to protect a once-living mollusc. In this way, through teleological theological reasoning as much as by empirical observation, seventeenth-century naturalists were led to the hypothesis of the organic origin of fossils. The leading advocates of this hypothesis were the Englishman Robert Hooke (1635–1703) and the Dane Nicolaus Steno (1638–1686).[14]

The new hypothesis did not gain immediate acceptance. Athanasius Kircher's (1602–1680) widely read *The Subterranean World* (1664) continued the Neoplatonic explanation of the origin of fossils in the moulding force and 'lapidifying power' of Nature.[15] But more important than the afterglow of the symbolic worldview, at least among naturalists, were two theologically problematic implications of the hypothesis of organic origin itself. First, the resemblance of certain fossils to living species was close but not exact. Fossils had been found, for example, that resembled living molluscs but were vastly larger than any known species. If such fossils originated as living beings then the species to which they belonged no longer existed and the inescapable conclusion must be that some species have become extinct. Extinction was a shocking thought, however, because that implied some imperfection or incompleteness in the divine plan of creation, and thus imperfection in either its Designer or his providential oversight. This problem was compounded by the widespread acceptance of the great chain of being. The idea of extinction, in other words, which was made thinkable by the teleological argument that all natural objects must display their divinely intended function, ran up against the equally theological objection that extinction casts doubt on divine perfection and providence. The force of these considerations may be seen in the reluctance of John Ray and Martin Lister (1638?–1712) to accept the organic hypothesis despite their recognition of its prima facie plausibility. Lister, a highly respected naturalist, accepted an organic origin for fossils that exactly resembled living species but denied it for those that would imply the reality of extinction. Ray, for his part, suggested that rather than having become extinct the unknown species might still exist in unexplored parts of the world and especially deep in the oceans.[16]

Ray, it would seem, could thereby accept the organic-origin hypothesis, but here the second problem came into play: the location of fossils. The fact that fossils were found on high hilltops and deep within rock was not a problem for Renaissance naturalists because they could have been produced *in situ*. But now, as Ray realized with profound uneasiness, anyone holding that fossils were the remains of once-living organisms had to explain how they had gotten to their present emplacements. Steno and Hooke grasped this as fully as Ray, and worked out parallel answers. Steno, in his *Forerunner to a Dissertation concerning a Solid Naturally Contained in a Solid* (1669), argued that the geology of the Earth had been built up by the successive accumulation of layers of sediment, which in turn had precipitated out of a fluid (thereby including a place in his scheme for the biblical Flood). As each layer formed it enclosed organic remains such as shells or shark teeth. The layers of sediment had formed horizontally over time – Steno identified six ages of the Earth – but episodes of crustal collapse had tilted the layers, thereby elevating fossil-bearing rock high above sea-level. Hooke, for his part, while believing in the reality of the biblical Flood, considered it an inadequate explanation for the placement of fossils on the grounds that the transient event recorded in the Bible could hardly have done all that was required. Hooke instead attributed to massive earthquakes both the destruction of now-extinct species and the transformations of the Earth that had embedded their remains within rock and at high altitudes.[17]

Hooke's and Steno's efforts to defend the hypothesis of the organic origin of fossils led them to the revolutionary idea that the Earth has a history. In a paper on fossils read to the Royal Society in 1668 Hooke expressed, in an image that would soon become a cliché, the new idea that Nature has a history in terms of the familiar evidence for human history:

> There is no Coin can so well inform an Antiquary that there has been such or such a place subject to such a Prince, as these [fossils] will certify a Natural Antiquary, that such and such places have been under Water, that there have been such kind of Animals, that there have been such and such preceding Alterations and Changes of the superficial Parts of the Earth: And methinks Providence does seem to have design'd these permanent shapes, as monuments and Records to instruct succeeding Ages of what past in preceding. And these written in a more legible Character than the Hieroglyphicks of the ancient Egyptians, and on more lasting Monuments than those of their vast Pyramids and Obelisks.[18]

Fossils, as for the Renaissance, are signs but they are now signs of Earth *history* rather than of the correspondences among things. Like Galileo and Kepler, Steno and Hooke were reading the divinely inscribed Book of Nature, but their Book of Nature was a history book because they recognized Nature as a realm of becoming and radical change rather than a cyclic world-machine. Mother Nature had become a woman with a past.

Neither Steno nor Hooke doubted the concordance between the Two Books. Hooke, as the passage just quoted attests, read a providential intention into the function of fossils as signs of the history of the Earth. Steno similarly accepted that what we learn about nature both confirms and is confirmed by the Bible. Both men, therefore, unhesitatingly placed their reconstructions of Earth history within the roughly 6,000-year time-span of biblical chronology.[19] Their landmark recognition that the Earth has a history did not, therefore, lead directly to the idea of an ancient Earth.

The identification of fossils as the remains of once-living animals and plants became widely accepted over the next couple of generations. Pious naturalists were quick to see that fossil evidence could be enlisted in support of the historical veracity of the Flood story. The Swiss physician and naturalist Johann Jacob Scheuchzer (1672–1733) is representative of this view. In his *Complaints and Claims of the Fishes* (1708) fossil fish themselves both confute those who deny their organic origin and proclaim themselves witnesses to the Flood. Since speaking plants seemed somehow less plausible than speaking fish, Scheuchzer spoke in his own voice in *Herbarium of the Deluge* (1709) in order to identify fossils of plants as relics of the Flood and again insist on their value as empirical evidence for its reality. He even deduced, on the basis of fossil botanic evidence, that the

Flood must have begun in the month of May. Scheuchzer directly echoed Hooke in his appreciation of the evidential value of fossils (though of course it is scriptural veracity as much as the history of the Earth to which fossils attest): 'Here are new kinds of coins, the dates of which are incomparably more ancient, more important and more reliable than those of all the coins of Greece and Rome.'[20]

The recognition of fossils as the remains of once-living organic beings together with the acceptance of the Genesis Flood narrative raised the possibility of human fossils. After all, if, as Scheuchzer and others assumed, the Flood was the principal explanation for the origin of fossils, and since all but seven members of the human race had perished in that event, their remains ought to be preserved along with the other fossil testators to the divine wrath. And yet, human fossils seemed to be utterly lacking. While their absence would later comfort nineteenth-century Christians once geologists had vastly extended the age of the Earth and of non-human life, in the seventeenth and early eighteenth centuries it suggested a regrettable omission in the dossier supporting the truth of the biblical account. The more pious the naturalist, the stronger the desire to identify at least one human fossil. Scheuchzer – alas for his reputation – yielded to the desire and declared a recently discovered fossil specimen to be the skeleton of *A Man, a Witness of the Deluge, and Divine Messenger* (1726). Georges Cuvier later identified the skeleton as belonging to a large Cenozoic amphibian of the salamander group.[21]

A former world

Agostino Scilla, a seventeenth-century Sicilian painter and naturalist whose views on the organic origin of fossils allied him with Hooke and Steno, observed in a treatise on marine fossils that people are so familiar with the apparently immutable landscape around them that they are simply unable to see the history that is written in nature: 'they are unable to grasp with their eyes the true history that the Omnipotent clearly registered in every place and offers to us.'[22] One seventeenth-century man who most certainly could see the history written in the landscape was the Englishman and Anglican divine Thomas Burnet (1635–1715).

Burnet's *The Sacred Theory of the Earth* (Latin 1681, expanded in English 1684–90) was premised on the recognition that various features of the Earth – notably caves and mountains – are more intelligible as marks of fracture and ruin than as cogs in a smoothly working machine. Caves, he noted, are neither useful nor beautiful, and as such could not have been a feature of the original Earth. Mountains, for their part, are nothing but great ruins; they bespeak a ruined grandeur as surely as the decayed temples and broken amphitheatres of the Romans bear witness to the former greatness of that people.[23] Caves and mountains, in short, are signs that the Earth was once radically different to what it is today. Burnet's summarizing image of our disfigured planet picks up the analogy of the Earth to architectural ruins:

> I confess that when this Idea of the Earth is present to my thoughts, I can no more
> believe that this was the form wherein it was first produced than if I had seen the
> Temple of Jerusalem in its ruines, when defac'd and sack'd by the Babylonians, I
> could have persuaded my self that it had never been in any other posture, and that
> Solomon had given orders for building it so.[24]

Lest his readers scent impiety in this line of thought, Burnet offered scriptural
confirmation. His proof-text, which he cited repeatedly in *The Sacred Theory of
the Earth*, is 2 Peter 3:5–7:

> For this they are willingly ignorant of, that by the word of God the heavens were of
> old, and the earth standing out of the water and in the water: Whereby the world that
> then was, being overflowed with water, perished: But the heavens and the earth, which
> are now, by the same word are kept in store, reserved unto fire against the day of
> judgement and perdition of ungodly men.

In Burnet's reading, the Petrine assertion that whereas the world was formerly
destroyed by water it will be destroyed in the future by fire implies that the present world, which will perish in a conflagration, is somehow different from the
world that perished in the Flood and different in such a way that an alternative
mode of destruction is necessary. Burnet's proof-text served a double function: it
provided a scientific problem to be explicated by his theory while at the same
time legitimating the premise on which his scientific project is built.

The Flood is one of 'the great Turns of Fate, and Revolutions of our Natural
World' that the Bible establishes as 'the Hinges upon which the Providence of
this Earth moves'.[25] (The other three are Paradise, the universal conflagration to
come, and the new Paradise that is to follow it.) Burnet's account of the Earth is
a 'sacred theory' because it explicates these hinges of Providence in terms of
seventeenth-century physics. Scheuchzer later wrote a *Sacred Physics* in precisely this sense.

Burnet's account of the former Earth begins with the problem of how to find
the eight oceans' worth of water that he calculated would be required to flood
the present Earth. Short of a miraculous creation and subsequent evacuation of
additional waters, the required mass of water simply was not available. One
solution to this difficulty would be to reduce the Flood to a local event rather than
a worldwide cataclysm, but Burnet considered this an impious solution since the
Bible clearly states that the Flood was universal. Happily, one need not fall back
on impiety once it is recognized that the Earth which was flooded was not the
irregular, mountainous Earth of today but a radically different one. Burnet's task
becomes that of reconstructing the Earth as it originally emerged from the chaos
of disorganized matter in such a way as to match its form with a source of water
sufficient to overwhelm it.

In Burnet's scientific gloss on the Genesis creation story, the utterance of the
divine Word set in motion physical laws of nature that by their operation transformed chaos into an ordered world. Heavier parts sank down in the order of
their specific gravity to form the core of the Earth while lighter matter separated
into liquid and air. The newly formed globe stabilized as a central fire surrounded

by an immense mass of waters, or the 'great Abyss', which in turn was surrounded by air. For a time the air was full of particles of dust or matter, but as they settled these particles mixed with the oily surface of the waters to form a level, even crust all over the globe, which the heat of the sun then hardened into a perfectly smooth surface over which the air was perennially calm. Such was the original Earth: smooth, regular and uniform, without mountains or seas, and free of climatic irregularities. Burnet's extensive description of the original Earth included an explanation of how rivers flowed despite the absence of rain. And while he discussed the site of the Garden of Eden, he pointed out that wide swathes of the original Earth were paradisal. Even after the expulsion from Eden antediluvian humanity, as myths of a Golden Age dimly recall, lived in simplicity, purity and innocence. Burnet made a particular point of explaining the longevity attributed to the patriarchs in Genesis by the salubrious material conditions of the original Earth.

While it would be unjust to dismiss his explanation of the physical nature of Paradise as a secondary matter, the real test of Burnet's reconstructed original Earth is that it solved the problem of the source of the Flood waters. Over time the expansion of the vapours generated in the liquid interior of the Earth slowly expanded the crust, which began to crack as heat from the Sun evaporated the water cementing it together. Crevices opened up and were then exacerbated by earthquakes. As the crust began to break apart the internal vapours escaped, condensed at the poles, and precipitated near the Equator as torrential rains. Finally, catastrophically, huge blocks of crust collapsed into the Abyss and the hitherto subterranean waters surged over the sinking and fracturing Earth. When the waters drained away the Earth that re-emerged was not a smooth globe but the irregular, mountainous terrain we know today. Let us suppose, Burnet wrote,

> that at a time appointed by Divine Providence, and from causes made ready to do that great execution upon a sinful World, that this Abyss was opened, or that the frame of the Earth broke and fell down into the Great Abyss. At this one stroke all Nature would be changed, and this single action would have two great and visible Effects. The one transient, and the other permanent. First, an universal Deluge would overflow all the parts and Regions of the broken Earth, during the great commotion and agitation of the Abyss, by the violent fall of the Earth into it ... Then, when the agitation was assuaged, and the Waters by degrees retired into their channels, and the dry land appeared, you would see the true image of the present Earth in the ruines of the first.[26]

The present Earth resembles a ruin because it is a ruin: 'a broken and confused heap of bodies, a great Ruine, a World lying in its rubbish'.[27] Burnet's cosmogony is a variation on the seventeenth-century theme of the ageing and corruption of the world.[28] Compare it with the lines of the Metaphysical poet John Donne, in which the contrast of the present Earth with the original serves to expresses his sense of moral decay:

> But keepes the Earth her round proportion still?
> Does not a Tenarif, or higher Hill
> Rise so high like a Rocke, that one might thinke
> The floating Moone would shipwrack there, and sinke?
> Seas are so deepe, that Whales being strooke to day,

> Perchance tomorrow, scarce at middle way
> Of their wish'd journies end, the bottom, die.
> And men, to sound depths, so much line untie,
> As one might justly thinke, that there would rise
> At end thereof, one of th' Antipodies:
> …
> Are these but warts, and pock-holes in the face
> Of th' Earth? Thinke so; but yet confesse, in this
> The world's proportion disfigured is;
> That those two legges whereon it doth rely,
> Reward and punishment are bent awry.[29]

Burnet magnificently demonstrates the seventeenth-century tendency to treat the Bible in general and Genesis in particular as a textbook of cosmology and geology, which followed from the shift from symbolic to plain-sense readings of the Bible. Whereas the Church Fathers and medieval theologians had interpreted the Flood as, in addition to literal waters, a flood of passions which brought death and destruction or the cleansing waters of baptism, the Flood story was now regarded as testimony to the history of the Earth, albeit expressed in language accommodated to people ignorant of science. The task of natural philosophers was to 'unaccommodate' the biblical language by explaining the facts narrated in Scripture in terms of the operation of secondary causes. Conversely, the questions raised by treating the Flood story as natural history – Where did the waters come from, and where did they go? How did the Flood change the Earth? How was the Ark constructed and navigated? How were so many animals housed and fed on the Ark? – were thought to have scientific answers.[30]

While Burnet's *The Sacred Theory of the Earth* fits squarely within the seventeenth-century conception of science, theologians and many naturalists sensed something impious in supposing that a catastrophe, even one willed by God, could upset the divine plan and the original harmony of creation. John Ray, for one, insisted that mountains are both beautiful and useful to human beings. And Isaac Newton, to whom Burnet had showed his theory in manuscript and who was generally enthusiastic about it, nevertheless thought that Burnet had abused the principle of accommodation by passing off his own totally unbiblical theory as an explication of the Mosaic account. Newton pointed out that since, according to Burnet's theory, oceans did not exist until after the Flood, fish and other marine life were not created with the rest of the cosmos and there would had to have been a second episode of creation – for which there is no biblical warrant – after the Flood.[31] These were not, however, conflicts between science and religion. Burnet, Ray and Newton all shared the general seventeenth-century assumption that the task of natural philosophy is to uncover the mode of divine creation. Burnet spoke for his century when he asserted that the very possibility of science requires a Creator:

> without God and a First Cause, there is nothing but darkness and confusion in the Mind, and in Nature; broken views of things, short interrupted glimpses of Light, nothing certain or demonstrative, no Basis of Truth, no extent of Thought, no Science, no Contemplation.[32]

The controversy over Burnet's theory was played out within the seventeenth-century conception of science as description of the contingent order of divine creation and within the hermeneutic framework of accommodationism.

Burnet warned early on in *The Sacred Theory of the Earth* against engaging the authority of Scripture in disputes about nature in opposition to reason. He was in no way elevating reason above revelation, but rather offering yet another expression of the doctrine of the Two Books: 'We are not to suppose that any truth concerning the Natural World can be an Enemy to Religion; for Truth cannot be an Enemy to Truth, God is not divided against himself.'[33] And yet, it was not simply a matter of collating the two books. For Burnet, as for Galileo, correct interpretation of Scripture now depended on a proper understanding of nature:

> concerning these passages of Scripture, which we have cited, we may truly and modestly say, that though they would not, it may be, without a Theory premised, have been taken or interpreted in this sense, yet this theory being premised, I dare appeal to any unprejudiced person, if they have not a fairer and easier, a more full and more emphatical sense, when applied to that form of Earth and Sea, we are now speaking of, than to their present form, or to any other we can imagine.[34]

An example of how Burnet's science guides the interpretation of Scripture is his discussion of the book of Job. With Bacon and all the natural theologians, he regarded Job as containing scientific descriptions of the Earth, but uniquely insisted that the book makes sense only if the Earth it describes is the antediluvian Earth:

> There is another remarkable discourse in *Job*, that contains many things to our present purpose, 'tis Chapt. 38, where God reproached Job with his ignorance of what pass'd at the beginning of the World, and the formation of the Earth, vers. 4,5,6. *Where was thou when I laid the foundations of the Earth? Declare if thou hast understanding: Who hath laid the measures thereof, if thou knowest; or who hath stretched the line upon it? Whereupon are the foundations thereof fastened, or who laid the corner-stone?* All these questions have far more force and Emphasis, more propriety and elegancy, if they be understood of the first and Ante-diluvian form of the Earth, than if they be understood of the present; for in the present form of the Earth there is no Architecture, no structure, no more than in a ruine; or at least none comparatively to what was in the first form of it. And that the exteriour and superficial part of the Earth is here spoken of, appears by the *rule* and *line* applied to it; but what rule or regularity is there in the surface of the present Earth? What line was us'd to level its parts? But in its original construction when it lay smooth and regular on its surface, as if it had been drawn by rule and line in every part; and when it hung pois'd upon the Deep, without pillar or foundation stone, then just proportions were taken, and every thing placed by weight and measure: And this, I doubt not, was that artificial structure here alluded to, and when the work was finisht, *then the morning Stars sang together, and all the sons of God shouted for joy* (verse 7).[35]

At times Burnet pushed the principle of interpreting Scripture in the light of science almost into heterodoxy. We have seen one example in the need for a second episode of creation for marine life after the Flood had brought oceans into existence. Another example is his account of the origin of the peoples of America. The problem, and it was one that vexed many seventeenth-century minds beside Burnet's, was that the Bible states that Adam is the father of all humanity and that the world was repopulated after the Flood by the descendants of Noah. Burnet first pointed out that his theory easily explains how people got to America before the Flood: since the Earth was not yet broken into continents and seas, Adam's descendants could have walked unimpeded over the entire surface of the globe (actually, a torrid zone prevented movement from the northern to the southern hemisphere). But, some may ask, how did the posterity of Noah, whose Earth was our broken Earth, reach America? Burnet's answer shocked many readers. It may be, he said, that the first descendent of Noah ever to reach America was Christopher Columbus. The view that all humanity descends from Noah, he insisted, is not a doctrine of faith, however much it may be strongly implied in Genesis. We are free to suppose that in each of the regions that became the continents a few people survived the Flood, unrecorded by Scripture, and that the peoples of America descend from such posterity of Adam.[36] The interesting point here is that Burnet was pushed into this highly contentious, if not outright heretical, claim by the implications of his theory of the Earth. Since there was no way the descendents of Noah could have reached America given the state of his postdiluvian Earth, he abandoned a plain-sense reading of the Bible on this par-ticular point.

A further charge levelled against Burnet was that his explanation of the Flood by natural causes denied the clear biblical teaching that the Flood was God's punishment on a sinful humanity. Burnet had anticipated this charge and assured his readers that 'Nature does not fall into disorder till Mankind be first degenerate and leads the way'.[37] That is, a pre-established harmony between the history of the Earth and the history of humanity ensured that the Earth's crust crashed into the Abyss as a result of natural causes at the precise moment as, in the moral order, the sinfulness of humanity provoked divine wrath. Burnet hailed this har-mony, or Synchronism, as evidence of

> the great Art of Divine Providence, so to adjust the two Worlds, Humane and Natural, Material and Intellectual, as seeing through the possibilities and futuritions of each, according to the first state and circumstances he puts them under, they should all along correspond and fit one another, and especially in their great Crises and Periods.[38]

Burnet here distinguished between two types of providence. Natural providence governs the usual course of nature according to the general laws divinely estab-lished at creation. Sacred or theological providence concerns human salvation. The only recourse to sacred providence in *The Sacred Theory of the Earth* is the divine intervention that Burnet thought must have been required to preserve the Ark from capsizing during the collapse of the first Earth into the Abyss. This event, however, pertains to the salvation of humanity rather than to the history of the Earth and therefore is not part of the explanatory structure of the treatise. Conversely, the investigation of nature can uncover how God ordered the universe and thereby demonstrate his wisdom and benevolence, but it can-not tell us about God's essential nature or his ultimate purpose in creating. Questions about ultimate purpose lead to 'an Abyss of Sacred Wisdom' and the few answers to them we are permitted to know in this life we learn through Scripture.[39]

The synchronism manifested in the Flood between the natural and moral orders, or between natural and sacred providence, was, to Burnet's mind, better evidence of design in the universe than the form of the present Earth so highly praised for its order and beauty by natural theologians. He pointedly contrasted a rhetorical to a philosophical portrait of our Earth:

> if I was to describe it as an Oratour, I would suppose it a beautiful and regular Globe, and not only so, but that the whole Universe was made for its sake; that it was the darling and favourite of Heaven, that the Sun shin'd only to give it light, to ripen its Fruit, and make fresh its Flowers; And that the great Concave of the Firmament, and all the Stars in their several Orbs, were designed only for a spangled Cabinet to keep this Jewel in. This *Idea* I would give of it as an Oratour; But a Philosopher that overheard me, would either think me in jest, or very injudicious, if I took the Earth for a body so regular in it self, or so considerable, if compar'd with the rest of the Universe. This, he would say, is to make the great World like one of the Heathen Temples, a beautiful and magnificent structure, and of the richest materials, yet built only for a little brute Idol, a Dog, or a Crocodile, or some deformed Creature, plac'd in a corner of it.[40]

Burnet advocated in passing the manufacture of topographical globes so that we should easily see 'what a rude lump our World is, which we are so apt to dote upon'.[41] And yet, Burnet did not intend to overthrow natural theology with its emphasis on the marvellous contrivances of nature that lead us to adore its Creator. The penultimate chapter of book 2 recuperates the design argument on the grounds that despite its aspect of a ruin there is enough evidence of contrivance in the frame of our world (and elsewhere) to require an intelligent Creator. Even a broken ruin of a world still displays a designer, just as a ruined building still implies an architect. Burnet's concern with design and providence mitigates somewhat the contrast between the Earth-as-machine and the Earth-as-ruin models. Just as Ray qualified the perfect functioning of the world-machine in order to refute the Mechanick Atheists who had no need of a caring deity, so Burnet's ruined world still pointed to a designer. Moreover, Burnet thought that since the Flood the Earth has changed very little.[42]

Most seventeenth-century natural philosophers and theologians thought that time was incidental to the structure of the universe; the Earth upon which they walked had changed little since the Creation-week. Hooke, Steno and Burnet accomplished a revolution in historical consciousness by recognizing in the Earth itself signs of its history. Yet, no more than Hooke and Steno did Burnet question the biblical chronology. He explicitly rejected a uniformitarian geological explanation for the formation of mountains on the grounds that the thousands of ages required for geological agency to uplift mountains are more than Scripture will allow.[43] That historically minded thinkers as daring as Hooke, Steno and Burnet could not imagine an ancient Earth attests to the hold of the biblical chronology on early modern minds.

Chapter 3

BIBLICAL EXCEPTIONALISM

The Bible entered the early modern period as a uniquely authoritative text. Catholics and Protestants might disagree violently over its proper interpretation, but all parties recognized the Bible as the unquestioned source of knowledge for everything it addressed: salvation and spiritual truths, of course, but also cosmology, chronology, geography, history, and so on. This authority rested on the doctrine of biblical 'exceptionalism', or the idea that the Bible is an incomparable book because, since it is divine revelation and not a merely human composition, its assertions cannot be questioned in the way that merely human assertions can, nor does it have a history of composition or transmission like other books. The unique status of the Bible was further exalted, as we saw in Chapter 1, by Protestant Reformers who countered the claims of Catholic tradition by postulating a Bible untainted by error and understandable by all readers. And yet, even as sixteenth- and seventeenth-century Protestant theologians were exalting the Bible, a flood of new knowledge threatened to undermine its exceptional status. Two categories of the new knowledge were particularly threatening. First, the massive expansion of knowledge produced by humanist scholarship and voyages of exploration about human cultures, both ancient and modern, raised difficulties for the biblical account of a world created between 6000 and 4000 BCE, destroyed by the Flood about 2300 BCE, and then repopulated by the descendants of Noah. This new knowledge coalesced around the problem of chronology. Second, textual scholarship, applying to the Bible itself philological techniques developed in the study of secular texts, produced the daring new science of *critica sacra*, or biblical criticism.[1]

Chronology

The Bible was assumed to contain the complete history of the world. It was not a detailed history, to be sure, but all major events and peoples were present and accounted for. Ancient and medieval Christians (and Jews) had been well aware that the chronicles of various pagan peoples claimed both a content of and duration to history far exceeding that of the Bible. But Augustine and other Church Fathers had provided a satisfying answer to these claims: the pagans were lying. Their accounts were not history but fanciful stories, and how could tales made up by humans (or, more likely, at the instigation of demons) challenge revelation?[2] As new information about the ancient world and discoveries about the peoples of other continents accumulated, however, it became more and more difficult to reject out of hand the detailed historical records now coming to light.

The newly encountered civilizations of Meso-America and China posed particular challenges. While Meso-American religions might be attributable to the work of the Devil, Europeans recognized the Aztec, Mayan and Inca calendars as significant technical achievements and thus their astronomical data implying observations going back tens of thousands of years could not be dismissed out of hand. Similarly, Chinese records, transmitted to Europe by Jesuit missionaries, presented an uninterrupted historical chronicle of a length exceeding the limits of biblical chronology.[3] These newly discovered chronologies prompted reconsideration of classical historical sources, particularly those of Berossos and Manetho. Berossos, a Babylonian priest of Bel (Marduk), and Manetho, an Egyptian priest and scribe of Heliopolis, each wrote accounts in Greek of their respective nations in the early third century BCE. Their histories, conceived in the aftermath of Alexander the Great's conquests and the subsequent incorporation of their civilizations into the Hellenistic world, were written to assert that their respective nations were far older than and culturally superior to the Greek civilization of the conquerors. Neither Berossos' *History of Babylonia* nor Manetho's *History of Egypt* is extant. Our knowledge of them, as in the seventeenth century, comes from extensive extracts quoted by ancient Jewish and Christian authors in the course of attempting to refute their chronological claims. And indeed, Berossos and Manetho not only exceeded the limits of biblical chronology in their histories, but did so on a massive scale. Berossos began his narrative with the creation of the world (roughly paralleling the creation story in the *Enuma elish*), passed on to the list of kings who reigned in Babylon before the Flood, and then proceeded through the post-diluvial kings. For the time span of the antediluvian kings alone Berossos gave the astonishing figure, based on astronomical archives, of 432,000 years. Manetho, for his part, divided the rulers of Egypt into the human rulers, whose reigns he grouped into 31 dynasties (he invented the concept of dynasties, in use ever since), and the divine or otherwise not fully human rulers who had preceded the human dynasties. Adding up the duration of the reigns attributed to each ruler yielded a figure of 24,925 years for the list of predynastic kings, and of another 11,600 years for the dynasties. If not of Babylonian magnitude, Manetho's total of 36,525 years nonetheless immensely exceeded the biblical chronology.[4]

The question of whether and how biblical history could be reconciled with world history as it was being newly reconstructed became a critical issue of the day. Christian scholars did not fundamentally question the Hebrew chronology; the problem as they perceived it was to synchronize the events reported in the various Gentile (the polite word for 'pagan') chronicles with sacred history. The discipline of Chronology emerged to take up this challenge by attempting to relate all of world history to a divinely ordered plan by establishing firm dates for historical events and synchronizing the various calendars. Institutionalized in both Protestant and Catholic universities, Chronology was both a technical discipline and a defence of the reliability of sacred history. The first step in relating world history to a divinely ordained plan was to establish the order of events, even in the remotest ages. But how could that be done? The Bible was an authoritative text, but its lists of the generations and ages of the patriarchs and the duration of royal reigns supplied no fixed dates. And could one be sure that the biblical years were solar years rather than lunar, and if solar, how many days were in a year? Turning to the Gentile histories, how did the various nations measure their time: years of a king's reign, years since the founding of a city, years of a dynasty? And how did they measure their years?[5] These difficulties had caused Church Fathers such as Eusebius of Caesarea to despair of ever establishing a firm chronology back to the origin of the world. But early modern chronologers were confident that they could succeed where the ancients had failed because they possessed a key to the labyrinth of ages and generations: modern astronomical calculations. Astronomy thus became the second pillar, along with sacred history, of the new discipline of Chronology.

Copernicus himself had realized the significance of astronomy for chronology. In *On the Revolutions of the Celestial Spheres* (1543) he had noted that the biblical narrative could be connected to Gentile history because the Babylonian king Nabonassar, from whose accession on 26 February 747 BCE the Greek astronomer Ptolemy had dated his observations, was the biblical Shalmanassar, the Assyrian king whose destruction of Israel is narrated in 2 Kings 17. Copernicus himself did not elaborate on this moment of concordance between biblical and Gentile history, but other sixteenth-century scholars such as Theodore Bibliander, Johann Funck and Andreas Osiander exploited Copernicus' key to produce systematic chronologies that linked as far as possible the certain periods of biblical history to the certain dates provided by Ptolemaic astronomy.[6] The period's greatest chronologer, however, was Joseph Justus Scaliger (1540–1609), a French Huguenot who found refuge from Louis XIV's persecutions in the new Dutch university of Leiden. Scaliger's *New Work on the Rectification of the Epochs* (1583) revolutionized Chronology by bringing the remotest periods into firm chronology and incorporating into it all known Gentile histories.

Scaliger was personally devout and accepted without question the reliability of the biblical chronology and the historical veracity of the events it narrated. But he also thought that sacred history could not be made into a scientific chronology without the supplementary information provided by Gentile historical records and modern astronomical calculations. In *On the Rectification of the Epochs* he set out to synchronize sacred history, Gentile histories and astronomical data into one master chronology. His first step was philological. He studied classical and biblical texts in order to establish coherent timelines for each people. This involved tackling an enormous number of problems over such matters as textual corruptions and forged documents, distinguishing history from myth, contested dates, confused dynastic successions, duplication of names or dynasties and the reliability of sources. The result of his philological labours was a set of internally reliable, but not yet synchronized, chronologies for the principal nations of the world. Turning to the problem of synchronization, Scaliger combined biblical authority with astronomical data. Once again, the Ptolemaic date of 747 BCE for

Nabonassar provided a fixed date. (Scaliger showed that Copernicus had confused a Babylonian king with an Assyrian one in identifying Nabonassar with Shalmanassar, but his insight remained valid and once the misidentification was cleared up the astronomically attested date could be used for the purposes of calendrical synchronization.) Scaliger then established, again by astronomical calculations, certain dates for Nebuchadnezzar and Cyrus the Great, thereby bringing the internally reliable Babylonian and Persian calendars into harmony with the Assyrian and biblical ones. After that, synchronizing Greek and Roman chronologies was child's play. In this way, Scaliger established accurate dates for all major historical events and personages in Gentile history from the reign of Nabonassar onwards by poring over records of eclipses, planetary conjunctions, and other astronomical data. This left the ages preceding Nabonassar. For them Scaliger relied on the authoritative account supplied by the Bible. Working backward from the books of Kings to Genesis, Scaliger calculated that the period from King Jehoiachin to the creation was 3,350 years. The accuracy of this figure could not be doubted since it was guaranteed by the authority of the biblical narrative. But how was one to provide fixed dates for the events of this span of time? Scaliger knew, by combining information in the books of Ezekiel and 2 Kings, that King Jehoiachin had been taken into exile by Nebuchadnezzar in the twenty-fifth year after the accession of Nabopallaser of Babylon, Nebuchadnezzar's father. Ptolemy's astronomical calculation had identified the twenty-fifth year after Nabopallasar's accession as 600 BCE. All Scaliger then had to do was to add 3,350 to 600 in order to arrive at a date of 3949 BCE for creation. The certain but undated intervals of sacred history were thus connected to the astronomically fixed dates of Gentile history, producing a single, comprehensive chronology in which all major events of the principal ancient nations were assigned a fixed date and placed in their proper relation to each other.[7]

But Scaliger did not rest with this accomplishment. In order to clarify and make more useful his system, Scaliger wanted a single universal calendar in which a given event or ruler could be unambiguously located. He therefore devised the 'Julian period', which was a mathematically derived duration in which no day ever has exactly the same position. Scaliger intended the Julian period simply as a tool for dating; the number produced by his system indicated only where in time a specific event occurred, and took no account of its religious meaning. (Scaliger here closely approximated early modern naturalists who sought to place a natural object in the divinely inscribed order of nature rather than to interpret its symbolic meaning.) In constructing his Julian period Scaliger began with Dionysius Exiguus' Easter table, a 532-year cycle used to calculate the date of Easter. The table had been created by multiplying the 19-year lunar cycle by the 28-year solar cycle so that any date can be fixed to a certain year if one knows the phase of the moon and the day of the week. Since Scaliger needed a larger cycle in order to establish unambiguously all the years of history, he multiplied the 532-year cycle of the Easter table by the 15-year cycle of the Roman Indiction (a taxation cycle still used in the Middle Ages to date legal documents). The product was a cycle of 7,980 years, which he called the Julian period because its years consisted of the 365.25 days of the solar year that Julius Caesar had introduced to Rome in 45 BCE. Scaliger's Julian period synchronized all chronologies and provided unambiguous dates – because fixed on a single time line – for every significant historical event in both sacred and Gentile history. Finally, in order to fix the dates of his Julian period in relation to all other chronologies Scaliger had simply to find an event that was dated in all three cycles. He chose the birth of Christ, and calculated that the Nativity had occurred in the Julian year 4713. That the Julian period extended well back beyond the creation of the world in 3949 BCE was not a problem because the Julian period was a purely numerical system. As such, it was appropriate that it should exceed the age of the world, since the goal was to construct a system into which all possible events of antiquity could be placed.[8]

On the Rectification of the Epochs was not Scaliger's final word on chronology. He took up the problem posed by Manetho's *History of Egypt* in *Treasury of the Epochs* (1606). While Scaliger dismissed the tens of thousands of years Manetho attributed to the pre-dynastic rulers as mythological nonsense, his philological studies convinced him that Manetho's account of 31 human dynasties was reliable. The problem was that, since these records attested to the historical existence of Egypt over a period of 5,355 Julian years before the termination point of Manetho's narrative in 329 BCE, Egyptian history predated the Julian period itself. Scaliger's response was to place another cycle of 7,980 years (known as the 'postulated' Julian period) before the original Julian period, and to assign Manetho's first four dynasties to the 'postulated' period. But the theological problem Manetho posed was not so easily solved. Egypt, it would appear, had been flourishing over a thousand years before creation itself. Scaliger refused to tamper with the Egyptian records because his scholarship had them deemed sound, yet there could be no question of doubting the authority of the biblical date for creation. His solution was another conceptual innovation, this one in equal parts ingenious and desperate: 'proleptic time'. 'Proleptic', from the Greek *prolepsis*, is usually used in a forward-looking sense to treat as done something that has not yet been done (anticipating the act). Scaliger used it in a backward-looking sense. Proleptic time treats as having actually occurred events that did not and could not have occurred because time did not yet exist. While the 'postulated' Julian period merely preserved the uniqueness of each date in a purely numeric scale, proleptic time defended the reliability of the biblical chronology of actual, lived history. But Scaliger had to acknowledge that he had saved the biblical chronology only by means of an oxymoronic category – time before time.[9]

The best-known of the seventeenth-century chronologies is the one worked out by James Ussher, Archbishop of Armagh and Professor of Divinity at Trinity College, Dublin. Ussher's chronology was incorporated into the annotations to the King James Version of the Bible, and was therefore widely and authoritatively disseminated throughout the English-speaking world. Ussher was no obscurantist cleric; he was a widely respected scholar, if not an intellect of the first water like Scaliger. Ussher drew heavily on Scaliger in his work, but prided himself on being a more careful reader of Scripture than the master. He triumphantly convicted Scaliger of a careless error on precisely this terrain. The patriarch Terah was Abraham's father; both scholars agreed that the creation had occurred 1,949 years before the birth of Terah's eldest son. Scaliger had supposed that Abraham was Terah's eldest son, but Ussher pointed out that Abraham's mother was Terah's second wife and Abraham was not his eldest son. Ussher calculated the number of years between Abraham's birth and that of his eldest brother, and adjusted all of Scaliger's pre-Abrahamic dates by that number. The result, announced in *Annals of the World* (1650), was that creation had occurred on early Sunday evening, 23 October 4004 BCE, which corresponds to the Julian year 710.[10] (The BC/AD system, which was worked out in the seventeenth century by the Jesuit scholar Domenicus Petavius as an alternative to the Julian period, became standard only in the eighteenth century.)

Scaliger had reconciled sacred history with Gentile chronologies, but in doing so had magisterially demonstrated that the Bible was neither complete nor self-contained as a history of humanity. Worse, the fact that the greatest scholar of the day had been forced to have recourse to the idea of proleptic time (which not even liberal-minded contemporaries like Isaac Casaubon could bring themselves to accept) shows that cracks were beginning to form in the edifice of biblical exceptionalism.

Biblical criticism

The rise of biblical criticism similarly led to doubts about the exceptional status of the Bible. Renaissance humanists, recognizing that the ancients had inhabited a world different from theirs, devised what we would now call the methods of historical philology – rules for testing the external form, internal consistency, and vocabulary of documents – in order to bring themselves closer to it. Petrarch's work on the text of Livy, Lorenzo Valla's exposure of the 'Donation of Constantine' as a forgery, and Isaac Casaubon's redating of the *Corpus Hermeticum* to the early Christian era exemplify this historical insight.[11]

Erasmus and Valla applied the techniques of historical research and textual criticism to the Bible in pursuing the pious aim of restoring the sources of primitive Christianity. While their treatment of the Bible as a document subject to error and corruption disturbed many Christians, no church in the sixteenth century could avoid questions about the reliability of the biblical text. The Vulgate Bible used by the Roman Catholic Church, a Latin translation made by St Jerome in the fourth century, had long been recognized as needing emendation and correction. Luther and Protestants in general went back to the Hebrew, Greek and Aramaic texts, including the Septuagint (a Greek translation of the Hebrew Bible made in Hellenistic Alexandria for Greek-speaking Jews), but they discovered that the editions of all these texts, and the manuscripts on which they were based, varied from one to another. Amid the theological polemic of the age, a succession of great scholars, Catholic and Protestant, rose up to grapple with the textual difficulties in an attempt to establish the authentic text of the Bible. They studied the biblical languages, they weighed questions of authorship and transmission, and they brought extra-biblical knowledge to bear on the sacred text. The discipline they created is called *critica sacra*, 'criticism of the sacred text' or simply 'biblical criticism'.[12]

The work of the Jewish scholar Elijah ben Asher Levita (1468–1549) was fundamental to their work. In his *Massoret ha-Massoret* of 1538 he had demonstrated that the accents and points that tell the reader where to insert vowels and divisions in the Hebrew text of the Bible were not part of the original but rather added by a group of rabbis known as Massoretes who worked in the Palestinian city of Tiberias in the fifth and sixth centuries CE. Levita's revelation meant not only that before the work of the Massoretes the biblical text had been transmitted devoid of vowels, punctuation and other textual divisions, and therefore that no existing texts incorporating the Massoretic points correspond to the original unpointed text, but also that, since the Massoretes had used their human judgement in constructing their critical apparatus, the Bible cannot be considered immune from human fallibility. Levita's scholarship, while read in his Hebrew by scholars like Scaliger (who accepted its implications for the biblical text but refrained from publicizing them), reached a broad Christian audience in Louis Cappel's *The Mystery of the Points Unveiled* (1624). Cappel (1585–1658), a French Calvinist professor of biblical studies at the Academy of Saumur, pushed Levita's historical arguments further in his massive *Sacred Criticism* (1650). After thoroughly examining thousands of obscurities, errors and variants in the biblical text, Cappel concluded that the Bible has been subjected to the same historical vicissitudes as all other ancient books. While he firmly believed that there was an inspired original text, he also claimed that none of the variant texts of the Old Testament now extant correspond to it, and no recovery of any version that even approximates the error-free original is possible. The work of Levita and Cappel undermined the perfect Bible posited by Protestant theologians by demonstrating that the Bible was a book with a human history. Attacked by fellow Protestants such as Johannes Buxtorf as a dire threat to true religion, Cappel defended his work on the twofold principle – also invoked by Thomas Burnet – that piety cannot overrule facts or annul history and that it is inadmissible to overcome inconvenient facts by having God produce new miracles on demand.[13]

This same combination of piety and critical thought recurs in the greatest of the seventeenth-century practitioners of *critica sacra*, Richard Simon (1636–1712). A member of the French Catholic order of the Oratory, Simon possessed a greater knowledge than just about anyone else in his day of the biblical documents, the languages in which they were written, and the history of the biblical period. He undertook his critical examination of the Bible when his superiors requested him to provide scholarly arguments against Calvinist biblicism. Calvinists (the dominant Protestant group in France) professed to gain their understanding of religious truth from the Bible alone and therefore dared to reject the authority of the Catholic Church. Simon's strategy was to refute the Calvinists and defend Catholicism by raising all sorts of difficulties about the biblical text itself. Simon first turned his attention to the Pentateuch, or the first five books (lit. 'five scrolls') of the Old Testament (the Jewish Torah). His *Critical History of the Old Testament* (1678), building on the foundation of the historicity and textuality of Scripture as established by earlier critics like Levita and Cappel, denied that Moses was the author of the Pentateuch. Instead, Simon argued – on the basis of the conflicting literary styles in which the first five books were written, the factual conflicts, obscurities and repetitions in the texts, and the logical difficulty in supposing Moses to be the author of the account of his own death – that the biblical text most probably was written down by a series of scribes over a long period of time, in the vicinity of eight hundred years. Since then it has been copied and added to, and all sorts of transcriptional, lexical, grammatical and translational errors have crept in as books, chapters, sentences, words and vowels have been misordered, lost, added, mutilated and corrected. Simon's subsequent *Critical History of the Text of the New Testament* (1689), and its sequel, *A Critical History of the Versions of the New Testament* (1690), showed that the New Testament was in as poor a textual shape as the Old: no original survived, doubtful readings were rife, and the Gospels showed variations and contradictions.[14]

Simon's attack on Calvinism – devastating if accepted, because if the biblical text is not sound then the Calvinists' claim to justify their separation from the Catholic Church on the Bible collapses – was so corrosive that many Catholics found it could be turned against Catholicism itself. In defending himself against Catholics outraged by his work Simon insisted – sincerely – that he believed the real biblical text to be divinely inspired, but he just did not know which of the present-day versions corresponds to that inspired text. The task of critical scholarship, as he understood it, is precisely to try to separate out the Word of God from the human accretions, variations and errors that have crept into the biblical text. Simon was adamant that this enormously difficult task must be carried out independently of theology; that is, any attempt to supply or justify a particular textual reading because it supports an orthodox theological position is inadmissible. Textual criticism must operate by scholarly methods, and they are theologically neutral. Scholars establish what the Bible *says*; theologians then tell us what it *means*. Simon insisted that his work touched only matters of scholarship and that he left theological interpretation to the magisterium of the Church. Most contemporaries were unable or unwilling to grasp Simon's distinction between textual criticism and theological interpretation; he was attacked by Catholic theologians and exegetes, including the powerful Jacques-Benigne Bossuet, who succeeded in having *Critical History of the Old Testament* placed on the Index of Forbidden Books. Simon himself was expelled from the Oratorians and ended his life as a *curé* in rural Normandy.[15]

The rise of biblical criticism is a good example of historical irony: Cappel and Simon were neither sceptics nor rationalists; their critical work was motivated by piety. But though they truly believed that Scripture contained the Word of God, their work began the process that dethroned 'the Book' from its inerrant, universal and ahistorical exceptionalism and made it one more fallible, particular and historical book.[16]

La Peyrère

The challenges to the status of the Bible from Chronology and biblical criticism came together in a particularly dramatic fashion in the writings of the French Calvinist Isaac La Peyrère (1596?–1676). La Peyrère's two major works, *On the Recall of the Jews* and *Men Before Adam*, were written by 1640 and 1641 respectively but not published until later, respectively 1643 and 1655. The former title refers to his messianic theology, in which the Jews receive a leading role, and the latter to his conviction that there were people in the world before Adam.

On the Recall of the Jews lays out a three-stage theory of sacred history. The Old Testament chronicles the first stage, in which the Jews, as God's chosen people, were the sole actors in sacred history. The second stage begins when the Jews, having rejected Jesus, are cast aside and the Gentiles take their place as the elect. This middle stage of sacred history has lasted from New Testament times to the present (the mid-seventeenth century), but now the third stage is about to commence. The Jews will soon convert to a simplified form of Christianity (their recall) and join together with the Gentiles in one election. Led by the King of France, the new Jewish Christians will return to the Holy Land, which they will cleanse and restore in preparation for the imminent return of the Messiah. La Peyrère's pre-Adamite theory, for its part, asserts both that there were human beings in the world before Adam and that not all present-day peoples are descended from Adam. The Gentile peoples were created earlier, possibly far, far earlier, than the creation of the Jews, although they enter sacred history only much later, after the (temporary) rejection of the Jews. The history of the Gentiles prior to their entrance into sacred history is of no interest in itself to La Peyrère, but it serves to prove that the Bible does not tell the story of all humanity. Once we realize that the Old Testament is the history of the Jews only and not of all humanity, then we will not be surprised that it makes no mention of all those nations that were outside its narrative scope. True to this principle, La Peyrère interprets even the cosmological sections of Genesis as referring only to local phenomena. Most notoriously, he identified the Flood as a local event designed to punish only the Jews of the time. (Thomas Burnet wrote *The Sacred Theory of the Earth* in part to refute La Peyrère's claim that the Flood was merely a local event.)[17]

La Peyrère's pre-Adamite theory was not simply a rejection of the authority of the Bible in light of extra-biblical evidence. While he did indeed draw on the historical records of classical antiquity and contemporary ethnographic data as supporting evidence for his theory, he also offered a theological justification for it. Even as a child, La Peyrère recalled, his mind had been full of doubts about the Genesis stories arising from problems such as where Cain's wife had come from. These doubts crystallized into his pre-Adamite theory when he realized that a biblical text itself suggested that there had been human beings in the world before Adam.[18] The text was Romans 5:12–14. As translated in the 1656 English edition of *Men Before Adam*, it reads:

As by one man sin entered into the world, and by sin, death: so likewise death had power over all men because in him all men sinned. For till the time of the Law sin was in the world, but sin was not imputed, when the Law was not. But death reigned from Adam to Moses, even upon those who had not sinned according to the similitude of the transgression of Adam, who is The Type of the future.[19]

In this difficult passage, Paul sets up a double comparison, principally between Adam and Christ and secondarily between Adam and Moses. A standard present-day exegesis, to which most Christians of La Peyrère's day would have assented, interprets the passage as follows. Just as sin and death came into the world through Adam, so through Christ they are overcome. Adam sinned because he disobeyed a divine injunction, but during the period of history between Adam and Moses the evil that human beings did was not considered sin because the Law was not in effect until it was given to Moses on Mount Sinai.[20] La Peyrère, however, interpreted the passage as saying that the Law came into the world with Adam, rather than with Moses. With this one modification, the Pauline text now provides biblical support for a pre-Adamite theory: since sin was in the world before Adam but only took on moral significance with him, there must have been people before Adam who inhabited a lawless world anterior to and outside the jurisdiction of sacred history.[21]

Sacred history occurs within the biblical chronology, but since the Gentile peoples do not participate in sacred history until the time of Jesus their actual (but theologically irrelevant) history need not fit within the limits of biblical chronology. La Peyrère seized on the same Gentile historical records that spurred the activities of the Chronologists, but with opposite intent. He cited Berossos and Manetho on the dynastic and astronomical records of the Babylonians and Egyptians stretching back tens of thousands of years; he pointed to the Aztec and Chinese data chronicling cultures that antedate biblical history; and, finally, he conducted his own researches into peoples unknown to the Bible (La Peyrère, in fact, was recognized by contemporaries as the expert on the cultures of Iceland and the Greenland Inuit). La Peyrère accepted – avidly – as real lived history the vast antiquity of Gentile nations that Scaliger was forced to disembody as proleptic time. La Peyrère always insisted that the purpose of his pre-Adamite theory was not to destroy belief but to reconcile the Bible with all known histori-cal evidence. In his view, the fact that he could so easily reconcile Gentile historical records with the Bible was strong evidence for the truth of his theory.[22]

Having made a plausible case for his pre-Adamite theory from the internal data in the Bible and from the historical records of ancient and modern Gentile nations, La Peyrère turned to biblical criticism (he was a contemporary of Cappel and had worked out his criticism before Simon's great works were published). La Peyrère's method was to point out the conflicts, obscurities and repetitions in the text of the Pentateuch, notably in that section which was supposedly written by Moses about the death of Moses. These sorts of internal inconsistency had been known long before La Peyrère, and rabbis and Christian theologians had devel-oped various means of reconciling them without raising any doubts about the Bible itself. La Peyrère obviously did not want to harmonize Scripture with his data, but rather to raise doubts about the reliability of the biblical text in order to justify his own religious views. From various textual examples he showed that there seemed to be different authors of different portions of Scripture, although he was willing to consider that Moses might have made a diary that had been incorporated into the Pentateuch. La Peyrère insisted that he believed that the Word of God is contained in Scripture, but because the text which has come down to us has been transmitted through fallible human copiers and transcribers we now have an inaccurate text. La Peyrère's imperfect Bible, which corresponds to Burnet's 'broken globe' of the Earth as a sign of historical-mindedness, served to justify his messianism. La Peyrère's biblical criticism, like his pre-Adamite theory, was a consequence of his messianic vision.[23]

La Peyrère's pre-Adamite theory, which circulated for some time among scholars before it was published, caused a stir among biblical critics but failed to convince them. Simon, for example, argued that La Peyrère had been lamentably uncritical in accepting the immense ages claimed by Gentile records. Further, while La Peyrère's principles of biblical criticism resembled his own (as his own critics delighted in pointing out), Simon described La Peyrère as a man of very limited scholarship, ignorant of both Greek and Hebrew, whose application of those principles was highly suspect.[24] Disappointing as this reception of his theory was to La Peyrère, of more immediate concern was the response of the Church. *Men Before Adam* had scarcely left the printer's shop before Church authorities and theologians condemned it for demeaning the Bible to the same level as the profane historical records of the Mexicans, Babylonians and Chinese. A few months later La Peyrère was arrested by order of the Catholic Archbishop of Malines. Things looked grim, until it was suggested to him that he might be released from prison if he became a Catholic and apologized to the Pope. La Peyrère quickly converted and on 11 March 1657 was on his knees before Alexander VII abjuring his heresy and explaining that Calvinism had led him astray. As a Calvinist he had had to interpret Scripture according to reason and according to individual conscience, and by these lights the pre-Adamite theory carried conviction. But now, as a Catholic, he recognized that the authority of the Church transcends the claims of reason and conscience. Humbly yielding to the authority of the Pope, La Peyrère abjured his theory, even though he contended to the end of his life that no one had shown him any evidence, natural or scriptural, that opposed his theory or any arguments that disproved it. After his adventure in Rome La Peyrère returned to France and became a lay brother in a seminary of the Oratorians near Paris. Here he lived out the rest of his life, spending most of his time searching the Bible for more evidence for his pre-Adamite theory and reworking his *On the Recall of the Jews*. Simon, his fellow Oratorian, got to know La Peyrère well during this period. The two men passed many enjoyable hours discussing biblical criticism and La Peyrère's theories.[25]

Status of the Bible

By the end of the seventeenth century the labours of the Chronologists and biblical critics had seriously undermined the claims of biblical exceptionalism by amassing considerable evidence for two unsettling claims: that the Bible is a book with a history and that the history of the world vastly exceeds in length and scope the limits of sacred history. Despite the genuine piety of all of the principal actors surveyed in this chapter, the result of their work was an epochal reversal in frameworks of interpretation. At the beginning of the seventeenth century interpretation was a matter of incorporating information about world history into the framework provided by the biblical narrative; by the end of the century it had become one of fitting the biblical stories into a more comprehensive historical narrative. La Peyrère had gone even further; by separating Gentile antiquity from sacred history he had opened up the possibility of studying such peoples apart from the providential context of sacred history (for which he is recognized as an unwitting pioneer of modern anthropology). The orthodox, it is true, continued to defend and refine the doctrines of the verbal inspiration and inerrancy of Scripture; and yet the biblical criticism of Cappel, Simon and La Peyrère had founded an academic discipline that would eventually reclassify the Bible, for many, from an incomparable book of divine revelation to a collection of the tales and beliefs of the Hebrews and early Christians, comparable in its content to the tales and beliefs of other Near Eastern groups and in its historicity to any other document embedded in human history.[26]

A century later Tom Paine, attacking the truth of the Bible in the name of the Enlightenment in *The Age of Reason* (1795), wrote:

> Take away from Genesis the belief that Moses was the author, on which only the strange belief that it is the word of God has stood, and there remains nothing of Genesis but an anonymous book of stories, fables, and traditionary or invented absurdities and down-right lies. The story of Eve and the serpent, and of Noah and his ark, drops to a level with the Arabian tales, without the benefit of being entertaining; and the account of men living to eight or nine hundred years becomes as fabulous as the immortality of the giants of the Mythology.[27]

Such indeed would be the monumental effects of the historical challenge to biblical exceptionalism. But although, as the culmination of Simon's distinction between theology and scholarship of the Bible, history eventually became a secular discipline and sacred history a province of theology, the work of the Chronologists and biblical critics did not go unchallenged. We turn to this story in Chapter 4.

Chapter 4

HISTORIES OF THE GENTILES

The work of Chronologists and critics threatened both the exceptional status of the Bible and its claim to provide the authoritative history of the world. The genre of 'universal history' emerged in the second half of the seventeenth century as a backlash against the subversive implications of their work. Before turning to the universal histories themselves we must note that anyone who discussed the oldest Gentile civilizations risked the accusation that their writings, intentionally or not, gave aid and comfort to La Peyrère and other 'atheists'.[1] Two groups of seventeenth-century writers fell particularly under this suspicion: the proponents of the ancient theology and the China Jesuits.

Proponents of the ancient theology, including the Jesuit polymath Athanasius Kircher and the English Hermeticist and Christian Kabbalist Robert Fludd, carried the practice of symbolic exegesis into the early modern period, but the aspect of their thought that concerns us here is their single-source theory of culture and religion. They posited an original revelation to the first human beings of fundamental religious truths, or a primitive monotheism, which was then transmitted to such figures as Zoroaster, Hermes Trismegistus, Orpheus, the Brahmins, the Druids, Pythagoras, Plato and the Sibyls. These figures, the ancient theologians themselves, comprise a genealogy of wisdom, and the writings attributed to them – including the *Hermetica*, *Orphica*, the *Golden Verses*, and the *Chaldean* and *Sibylline Oracles* – were treasured as sources of profound wisdom and true religion. A sophisticated and learned few among the Gentile peoples, so the theory went, preserved the ancient wisdom for a considerable time under the veil of the mysteries, while outside the mysteries it was corrupted into the exoteric religions of antiquity. Further divine revelations successively restored the purity of the original revelation in Judaism and above all Christianity. Present-day paganisms, like ancient ones, are therefore degenerate corruptions of the universal primitive revelation rather than human inventions or demonically inspired frauds.[2] An important, indeed crucial, question for a proponent of the ancient theology was whether the ancient theologians had received their wisdom from Adam, Noah, Moses or some other Hebrew patriarch or, conversely, had the patriarchs been taught by Gentiles? The biblical story of the sojourn of the Hebrews in Egypt made the most common point of transmission a presumed encounter between Moses and Hermes Trismegistus. The orthodox majority insisted that the transmission had flowed from Moses to Hermes; the more daring, such as John Marsham in his *On Egyptian, Hebrew, and Greek Chronology* (1671), reversed the direction of the flow.

The theory of the ancient theology encountered a major stumbling block as a result of advances in textual scholarship. In 1614 the Greek scholar and Church historian Isaac Casaubon redated the *Hermetica* to the second or third century CE. Other scholars similarly debunked the claims of immense antiquity made for the writings attributed to several of the other ancient theologians. Kircher and Fludd, for their part, ignored Casaubon's demonstration and continued to believe that Hermes Trismegistus had authored the works attributed to him. Other proponents of the ancient theology responded with the resourceful claim that while the documents themselves may be relatively recent, the wisdom they contain is far, far older. Despite such ingenuity, however, the combination of philological criticism and the general decline of symbolic exegesis shifted scholarly attention away from Hermes, Orpheus and others of that kind and toward the historical records of China.[3]

The source of European knowledge of China was the Jesuit missionaries who had settled in the Middle Kingdom since the late sixteenth century. These China Jesuits, recognizing that the Chinese would not listen to the religious views of barbarians, sought to accommodate Christianity as much as possible to Chinese values and traditions. This practice eventually so alarmed the Church that the Jesuits were recalled from China. But the point for us is that the Jesuits, in undertaking extensive study of the Chinese language and culture, were forced to come to terms with the historical records of their hosts. Martino Martini's account of the early history of China, *The First Ten Divisions of Chinese History* (1658), which was widely read in Europe, showed that Chinese records, even conservatively interpreted, date the unbroken line of Chinese history to the accession of the first emperor, Fu Hsi, in 2952 BCE. Just a few years prior to the appearance of Martini's work, Archbishop Ussher had published his chronology dating the Flood to 2349 BCE and Creation to 4004 BCE. More seriously for the Jesuits, the Vulgate version of the Bible used by the Catholic Church supported Ussher's chronology. Martini's presentation of Chinese history appeared to contradict the biblical assertion that all humanity except for Noah and his family had been destroyed in the Flood. Noah could not be the father of all humanity if the Chinese records attesting to an unbroken history stretching back before the date of the Flood were valid. Here was a dilemma. If the Jesuits contested the accepted date for the Flood in order to place it before the Chinese date for Fu Hsi, they would face serious problems in Europe; but to contest the traditional Chinese date for Fu Hsi in order to place him after the Flood would be a terrible insult to the Chinese and thereby severely jeopardize any hope of missionary success. The Jesuits had attempted to cut this Gordian knot two decades before Martini wrote by seeking permission from Rome to use the Septuagint chronology in place of the Vulgate's. Permission was eventually granted, and since the Septuagint chronology dated the Flood to approximately 2957 BCE, the additional few centuries it allowed permitted the Jesuits to present Fu Hsi as post-diluvial rather than pre-diluvial and thereby to preserve Noah's universal patriarchy. But even this strategy did not solve all the problems posed by the Chinese historical records. In particular, the Chinese had preserved an account of a flood occurring during the reign of Emperor Yao (2357–2257 BCE). While this date would be chronologically reconcilable with the Ussher dating of Noah's Flood, Martini recognized that the problem of Noah's universal patriarchy remained, since the Chinese records asserted that descendants of Yao survived the Flood to propagate the Chinese race. Martini never clearly resolved this problem. Worse, he doubted that the flood described in the Chinese accounts was identical with the biblical Flood.[4]

For all their differences, the proponents of the ancient theology and the China Jesuits, while not necessarily claiming an immense age for the world, lent support in other respects to La Peyrère's threat to the authority of the biblical narrative: the Bible is not the sole source of true history; there are people in the world not descended from Noah; the Bible does not contain the history of all peoples; and the Bible is the local history of one people only.[5]

Universal histories

By the late seventeenth century the threat which Gentile historical records posed to biblical history and chronology had become a spectre haunting Christian Europe. The genre of universal history emerged as an attempt to exorcise this spectre by expanding the scope of sacred history beyond the Hebrews to include the entire historical record. As such, it is analogous to the response of the Hebrew prophets to the Exile. When in 586 BCE the Babylonians captured Jerusalem, destroyed the Temple, and exiled the elites, prophets like Second Isaiah (Isaiah 40–55) wondered how Yahweh as national God of Israel could have permitted the destruction of his city, his Temple and his people. Isaiah's answer was that Yahweh is not just a national God but the universal God and sovereign Lord of history who uses other nations to accomplish his designs. Universal histories similarly combined Hebrew and Gentile history into a single coherent story – only this time it was the historical records of the Babylonians rather than their armies that had to be reconciled with divine providence. Universal history falls within the seventeenth-century understanding of Chronology, but is distinct from the technical chronology of Scaliger and Ussher. Rather than establishing firm dates and synchronizing calendars the authors of universal histories tended to follow one of two basic strategies in their attempt to reconcile Gentile historical records with biblical chronology. One strategy identified the various rival histories as derived from the biblical narrative itself, thereby reducing the histories of the Egyptians, the Babylonians, the Chinese and the Aztecs to plagiarized and distorted versions of sacred history. The other flatly denied any historical truth to these rival histories, thereby dismissing all Gentile histories that deviate from the content or chronology of sacred history as 'imaginary' or 'fabulous'.[6]

Isaac Vossius (1618–1689), in his *Dissertation on the True Age of the World* (1659), may serve as an example of the first strategy. Setting out to confound all those who would use Babylonian, Egyptian or Chinese records as proof of the immense antiquity of the world and thereby destroy the truth of the Mosaic history, Vossius simply dissolved many of the chronological difficulties by using the Septuagint chronology. He treated the Gentile records as genuine historical documents and argued that where possible they should be used to confirm, rather than oppose, sacred history. Once the Gentile records were accommodated by means of the Septuagint chronology into the biblically authorized time span then the events those records memorialized could be used as confirmation of the events narrated in sacred history. While the bulk of Vossius' work demonstrates how Gentile history lends support to the biblical account, at times he accepts some Gentile testimony over the biblical, most notoriously in his view that the Flood was not universal.[7]

Whereas Vossius, like most universal historians, drew on historical records, the Huguenot pastor Samuel Bochart (1599–1667), another prominent representative of the identification strategy, won the admiration of his contemporaries by pioneering a new field of evidence: geographical names. In his *Sacred Geography* (1646) Bochart read Greek and Roman geographical literature in light of the tenth and eleventh chapters of Genesis, which list the descendants of Noah and the direction of their scattering after the episode of the Tower of Babel and the confusion of language. Bochart argued that many place-names throughout the ancient world are Phoenician in origin, and as such are evidence that the various civilizations of antiquity had been founded by Phoenician wanderers who carried with them their civilization and language. He argued by ingenious (and for the most part fanciful) etymological analysis that the legacy of Phoenician culture survived, in severely distorted form, in the mythologies of the Greeks, Romans and other ancient peoples. Moreover, Bochart declared that the cause of Phoenician wandering could be known with certainty because it was recorded in the Bible. The Hebrew conquest of the Promised Land drove the Phoenicians from their homeland. Importantly, for Bochart, the Phoenicians shared their civilization – religion aside – with the Israelites, to whom they were closely related. The net result is that the Phoenicians served Bochart as a proxy for the diffusion of Hebrew civilization throughout the ancient world and guaranteed the primacy of Hebrew chronology. Phoenician place names show that all the Gentile civilizations both postdate the Hebrew conquest of Canaan and are culturally derivative from ancient Israel and its Near Eastern neighbours.[8]

Universal histories following the identification strategy, whether working with historical records like Vossius or place-names like Bochart, assimilated the content of Gentile histories and mythologies to sacred history. Gentile history and myth possess meaning only in that they point to the history narrated in the Bible; they have no meaning in themselves. Their authors read Gentile chronicles as distortions of sacred history, and attributed all significant departures from it (above all, claims of a vast antiquity) to their corrupt status. These universal historians clinched their thesis by systematically identifying the personages and events of Egyptian, Babylonian, Greek and Chinese history and mythology with those of the Bible (this strategy made no distinction between history and myth; they were simply the two registers in which the Gentiles had at once corrupted and preserved sacred history). The biblical Nimrod, for example, was the original to which the Babylonian Belus and Greek Bacchus correspond as more or less

distorted copies. Similarly, Magog is the original of Prometheus; various patriarchs of the early Chinese emperors; and Noah of Deucalion, Atlas, Osirus and
Dionysos. Above all, disguised versions of Moses circulate through Gentile
myth and history like a plagiarized essay through a diploma mill: he is the original of (and this is a very partial list) Thoth, Zoroaster, Adonis, Hermes, Mercury, Teutates, Cecrops, Amphion and Agamemnon.[9]

Isaac Newton's work on Chronology, which combines technical chronology
with universal history, is an excellent example of the identification strategy,
although it was largely unknown to his contemporaries (his *Chronology of Ancient
Kingdoms Amended* appeared posthumously in 1728, and represents only a small
fraction of his manuscript writings concerning the Bible and ancient history).
Newton shared the goal of defending the biblical chronology, but because he
believed that the Bible itself had suffered doctrinal corruption (see Chapter 1) his
universal history is less concerned with defending the content of sacred history
than with using Gentile historical records to support his own anti-Trinitarian
monotheism. Newton proceeded in two steps. The first task was to establish at
least one fixed date linking Gentile and sacred history so as to permit correlations
among historical records. Newton anchored his literary evidence – in part derived
from contemporary sources such as Bochart's *Sacred Geography*, but mostly
from his own exhaustive reading in classical and patristic authors – to a complex
astronomical argument dating the expedition of Jason and the Argonauts to 939
BCE. The quest for the Golden Fleece, whose historical core Newton identified as
a Greek diplomatic mission to eastern lands, served as the key to his scientific
chronology. All dates can be fixed with certainly by relating them to this date.[10]

Newton's second step was to synchronize the various Gentile histories and fit
them into the biblical chronology as established by Ussher. This entailed repeatedly overcoming their claims to an antiquity exceeding that permitted by the
Bible. A good example of his procedure is his treatment of the Egyptian pharaoh
Sesostris, whom Herodotus had celebrated as the creator of the first great Egyptian empire on the basis of Manetho's list of dynasties. Newton had to refute the
assertion that Sesostris lived in remote antiquity and therefore that Egyptian
civilization predated that of the Hebrews. His solution was to identify Sesostris
with another, much later Egyptian king and conqueror, Sesac (or Shishak).
Newton provided various kinds of evidence for this identification. First, he cited
an ancient authority, namely Josephus, whose *Jewish Antiquities* attributed to
Sesac the exploits Herodotus had credited to Sesostris. He then buttressed this
argument from authority with one from historical method. Newton regarded it as
axiomatic that only those individuals or events memorialized in historical records
were remembered; where there were no records there was no history. If Sesostris
had been as early as Manetho and Herodotus claim he would predate the invention of writing and therefore would not have been remembered. The very fact
that historians recorded his achievements in detail assures us that he was a relatively recent pharaoh, and confirms Josephus' identification of him with Sesac. It
now remained only to link Sesac/Sesostris to the biblical chronology, and this
was the simplest task of all since 1 Kings 14 narrates Sesac's (Shishak's) inva

sion of Israel during the reign of Rehoboam, son of Solomon. The relative antiquity and cultural primacy of the Hebrews over the Egyptians was thus preserved. Newton performed similar operations in order to bring the histories of the other Gentile nations into line with the biblical chronology.[11]

Turning now to the content of Newton's universal history, Newton argued in his Latin treatise on *The Philosophical Origins of Gentile Theology* and its later English variants such as *The Original of Religions* that knowledge of true religion had been possessed by Noah and his sons after the Flood and had subsequently been transmitted to the Egyptians. This true religion, a form of natural theology, consisted of a rational monotheism based on astronomical observation of the heliocentric cosmos. The Sun and the planets were not, of course, objects of worship; rather, the mathematical laws governing their motions bore witness to a divine designer who had established them. Ancient Egyptian priests, descendants of Noah's grandson Mizraim, esoterically symbolized this rational monotheism by encoding in the very design of their temples around a central hearth and fire the mathematical laws governing the heliocentric cosmos. From Egypt these temples (called Prytanea) and the knowledge of the divine order they encoded spread throughout the world. Newton identified all temples containing a fire – from the fire temples of the Zoroastrians to the Roman temple tended by the Vestal virgins to the sacred fires of the Brahmins – as Prytanea. The finest example, although not the oldest, was the Temple of Solomon in Jerusalem, in which an eternal flame burned on a sacrificial altar at the centre of a geometrically precise representation of the heliocentric solar system.[12]

Brotherhoods of priests in various parts of the world preserved the true religion, Newton continued, but outside their sacred precincts the primitive rational monotheism degenerated into the familiar paganisms of the ancient and modern worlds. Inevitably, the popular mind could not sustain the focus on the mathematical principles that demonstrate the divine wisdom manifest in creation, and began to worship the Sun, Moon, stars and planets as deities. In fully developed (that is, fully degenerate) mythological systems, deceased rulers and heroes became identified with celestial objects. Corrupt religion in turn corrupted the understanding of nature. Heliocentrism degenerated into the belief that there was a fire in the core of the Earth that was the centre of the geocentric cosmos. Judaism and Christianity, in Newton's system, restored, but only partly, the true religion of rational monotheism. The Law given to the Jews by Moses purged many of the idolatrous accretions and restored the original monotheism, as did Christianity at a later date. Note that Christ does not represent for Newton a new dispensation; nothing is added with Christ that was not already present in the primitive revelation. And in any case, early in the history of the Church Christianity itself was corrupted by the nefarious Trinitarians. Happily, however, a new Moses has arisen to restore the true religion: Newton himself. That he has been able to restore the true religion of rational monotheism is one more sign, along with his decoding of the laws of nature and of prophecy, that the Last Days are drawing near.[13]

The second strategy in writing universal histories followed the identification strategy to a certain extent but diverged at points where some Gentile history resisted reconciliation with the biblical chronology that did not either travesty the Gentile records or unduly stretch the biblical account. That the status of the Bible lay in the balance accounts for the sometimes vicious rivalry between representatives of the two strategies. The defining characteristic of the second strategy was its sharp distinction between facts and fable; between, that is, the real events and personages of sacred history as well as the genuine, because recent, history of the Gentiles, and the fanciful claims of events and personages belonging to a remote antiquity that are properly described as myth or fable. Thus, Georg Horn, arguing against Vossius in his *Dissertation on the True Age of the World* (1659; same title, same year as Vossius' treatise), insisted that anything in the annals of the Babylonians, Egyptians, Chinese, etc. that could not be immediately reconciled with Mosaic chronology must be declared to be 'fabulous'. Melchior Leydedder's twelve-volume *On the Republic of the Hebrews* (1704) took up Horn's position at length, defending the biblical narrative by demonstrating that of all ancient peoples only the Hebrews, thanks to divine revelation, knew their own past. The accounts of the Egyptians, Phoenicians, Arabs, Babylonians, Greeks and Romans become reliable only where sacred history leaves off (more or less with the rise of Persia). Before then, and especially for earliest times, the past of the Gentile peoples is uncertain, fabulous and wrapped in thickest darkness. Horn, Leydedder and the other champions of the second strategy denied that Gentile accounts of the earliest periods of their history document a genuine historical reality. The earliest rulers of Egypt, the first emperors of China, and the heroes of the Trojan War were not men who had really lived and therefore require assimilation into sacred history, but mythical characters. Helen of Troy was a fabulous babe. All the earliest rulers and heroes of the Gentile nations had been invented in the more recent times of human history in order to pander to the pride of the various peoples, each of which flattered itself as being the oldest and wisest. The transformation of La Peyrère's pre-Adamite centuries into imaginary or fabulous time proved a more palatable alternative than Scaliger's concept of proleptic time.[14]

Vico's new science

Giambattista Vico (1668–1744) held for more than forty years the relatively minor post of professor of Latin Eloquence at the University of Naples. It was one of the two great disappointments of his professional life that he was never raised to the prestigious Chair of Law. The other great disappointment was the reception accorded his masterwork, the *New Science*. Upon the first edition of the treatise (1725) being largely ignored, Vico continued to revise and enlarge it, publishing a second edition in 1730, and preparing a third, definitive edition, which appeared in 1744, a few weeks after his death. While it gained some recognition among Italian jurists, Vico's work did not come to the attention of Europe until it was taken up by the Romantics – notably the historian Jules Michelet, who translated it into French – in the nineteenth century. The Romantics seized on those aspects of the *New Science* that resonated with their own projects, and since then Vico has been hailed as an isolated genius, a stranger to his own times whose message was for later generations. While there was indeed much in the *New Science* for later generations, the work nevertheless grapples with the same problems and pursues the same goals as the authors of universal histories: to reconcile the historical records of the Gentile nations with the history and chronology of the Bible and to demonstrate the providential governance of history. And indeed, with its didactic frontispiece and Descartes-inspired format of deductions from axioms the *New Science* formally resembles seventeenth- and early eighteenth-century treatises. And yet while Vico's problems and goals were those of his time, there is some truth to the legend of the isolated genius because his solution to these problems was profoundly original.

The *New Science* concerns itself solely with the history of the Gentiles. Sacred history provides the setting but not the template for this history. Vico asserted that while sacred history is more ancient and more reliable than all the profane histories of the nations, it is not, with the exception of the first few chapters of Genesis, a universal history. From creation to the Flood the Bible records the history of the entire human world but with the renewal of human history after the Flood the history of the Gentiles separates from sacred history. All humanity truly descends from the sons of Noah but only one lineage, the Hebrews, remained in direct contact with God through revelation and preserved their civilization. The rest of post-diluvial humanity, bereft of direct divine guidance, scattered throughout the primeval forests where within a few generations the harsh conditions of life in the forests had transformed them from rational beings into feral brutes of gigantic stature and bestial behaviour. Vico calls these ancestors of the Gentile nations *bestioni* (man-beasts). The history of the Hebrews is told in the Bible; how can the early history of the Gentiles, the *bestioni*, be told? This is a problem of method even more than of content. It occupied Vico for two decades, and his triumphant solution provided the 'master-key' of his 'new science'.

As he thought about the problem Vico became convinced that his predecessors had been guilty of a fatal anachronism in imagining the ancient Gentiles to have been rational beings like ourselves. One must somehow discover a method by which to comprehend the nature, so alien to our own, of those 'stupid, insensate, horrible beasts'.[15] Vico's insight was that the first Gentile peoples, having lost their reason in the trauma of the Flood and its aftermath, would have been entirely subject to their powerful imaginations. Their languages, traditions and myths accordingly must be understood not as rational discourses or esoteric wisdom, but as 'poetic characters'; that is, as the products of crude mythopoeic minds. The task of their would-be historian is to decipher the historical content of these fanciful, bizarre and often disturbing poetic characters. 'For the purposes of this enquiry', Vico declared, 'we must reckon as if there were no books in the world.'[16] That is, we must turn from scholarly traditions about ancient wisdom to the historical testimony offered by the words and myths of the ancient Gentiles themselves. And yet the claims of the ancients cannot be taken at face value; they can serve as historical documents illuminating earliest antiquity only once they have been deciphered by means of Vico's master-key, which recognizes them as poetic characters.[17]

Vico's master-key to the labyrinth of ancient history recognizes that the human mind has undergone radical change over time. His new science, therefore, is properly a study of the cultural creations of the human mind over the course of its development. And this is precisely what qualifies it as science because, in Vico's view, science is true knowledge of what we ourselves have made:

> But in the night of thick darkness enveloping the earliest antiquity, so remote from our-
> selves, there shines the eternal and never failing light of a truth beyond all question:
> that the world of civil society has certainly been made by men, and that its principles
> are therefore to be found within the modifications of our own human mind. Whoever
> reflects on this cannot but marvel that the philosophers should have bent all their
> energies to the study of the world of nature, which, since God made it, He alone knows;
> and that they should have neglected the study of the world of nations, or civil world,
> which, since men had made it, men could come to know.[18]

Vico sent Isaac Newton a copy of the first edition of the *New Science* in the hope that the great man would recognize it as having brought order to the apparent chaos of civil history, just as the *Mathematical Principles* had brought order to the realm of nature. (It is not known if Newton received it, and in any case Vico's theory would have invalidated his own chronological and historical studies, of which Vico was unaware.)

Turning now to Vico's reconstruction of the early history of the Gentiles, Vico presented the origin of Gentile religion in the encounter of the robust imagination of the gigantic beast-men with the post-diluvial natural environment. When the Earth had dried out after the Flood, a process Vico estimated to have taken a couple of hundred years in most parts of the world, thunderstorms crashed over the forests through which the feral ancestors of the Gentile nations prowled. Terrified of the thunder and lightning and ignorant of its true cause, the *bestioni*, owing to the tendency of the human mind to attribute its own nature to unknown things, imagined them to be the decrees of beings analogous to themselves but hugely superior in strength, whom they must placate and obey. At this moment the first gods of the Gentiles were born – not as an idolatrous corruption of true, revealed religion, but naturally from the fearful imaginings of the first peoples. The same theogony was played out again and again all over the primeval forest and so the first Gentile religion, or 'poetic metaphysics' as Vico calls it, was born from attempts to divine the wishes of the frightening gods conjured up by the terrified imaginations of the *bestioni*.[19]

Two particularly important consequences followed from the birth of the gods because fear of them induced the *bestioni* to restrain their hitherto unbridled passions: they abandoned their open-air promiscuity in favour of a rude domes-ticity with one woman, and they began to bury the dead rather than abandoning them. In this way the fearsome religion created by the imaginations of the *bestioni* gave rise to the institutions of marriage and burial. Over time the civilizing effects of these three institutions transformed them back into rational human beings. It was 'that frightful thought of some divinity which imposed form and measure on the bestial passions of these lost men and thus transformed them into human passions'.[20] In Vico's system the historical process transformed human nature itself; today we are no longer *bestioni*, but we developed out of them and by means of the institutions of religion, marriage and burial that they unwittingly created.

The wisdom of the first age corresponds to the brutish, poetic nature of the first peoples. Ancient wisdom, like ancient religion, consisted of poetic fantasies born of ignorance and conceived through the conjunction of the objects of the external world and imaginations untrammelled by reason. Vico harboured a special contempt for scholars whose traditionalist reverence for 'the matchless wisdom of the ancients' leads them anachronistically to read the rational philosophy or esoteric wisdom of later ages into these frightful fantasies.[21] More urgently, the *New Science* defended sacred history and chronology against those who would use the historical records of the Egyptians, Babylonians, Chinese and other Gentile nations to subvert them. Vico explicitly presented his work as a refutation of scholars, including John Marsham, Martino Martini and not least La Peyrère himself, who cast doubt on the truth of the Bible.[22] All claims for the immense antiquity of this or that Gentile nation rest, Vico argued, on a misinterpretation of the Gentile records, a misinterpretation now overcome by means of his master-key that recognizes them as poetic characters. Correctly interpreted, they are indeed genuine historical documents, but documents that attest not to a vastly remote antiquity but to the centuries of post-diluvian barbarism. Far from there being pre-Adamites, no Gentile nation predates even Noah; Moses could not have learned from Hermes Trismegistus because Hermes Trismegistus is a poetic character representing the crude, fearsome metaphysics of the first post-diluvial Egyptians. The entire regression into brutishness and reattainment of rationality took little more than a millennium to complete. The Chronological Table Vico inserted at the beginning of book 1 drives home this point by locating all the major personages and events of the Chaldaeans (Babylonians), Scythians, Phoenicians, Egyptians, Greeks and Romans in the time since the Flood, which itself is dated to 1,656 years after the creation of the world. The discovery of poetic characters, Vico proudly (and polemically) declared, clears away the rough chronological tempests,[23] allowing the *New Science* to succeed where all previous universal histories failed, and thereby to supersede them.

Vico designated the first period of history the age of the gods, or the divine age, because the early Gentiles imagined all things to be decreed by the gods. Although he devoted the bulk of the *New Science* to interpreting the poetic wisdom of the divine age, Vico outlined two further ages of Gentile history. The divine age was succeeded by the heroic age, in which nobles who believed themselves to be descended from gods ruled over a multitude whom they did not recognize as human. The heroic age, whose values were those of war and the hunt, in turn yielded to the human age, in which all people are recognized as equal, and the humane values of reason, justice and duty prevail.[24] All nations pass through the sequence of three ages, and all aspects of culture go through three stages corresponding to the three natures. The sequence of divine, heroic

and human ages traversed by all Gentile peoples in the course of their development comprises what Vico called the ideal, eternal history.[25] This immutable
sequence of ages functions for Vico as did the Julian period for Scaliger: it
allows one to fix events in their proper sequence. The order of ideas, Vico noted,
must follow the order of institutions. First came forests, then huts and villages,
and finally cities and academies. We can assign any cultural artefact to its correct
period by paying attention to the words and ideas it contains because the meanings of words and ideas shifts according to the order of institutions. Vico offered
the example of the Latin word *lex* and its cognates. During the divine age, when
the feral ancestors of the Latins lived in the forest, *lex* meant a collection of
acorns. As they settled down to an agricultural way of life, *lex* came to mean a
collection of vegetables, or *legumina*. Later on, but still before the Latins became
literate and therefore before they could write law codes, *lex* meant a collection of
citizens and by extension their collective decisions, or 'law'. Finally, the attainment of literacy itself was expressed as collecting letters and making, as it were,
a sheaf of them for each word: hence *legere*, 'reading'.[26]

Neither the ideal eternal history nor the civilizing efficacy of the institutions of
religion, marriage and burial were recognized by the human beings who lived
them. Every individual and collective human act was motivated by some combination of self-interest, desire, fear, fantasy or superstition. And yet, the end result
was the creation of civilization and the humanizing of the *bestioni*. The gulf
between the intent of the actors and their achievement (philosophically expressed
as the 'heterogeny of ends') led Vico to the second great contemporary concern
of the *New Science*: providence. Vico's reconstruction of the history of the
Gentiles demonstrates 'what providence has wrought in history'; as such, the
New Science is 'a rational civil theology of divine providence'.[27] Vico's providentialism in no way cancels the fact that history is the creation of human beings
themselves. Rather than dictating their actions directly, providence uses selfish
human actions for its own purposes:

> It is true that men have themselves made this world of nations ..., but this world
> without doubt has issued from a mind often diverse, at times quite contrary, and
> always superior to the particular ends that men had proposed to themselves; which
> narrow ends, made means to serve wider ends, it has always employed to preserve the
> human race on this earth.[28]

The Gentiles, that is, lived under an indirect or immanent providence. Vico distinguished (in a manner strongly reminiscent of Thomas Burnet) between the
'extraordinary' (direct, transcendent) providence of the Hebrews and the 'ordinary' (indirect, immanent) providence of the Gentiles.[29] His immanent
providentialism (again like Burnet's) is itself a form of the design argument. The
universality of the ideal eternal history proves that there is an order, a design to
human history that is unattributable to human intention. This order, in turn,
proves the existence of an intelligent designer, or in Vico's phrase, a 'divine
legislative mind'.[30] Universal histories that identified Gentile history as distorted
versions of sacred history granted it meaning only insofar as it conformed to
sacred history. La Peyrère, we recall, thought that the history of the pre-Adamites

was theologically meaningless. Vico's attribution of an immanent providence to Gentile history permits him to discover meaning *in*, as well as *to*, Gentile history.

In 1691 the Inquisition had tried four men at Naples on charges of believing that the universe was composed of atoms, that there were men on Earth before Adam, and that Christ was an impostor. Two of the accused were friends of the 23-year-old Vico. The dangers of unorthodoxy in early modern Italy must not be forgotten, and the possibility has to be borne in mind when reading Vico that while he always claimed to be an orthodox Catholic and was on good terms with the local clergy he may have harboured more unorthodox views that he was prepared to publish. Jules Michelet, speaking for the nineteenth century, assumed that Vico's talk of providence was a sop to the orthodox and read the *New Science* as a Promethean tale of humanity's self-creation. The degree to which Vico intended or even recognized his work as a naturalistic theory of culture detachable from its providentialism continues to be debated among scholars. While Vico did leave questions of salvation outside the explanatory structure of the *New Science*, and while it therefore offered a potentially secular explanation of history, at least an immanent providentialism is fundamental to the *New Science* because it serves as the guarantee that Gentile history has a discoverable order in the first place. Without this residual Platonism in Vico's thought the ideal eternal history would be no more than another scholarly conceit.

Between sacred and secular history

Vico both affirmed the biblical chronology and limited our knowledge of the early history of the Gentile nations to the indirect knowledge derived from interpreting words, myths and other cultural artefacts. Metaphorically, Vico's new science may be seen as an archaeology of language. While this metaphor linking philology to archaeology became a commonplace in the nineteenth century, it would not have occurred to Vico or to any of his contemporaries because the discipline of archaeology did not yet exist. Most universal historians, in fact, ridiculed such non-literary artefacts as had been unearthed. Isaac Newton, for example, mocking the Earl of Pembroke as 'a lover of stone dolls' for his collection of classical statuary, dismissed such artefacts as mere amusements of connoisseurs and as such to be despised by serious historians engaged in decoding biblical prophecy.[31] Remember that for Newton the only history was that recorded in written records; he lacked both the concept of 'prehistory' and an appreciation of types of evidence appropriate to it.

By the early eighteenth century, however, some historians had come to realize that artefacts dug out of the earth (coins, burial urns and ruins, as well as statuary) could usefully supplement literary sources as historical evidence or even offer precious glimpses into the past of societies that had not left written records. English antiquarians in particular drew on this material evidence for Britain's otherwise inaccessible Roman and Celtic past. William Stukeley's (1687–1765) excavations of Avebury and Stonehenge, ancient stone monuments in the west of England, are excellent (if slightly later) examples of the use of what we would now call archaeological (along with literary and astronomical) evidence to locate ancient Britain within sacred history. This motivation is important. Stukeley was not anticipating modern archaeology; he was looking for evidence to connect the Britons of Celtic times with the people and chronology of the Bible. The titles of his books – *Stonehenge: A Temple Restor'd to the British Druids* (1740), *Abury: A Temple of the British Druids* (1743) – testify to his obsession with the Druids. In part, this was a patriotic obsession inasmuch as the Druids were Britain's only claim to an indigenous high culture (although how many other patriotic antiquarians built a Druid temple complete with a mistletoe-draped apple tree at the centre of their gardens?). More significantly, the Druids provided Stukeley with a link between ancient Christianity and the modern Church of England. The early Hebrew patriarchs, he claimed, had possessed a version of Christianity. This pure ancient Christianity had been corrupted not by ancient Gentiles but by Moses before being restored for the world by Christ. England, however, had been spared the corruption of the primitive religion because descendants of the patriarchs had come to Britain, where, under the name of Druids, they carried on the practice of their early and pure Christianity in temples such as Avebury and Stonehenge. Their doctrines were transmitted from generation to generation down the ages and passed smoothly into the teaching of the Church of England.[32]

Like Stukeley, the authors of universal histories strove heroically to defend the biblical narrative. Dominic Perrenin, one of the China Jesuits, paid them a backhanded compliment when he lamented that it had been easier to pass from the Ptolemaic to the Copernican system than to extend the biblical chronology by even brief periods. And yet, their efforts ultimately served to relativize the Bible by implying that the authority of sacred history needed to be confirmed by outside sources.[33] Worse, whether they reduced all history to sacred history or rejected Gentile histories of early times as fabulous, the work of the universal historians carried the seeds of impiety (seeds whose germination the Enlightenment critics of Christianity would lovingly nurture in the next century). If all histories are really distorted versions of sacred history, perhaps the Bible itself is a distorted version of an even earlier teaching. This idea, which was at the heart of Deist and rationalist attacks on revealed religion, was programmatically set out in Matthew Tindal's *Christianity as Old as the Creation: or The Gospel, a Republication of the Religion of Nature* (1730). If, on the other hand, the creation stories and early history of the Gentile peoples were fabulous or mythic, perhaps those of the Hebrews were too. On this view, powerfully argued by a long line of Enlightenment theorists of religion, Christianity itself becomes fabulous, simply one more among the irrational fantasies that have hobbled humanity and that the light of reason will expose and banish.[34] Similarly, Vico's *New Science* could be read as a naturalistic theory of culture. In spite of themselves, in short, universal historians participated in the transition from sacred history to modern sciences of culture begun by La Peyrère. Both the universal historians' fusion of Gentile and biblical history and Vico's application of indirect providence to the history of the Gentiles indicate the transitional nature of their work; seen in retrospect, universal histories occupy an intellectual space midway between the theological meta-narratives that were once unquestioned and the secular disciplines of archaeology, prehistory and anthropology that had not yet been born.[35]

Subsequent critical historical scholarship eventually demonstrated that much of the vast age claimed for the Egyptians and other Gentile nations on the basis of their historical records was indeed fabulous. To take as an example the astronomical records of the Egyptians, Babylonians and Aztecs that had so shaken seventeenth-century Europe, scholars in the nineteenth century came to realize that the key issue was not whether they were true or false, historical or fabulous, but rather the kind of historical evidence they represent. In the earlier period star maps such as zodiacs were thought to be planispheres, or projections of the night sky as seen by the people who produced them. As such they were valued precisely because they reflected direct empirical observation of nature rather than being filtered, like so many other historical records, through human beliefs and traditions. Chronologists dated star maps by applying the astronomical principle of precession, according to which the position of the Sun at the equinoxes and solstices changes over time in relation to the zodiacal constellations. By establishing the relative position of the Sun in relation to the signs of the zodiac in a given star map one could calculate, given the known rate of precession, the numbers of years before the present when the sky had displayed that particular alignment and so arrive at the date when the planisphere had been produced. When a date so derived vastly exceeded the biblical chronology, those who wished to undermine biblical authority celebrated the star map as sound historical evidence while pious scholars dismissed it as a lie or forgery. Nineteenth-century scholars revolutionized the study of antiquity by recognizing that the star maps of ancient peoples were not planispheres at all but rather cultural artefacts; they did not reflect the sky at the time they were made but rather expressed the religious and other cultural values of the people who produced them.[36]

Meso-American calendars, for example, proved to be fusions of observation and mathematics with ritual and divination and as such are inseparable from the religion and astrology of the Maya and Aztecs. These peoples used astronomy in order to establish divine genealogies and sanction rulers, to locate auspicious dates for war and planting, to situate temples and cities, and so on. The Maya and Aztecs located all significant events within a cosmological framework of repeating cycles tied to the periodic regeneration of life and time itself. They projected cyclically recurring events ahead into the future and, more relevantly for our purposes, far back into the past – tens of thousands of years in the case of the Maya Long Count calendar. Their records of planetary cycles, eclipses and other astronomical events occurring in the remote past were not direct observations, and therefore not evidence of the existence of high cultures in Meso-America tens of thousands of years ago, but rather mathematically derived reconstructions of long-ago skies created much, much later for religious purposes. Their star maps fused real (and historically recent) and fabulous (vastly ancient) history. In recent decades the new academic discipline of archaeoastronomy, which studies the astronomy of ancient peoples in relation to their religion and culture, has systematized the early nineteenth-century recognition of star maps as cultural artefacts.[37]

In the early 1820s Jean-François Champollion himself exemplified the cultural approach to star maps. The massive stone zodiac of Dendera was one of the prizes brought back to Europe as a result of Napoleon's Egyptian campaign. Scholars who continued to treat it as a planisphere dated the Dendera zodiac to many thousands of years before the biblical date of creation (more soberly, the astronomer Jean-Baptiste Biot hazarded a date of 800 BCE). Champollion, who would shortly announce his decipherment of Egyptian hieroglyphics, refuted all claims of a vast antiquity for the Dendera zodiac by showing, first, that it was not a planisphere but an astrological chart and, second, that it could be dated to the first century BCE by means of the royal names enclosed in adjacent cartouches that he was now able to read. The Pope was so grateful to Champollion for thereby salvaging the biblical chronology that he offered to make him a cardinal, despite the fact that Champollion was an unbeliever.[38]

Historical scholarship would eventually reinstate the remote antiquity of humanity, if not of high civilizations, but not until the reality of deep time had been established by other means. The limits of the biblical chronology were finally shattered not by evidences of human prehistory but by the nineteenth-century historical sciences of geology and palaeontology.

Chapter 5

THE BIRTH OF DEEP TIME

The essayist John McPhee coined the phrase 'deep time' for the immense duration of the history of the Earth as established by modern geology. The 4.6 billion
years since the formation of our planet is so alien to our human experience of
lived time, McPhee observes, that it is almost impossible for us to comprehend.
He therefore offers analogies: the calendar year, in which the Precambrian period
(4.6 billion to 545 million years ago) runs from New Year's Day until Hallowe'en,
and the ice sheet from the most recent ice age melts at 11:59 p.m. on 31 December; or the span of one's arms spread wide, in which the Precambrian extends
from one hand to the wrist of the other hand, and human history is limited to the
outer edge of a fingernail and could be eradicated with a single stroke of a nail
file.[1] This chapter discusses the early history of the discovery that the Earth is
vastly older than the six to ten thousand years of the various calculations based
on biblical chronology. While the estimates at issue here are much, much less
than the currently accepted age of the Earth, the subsequent extension from
hundreds of thousands or a few million years to billions of years was both psy-
chologically and religiously far less dramatic than the initial bursting of the limit
of a few thousand years. Excellent books on the history of geology are available;
this chapter merely surveys those aspects of it relevant to the birth of deep time
and places them in the context of attitudes toward the Bible.

Time and the machine

Orthodox defenders of the biblical chronology received reinforcement from an
unlikely ally in the seventeenth and early eighteenth centuries. Classical physics,
conceiving of the universe as a machine operating by immutable laws, was
concerned with the world as it is and always has been – the world that had been
put in motion by God and had not fundamentally changed since that origin. In
this framework it made no sense to pose the historical questions of the formation
of the world or the history of the Earth; such questions were beyond the limits
of the empirical method, and therefore outside of science. Naturalists inclined
toward natural theology, such as the Abbé Noël Antoine Pluche in his highly
popular *Spectacle of Nature* (1732) and *History of the Heavens* (1743–53), at
once celebrated the perfection of the world-machine and rejoiced that sound
empirical method ruled out speculations on its origin that might conflict with
the Mosaic account.[2] More surprisingly, the same enlightened *philosophes* who

extended the fabulous nature of Gentile mythologies to Christianity in their campaign to eradicate superstition also dismissed the possibility of an historical approach to the age of the Earth, because they shared the conceptualization of the universe as a machine. In short, the prestige of Newtonian physics allied pious naturalists and critical Enlightenment thinkers against the ideas that the Earth had undergone radical change and possessed a discoverable origin.

And yet, the first compelling scientific demonstration that the Earth is both ancient and has massively changed since its origin was accomplished by a great Newtonian naturalist who asked himself what could be deduced about the history of our planet from the principles of physics. Georges Leclerc, comte de Buffon (1707–1788), the leading French naturalist of his day, integrated his ideas about the history of the Earth into his 36 volume *Natural History* (1749–89), which was to cover cosmology, geology and zoology. In the opening volumes Buffon argued that the Earth had originated as an incandescent body produced by the near-collision of a comet with the Sun and gradually cooled to become what it is today. He did not estimate the length of time required for a molten, incandescent globe to become the modern Earth, but clearly the cooling process demanded a very long period of time. Sensing impiety, the Faculty of Theology of the Sorbonne censured his work and compelled Buffon to issue a formal retraction on the several points they declared to be contrary to revealed religion. For the next quarter century Buffon avoided direct conflict with the theologians, but continued to work out a natural history independently of biblical constraints. Finally, in 1775, he returned to chronology in *Introduction to the History of Minerals*. His method, tested by a set of experiments on the cooling rates of spheres of various sizes and substances, was to calculate the length of time needed for the different planets and their satellites to cool from a white heat to a habitable temperature. His conclusions, offered without so much as a nod to the theologians, shattered the Genesis time-scale: the Earth had taken 2,936 years to become solid to the core, 34,270.5 years to become cool enough to be touched, 35,983 years for life to appear, 74,832 years to reach the temperature it now has, and in another 93,291 years it will have become too cool to support life. Buffon thus dated the age of the Earth at about 75,000 years (though privately he estimated it to be nearly half a million years old). This is clearly deep time if not the billions of years of present-day geology. When no theological condemnation greeted these calculations, Buffon followed them up in *Epochs of Nature* (1778) with a seven-stage history of the geological ages through which the Earth had passed from its distant origin to its present appearance.[3]

While the seven ages of his *Epochs of Nature* could be correlated with the seven days of creation in the Genesis narrative, Buffon himself, holding science to be independent of theology, gave no place to the authority of the Bible in his history of the Earth. He did not, for example, grant the Flood any geological agency. In terms of chronology, Buffon sought to dampen potential outrage by pointing out that there would be no conflict between his science and Genesis if the 'days' of creation are not taken literally. Once again the venerable principle of accommodation came to the aid of science. The book of Genesis, he argued, was written for the unlearned; since it was not intended to contain scientific truth it should not be interpreted literally on matters that touch on cosmology and Earth history. There is no cause, therefore, to understand the 'days' of creation as literal 24-hour days; rather, we should read the biblical word for 'days' as referring to periods of indefinite duration. Once, however, Genesis turns from the narrative of creation to that of human history, Buffon accepted a literal reading. His seventh epoch, which corresponds to the geologically modern world and the appearance of human beings, covers precisely the last six thousand years and thus agrees with the biblical chronology. Buffon's accommodationist strategy effectively substituted two distinct chronologies for the single traditional chronology by detaching the vast pre-human history of the Earth from the 6,000-year history of humanity. Buffon claimed the former for geology, but left the latter as the province of Scripture.[4]

While Buffon must be credited with firmly establishing the idea of deep time within respectable science, his Newtonian approach and system of seven ages proved marginal to the spectacular accomplishments of the newly emerging science of geology (to which we shall turn shortly). In the decades during which Buffon was writing the volumes of his *Natural History* other men were attempting to piece together the history of the Earth from the evidence of the Earth itself rather than as deductions from the principles of physics. The transitional figure between the world-machine view of the eighteenth century and the historical geology of the nineteenth was the Scot James Hutton (1726–1797).

Drawing on evidence such as unconformities in rock strata and fossils, Hutton presented to the world, in his *Theory of the Earth* (1788), a vision of the Earth as a self-renewing machine. While most previous thinkers, including Nicolaus Steno, had thought of the (short) history of the Earth in terms of the gradual erosion of the original creation, Hutton countered the agency of decay with one of uplift. The result was a repeating cycle: erosion washes continental rock into the ocean, where it is deposited as strata of sedimentary rock; eventually the weight of accumulated strata generates so much heat that the sedimentary rock melts and, thereby transformed into igneous rock, erupts upward to form new continents. Then the newly created continental rock begins to erode into the oceans, and the cycle starts again. The reality of deep time follows from the cyclical nature of Hutton's world-machine. Worlds are built up by volcanic uplift and ground down by erosion in an endlessly repeating cycle that may have been going on throughout eternity. Not that Hutton believed it had; the world is truly very old, but there had been an original Day of Creation, as there will be a Last Day. Geology, however, can tell us nothing about these framing events; in his famous phrase, 'The result, therefore, of our present inquiry is, that we find no vestige of a beginning, – no prospect of an end.' Just as in the Newtonian account of celestial mechanics the planetary orbits were established by God and tell us nothing about the process of creation itself, so for Hutton God established the present geological order at an unknowable date in the past and will terminate this dispensation at an undetermined moment in the future. Questions of origin and end are therefore metaphysical questions and as such lie outside the bounds of empirical science.

Hutton similarly belonged to the outlook of the eighteenth century in denying any direction to the world-machine. The fluctuating cycles of erosion and uplift effect no development; the Earth has not passed through a set of unique ages, as for Buffon, nor has its operation changed in any significant way from the moment it was put into motion. Whereas in the seventeenth century Steno, Robert Hooke and Thomas Burnet had given the Earth a history but denied deep time, Hutton posited deep time but denied history. Although Hutton built his Newtonian theory of the Earth on the very evidence (strata and fossils) that would form the basis of historical geology in the nineteenth century, he never interpreted this evidence as signs of history. (The astronomer John Playfair, whose *Illustrations of the Huttonian Theory of the Earth* (1802) popularized his friend's theory, disguised its distance from the rising discipline of historical geology by blunting Hutton's denial of history.)[5]

Hutton's denial of radical change, itself a late example of the machine-versus-ruin schism that characterized the earlier period, was motivated as much by theological as by scientific considerations. Hutton, like John Ray earlier, insisted that the Earth is a perfectly functioning machine: erosion is always followed by uplift, and as such its perfection implies both its essential changelessness and the wisdom of its Creator. To posit real change would insinuate imperfection in the design of the machine and therefore improvidence in its Designer. Hutton, then, shared the conviction of Ray and the natural theologians that the structure of the world, in which nothing is lacking or superfluous, displays the wisdom of God, just as he shared their conception of the Earth as a body with a purpose. The cycling of Hutton's world-machine ensures that it is a fit habitat for life, and especially for human beings, whom God, according to his inscrutable will, decided to create approximately six thousand years ago. Geological processes are the secondary causes through which the Creator works to accomplish his ends.[6] Hutton's God, like Newton's, is the God of order:

> It is with pleasure that he [Man] observes order and regularity in the works of nature, instead of being disgusted with disorder and confusion; and he is made happy from the appearance of wisdom and benevolence in the design, instead of being left to suspect in the Author of nature, any of the imperfection which he finds in himself.[7]

Historical geology

Hutton used the evidence of rock strata and fossils to depict an endlessly repeating world-machine. Other researchers, however, were beginning to realize that this same evidence pointed to a history in which the present Earth has come into being out of former worlds massively unlike it. We must retrace our steps in order to introduce properly two areas of geological work that from the mid-eighteenth century contributed importantly to the recognition of both deep time and the historicity of the Earth: rock strata and the action of volcanoes. We should note in advance that once radical geological change was accepted the question of the agencies responsible for it and the manner of their operation came to the forefront. The principal battlelines pitted water against fire and catastrophism against uniformitarianism: was the principal agent flood water or volcanic eruption? was the history of the Earth one of long periods of stasis periodically shattered by violent catastrophes of a force exceeding present-day agencies or one of the action over immense time of the same geological forces operative today? While these questions are capital issues in the history of geology, they are tangential to our interests; we shall touch on them only as they affect the establishment of deep time and historicity or carry implications for the status of the Bible.

The first efforts to map the layers of rock exposed in sea-cliffs and mountains, and by human activity in road-cuts, mines and the like, were motivated by the practical demands of mining and other industrial interests rather than by scientific curiosity, though their theoretical implications were quickly apparent. The pioneers in the mapping of rock strata were Abraham Werner (1749–1817) and the students he trained at the Freiburg School of Mines in Saxony. Their classificatory labours yielded both a sense of the vast scale of Earth history (many of the thick strata appeared to have been built up very slowly) and a temporal framework. Partly on the basis of the fossil content of rocks, but more on their relative position and mineralogical composition, Werner identified three broad divisions of Earth history, each with many subdivisions. The oldest, with the Primary rocks, are the crystalline formations such as granite and gneiss in which fossils never occur and which form the core of mountains. Overlying Primary rocks are the Secondary strata formed at later periods. Loose deposits found on valley floors such as river gravels and beds of sand and silt comprise the Tertiary strata. Later, he added a fourth, or Transition, division between the Primary and Secondary in recognition of the oldest formations with any trace of fossils.[8]

Werner taught that deposits of rock strata had been formed almost entirely by sedimentation at the bottom of oceans. He considered volcanic activity to be a recent phenomenon that had contributed only superficial layers to the suite of rock strata. Other investigators, however, were connecting basalt formations in Scotland, the Rhineland and central France to similar formations in regions of present-day volcanic activity such as Iceland and southern Italy. One of the earliest was the French naturalist Jean-Etienne Guettard (1715–1786). In 1751 Guettard observed that the hexagonal basalt stone used for paving streets in some towns in central France strongly resembled rocks he had recently seen in the volcanic regions around Mount Vesuvius. Guettard traced the origin of these paving stones to the Massif Central region of France, where he easily identified the characteristic signs of former volcanic activity: basalt cliffs, a range of conical mountain peaks, and paths made by lava streams. Just as Vico had transformed the picture of early Gentile history by identifying familiar myths as poetic characters, so Guettard's identification of the black stones familiar to generations of Auvergnois as in fact ejecta of extinct volcanoes transformed the picture of the Earth's past. Similar regions of extinct volcanoes were recognized in many countries over the following decades. In themselves, the discovery of extinct volcanoes need not have led to the postulate of deep time. But their discoverers reasoned that if the volcanoes had been active during the span of human memory surely some record of this spectacular activity would exist, as it did for eruptions of Etna and Vesuvius in classical times. The absence of any such records suggested that the period of their activity must predate human existence and therefore exceed both, temporally, the biblical limit of 6,000 years and, geologically, the deposition of Werner's superficial strata.[9]

Until the early nineteenth century, 'history' in the phrase 'natural history' meant simply 'enquiry' or 'investigation'; hence natural history signified the investigation of nature in general and carried no connotation that the natural world had undergone radical change. This usage was clearly compatible with the nature-as-machine view. The accumulating evidence from rock strata and extinct volcanoes of deep time and radical change transformed the investigation of the Earth into a natural *history*; geology, that is, became a historical study in the modern sense of the term. And yet, before geology could truly become a historical science, interpretive techniques were needed to transform the record of the rocks into reliable historical evidence. The technique of stratigraphy, developed in England by William Smith (1769–1839) and in France by Alexandre Brongniart (1770–1847) and Georges Cuvier (1769–1832), provided the interpretive key that more than anything else transformed geology into a historical science.

Smith, a surveyor and engineer for coal-mining and canal-building companies, mapped the strata he encountered in the course of his professional work. By the mid-1790s he had recognized both that strata had been deposited in the same order everywhere in Britain and that – and here he moved beyond the Freiburg school – a unique assemblage of fossils corresponded to each stratum. Smith drew superb geological maps of England and Wales based on his principle – the basis of stratigraphy – of identifying strata by their characteristic fossils. His maps, however, did not begin to be published until 1815, by which time stratigraphical analysis had been independently invented and applied to the geology of the Paris basin by Brongniart and Cuvier. Their work, appended to Cuvier's landmark *Researches on the Fossil Bones of Quadrupeds* (1812), was widely disseminated. Not only did Cuvier and Brongniart's correlations of fossil assemblages to the strata of the Paris basin represent the first published stratigraphical analysis, but, and more importantly, they used the technique to ask different questions than Smith was asking. For Smith, the relationship between strata and the fossils they contained yielded practical knowledge of the sort useful to the Industrial Revolution: is a given formation likely to contain coal seams; how much reinforcement will a railway tunnel bored through it require? Cuvier and Brongniart, however, used the relationship between strata and fossil content to decode the history of the Earth by defining a set of time markers.[10]

Armed with the technique of stratigraphy, historical geologists set out to decipher the history of the Earth and its inhabitants by reading the record of the rocks. They learned how to trace formations over long distances despite obstacles such as local unconformities or particularly complex crustal folding through the use of distinctive and therefore easily traceable marker formations such as chalk. And yet, historical geologists faced a problem analogous to that faced by the Chronologists of an earlier century who possessed lists of biblical generations or

Egyptian dynasties but lacked fixed dates for them. The generations correspond, of course, to the succession of rock strata; what would correspond to Scaliger's astronomy or Vico's discovery of poetic characters as the interpretive key permitting the alignment of local histories into a single master history? The answer proved to be the integration of stratigraphy and palaeontology. Fossils, now firmly identified as (and the term restricted to) the remains of organisms that had lived in the past, took centre stage. The principal dramaturge here was Cuvier, whose work synthesized comparative anatomy and palaeontology with stratigraphy.

Cuvier's anatomical research, carried out amid the unequalled anatomy and fossil collections at the National Museum of Natural History in Paris, had begun independently of his interest in stratigraphy. His approach to anatomy, heavily indebted to Aristotle's teleological biology, was based on two rational principles: the correlation of parts and the conditions of existence. The former principle states that an animal's organs are interdependent; a carnivore possesses not only teeth but also claws, leg muscles, eyes, intestines, and so on suitable for catching, devouring and digesting its prey. The latter principle states that an animal possesses the attributes appropriate to survival in its particular environment. The application of these principles allowed Cuvier to deduce the nature of an animal from a small portion of its skeleton such as a tooth or femur.[11] This skill, which he publicized with the flair of a Barnum, greatly impressed his contemporaries. A famous story tells how one of Cuvier's students dressed up in a devil's costume and awakened the great man in the middle of the night with the cry, 'Cuvier, Cuvier, I have come to eat you!' Cuvier reportedly opened his eyes and replied, 'All creatures with horns and hooves are herbivores. You can't eat me,' and went back to sleep. In the daylight hours Cuvier applied his anatomical skills to fossil animals, particularly those found in the Tertiary formations around Paris. One of the first fruits of his palaeontological work was to establish beyond reasonable doubt the reality of the extinction of species. Cuvier's 1796 paper 'On the Species of Living and Fossil Elephants' demonstrated that the fossil elephants found in Tertiary gravel deposits in Siberia and northern Europe belonged to neither of the two present-day species of elephants (African or Indian). These mammoths, as the fossil elephants were named, comprised a third species that no longer existed anywhere on the Earth. The mammoth thus became the first species to be recognized as extinct.[12]

The mammoths found in geologically recent strata were anatomically similar to (if crucially different from) living species. The creature Cuvier unearthed in 1804 from a gypsum quarry outside Paris was another matter altogether. By applying his anatomical principle of the correlation of parts Cuvier determined it to be a mammal of a totally unknown genus that combined some of the features of the tapir, the rhinoceros and the pig. As such the creature, which he named *Palaeotherium* ('ancient beast'), was stranger than any fossil he had studied hitherto. As to the question of the creature's relative age, the critical element was the rock in which its bones had been found. The gypsum beds were part of a thick series of regular strata belonging to the Tertiary period, but much older than the superficial gravels that had yielded the mammoth bones. It followed, therefore, that *Palaeotherium* predated the mammoth. Cuvier generalized the case of *Palaeotherium* into an interpretive principle: the stranger an animal appears in relation to present-day fauna, the more ancient it must be.[13] Cuvier's principle of strangeness may be conceived as corresponding to Vico's discovery of poetic characters: both keys interpret remoteness from present-day standards as the index of historicity.

Cuvier presented himself as a 'new species of antiquarian'. In part, this is the by-now-expected trope of fossils as the coins or inscriptions naturalists use to reconstruct the history of the Earth. But Cuvier transcended the commonplace metaphor by emphasizing that fossils, as the documents of Earth history, require decoding before they can be read. If fossils are documents, they are like the Egyptian hieroglyphic inscriptions that were then fascinating France in the aftermath of Napoleon's expedition to Egypt. Both are written in a language that must be deciphered before their meaning can be understood. Cuvier's anatomical principles made him the Champollion of fossils because they provided the interpretive key that allowed the fossil documents to be read as testimony to the remote past of the Earth. Once Cuvier had demonstrated the reality of extinction and sequential biological change, it became compellingly plausible to treat the fossils that had previously been identified as characteristic of given strata as essential to them in the sense that, since the history of life was now recognized to be unique and irreversible, they had existed within a certain span of time. It was now possible to order temporally, rather than simply correlate, strata based on their fossil content.[14] Stratigraphy thus provided the key to another historical labyrinth, that of the history of the Earth. From this point on, palaeontology became indispensable to geological research.

As early as 1801 Cuvier had realized that an alliance between palaeontology and stratigraphy could form the basis for a truly scientific history of the Earth. After a further decade of work he published his theory of the Earth in the 'Preliminary Discourse' to his *Researches on the Fossil Bones of Quadrupeds*. This preface, reprinted separately as *Discourse on the Revolutions of the Globe*, was massively influential, and, as Cuvier had intended, widely read beyond scientific circles. His essay was designed to convey a sense of both the immensity of geological time and the magnitude of the changes the Earth and its denizens have undergone over the course of its history. The thickness and evenness of many of the strata testified to long periods of stability during which the familiar geological processes operated. But the sudden and abrupt discontinuities between strata equally testified to periodic catastrophes that transformed the Earth's crust and wiped out living things. The geological agents responsible for these catastrophes were water or sometimes ice, but operating at a force beyond that of present-day agencies. Each of the ages, or revolutions of the globe, possessed its own distinctive fauna. Cuvier joined a physical theory of the successive revolutions of the Earth to an unrepeatable history of life. He identified the most recent catastrophe, the one that produced our present world and that separates our fauna from that of the age of the mammoths, as a sudden and prolonged inundation by the sea; in short, a catastrophic flood. The catastrophes that separate successive ages of the world explain the fact of episodes of mass extinction, but Cuvier refused to offer an opinion on the question of the creation of species (or the re-creation of species) after each catastrophe. Such a question belongs to 'metaphysics' or speculation; since no evidence relevant to the question exists, it thereby falls outside the realm of science.[15]

Palaeontological work over the next few decades, much of it at first carried out by Cuvier himself, confirmed the applicability of the principle of the correlation of the distance of an animal from the appearance of present-day fauna to its temporal remoteness. Superficial Tertiary deposits yielded the bones of mammals of extinct species but known genera such as hippopotamus, rhinoceros, tapir and mastodon. Remains recovered from lower Tertiary strata were mostly of mammals and tended, like *Palaeotherium*, to belong to genera unknown among living animals. The *Megatherium* discovered in Paraguay was another such instance. These two groups made up the bulk of the vertebrates reconstructed in Cuvier's *Researches on the Fossil Bones of Quadrupeds*. The dominance of mammals dramatically ended in the transition from Tertiary rocks to those of the Secondary period. As researchers turned their attention to Secondary formations they brought to light the remains of a number of enormous reptiles unlike anything hitherto observed. Landmark discoveries included the crocodile-like *Mosasaur*, the fish-like *Ichthyosaurus*, the winged *Pterodactylus*, the marine *Plesiosaurus* with its long snake-like neck, and the terrestrial herbivore *Iguanodon* (some of these names, like the collective term 'dinosaur', postdate the initial discovery). The utter strangeness of these creatures recovered from Secondary strata indexed the remoteness of the times at which those strata had formed. At the opposite end of the time-scale the continuing failure to unearth any human fossils led Cuvier to assign humanity to the most recent age of the Earth. Human beings, he pronounced, had not co-existed even with the mammoths found in superficial Tertiary deposits. The most recent catastrophe separated a relatively short human history from the vast reaches of prehuman history.[16]

Cuvier's advocacy of a short span of human history and his catastrophism, together with his refusal to speculate on the creation of species, might be taken as support for the historical veracity of the Genesis narrative. In fact, the Protestant Cuvier, no less than Buffon, considered science to be independent of theology. Three points warrant comment here. First, Cuvier simply assumed deep time; he estimated that even the relatively recent Paris basin fossils were probably 'thousands of centuries' old. In order to accommodate such deep time the days of the Genesis creation narrative would have to be interpreted as staggeringly long ages. Second, while his most recent catastrophe does suggest the biblical Flood, Cuvier described an inundation that was not universal and lasted far longer than forty days. More significantly, Cuvier's evidence for it was entirely drawn from geology. Further, if Cuvier had intended to offer a scientific defence of the Flood story he would have accounted somehow for the absence of the human fossils that ought to exist as testimony to the antediluvian humans who perished in it. In fact, Cuvier regarded the biblical Flood story as a distorted recollection of the most recent catastrophe, whose true account is provided by his geological research. While not 'fabulous', the Genesis narrative is no more authoritative *as science* than the Flood stories passed down in other cultures; all such tales are distorted legends whose small core of historical truth is only apparent retrospectively in light of science. Third, while Cuvier's anatomical principles of the correlation of parts and the conditions of existence express his (ultimately teleological) conception of the suitability of an animal to its environment, he never used the language of design. His refusal to attribute the matching of form and function to a divine designer sharply distinguishes the protocols of French professional science from those of contemporary British science, which was strongly marked by the Anglican tradition of natural theology.[17]

Diluvial geology

It is precisely this distinction that the English translation of *Researches on the Fossil Bones of Quadrupeds* elided. Robert Jameson's rendering of it as *Essay on the Theory of the Earth* (1813) freely added design language to Cuvier's text, and his introduction presented Cuvier's work as scientific confirmation of the veracity of Scripture. Jameson's harmonization of Cuvier and the Bible was taken up by a group of British geologists who identified Cuvier's most recent catastrophe as the biblical Flood. These men, who came to be known as the diluvial geologists, were at once Anglican clergymen and scientists. They were most prominently represented by the Reverends William Buckland, mineralogist and geologist at the University of Oxford and canon of Christ Church, Adam Sedgwick, professor of geology at the University of Cambridge and prebendary of Norwich, and William Conybeare, rector of parishes in Glamorgan and later Devon and a gentlemanly geologist. It is important to note that these men were not literal-minded biblicists who dabbled in a science they did not fully understand. Buckland and Sedgwick in particular were highly respected scientists and teachers. Buckland's stratigraphical mapping was universally recognized as first-rate and he was the acknowledged expert on the geology and palaeontology of caves, while Sedgwick's work helped to clarify the stratigraphy of the oldest Secondary rocks. And if Conybeare was not a scientific giant like Buckland and Sedgwick, he was a competent researcher (it was he who first reconstructed the plesiosaur). All of these men accepted the reality of deep time.[18]

The diluvial geologists reconciled geology with Genesis by means of a two-step operation. The first step was to identify the most recent catastrophe of Cuvierian geology with the biblical Flood by transforming Cuvier's prolonged inundation of much but not all of the planet's land masses into a brief but universal deluge. Buckland's research on caves and the bones found in them provided the principal scientific authority for this (significant) modification. His conclusion, presented in *Relics of the Flood* (1823), was that the geological and palaeontological evidence from caves, plus that of erratic boulders, gravel deposits, and valleys far exceeding in size the rivers that flow through them, testified to a massive flood about six to ten thousand years ago that marks the boundary between the human world of today and the prehuman worlds of the remote past. Buckland referred collectively to all this evidence for the Flood as the 'Diluvium'. (Most of it would soon be reassigned to the effects of ice, most notably as a result of Louis Agassiz's *Studies on Glaciers* (1840), and Buckland himself came to accept that an ice age rather than a flood accounted for most of his non-cave data.)[19] The second step in the programme of the diluvial geologists was to interpret Genesis non-literally so as to permit the vast time-scale. This they did without hesitation or scruple, in large part because their acceptance of deep time in no way threatened their belief in design and providence (see Chapter 6). They firmly believed, as clergymen and as scientists, that God had created the natural world and established the secondary causes by which it operates, secondary causes that it is the honour and pious duty of geologists to discover and publish.

Their piety notwithstanding, Buckland and his colleagues were chastised by a group of writers who objected to the liberties they took with the biblical text. These writers – known as Mosaic or scriptural geologists – insisted that the history of the Earth must be confined to the 6,000-year time-scale of a plain-sense interpretation of the Genesis narrative. They attacked the diluvial geologists as infidels, atheists, heretics and corrupters of youth. Where the diluvial geologists sought to reconcile the data of geology with the Mosaic account, the scriptural geologists subordinated it to the Bible. And here we must acknowledge that the term 'scriptural geologists' is somewhat misleading because they were not geologists in a professional sense (even by early nineteenth-century standards). That is, however much they might convince the general public of their authority, and therefore however seriously they must be taken in terms of the public opinion of science, no working geologist gave them the slightest credence. All geological work that was taken seriously by experts took for granted the reality of deep time.[20]

If the diluvial geologists were attacked on one side by the scriptural geologists, a far more formidable threat to their conciliationist programme emerged from the opposite direction by the early 1830s. Charles Lyell's widely read *Principles of Geology* (1830–33) was the standard-bearer for this position (as it was for several others of great import for the history of geology but which do not concern us directly). Lyell argued that attempts to reconcile geology with the Bible are misguided, though his goal was not to undermine the Bible but to defend the scientific integrity of geology by limiting it to the study of natural causes.[21]

Lyell appears in histories of geology as the great champion of uniformitarianism. We note here only that Lyell's thoroughgoing uniformitarianism led him to promote vigorously the reality of both radical change and deep time (both of which Buckland accepted). Parallel to Cuvier's principle of strangeness, Lyell noted that the succession of geological and palaeontological change conveys to us the immensity of time far more effectively than numerical calculations. He then reversed the direction of the logic in order to show, on the analogy of Egyptology, that refusing to accept deep time encourages supernatural explanations. Let us imagine, he wrote, that Egyptologists pursue their investigations under the delusion that Egypt has been inhabited by human beings for only one generation before the present. Faced with the astonishing sight of pyramids, obelisks, colossal statues and ruined temples, they might attribute their construction to superhuman powers. Or, confronted with mummies, they might theorize that they could not have been once-living human beings but had been generated in the Earth by some plastic virtue.[22] Lyell was arguing here against catastrophism itself as well as against its use by biblical literalists. Modern-day geologists do, in fact, accept that the history of the Earth attests to occasional catastrophic events – most famously, the impact of a meteor or comet off the Yucatan Peninsula approximately 65 million years ago that brought about the extinction of the dinosaurs and much other Mesozoic life.[23] But such departures from an absolute uniformitarianism, of course, in no way support claims for a young Earth or the supernatural intervention posited by biblical catastrophism. What, in any case, is most important for our purposes here is that Lyell's book was an authoritative declaration in language easily comprehensible to the educated public of the reality of deep time on a scale of millions of years. His concluding remarks in *Principles of Geology* fused the recognition that the Earth is incomprehensibly old with natural theology (but not biblical cosmology):

> In vain do we aspire to assign limits to the works of creation in *space*, whether we examine the starry heavens, or that world of minute animalcules which is revealed to us by the microscope. We are prepared, therefore, to find that in *time* also, the confines of the universe lie beyond the reach of mortal ken. But in whatever direction we pursue our researches, whether in time or space, we discover everywhere the clear proofs of a Creative Intelligence, and of His foresight, wisdom, and power.[24]

Deep time and the history of life

The episodes in the historiography of the Earth with which this chapter will conclude pertain to the clarification of the Transitional strata that Werner had posited between the Primary and Secondary strata, and to the classificatory fusion of deep time with the history of life.

The two men primarily responsible for bringing order to the geologically complex Transition strata were Adam Sedgwick and Roderick Murchison (1792–1871). Murchison, a member of the land-owning gentry who had taken up geology in lieu of fox-hunting, began work in 1831 on a formation straddling the border between England and Wales to which Buckland had directed him. The Transition strata here proved relatively easy to sort out and contained well-preserved fossils. What was particularly exciting was that the fossils were entirely of marine invertebrates. Murchison concluded that the Transitional rocks, which he named Silurian in honour of the people who had inhabited the region in Roman times, bore witness to an age of the Earth predating the first appearance of either vertebrates or terrestrial vegetation. By 1839, when Murchison's *The Silurian System* announcing his discovery appeared, its importance had been confirmed by other geologists who had identified the distinctive Silurian strata and fauna in other parts of Europe and particularly in North America. Sedgwick, meanwhile, proposed a Cambrian era that was even earlier than Murchison's Silurian as a result of his work on older and more complex Transition rocks in central Wales. Murchison responded by extending the Silurian period to include Sedgwick's Cambrian as 'lower Silurian'. Relations between the two men soon deteriorated to the point of total estrangement. In part, this was a quarrel over technical science. If Sedgwick could not produce fossil evidence of a distinctive Cambrian fauna, then why insist that it be recognized as a separate formation? (In fact, a distinctive Cambrian fauna of trilobites was eventually discovered; hence modern geology recognizes the Cambrian as an era in its own right.) But the quarrel was also over who could claim to have discovered the temporal origin of life – and this was the real source of its bitterness. Murchison had traced the gradual disappearance of fossil fauna as he moved downward through the lower Silurian (that is, Cambrian) strata until all vestiges of life vanished at the boundary of the crystalline Primary rocks such as gneiss and schist on which the Silurian strata lay. Life, in short, had begun in the early Silurian era. Sedgwick, of course, claimed the same for his Cambrian age.[25]

Meanwhile, other researchers were adding eras to the geological column based on distinctive fauna. The English county of Devon gave its name to the era succeeding the Silurian, an era characterized by the appearance and proliferation of species of fish. The Devonian era, in turn, was shown to have given way to the Carboniferous, named for the massive explosion of terrestrial vegetation that marked the conquest of land by living things. Finally, the geology of the formerly mysterious Transition rocks was wrapped up in 1841 when Murchison assigned the Red Sandstone rocks of eastern Russia, whose fossils included those of the earliest reptiles, to the Permian era. The result of all this work was not only an orderly classification of geological ages but also a history of life. To move from Primary granite to Tertiary deposits was to pass from a complete absence of life through marine invertebrates to an age of fish, then on through an age of reptiles that began in the Permian and extended through eras that were beginning to be called Triassic, Jurassic and Cretaceous and to which had belonged the *Ichthyosaurus* and the other reptilian monsters that had astounded Cuvier's generation, and finally, entering the Tertiary, to arrive at an age of mammals crowned by the recent appearance of human beings. The fusion of geology and palaeontology inherent in this framework received formal expression in the classificatory system devised in 1841 by the nephew of William Smith, John Phillips (1800– 1874), and still in use. Phillips replaced the old divisions of Primary, Transition, Secondary and Tertiary with Azoic, the era before life (Precambrian), Palaeozoic, the era of ancient forms of life (Cambrian invertebrates to the early reptiles), Mesozoic, the era of middle forms of life (reptiles and molluscs), and Cenozoic, the era of new forms of life (mammals and modern plant and invertebrate species).[26]

Chapter 6

'CREATION'S FINAL LAW'

This chapter shifts our attention from geological and palaeontological science to its popular reception, and to the doubts it raised among Christians as to whether, in the poet Alfred Tennyson's phrases, divine love or 'nature red in tooth and claw' is 'Creation's final law'.

Deep time and the divine order

Lord Byron (1788–1824) drew on Cuvier for his assault on orthodox Christianity (especially its Scottish Presbyterian form in which he had been raised) in his speculative poetic drama *Cain: A Mystery* (1821). Cuvier's science, to be sure, was more of a useful ally than a primary resource; Byron was not attempting to come to grips with geology and palaeontology in the poem, and his objections to orthodoxy were independent of science. While *Cain* brought down on Byron's head charges of blasphemy and impiety (the result of a combination of its content and Byron's prior notoriety), Byron's own beliefs can best be described as Deist. Like the eighteenth-century religious rationalists whom he had read since his student days at Cambridge, Byron rejected much of the Bible and Christian doctrine but retained belief in the existence of God, the immortality of the soul, and judgement in another life.

The poem opens with the first family at their prayers, still within sight of Paradise, from which they have been disbarred by Adam and Eve's transgression of the divine command not to eat of the tree of the knowledge of good and evil. Only Cain dissents from the chorus of praise for their Maker. His problem is that of theodicy, or divine justice amid a world in which evil occurs. He does not understand why he should have to suffer for something that his father and mother did, nor why he should worship a being unjust enough to punish the innocent. The whole system, over which hangs inevitable though as yet unknown death, seems to him the product not of a benevolent deity but a cruel tyrant. Lucifer soon appears before Cain to echo and amplify his protests. He casts himself as the champion of humanity against an authoritarian and arbitrary deity and urges Cain to a similarly Promethean resistance against an unjust God. Lucifer, who promises Cain knowledge as the worthy contrary to grovelling obedience, is opposed in the poem by Adah, Cain's sister and wife (Byron, suspected of an incestuous relationship with his sister Augusta, flaunts the biblical warrant for Cain's). Adah counters Lucifer's promise of knowledge with a plea that he be content with their love for each other and for their children. But Cain is tormented by the thought that his son and all subsequent generations must inherit the unhappiness of an unjust order. And so he flies off with Lucifer into the Abyss of Space in search of knowledge.

Cain sees the Earth gradually diminish in size to a faint spark and then disappear altogether. Lucifer, however, intends to show Cain not other planetary systems but shadowy visions of the earlier ages of the Earth itself; it is a journey through time as much as through space. Just as the cosmic distances drive home the physical insignificance of the Earth, so Cuvier's theory of the revolutions of the globe serves Lucifer's assertion that the present Earth is insignificant in relation to its former states. So, then, on the ostensible grounds that he had promised to teach Cain about death, Lucifer shows him the extinct denizens of the pre-Adamite Earth: 'the world of phantoms, which | Are beings past'.[1] Cain first sees glorious rational beings:

> What are these mighty phantoms which I see
> Floating around me? – they wear not the form
> Of the intelligences I have seen
> Round our regretted and unenter'd Eden,
> Nor wear the form of man as I have view'd it
> In Adam's, and in Abel's, and in mine,
> Nor in my sister-bride's, nor in my children's:
> And yet they have an aspect, which, though not
> Of men nor angels, looks like something, which
> If not the last, rose higher than the first,
> Haughty, and high, and beautiful, and full
> Of seeming strength, but of inexplicable
> Shape; for I never saw such. They bear not
> The wing of seraph, nor the face of man,
> Nor form of mightiest brute, nor aught that is
> Now breathing; mighty yet and beautiful
> As the most beautiful and mighty which
> Live, and yet so unlike them.[2]

Byron later explained that he had drawn on Cuvier's notion that the world has been destroyed three or four times, and that the creatures discovered by palaeontology were the inhabitants of these pre-human worlds: 'I have, therefore, supposed Cain to be shown, in the *rational* Preadamites, beings endowed with a higher intelligence than man, but totally unlike him in form, and with much greater strength of mind and person.'[3]

Lucifer's explanation of how the rational pre-Adamites perished equally derives from Cuvier:

> By a most crushing and inexorable
> Destruction and disorder of the elements,
> Which struck a world to chaos, as a chaos
> Subsiding has struck out a world: such things,
> Though rare in time, are frequent in eternity.[4]

His summary of the resulting transformation of the Earth almost quotes Cuvier word for word:

> Their earth is gone forever –
> So changed by its convulsion, they would not
> Be conscious to a single present spot
> Of its new scarcely harden'd surface – t'was –
> Oh, what a beautiful world it was![5]

In Cain's subsequent vision of a later but still pre-Adamite world, Cuvier's palaeontological researches are used to underscore Lucifer's point about our insignificance:

Cain: And those enormous creatures,
            Phantoms inferior in intelligence
            (At least so seeming) to the things we have pass'd,
            Resembling somewhat the wild inhabitants
            Of the deep woods of earth, the hugest which
            Roar nightly in the forest, but ten-fold
            In magnitude and terror; taller than
            The cherub-guarded walls of Eden, with
            Eyes flashing like the fiery swords which fence them,
            And tusks projecting like the tree stripp'd of
            Their bark and branches – what were they?
Lucifer: That which
            The Mammoth is in thy world – but these lie
            By myriads underneath its surface.
Cain: But
            None on it?
Lucifer: No: for thy frail race to war
            With them would render the curse on it useless –
            'Twould be destroy'd so early.[6]

In terms of the development of the action of the poem, Cain's journey through space and time leads to the tragedy of Act III. Returning to his family, his sense of injustice now fanned to white heat by Lucifer, Cain finds his brother preparing a sacrifice to God. He tries to deflect Abel's suggestion that he too should offer a sacrifice, but Abel insists. When God accepts Abel's bloody offering of a lamb but scatters Cain's fruit-laden altar, Cain denounces God and begins to knock over Abel's altar. Abel tries to prevent the sacrilege and in the struggle Cain kills him. Cain's remorse is instant and total. Whatever the justice of his complaint against God, we have inviolable obligations to our fellow human beings.

The problem of theodicy at the heart of *Cain* is a venerable philosophical problem independent of the discovery of deep time. Yet, Byron's use of Cuvier links doubts about design and providence raised by geology and palaeontology to the philosophical problem of theodicy. We recall that natural theology, which took it upon itself to defend design and providence by evidence from nature, had traditionally been associated with the world-as-machine viewpoint. If Burnet's broken world had troubled natural theologians, how would they cope with multiple destroyed worlds and their monstrous inhabitants? An answer was provided by William Buckland himself in *Geology and Mineralogy, Considered with Reference to Natural Theology* (1836). This volume was one of the series of Bridgewater Treatises (sponsored by the will of the Reverend Francis Henry Edgerton, a

Fellow of the Royal Society and eighth Earl of Bridgewater), charged with bringing natural theology up to date by showing how modern scientific knowledge provides evidence of 'the power, wisdom, and goodness of God, as manifested in the Creation'.

Before discussing Buckland's pastoral arguments, we must note that he was writing a generation after but very much in the shadow of the most successful statement of natural theology, William Paley's (1743–1805) *Natural Theology, or Evidences of the Existence and Attributes of the Deity Collected from the Appearances of Nature* (1802). Paley's work opens with his famous analogy of the watch. Suppose that, in crossing a heath, I kick my foot against a stone. If I were asked how it came to be there, I might reply that for all I knew it had lain there for ever. But should I stumble on a watch, I would not give that answer because it is obvious that the watch has been contrived for the purpose of telling time. Such a contrivance, so marvellously designed for a purpose, must surely be the work of an artificer. The universe, Paley suggested, is like the watch rather than the stone; it is a complex, ordered entity, and from this one must infer that it had an artificer or designer – in short, the universe was created by an intelligence vastly greater than our own, but yet not wholly dissimilar. The rest of the book itemizes instance after instance of contrivance in nature, or natural phenomena in which parts work together in an arrangement that is essential to their function and in which the function of the whole has a discernible and beneficial use. The webbed feet of a swimming duck and the barbed tongue of an insectivorous woodpecker are both examples of the matching of form to function, but Paley's favourite example – and, to his mind – irrefutable proof of an intelligent designer of the universe – is the eye. The exemplary nature and subsequent popularity of this passage warrants extensive quotation:

> Were there no example in the world of contrivance except that of the eye, it would be alone sufficient to support the conclusion which we draw from it, as to the necessity of an intelligent Creator ... Its coats and humours, constructed as the lenses of a telescope are constructed, for the refraction of rays of light to a point, which forms the proper action of the organ; the provision in its muscular tendons for turning its pupil to the object, similar to that which is given to the telescope by its screws ...; the further provision for its defence, for its constant lubricity and moisture, which we see in its socket and its lids, in its gland for the secretion of the matter of tears ...; these provisions compose altogether an apparatus, a system of parts, a preparation of means, so manifest in their design, so exquisite in their contrivance, so successful in their issue, so precious and so infinitely beneficial in their use, as, in my opinion, to bear down all doubt that can be raised upon the subject.[7]

This natural world that bears witness to the existence of the Creator also for Paley testifies to his attributes, especially his goodness: 'It is a happy world after all', he remarks in the course of a long passage enumerating the various Disney-like joys of being a fly, an aphid, a fish and a shrimp.[8] As marks of design and evidences of benevolence are everywhere discernible in the natural order, 'the world thenceforth becomes a temple, and life itself one continued act of adoration'.[9]

Buckland's Bridgewater assignment was to discern and celebrate marks of design and evidences of benevolence in the former ages of the Earth; he was to be the Paley of deep time. *Geology and Mineralogy* opens with a preliminary chapter in which he acknowledged (as he must in a book intended for the general public) that the necessary acceptance of deep time requires one to abandon a literal interpretation of Scripture. Buckland assured his readers that the vastly expanded range of natural theology accomplished by such a concession more than adequately compensates for the loss of literalness. His preferred strategy of reconciliation was not to interpret the 'days' of creation as ages, but what came to be called the 'gap theory'. The idea here is that all of deep time may be placed in an interval or gap posited between the second and third verses of the first chapter of Genesis. Accordingly, he interpreted 'In the beginning' as referring to the millions of years antecedent to the most recent catastrophe and judged that Moses had omitted the events of these epochs from his account because they are irrelevant to the history of humanity. The Earth 'without form and void' of verse 2 then refers to the wreck and ruins of a former world out of which God created our world. With verse 3 ('And God said, "Let there be light"') begins the account of the creation of our world, which dates back only to the most recent catastrophe and thus lies within the limits of the traditional biblical chronology. At this point the gap theory rejoins and affirms a literal reading of the Mosaic narrative. Buckland later noted that it is the total absence of human fossils that permits the reconciliation of the geological and Mosaic chronologies. He concluded his excursus on biblical interpretation with the twofold reminder that in such matters it is not a question of the correctness of the Mosaic narrative but of our interpretation of it, and that Moses' object was not to state *in what manner*, but *by whom*, the world was made. The Bible teaches religious and not scientific truths.[10]

Buckland's geological evidences of design fall into the two categories of purpose and temporal origin. The result of the operation of geological agencies has been to form dry land and so furnish it as to anticipate the needs of the future species of terrestrial creatures that were to inhabit it. Human beings have been the beneficiaries, not only of this general providential design, but also of the particular geological processes that produced deposits of coal, iron and the other natural resources needful to our safety and well-being. It should be noted that Buckland is not claiming that geological phenomena exist solely and exclusively for our benefit. Their future value to us was foreseen by God, but we must confess that they may have some other role independent of us in God's plan for creation. Turning to the second category, geology's demonstration that there was a period before organic beings existed proves that living beings must have been created at a certain moment in time by an intelligent and all-wise Creator.[11]

When he moves on to consider the palaeontological evidence for design, Buckland finds himself awash in a sea of evidence so vast that it requires almost four hundred pages to pass from 'Proofs of design in the structure of fossil vertebrate animals' through molluscs and invertebrates to 'Proofs of design in the structure of fossil vegetables'. Buckland's discussion of fossil vertebrates featured two mammals (*Dinotherium* and *Megatherium*) and several reptiles: *Ichthyosaurus*, *Plesiosaurus*, *Mosasaurus*, *Pterodactylus*, *Megalosaurus* and *Iguanodon*. His words about pterodactyls apply programmatically to the entire section: those creatures of exceedingly remote ages may at first seem monstrous to us, but examination of their remains shows that they were as carefully designed as any being living today. In drawing explicitly on Cuvier's anatomical principles of the subordination of characters and the correlation of parts in his demonstration of the wise design of extinct monsters, Buckland exemplifies the English appropriation of Cuvier to natural theology.[12] The summary of the *Megatherium* may stand for his approach throughout:

> His entire frame was an apparatus of colossal mechanism, adapted exactly to the work it had to do; strong and ponderous, in proportion as this work was heavy, and calculated to be the vehicle of life and enjoyment to a gigantic race of quadrupeds; which, though they have ceased to be counted among the living inhabitants of our planet, have, in their fossil bones, left behind them imperishable monuments of the consummate skill with which they were constructed. Each limb, and fragment of a limb, forming co-ordinate parts of a well adjusted and perfect whole; and through all their deviations from the form and proportion of the limbs of other quadrupeds, affording fresh proofs of the infinitely varied and inexhaustible contrivances of Creative Wisdom.[13]

While Buckland often echoed Paley, as in his inference of design from the structure of the eye of the Cambrian trilobite, he thought that geological evidence allowed him to improve on Paley's natural theology. After rehearsing in his conclusion Paley's opening scene contrasting a watch to a stone and noting that Paley had observed that if I were asked how the stone came to be there I might reply that for all I knew it had lain there for ever, Buckland trumped him with the exclamation 'Nay': geology has demonstrated that the Earth is not eternal. He then went on to offer a set of scenarios in which he assigned a geological classification to the stone that Paley had left unidentified. Perhaps it is a pebble or a sandstone or conglomerate, perhaps it is fossil-bearing, or even granite or other Primary rock. For each hypothetical identity Buckland showed that the stone had not been lying in wait for Paley's foot from eternity but must have come into its present state and location as a result of historical processes. Geology thereby confounds the pernicious doctrine of the eternity of the world and establishes that even rocks come into existence by an act of creation at a particular moment in time. Geology and palaeontology, Buckland assured his readers in his concluding peroration, in offering abundant proofs of the direct agency of a Creator, have 'lighted a new lamp along the path of Natural Theology'.[14]

Scenes from deep time

What sort of idea did the educated general public of the second quarter of the nineteenth century have of deep time and its denizens? What did they picture in their mind's eye when they tried to imagine Buckland's extinct monsters or Byron's phantoms? The answer lies in large part in the new pictorial genre of 'scenes from deep time'. These early ancestors of *Jurassic Park* typically featured one or more of the great reptiles such as an ichthyosaur, plesiosaur or pterodactyl in an environment indicated as prehistoric by the presence of various extinct invertebrates, shells and plants. While the dramatis personae of the scenes changed little, Martin Rudwick has identified a clear divergence in affect within the genre between pastoral and gothic. In the earliest scenes even incidents of predation did not disturb their overall peacefulness. An example is the scene chosen by George Richardson, curator of the Mantellian Museum (which housed the fossil collection assembled by the physician Gideon Mantell), as the frontispiece to his *Sketches in Prose and Verse* (1838). 'The Ancient Weald of Sussex' featured an iguanodon, but the gleam in the iguanodon's eye, as Rudwick remarks, belies its fearsome appearance. Richardson epitomized the pastoral side of the genre in some lines of verse that he offered as a general commentary on the Museum's collection, lines that would have warmed the heart of the most sentimental of natural theologians:

> Yet these giant forms tremendous,
> Creatures wondrous, wild, stupendous, –
> Huge, – that fancy cannot frame them;
> Wild, – that language may not name them,
> Differing from a world like this,
> Each and all were framed for bliss;
> Form'd to share, without alloy,
> Each its element of joy,
> By that Power that rules to bless,
> All were made for happiness![15]

Gideon Mantell himself published his *Wonders of Geology* (1838) in the same year as Richardson's *Sketches in Prose and Verse* appeared. Mantell's frontispiece also features iguanodons, but 'The Country of the Iguanodon' depicts a truly terrifying scene of ferocious creatures tearing at each other in an eerie landscape. The creator of this image, John Martin (1789–1854), was an established artist who specialized in 'Gothick' or 'Romantic' scenes of tragedy and destruction. Martin quickly became a sought-after illustrator for scenes of deep time.[16] The choice between pastoral or gothic representations of the world of deep time had little to do with the scientific evidence itself. After all, a gleam in an iguanodon's eye does not fossilize. Nor was it the case that the gothic images were more troubling to Christians or more faithful to the palaeontological evidence. The genre itself, and not the tone of its presentation, conveyed the strangeness of the creatures and therefore the vast remoteness of deep time. Moreover, the artistic conventions that Martin and others used to make their creatures so terrible were largely derived from traditional Christian iconography of Saint George and the Dragon. Mantell, at least, chose Martin to illustrate his book because he thought a dramatic illustration would help increase its sales. This bit of calculation strongly suggests that gothic pictures were not linked to religious doubts in the public mind, as such a connection would presumably have harmed sales.[17]

In cataloguing mid-century depictions of extinct monsters one must not neglect to mention Jules Verne's 1864 adventure story, *Voyage to the Centre of the Earth*. In this dramatization of the new nineteenth-century historical sciences a philological mystery leads to a geological adventure for Professor Hardwigg and his nephew. In the chapter that concerns us, 'Terrific Saurian Combat', the adventurers' raft is almost destroyed in crossing the Central Sea deep in the Earth when they are caught in a terrifying fight between an ichthyosaur and a plesiosaur. Verne's vivid description of the fury of the monsters brought John Martin's gothic images to life.

The circulation of these scenes throughout Europe was an important means by which consciousness of deep time began to spread beyond the ranks of geologists and palaeontologists. Two additional means by which deep time took its place within the imagination of the period were the massively popular introductory textbooks on geology and, especially in Britain, the reconstructions of extinct creatures displayed on the grounds of the Crystal Palace from the early 1850s. The models of *Iguanodon*, *Ichthyosaurus*, *Megatherium*, *Mastodon*, and others were wildly popular, spinning off articles and cartoons in popular magazines and even, in what must mark the birth of the blockbuster museum show, small souvenir reproductions. While the general public did tend to collapse the carefully demarcated eras of geological history into a single, undifferentiated 'ancient world', the fundamental distinction between the human world of today and a radically different prehuman world of immense if uncertain duration had been assimilated.[18]

The establishment of deep time presented the mid-nineteenth century with two distinct issues: it challenged both a plain-sense reading of the Mosaic creation narrative and belief in divine design and providence. On the first issue, the fault-line ran between those like Buckland who accepted deep time and therefore interpreted the Genesis narrative in a non-literal manner and those who defended the literal truth of the Mosaic account. The popularity of Buckland's Bridgewater Treatise shows that at least a segment of the educated general public could follow him. But it is also true that Buckland's work was highly controversial; many people, including clergymen and educated laypeople, were offended by its rejection of biblical literalism and apparent subordination of Scripture to science. On the issue of design, on the other hand, Buckland and the literalists were in agreement. Buckland had no doubt whatsoever that geology and palaeontology bear witness to the same wise benevolence of God the Creator and to his continuing oversight of his Creation that the literalists affirmed in relation to a young Earth. The opposing party here is more difficult to define, yet there were those who found the geological evidence of deep time convincing but could not share Buckland's easy confidence that it left design and providence untouched. This position picked up on some of the difficulties Byron had instinctively grasped from reading Cuvier but, in the years before Darwin, it was more an unquiet foreboding than a reasoned conviction. Our canary in this coal mine will be Alfred Tennyson's (1809–1892) great poem, *In Memoriam*.

'Are God and Nature then at strife?'

The poem was published anonymously in 1850, but its authorship was an open secret. Its full title is *In Memoriam A. H. H. Obit MDCCCXXXIII*. A. H. H. was

Arthur Henry Hallam. The friendship of Alfred and Arthur, who had met as students at Cambridge in 1829, was an exercise in mutual hero-worship; Alfred saw in Arthur the intellectual brilliance of Samual Taylor Coleridge, while Hallam recognized Tennyson as the new Wordsworth. In 1833, shortly after becoming engaged to Alfred's sister, Emily, Arthur died suddenly while abroad. *In Memoriam*, in which Tennyson worked out his emotional and intellectual response to the death of his friend, fused private sorrow with metaphysical anguish. His desire to meet his friend again in another life led him to question whether we can be sure of immortality, while his suffering raised doubts about whether the world is really governed by a law of love; and these larger questions, in turn, demanded consideration of the evidence presented by geology and palaeontology. It was the confrontation within a private spiritual crisis of the challenges to faith posed by the new historical sciences that accounts for the massive popularity of the poem among Victorians.

The poem is divided into 131 sections, or groups of lyrics of varying length. In sections 31–36 Tennyson introduces the problem of faith in immortality, and establishes an important distinction between external and interior faith by means of a meditation on the Gospel story of Jesus raising Lazarus from the dead (John 11:1–44). When Lazarus returns home to his sister Mary's house, she, unlike the poet, does not wonder what he experienced during those four days among the dead; she is wholly absorbed in joy at his return and devotion to Jesus. The next section contrasts Mary's unquestioning faith in Jesus as an external authority with one whose faith no longer requires an external object:

> O thou that after toil and storm
> Mayst seem to have reach'd a purer air,
> Whose faith has centre everywhere,
> Nor cares to fix itself to form.[19]

Such an interior faith carries with it its own conviction, but those who have achieved this spiritual independence must not disturb the simpler external faith of those, like Mary, for whom it brings serenity and moves to perform good actions.

The poet, linking himself to the interior faith, next turns away from revealed truth to seek for some assurance of immortality in his own nature. Without that assurance, life would be meaningless and God irrelevant:

> My own dim life should teach me this,
> That life shall live for evermore,
> Else earth is darkness at the core,
> And dust and ashes all that is;
>
> …
>
> What then were God to such as I?
>
> …
>
> 'Twere best at once to sink to peace,
> Like birds the charming serpent draws,
> To drop head-foremost in the jaws
> Of vacant darkness and to cease.[20]

It is vain to reply that even then love might give a value to life, for the awareness of one's mortality would make it a fraudulent value. Tennyson expresses the destructive action of doubt in the imagery of geological erosion ('Aeonian' below refers to the remote past ages uncovered by geology):

> But I should turn mine ears and hear
>
> The moanings of the homeless sea,
> The sound of streams that swift or slow
> Draw down Aeonian hills, and sow
> The dust of continents to be;
>
> And Love would answer with a sigh,
> 'The sound of that forgetful shore
> Will change my sweetness more and more,
> Half-dead to know that I shall die.'[21]

We must have an assurance of immortality, then, or else life is pointless and love a fraud. Section 36 concludes the sequence with the observation that although spiritual truths, and especially that of our immortality, are accessible to us through our human nature, we owe thanks nonetheless to Jesus, who revealed them to everyone and embodied them in his life. This is an intriguing lyric because its very praise of Christ seems to reduce the Christian revelation to a story for those (labourers and savages)[22] who are unable to grasp the spiritual truths unaided.

Immortality being assumed, Tennyson turns in sections 40–47 to the question of whether the dead remember earthly life. Various metaphysical scenarios are considered, resulting in the conclusion that the nature of love, and particularly the possibility of an ultimate reunion with his friend, demand an affirmative answer. But soon his trust in immortality is again overwhelmed by a recurrence of doubt, this time caused by the thought that nature reveals a world ruled not by love but by suffering and waste. Tennyson must now face up to the appalling thoughts suggested by the discoveries of geology and palaeontology: 'Time, a maniac scattering dust, | And Life, a Fury slinging flame'.[23] Tennyson was knowledgeable about these sciences. His father, an unbelieving clergyman, had exposed him to Buffon early on; he read Lamarck and other pre-Darwinian evolutionary theorists at Cambridge; and while working on *In Memoriam* he carefully studied Lyell's *Principles of Geology* and the anonymous *Vestiges of the Natural History of Creation* (1844). In his poem Tennyson distills from his reading three powerful sections (54–56) evoking the complex emotions stirred by the new historical sciences in nineteenth-century hearts and minds unable to be assuaged by Buckland's hearty natural theology. They are of a piece with his friend John Ruskin's lament: 'If only the Geologists would let me alone, I could do very well, but those dreadful Hammers! I hear the clink of them at the end of every cadence of the Bible verses.'[24]

Tennyson struggles to trust in God's love against evidence that the world is ruled by pointless suffering:

> O yet we trust that somehow good
> Will be the final goal of ill,
> To pangs of nature, sins of will,
> Defects of doubt, and taints of blood;

> That nothing walks with aimless feet;
> That not one life shall be destroy'd,
> Or cast as rubbish to the void,
> When God hath made the pile complete;
>
> That not a worm is cloven in vain;
> That not a moth with vain desire
> Is shrivelled in a fruitless fire,
> Or but subserves another's gain.
>
> Behold, we know not anything;
> I can but trust that good shall fall
> At last – far off – at last to all,
> And every winter change to spring.
>
> So runs my dream; but what am I?
> An infant crying in the night;
> An infant crying for the light,
> And with no language but a cry.[25]

So far from the world being a temple and life itself one continued act of adoration, nature's carelessness with individual lives subverts the inference from the design of the world to a benevolent designer on which natural theology depends:

> The wish, that of the living whole
> No life may fail beyond the grave,
> Derives it not from what we have
> The likest God within the soul?
>
> Are God and Nature then at strife,
> That Nature lends such evil dreams?
> So careful of the type she seems,
> So careless of the single life,
>
> That I, considering everywhere
> Her secret meaning in her deeds,
> And finding that of fifty seeds
> She often brings but one to bear,
>
> I falter where I firmly trod,
> And falling with my weight of cares
> Upon the great world's altar-stairs
> That slope thro' darkness up to God,
>
> I stretch lame hands of faith, and grope,
> And gather dust and chaff, and call
> To what I feel is Lord of all,
> And faintly trust the larger hope.[26]

Worse, palaeontologists have shown that even species are not preserved from mass destruction:

> 'So careful of the type?' but no.
> From scarped cliff and quarried stone
> She cries, 'A thousand types are gone;
> I care for nothing, all shall go.'[27]

The next thought, terrifying but inevitable, must be: do we humans too belong to this dismal scene of violent struggle and ultimate extinction?

> And he, shall he,
>
> Man, her last work, who seemed so fair,
> …
> Who trusted God was love indeed
> And love Creation's final law –
> Tho' Nature, red in tooth and claw
> With ravine, shriek'd against his creed –
>
> Who loved, who suffer'd countless ills,
> Who battled for the True, the Just,
> Be blown about the desert dust,
> Or seal'd within the iron hills?[28]

If these doubts triumph, if our hopes and ideals are nothing but illusion, then John Martin's ferocious iguanodons are nothing in comparison to our raging despair:

> No more? A monster then, a dream,
> A discord. Dragons of the prime,
> That tare each other in their slime,
> Were mellow music match'd with him.
>
> O life as futile, then, as frail!
> O for thy voice to soothe and bless!
> What hope of answer, or redress?
> Behind the veil, behind the veil.[29]

Nature's brutality and waste are powerful obstacles to belief in the immortality of the soul and love as the law of creation. Reason is impotent to silence the doubts raised by scientific investigation of the Earth; in these sections the poet's hope that good will be the final goal of ill is sustained only by blind trust.

While Tennyson's hope hitherto has been that he will meet his friend beyond the grave, his struggle against doubt kindles a desire for contact here and now. He considers in section 92 the possibility of some kind of vision, but rejects the thought on the grounds that he could not be sure that such a vision was not a hallucination or a projection of his own memories or presentiments. Dismissing outright the possibility of visions since immaterial spiritual beings are incommensurate with our material senses (thereby repudiating Spiritualism and its séances even as it is being born), Tennyson accepts that direct spiritual communion of one spirit with another, an ineffable connection of soul with soul, is possible but only for one who is spiritually at peace. Tennyson himself fulfils this condition one summer evening while sitting alone on the lawn rereading Arthur's letters. Suddenly his wish for contact with his friend is fulfilled:

> So word by word, and line by line,
> The dead man touch'd me from the past,
> And all at once it seem'd at last
> The living soul was flash'd on mine,

> And mine in this was wound, and whirl'd
> About empyreal heights of thought,
> And came on that which is, and caught
> The deep pulsations of the world,
>
> Aeonian music measuring out
> The steps of Time – the shocks of Chance –
> The blows of Death. At length my trance
> Was cancell'd, stricken thro' with doubt.[30]

This direct experience not only provides assurance of immortality but also accomplishes what reason could not: Tennyson grasps the harmonious order behind the appearances of nature that seem to deny any such order. It has been granted to him, like an initiate in a mystery religion, to behold the truth behind the veil before which he stood at the end of section 56.

Doubt returns since human frailty cannot sustain the experience, but it no longer terrifies. Tennyson even suggests that doubt is inseparable from the higher sort of faith. Indeed, the very next section contains his famous defence of doubt against the charge that it is Devil-born:

> One indeed I knew
> In many a subtle question versed
> Who touch'd a jarring lyre at first,
> But ever strove to make it true;
>
> Perplex't in faith, but pure in deeds,
> At last he beat his music out,
> There lives more faith in honest doubt,
> Believe me, than in half the creeds.
>
> He fought his doubts and gathered strength,
> He would not make his judgement blind,
> He faced the spectres of the mind
> And laid them: thus he came at length
>
> To find a stronger faith his own;
> And Power was with him in the night,
> Which makes the darkness and the light,
> And dwells not in the light alone,
>
> But in the darkness and the cloud,
> As over Sinai's peaks of old,
> While Israel made the gods of gold,
> Altho' the trumpet blew so loud.[31]

Note here Tennyson's seemingly casual linking of the lower sort of faith, which needs external forms and fears honest doubt, with the idolatry of the Israelites before the Golden Calf.

Just as faith must progressively be won through struggling with doubt, so the struggle manifest in nature may now be seen as a progressive history in which humanity is the culmination of the natural order. Rather than reducing humanity to mortal nature, Tennyson merges the physical order with the moral order in a single teleological vision:

Contemplate all this work of Time,
The giant labouring in his youth;
Nor dream of human love and truth,
As dying Nature's earth and lime;

But trust that those we call the dead
Are breathers of an ampler day
For ever nobler ends. They say,
The solid earth whereon we tread

In tracts of fluent heat began,
And grew to seeming-random forms,
The seeming prey of cyclic storms,
Till at the last arose the man;

Who throve and branch'd from clime to clime,
The herald of a higher race,
And of himself in higher place,
If he so type this work of time

Within himself, from more to more;
Or, crown'd with attributes of woe
Like glories, move his course, and show
That life is not as idle ore,

But iron dug from central gloom,
And heated hot with burning fears,
And dipt in baths of hissing tears,
And batter'd with the shocks of doom

To shape and use. Arise and fly
The reeling Faun, the sensual feast;
Move upward, working out the beast,
And let the ape and tiger die.[32]

Section 123 caps a magnificent evocation of the no-longer-troubling geological transformations of the Earth with a reaffirmation of his spiritual experience:

There rolls the deep where grew the tree.
O earth, what changes hast thou seen!
There where the long street roars hath been
The stillness of the central sea.

The hills are shadows, and they flow
From form to form, and nothing stands;
They melt like mist, the solid lands,
Like clouds they shape themselves and go.

But in my spirit will I dwell,
And dream my dream, and hold it true;
For tho' my lips may breathe adieu,
I cannot think the thing farewell.

The poem's reliance on the inward evidence of personal experience constitutes Tennyson's direct rejection of Buckland's natural theology:

That which we dare invoke to bless;
Our dearest faith; our ghastliest doubt;
He, They, One, All; within, without;
The Power in darkness whom we guess –

I found him not in world or sun,
Or eagle's wing, or insect's eye,
Nor thro' the questions men may try,
The petty cobwebs we have spun.

If e'er when faith had fallen asleep,
I heard a voice, 'believe no more',
And heard an ever-breaking shore
That tumbled in the Godless deep,

A warmth within the breast would melt
The freezing reason's colder part,
And like a man in wrath the heart
Stood up and answer'd, 'I have felt'.

No, like a child in doubt and fear:
But that blind clamour made me wise;
Then was I as a child that cries,
But, crying, knows his father near;

And what I am beheld again
What is, and no man understands;
And out of darkness came the hands
That reached thro' nature, moulding men.[33]

The remaining sections of the poem celebrate love, now firmly recognized as creation's final law. The final section concludes that we must trust by faith truths that cannot be proven until experienced by the victory of love in the next life. This, then, is Tennyson's hard-won faith: trust in love sustained by feeling and personal experience. Such a faith is indeed able to overcome the doubts raised by geology and palaeontology, but it offers no intellectual solution to them. Tennyson, here, in dissociating religion from reason and placing it in the realm of feeling and experience, adds his thread to a major strand of nineteenth-century religious thought. From Immanuel Kant and Friedrich Schleiermacher onwards, religious thinkers attempted to protect religion from critical reason by isolating it in a realm in which the rational methods of science were said not to apply.[34]

With *In Memoriam* Tennyson became something of a Church Father for the Victorian Age, and yet we may legitimately ask just how orthodox his faith was? The general public for its part had no doubts on this score. Many found consolation in the poem, including Queen Victoria herself after the death of Prince Albert. The most important private voice also affirmed Tennyson's orthodoxy. He had been in love with, and intermittently engaged to, Emily Sellwood since before Arthur Hallam's death. At first, her father had forbidden the marriage, but later Emily herself became convinced that their religious beliefs were incompatible. It was her charge that doubt is Devil-born that Tennyson faced in section 96. *In Memoriam* convinced Emily of Tennyson's piety and they were married. Yet

Tennyson was clearly not orthodox in a narrow sense of the term, as his distinction between the lower and higher sorts of faith attests. He had been a liberal in theology since his student days at Cambridge, and it was because he had never interpreted the Bible literally that he was untroubled by the fact that the new historical sciences were incompatible with a plain-sense reading of the Mosaic account. His liberal understanding of theology and biblical interpretation allied him with a movement in the Anglican Church that by 1850 had become known as the Broad Church. This movement, led by such establishment figures as Thomas and Matthew Arnold, Archbishop Richard Whately, the Oxford don Benjamin Jowett, and the Cambridge 'gentlemen of science' under the leadership of Adam Sedgwick and John Stevens Henslow, sought to interpret Scripture and the Anglican doctrinal statements in a broad and liberal sense in order to minimize conflict between Christianity and modern culture. The Broad Church itself was a response to new currents in biblical criticism, to which we turn in the next chapter.

Chapter 7

THE HIGHER CRITICISM OF THE BIBLE

Tom Paine's attack on the authority of the Bible, cited at the end of Chapter 3, capped a century of rationalist attacks on the truth of the biblical narratives. Enlightenment thinkers no longer regarded the biblical claims as guaranteed by the authority of the Bible itself. The radical French Enlightenment, with which Paine was allied, sought the complete overthrow of Christianity, along with its partner in tyranny, the political order of the Ancien Régime. Rationalist movements in eighteenth-century England and Germany, which shared with the French the conviction that reason is the supreme value and that all traditional beliefs and claims must be examined before the tribunal of reason, similarly subjected the veracity of biblical claims to independent investigation. While English and German rationalists rarely wished to erase Christianity altogether in the manner of the French anti-clericals, they did want to eliminate its more irrational aspects. John Locke's *The Reasonableness of Christianity* (1695) is a good example of the goals and methods of the moderate camp. Situated between rational Christians like Locke and the French radicals were the Deists, who so rationalized religion as to leave nothing of the historical or miraculous content of Christianity. Deist works such as Matthew Tindal's *Christianity as Old as Creation* (1730) reduced true religion to belief in God, the immortality of the soul and a future judgement, and explained the various religions of the world as the result of the corruption of this natural, rational religion by priests and tyrants.

Enlightenment rationalists did not think historically. Operating on the hypothesis that Christianity is true if the Gospel narratives are reliable, they posed a stark alternative: either the Christian religion is factually true, or Jesus and his disciples were at best deluded fanatics or at worst deliberate deceivers.[1] Convinced of the latter, they set out to demolish the credibility of the Gospel narratives by means of rational criticism. And yet, the historical-critical method of biblical interpretation emerged out of the German Enlightenment, which itself drew heavily on English Deism.[2] We shall therefore begin this chapter with a look at the work of the most radical rationalist biblical critic of the German Enlightenment, Hermann Samuel Reimarus (1694–1768).

Progressive revelation

In his lectures and published writings Reimarus taught that Christianity was compatible with reason and promoted natural theology. But privately, above all in his closely guarded manuscript, 'Apology, or Defence for the Rational Worshippers of God' (*c.* 1767), Reimarus was a thoroughgoing rationalist who remorselessly exposed variations, contradictions and logical impossibilities in the Bible, dismissed prophecy and miracles as irrational, and denied the possibility of supernatural revelation. In effect, Reimarus applied the Enlightenment distinction between universal rational truth and particular contingent history to deny the possibility of historically mediated knowledge of God. Reimarus identified Jesus as a failed Jewish revolutionary who never claimed to be the Redeemer or the Son of God; Christ, the God-Man saviour of the Gospels, was a deception perpetrated by the disciples, who invented the doctrine of the resurrection and stole the body of Jesus from the tomb to further their fraud.[3]

The private Reimarus came to public attention between 1774 and 1778 when excerpts from the 'Apology' were published posthumously and anonymously as the *Wolfenbüttel Fragments* by Gotthold Ephraim Lessing. Lessing (1729–1781), along with Johann Gottfried Herder, is the key figure in the emergence of historical-mindedness from Enlightenment rationalism. Having made his name as a playwright and literary critic, Lessing turned to philosophical and theological studies in the last decade of his life when he was ducal librarian at Wolfenbüttel. Lessing accepted the rational critique of revelation and yet, while he did not wish to drag back all the 'rubbish', as he termed it, of orthodox Christianity, he had come to think that Christianity possessed a meaning and a value independent of its truth-claims. The form in which he chose to present his radically new position was to publish excerpts from Reimarus' 'Apology' as the most powerful example of the Enlightenment critique of Christianity, and then append to them a set of his own 'counter-assertions' in which he accepted Reimarus' criticism but rejected his conclusions. Lessing thereby separated the question of the factuality of the Christian revelation from its truth. While Reimarus is correct, he argued, in saying that the factual claims of the Christian religion are insupportable and the biblical accounts of these alleged facts hopelessly contradictory, Christianity is nevertheless intrinsically true.[4]

Lessing's separation of the value of Christianity from its historical or factual foundation was only the first of two steps. He then reunited value and history by reconceptualizing revelation as a historical process in his epochal work, *The Education of the Human Race* (1780; first 53 paragraphs published in 1777), which he appended to his 'counter-assertions' to the fourth fragment of Reimarus. As the title suggests, Lessing understood revelation as analogous to the education of a person from childhood to adulthood. The Old Testament constitutes a primer of our earliest education, in which God calibrated his teaching to the first stirrings of our intellectual life in its dramatic stories and depictions of a mighty deity. But then, just as a child outgrows his first books and teachers, so God sent a second teacher, the New Testament, when humanity had developed sufficiently. While the more spiritual doctrines of the New Testament supersede those of the Old, they mark only the adolescence, not the true maturity, of humanity. By degrees we begin to do without the New Testament as we find evidence of spiritual truths in our own reason. The progressive history of revelation is thus a passage from belief in stories through belief in spiritual doctrines to rational conviction of religious truths; a passage, in short, from mystery to reason. Formal religion, like any good teacher, becomes unnecessary once humanity has learned to think for itself. It is pernicious, Lessing warned, to remain at a stage one has surpassed in intellectual and spiritual development. Those, however, who have advanced beyond literal belief in the New Testament must be careful not to betray this to their 'weaker fellow-pupils' who are still working through its pages.

Lessing's concept of progressive revelation reinterprets revelation from being a miraculous communication of absolute and saving truth at a particular moment in time to a historical process. God, that is, has successively provided the degree of spiritual insight appropriate to the level of development of a given community at its time and place. The various religions and their scriptures represent particular stages in the development of the religious consciousness of humanity as a whole. Vico's model has here been extended to encompass sacred history inasmuch as Lessing discovered meaning *in* history, not just *to* history. From this historical standpoint the question of the factuality of any particular revelation becomes irrelevant. A given doctrine or narrative simply represents a particular stage in the development of the religious consciousness of the human race and must be evaluated and appreciated on its own terms. Correspondingly, contradictions or obscurities in the Bible are not evidence of fraud but of the historically conditioned character of the biblical books as indexes of the religious consciousness attained by the various biblical writers.[5]

This historical version of the condescension principle allowed Lessing to understand the Bible as containing religion rather than defining it, and to substitute the religious development of humanity for supernatural revelation.[6] The Christian revelation is no longer the absolute, universally binding word of God, but merely one of the many paths along which the human race has striven to understand the Divine. A doctrine of tolerance follows naturally from the idea of progressive revelation: since each religion contributes to the development of the religious consciousness of the human race, none is absolutely true and all are worthy of respect. Such a programme of toleration was precisely the theme of Lessing's 1779 drama, *Nathan the Wise*.[7]

A group of German theologians, led by Johann Salomo Semler (1721–1791) and Johann David Michaelis (1717–1791), adopted Lessing's concept of progressive revelation. Semler distinguished between the Bible and the Word of God (again, the Bible *contains* rather than *is* the Word of God). Those parts of the Bible testifying to salvation through Jesus Christ truly are the Word of God, but much of the rest of it reflects the history and customs of the ancient Jews and early Christians. As they studied the Bible these liberal theologians (known as the Neologians) tried to situate the biblical writings in the historical contexts in which they had originally been written in order to get beneath the biblical text itself and gain access to the real events that had inspired it. They regarded philological and historical scholarship as the means of freeing the Word of God from the historical matrix in which it is embedded. To an extent, the Neologians practised the liberation of biblical criticism from doctrine and theology advocated in the previous century by Richard Simon. And yet they never entirely freed themselves from a confessional framework, nor ever wished to do so. A tension between theological commitment and scientific scholarship, between orthodoxy and rationalism, runs through their biblical studies.[8] The next step toward a completely non-theological investigation of the Bible was taken by another group of German scholars, who practised what they called the higher criticism.

The higher criticism of the Bible

Emerging from the theological faculties of certain German universities, notably Göttingen, Halle and Altdorf in the late eighteenth century, 'the higher criticism' of the Bible received its name from the man who has as good a claim as anyone to be its founder, Johann Gottfried Eichhorn (1752–1827). Eichhorn, Professor of Oriental Languages at Jena and later Professor of Philosophy at Göttingen, intended the term to distinguish a new brand of historical criticism from the 'lower' or textual criticism that had been practised since the seventeenth century.

Eichhorn built on the work of Michaelis, his teacher, Semler, and J. G. Herder, who became a close friend. He was also deeply influenced by the classical scholar Christian Gottlob Heyne (1729–1812). Heyne studied the myths of the ancient world, often comparing them with the myths and rituals of contemporary primitives. He taught that myths offer insight into the world of archaic and primitive societies, and as such are key to understanding the childhood of the human race. Equating the mentality of ancient mythmakers with that of modern primitives, Heyne characterized it as, on the one hand, lacking the ability to place single observations in a wider context and to think in terms of cause and effect and, on the other hand, responding to simple phenomena with intense emotion. Lacking the capacity for abstract thought, ancient mythmakers and modern primitives express their emotions and needs in the concrete imagery of pro-creation, birth, warfare and death; their gods represent the elementary forces of nature and of human emotion. Mythology, as Herder declared, is the natural idiom of the childhood of the human race.[9]

Eichhorn applied Heyne's insights into myth to the Old Testament, reading it as literature from the childhood of the human race rather than as absolute truth. His *Introduction to the Old Testament* (1780–83) systematically compared biblical narratives with each other and with non-biblical narratives in order to place them in their own historical and intellectual contexts. He concluded that many biblical narratives, especially in the Pentateuch, are myths rather than factual historical accounts. Since Eichhorn's understanding of myth was, like Heyne's, that of the Enlightenment – fanciful embroidery of a historical event or philosophical teaching – he thought that the myths of the Old Testament veiled a core of historical truth, a core that could be displayed by applying to the Penta-teuch the method of literary and historical criticism. Eichhorn therefore attempted to provide rational explanations for those biblical stories judged to be mythical – such as the episodes of Lot's wife or the burning bush – in the belief that once this had been done the 'demythologized' Old Testament would provide an accurate history of Israel.[10] A further consequence of Eichhorn's identification of the Old Testament as a species of oriental literature was that that one could now recognize the literary style and characteristic language, and therefore the world of thought, of its various human authors. When Eichhorn separated out strands or layers within the text of the Pentateuch that display a common style and idiom, his literary stratigraphy revealed the presence of two distinct documents. Although the idea that the text of the Pentateuch is made up of more than one document or literary unit had been suggested before Eichhorn, it was his scholarship that established it on a sound footing.[11]

The higher criticism was further developed by Wilhelm Gesenius (1786–1842), who had studied under Eichhorn at Göttingen. Gesenius' research into Hebrew grammar and vocabulary, which remains the basis of modern grammars and dictionaries of biblical Hebrew, pioneered the scientific study of the Hebrew text of the Old Testament. Recognizing that the Hebrew language must be understood historically, Gesenius placed Hebrew within the family of Semitic languages and, by tracing how word-forms and word-meanings developed and changed over time in various Semitic languages, grounded the study of Hebrew grammar in the context of its historical development. Gesenius' work completed the demotion of Hebrew from a unique sacred language to a historically and morphologically located human language.[12]

While Eichhorn had pointed to the presence in the Pentateuch of more than one literary unit, he had not seriously questioned its Mosaic authorship. This step was taken by Wilhelm Martin Leberecht de Wette (1780–1849). De Wette's *Dissertation* (1805) on the book of Deuteronomy showed that it was closely related to the book discovered in the Jerusalem Temple in 621 BCE during the reign of King Josiah. He pointed out that Deuteronomy must date from around this time because the cultic practices it lays out as binding on Israel are those of the late seventh century BCE and not of Moses' day. Deuteronomy, therefore, cannot be the farewell address of Moses to his people that it purports to be. Similarly, in his 1803 presentation of the historical account of early Israelite religion in 1 and 2 Chronicles, de Wette demonstrated convincingly the anachronistic character of the cultic legislation attributed to the early monarchic age in these books. De Wette's two-volume *Contributions to Old Testament Introduction* (1806–07), rehearsing and extending his earlier studies, is a landmark in biblical scholarship because for the first time the practice of the higher criticism resulted in a presentation of the history of Israelite religion that differed radically from the Bible's presentation of that history. According to the Bible, Moses gave to the Israelites a fully developed legal system, sacrificial cult and priesthood. According to de Wette, Moses did none of these things; the legal, sacrificial and hierarchical systems set out in the Pentateuch and Chronicles date from a much later period than the time of Moses, and the ascription of them to Moses is an anachronistic back-projection of much later practices.[13]

Revolutionary as it was, de Wette did not intend his biblical criticism as an attack on faith. He saw his work as a continuation of the Reformation attempt to recover the original intention of the authors of the biblical texts. This view depended on his understanding myth in a Romantic rather than Enlightenment sense. Whereas myth for Eichhorn had meant fanciful embroidery of a historical or rational kernel of truth, de Wette followed F. J. W. von Schelling's revalourization of myth as the organic expression of a given people's worldview, analogous to a work of art, rather than as an inadequately expressed historical or philosophical statement of fact. The Romantic redefinition of myth totally recast the question of the historicity of the Old Testament. There was no longer any point in attempting to find the core of historical truth in the Old Testament narratives because these stories had not been written as a mythic mode of reportage of contemporary events but to express and sanction the beliefs and practices of much later generations of Israelites. Just as the *Aeneid* is not a historical source for the actions of real people named Aeneas, Turnus and Lavinia at the time of the founding of Rome, but instead reflects the self-understanding of Romans during the early Empire, so the Old Testament – Israel's national epic – is not a historical source for the actions of real people named Abraham, Moses and Deborah, but instead reflects the self-understanding of Israelites during the later monarchy. In this way de Wette shifted the historical focus of the higher criticism away from the content of the biblical texts and to the texts themselves; he asked not 'Who was Moses and what did he do?', but 'What does the depiction of Moses tell us about the beliefs and values of the people who wrote and edited the text?'[14]

De Wette was able to effect a revolution in historical scholarship of the Bible while retaining his faith because he separated historical-critical knowledge of the Bible from its true spiritual meaning. Here, again, contemporary German idealist philosophy – this time in the person of Jakob Friedrich Fries – was critical. De Wette embraced Fries's teaching that humans beings have access to certainty through three distinct and independent faculties – knowledge, faith and aesthetic intuition (corresponding to scholarship, religion and art). For de Wette, biblical criticism, as a matter of knowledge, could not erode truths known by faith; moreover, the reality of divine communication with humanity was affirmed by our aesthetic intuition, which subjectively grasps divine activity in history and nature. De Wette, in short, could be so daring in applying historical criticism to the Bible precisely because of his idealist conviction that scholarship is impotent to undermine spiritual truths grasped by faith and confirmed by aesthetic intuition.[15]

De Wette's conception of myth was taken up by another higher critic, David Friedrich Strauss (1808–1874). But whereas de Wette had applied it to the Old Testament narratives, Strauss raised the stakes dramatically in his *Life of Jesus, Critically Examined* (1835) by applying the category of myth to the Gospel foundation of the central Christian doctrines. Strauss was a tutor at the Protestant seminary of Tübingen University when he wrote the *Life of Jesus*. The theological context for the work was the question, initiated by Reimarus, of the relation of the idea of the Christ to the historical person of Jesus. Strauss's goal, originally conceived as a preliminary step toward a study of Christian doctrine, was to separate those elements of the Gospels that ought to be judged mythical from the historically reliable elements. His method was to examine each miraculous incident in the Gospel narratives from three successive points of view: the Enlightenment rationalist interpretation of miracles as non-miraculous factual events credulously or mendaciously presented as miracles by the biblical authors; the traditional interpretation, according to which the miracle stories are accounts of historical fact; and finally his own myth-criticism interpretation.[16]

As an example of Strauss's method, let us look at his discussion of the episode in Matthew 27:51 of the tearing of the veil of the Temple at the moment of Christ's death. Strauss began by identifying the veil as the inner curtain before the Holy of Holies. He then considered the rationalist naturalistic interpretation of the tearing of the veil as the effect of the earthquake mentioned by the Gospel writer a couple of verses later. Is it likely, he asked, that an earthquake should tear a pliant, loosely hung curtain? Rationalists therefore proposed that the veil was not loosely hung, but tightly fastened top and bottom, and side to side – to which conjecture Strauss countered that if the earthquake shook the walls of the Temple so violently as to tear a firmly fastened veil it would have also caused a part of the building to fall, which did not happen. Therefore, if the event really happened as recorded in Matthew's Gospel, it must have been a miracle. Strauss then turned to consider the traditional point of view. If it was a miracle, it must have had a divine purpose; specifically, to produce in the Jewish contemporaries of Jesus a deep impression of the importance of his death, and to furnish the first promulgators of the gospel with a fact to which they might appeal in support of their cause. But, Strauss then pointed out, nowhere else in the New Testament is this event mentioned, and therefore the divine purpose in ordaining this miracle must have totally failed; since, however, this is inconceivable it cannot have been ordained for this object, and so the tearing of the veil was not a miraculous event at all. The episode, in short, cannot be adequately explained by either the rationalists or the supernaturalists. Given, then, that the tearing of the veil cannot be explained either as a natural occurrence or as a miracle, Strauss declared that it had not happened at all, and turned to his own interpretation. In the Judaism of Christ's day only priests had access into the Temple sanctuary, and only the high priest might enter into the Holy of Holies once a year with the blood of atonement. The Epistle to the Hebrews presents Christ entering into the Holy of Holies behind the curtain as the eternal high priest, obtaining an eternal redemption for Christians (Hebrews 6:19–20, 9:6, 10:19–20). Strauss argued that the images in the Epistle to the Hebrews provide the key to interpreting the Gospel episode; it is a symbolic statement that by Christ's death the veil of Jewish worship was torn asunder and access to God opened to all by means of worship in the Spirit. Strauss urged his readers to renounce the historicity of the incident and recognize it as a myth produced by the first Christians as they reflected on the significance of Jesus in a milieu saturated with Jewish images and observances.[17]

Strauss presented his mythical interpretation as overcoming the difficulties of both the traditionalist and rationalist approaches to interpreting the Bible. In accepting miracle stories as literally true, traditionalists make unbelievable historical claims; the naturalistic explanations that rationalists provide for miracles are credible, but require one to abandon the meaning of the biblical text. The solution is to recognize each miracle story as an instance – in the context of the Jewish tradition and the anticipation of the coming of the Messiah – of the unconscious folk poetizing typical of 'pre-scientific' peoples who have not yet risen to the level of rational reflection. Since Jesus was believed to be the anticipated Messiah, mythical tales and Old Testament themes were bound to be applied to him – and this is precisely what happened in the case of the Gospel account of the tearing of the veil of the Temple. Myths, and therefore the biblical miracle stories, are not the result of deliberate invention or fraud, but arise spontaneously from the unconscious myth-making power of particular communities. Where Enlightenment rationalists jumped up and down and yelled 'fraud', the higher critics smiled indulgently at such childish story-telling. Strauss concluded, as de Wette would never have done, that the risen Christ of faith and the Saviour of the Gospels was a figure of myth and not of history. His daring conclusion made Strauss famous overnight, but orthodox outrage cost him his academic career.[18]

The various strands of the higher criticism were synthesized into a powerful critical tool by Julius Wellhausen (1844–1918). Drawing on the work of de Wette, Wilhelm Vatke and others, Wellhausen conceived the study of biblical history as the reconstruction of the development of the religious institutions of ancient Israel. He showed, in *The History of Israel* (1878; the second edition of 1883 was retitled *Prolegomena to the History of Israel*), how the various literary strata discernible within the Pentateuch encode the course of the historical development of Israelite religion. The Wellhausen documentary hypothesis posited the existence of four principal documents in the Hexateuch (Pentateuch plus the book of Joshua), designated as J (Yahwist), E (Eloist), D (Deuteronomist) and P (Priestly). Wellhausen correlated the four documents to three principal stages in the development of Israelite religion. He assigned the early narrative sections of J and E to around 870 and 770 BCE respectively, or the period of the divided monarchy, although he acknowledged that they underwent further editing until the early seventh century BCE. He dated D to the seventh century, and accepted de Wette's argument connecting it to the period and goals of King Josiah's reform. P, in which the post-exilic ritual system was projected back to the time of Moses, represented the triumph of the priests over the prophetic strand in Israelite religion. Its composition began, he said, with the Exile and continued until the final editing of the Hexateuch during the reforms of Ezra and Nehemiah around 450 BCE. Wellhausen's documentary hypothesis sharply distinguished between what the historical Israelites had actually believed and the beliefs of those who wrote or edited the Bible, whenever and wherever this had occurred. It radically departed from the account of the history of Israelite religion in the Old Testament itself by assigning the prophetic writings to a period before the composition of the Hexateuch so that the prophets became the originators of monotheism, not its renovators, while priestly ritual (and here one may discern the influence of Protestant suspicion of Catholic ritualism), no longer contemporary with Moses, became a late systematization of and rival to the prophetic teaching.[19]

Wellhausen himself thought that the documents had undergone further editing and supplementing over time, and his followers (and by the early twentieth century the 'Wellhausen School' had become the dominant critical school) continued to subdivide the documents. Modern biblical scholars have modified Wellhausen's dates for his four documents. In particular, they have placed the bulk of P before D, and therefore before the Exile.[20] But just as debates within geology over whether fire or water was the principal geological agent were secondary to the acceptance of the reality of deep time and radical historical change of the Earth, so disagreement about the exact number, date and identity of sources is less important than the recognition of the Old Testament as a historical document composed of several strands written by human beings at different times and in various places. This recognition is fundamental to all scholarly historical and literary study of the Old Testament/Hebrew Bible.[21]

Crossroads

The fundamental insight achieved by the higher criticism is that the biblical narratives reflect the political and social realities of the time and place in which they were written, and that these referents as uncovered by scholars, rather than their surface content, are the true indicators of their date and authorship. The higher criticism thereby set Western culture before a crossroads by separating historical-critical knowledge of the Bible from the historical claims made by the Bible itself. It had now become possible to detach the meaning of the Bible from the question of truth. The meaning of the Bible, for example, is that Jesus is the unique and necessary Saviour or that a great Flood destroyed all life except for the occupants of the Ark, but these claims need now carry no intellectual or religious relevance for the scholar just because the Bible asserts them. The biblical narratives may be regarded as simply historical evidence for what people believed in the past, and as such may be placed on a par with ancient Assyrian or Aztec stories.[22] But, as the case of de Wette indicates, this sort of thoroughly secular approach to the Bible did not happen immediately, any more than the increased knowledge about the world in the seventeenth century led directly to secular histories of the civil world.

One nineteenth-century response to the higher criticism simply rejected it outright and insisted on the traditional view of the Bible as true history. This Confessionalist reaction, led in Germany by the Lutheran Old Testament scholar Ernst Wilhelm Hengstenberg (1802–1869), continued to interpret the Old Testament narratives both as literally true and as typological prefigurations of New Testament persons and events. The Confessionalists made use of scholarship in order to defend traditional views of the authorship and authenticity of Old Testament writings, but regarded it as only a tool that must never be allowed to undermine revealed truths. The corruption of human understanding in the Fall, they affirmed, has rendered unaided reason deceptive and unreliable. When scholarship, as with the higher criticism, tries to free itself from theological constraints it transgresses the fundamental doctrine of original sin.[23]

A third road, increasingly well-travelled as the nineteenth century wore on, led to neither secularism nor Confessionalism. This middle way, known as biblical theology or salvation history (*Heilsgeschichte*), was paved by theologians who accepted many of the results of the higher criticism but continued to hold the Bible as religiously meaningful. Drawing on Lessing's conception of progressive revelation, biblical theologians sought religious meaning in the historical development of the Bible. Indeed, Wellhausen himself, unpersuaded by de Wette's Romantic theology, had argued instead that the Bible displays a clear progressive movement from the animism of the patriarchal period through the ethical monotheism of the prophets to the universal morality of Jesus. In reading the Bible as progressive revelation biblical theologians concerned themselves less with what the Bible said than with reconstructing the intentions of the biblical writers, which in turn reflected the stage of religious consciousness each had attained. They took seriously (and often literally) the words of the Bible, but treated them as evidence from which to reconstruct the various distinctive and historically conditioned minds and circumstances of its human authors. This interpretive focus on authorial intention made historical consciousness central; the biblical theologians were interested in what the writer of a passage was trying to convey to his original audience. If, for example, the text says that Jesus walked on water, the biblical theologians did not affirm that Jesus had indeed walked on water but instead asked themselves what the Gospel writer had wanted to communicate by depicting him as walking on water. The Bible was still a unique book – the story of the progressive deepening of humanity's consciousness of God – but its real meaning was distinct from the surface meaning of its words. Biblical theology, as a theological version of historical-mindedness, was a massive salvage effort that saved the churches from having to treat the Bible as just another human text. But its price was a drastic redefinition of the Bible's divine inspiration.[24]

Historical scholarship became the biblical theologians' principal exegetical aid. Since the words of the Bible can no longer be accepted as timeless truths addressed to the world at large (except in the case of general ethical rules), their real meaning cannot be understood apart from their historical context, which in turn must be established by painstaking linguistic and historical work. Biblical theologians adopted the historical techniques of the higher criticism in order to overcome the threat of reducing the Bible to just another human book posed by the higher criticism itself. And since the Bible may no longer be assumed to be unified in its surface meaning (its unity now lies in the reconstructed history of humanity's spiritual development it contains), it is no longer permissible to juxtapose passages from various parts of the Bible, since they belong to distinct phases of religious consciousness. The biblical theologians' historical consciousness, in short, outlawed the venerable practice of proof-texting, just as it similarly subverted the Protestant principle of 'the clarity of Scripture', or the ordinary Christian's sense that he or she can read the Bible without an interpreter and discover its unambiguous meaning (albeit already in practice highly muddied long before the higher critics arrived on the scene). Biblical interpretation was now a technical discipline practised by professionals trained in a variety of linguistic and historical disciplines.[25]

The biblical theologians, like the biblical critics of the seventeenth century, were pious; their intention was not to destroy but to strengthen the authority of Scripture. And indeed the labours of the biblical theologians eventually reconciled many educated Christians to the higher criticism. We may cite the testimony of the American theologian William Newton Clarke (1840–1912). The son of a New England Baptist minister, Clarke had graduated from seminary in 1863 firm in his belief in the timeless truth of Scripture as the revealed Word of God. Over the next two decades his encounters with biblical theologians and the higher criticism persuaded him, not without a struggle, that the Bible must be recognized as a historical document. In 1890 he gave up his parish to become a professor of theology at Colgate Theological Seminary. His *An Outline of Christian Theology* (1898) was the first systematic statement of Liberal Protestant theology to be written by an American. Years later, recalling his encounter with the higher criticism, Clarke's gratitude was palpable: he credited the higher criticism with having shown him that Christians need not attribute to the God of Christ all the acts and passions that the ancient Israelites attributed to the God of Israel, or approve the moral judgements that were recorded in days of inferior moral light.[26] Moreover, biblical theology had unified and Christianized his Bible:

> With what delight and satisfaction then did I welcome the message of the higher criticism! I was now led to see that the central thing in the religion of the Old Testament was not the law but the prophets and their teaching; and the prophets held forth essentially the same religion of spiritual inwardness and sincerity that Jesus preached ... In this light I saw that God had not held two contradictory attitudes in the two Testaments, or taken back his own teaching, or trampled upon his own earlier methods. Throughout the Bible religion was one, and God was one. His method of salvation was one in all ages, true to his own ethical nature ... For me the Bible was redeemed from this old division, and brought into clear Christian unity.[27]

Clarke here clearly illustrates two characteristics of biblical theology. First, the concept of progressive revelation replaced typology as the means of Christianizing the Hebrew Bible (as with the typological approach, the biblical theologians ignored post-biblical Judaism as a legalistic dead-end). Second, it placed the standard by which to evaluate the religious significance of the biblical books outside the Bible itself, in the criterion of moral progress. Here we see actualized the dictum that the Bible *contains* religion rather than *defines* it.[28] Clarke himself recognized the profound change in biblical interpretation brought about by historical consciousness:

> When a man is set to interpret the standard that he must obey, it means that henceforth he is to obey a standard that he has interpreted ... This, whatever the result may be, is on the face of it a profound change from the attitude toward the Bible that the fathers held. They said, 'This is the word: we must obey it.' Their children were saying, 'This is the word: we must find out what it means.'[29]

This insight represents an epochal moment in the intellectual history of the West. Recognition of the Bible as a historical document reversed the framework of interpretation: from having been a matter of incorporating the world into the biblical story, interpretation became one of fitting the biblical story into another world.[30]

Essays and Reviews

The higher criticism was slower to win recognition in England than in Germany (and was forbidden in Roman Catholic countries until the 1940s). While there were individuals like Buckland and Tennyson who were informed about German scholarship, the vast majority of English laity and most of the clergy well into the second half of the nineteenth century accepted without question the Mosaic authorship of the Pentateuch and were horrified at the suggestion that the New Testament narratives might be myths. English churchmen identified the German higher criticism with unbelief and charged 'German rationalism' with undermining Christianity. Further, the works of the Confessionalist opponents of the higher critics were translated into English, suggesting to receptive English minds that since the higher critics, whose works remained untranslated (except for the most notorious work of all, Strauss's *Life of Jesus*, translated by the equally notorious George Eliot in 1846), had already been refuted by German scholarship it would be pointless, indeed retrogressive, for English scholars to adopt the critical methods of the German higher critics.[31] As late as 1859 George Rawlinson, Camden Professor of Ancient History at Oxford, could declare in a University lecture that the historical narratives contained in Scripture were accurate and trustworthy eyewitness accounts: Moses' mother had probably met Jacob, who could have known Shem, son of Noah, and Shem was probably acquainted with Methuselah, who had known Adam.[32]

The small group of liberal-minded Anglicans known collectively as the Broad Church dissented from this orthodoxy. They maintained that the true Christianity of modern times is no longer an unquestioning faith in the Bible on the authority of external evidence such as miracles and the fulfilment of prophecy, but a moral Christian life in which an inner spirituality replaces literal biblicism. While these liberal Anglicans, under the leadership of Thomas Arnold (1795–1842) and Frederick Denison Maurice (1805–1872), drew on German critical scholarship, they were closer in spirit to the biblical theologians than to the more radical of the higher critics. They never doubted that the Bible told the story of divine providence guiding the People of God to a fuller and more complete comprehension of divine truth. They might admit that the Bible contains factual errors here and there, but they never questioned the claim that the account of Israelite history presented in the Bible is basically trustworthy. The higher critics' project of reconstructing the history of Israel as entirely different from the Old Testament account was alien to them; indeed, Maurice would be devastated when his protégé, John Colenso, demonstrated in *The Pentateuch and the Book of Joshua Critically Examined* (seven parts, 1862–79) the unhistorical nature of the Exodus and wilderness tradition.[33]

The higher criticism made a belated and somewhat timid appearance in England in 1860, in a volume that emerged out of the Broad Church movement. Bearing the deliberately bland title of *Essays and Reviews*, it consisted of contributions from six Anglican clergymen and one layman. Their goal was the Broad Church one of preserving Christianity among educated people by showing that it is compatible with modern scholarship.[34] As Benjamin Jowett, one of the contributors, observed: 'In a few years there will be no religion in Oxford among intellectual young men, unless religion is shown to be consistent with criticism.'[35]

Three of the essays are particularly relevant here: those by Frederick Temple on progressive revelation, by Benjamin Jowett on biblical interpretation, and by C. W. Goodwin on historical sciences and the creation narrative. The essay on 'The Education of the World' by Temple, at the time headmaster of Rugby school, presented a version of Lessing's progressive revelation that was shared by all the contributors (it was also indebted to Coleridge and above all Thomas Arnold).[36] Like an individual, Temple began, the world has passed through its childhood and youth into adulthood. In childhood, our education begins with the imposition of rules that we do not understand but must obey; in youth, we learn from the example of our teachers; in adulthood, we become our own instructors. In God's progressive revelation the Law corresponds to rules, Jesus to a teacher, and the Holy Spirit to self-instruction. In declaring that the office of the Spirit is not to give truth but to lead us to discover it within ourselves,[37] Temple was in effect offering another version of Tennyson's higher, interior faith in which the inner voice of conscience replaces external revelation as our religious authority. Temple argued that a progressive understanding of revelation in no way demeans the status of the Bible. Its very form as a historical document, he noted, is adapted to our present state. The books of the Bible are best studied by considering them as records of the time at which they were written, and as conveying to us the highest and greatest religious life of that time.[38]

While Temple's embracing of progressive revelation shocked conservatives, his reading of the broad outline of the Old Testament was entirely traditional. Genesis represents humanity's earliest instruction, and was followed in turn by the Law and then the Prophets.[39] The Oxford don Benjamin Jowett's 'On the Interpretation of Scripture', an essay partly written during his annual visit to Tennyson, raised the stakes by denying the Bible any special interpretive treatment. Jowett was a classical scholar and an authority on Plato. His life's work was to make the thought-world of ancient Athens intelligible to modern men and women. He recognized in the German higher criticism a parallel attempt to make intelligible to moderns the ancient thought-worlds of the biblical writers. In his own biblical criticism (such as his volume of commentary on 1 and 2 Thessalonians, Galatians and Romans), he applied to Scripture the same interpretive techniques he used on Plato's dialogues. His guiding precept was 'Interpret the Scripture like any other book'.[40] In studying Plato's text we want to know what Plato said and meant; no one would now dream of reading into it the later teachings of Neoplatonists or Christian Platonists and then declaring that this is what Plato had originally meant. To attribute to Paul or the Gospel writers the abstract formulations of fourth-century creeds or Reformation theology is just as anachronistic, and yet such has been and largely continues to be the practice of biblical interpreters. The consequences of these interpretive practices, which Jowett collectively referred to as 'read[ing] the Bible crosswise',[41] have been dire: the meaning actually intended by the biblical writers themselves has been lost, along with our own interpretive integrity. The higher criticism, which Jowett saw as completing the recovery of the plain sense of Scripture begun in the Reformation period, allows us to recover both.[42]

This dual recovery, Jowett argued, is critical because the very survival of Christianity depends on it. Traditionalists who refuse to accept the methods and conclusions of the higher criticism make it impossible for thoughtful people to remain Christians. The higher criticism, it is true, purges from Christianity dogmas and miracles (including the resurrection of Christ), as well as the practices of proof-texting and a typological interpretation of the Old Testament, but, Jowett insisted, none of this affects its ethical teaching. Jowett was known in his day as a remorselessly practical man. A contemporary cartoon showed him demanding of a dreamy Dante Gabriel Rosetti, 'And so, Mr. Rosetti, what do you intend to *do* with the Grail once you've found it?' He identified the 'eternal import' of the Gospels not in their doctrines or miracles but in the example of Christ. The life and death of Christ was an unequalled moral act, one that both inspires and enables us to re-enact it in our souls as we die to the world and sin and rise again in an ethical union with God.[43] This moral faith does not depend on historical accounts contained in the Bible, accounts which the higher criticism shows us we can no longer wholly trust. The divine truth of the Bible lies instead in its moral teaching, the contours of which are all the more recognizable once it has been detached from its obsolete historical matrix.

Jowett's faith that the Bible contains divine truth made the application of his precept that the Bible should be interpreted like any other book much less radical than it might have been. He did not mean by this that the content or the value of the Bible was just like that of any other book. Jowett believed that the Bible contains the Word of God and that the task of the exegete is to recover the original meaning intended by the biblical authors, a task that can only be carried out by applying the techniques of literary and historical criticism to the Bible. But Jowett did not, like the more radical of the higher critics, analyse the biblical text in an attempt to discover an alternative history to the one set out in the plain sense of the words themselves. He neutralized the more destructive potential of the higher criticism by subordinating its techniques to his commitment to progressive revelation and a subjective epistemology. The plain-sense meaning of the words of the Bible comprise a series of humanly mediated expressions of God-consciousness that together constitute a progressive revelation of God that culminates in the pure ethical consciousness of Christ. The modern-day interpreter, in turn, grasps the truth and beauty of the ethical message of the Bible by means of an interior, subjective faculty that is independent of and superior to rational knowledge. Jowett's version of the Broad Church religion of feeling allowed him to trust that 'When interpreted like any other book, by the same rules of evidence and the same canons of criticism, the Bible will still remain unlike any other book.'[44]

Jowett's conviction that only the ethical content of the Bible continues to have religious meaning, and not its historical or cosmogonic content, was the key to his hope that the higher criticism would reconcile the educated classes with revealed religion. Jowett was convinced that an epochal transition was under way in the intellectual forms by which the never-changing eternal truths of the Christian life are apprehended and understood in the modern world. Troubling as the higher criticism and other aspects of this transition may be for many people, he was confident that the end result would be a clearer conception of the moral power of the Bible. Moreover, without the re-evaluation of the Bible achieved by the higher criticism, revealed religion must oppose history and science. And Jowett had no doubt which would be the loser:

> The same fact cannot be true in religion when seen by the light of faith, and untrue in science when looked at through the medium of evidence or experiment. It is ridiculous to suppose that the world appears to have existed, but has not existed during the vast epochs of which geology speaks to us.

And again, more pithily: 'Doubt comes in at the window, when Inquiry is denied at the door.'[45]

Jowett's life mission – in his biblical criticism, in his theology, and in his efforts as head of Balliol College to reform intellectual life at Oxford – was to replace the traditional understanding of truth as a fixed body of received doctrine, and therefore of education as the faithful transmission of this body of doctrine, with the liberal or modern understanding of truth as tentative and provisional because it is mediated through human minds, and therefore of education as a disciplined enquiry after truth.[46]

The essay by Charles Wycliffe Goodwin, a lawyer by profession but an accomplished amateur geologist and Egyptologist,[47] picked up Jowett's remarks on science. 'On the Mosaic Cosmogony' protests against attempts by 'theological geologists' to reconcile, or 'harmonize', the Genesis creation narrative with the findings of geology. Goodwin first turned his attention to Buckland's Bridgewater Treatise. He noted that Buckland had claimed both that Moses simply omitted from his account the details of creation but that as far as it went the Mosaic account is accurate and that, further, the object of the Mosaic account was not to state *in what manner*, but *by whom*, the world was made. Goodwin countered that Buckland was wrong on both counts. The real difficulty is not that the details of creation are omitted from the Mosaic account but that what is told is contrary to the facts as described by modern science. Further, it is false to say that the object of the Mosaic account was to state by whom rather than in what manner the world was made because the greater part of the narrative consists in a minute and orderly description of the manner in which things were made.[48] The situation is no better with the alternative harmonizing scheme of the Scottish geologist and Evangelical Christian Hugh Miller (1802–1856). Miller's *Footprints of the Creator* (1847) and *The Testimony of the Rocks* (1857) were enormously popular versions of the interpretation of the first chapters of Genesis as the 'Mosaic vision of creation'. The underlying idea here is that Moses was an eyewitness to a vision of creation rather than the recipient of a verbal revelation.

The Genesis creation narrative bears the same relation to the events of the past as a prophetic vision bears to future events; it is a prophecy of the past. And just as prophecies of the future are only understood when the events they foretell come to pass, so the key to the correct interpretation of the creation narrative is the discovery of the Earth's past by modern geology. Modern science, that is, provides the true meaning of the days of creation: the first day was the Azoic period, the second the Silurian, the third the Carboniferous, the fourth the Permian, the fifth the Oolitic, and the sixth the Tertiary.[49] Goodwin was having none of this. Miller would have us believe, he said, that God granted Moses a vision of creation such that the account of it Moses gave has misled the world for centuries, and only now, and with difficulty, can the truth of it be recognized in light of modern science.[50]

Buckland and Miller both took it upon themselves to prove that the Mosaic narrative, however apparently at variance with our knowledge, is essentially and in fact true, although it had not been understood properly until modern science supplied the necessary interpretation. Goodwin, pointing out that both these theories assume that the factual account cryptically given in Genesis would never have been decoded had we not arrived at the truth from other sources, crowed that it would be difficult for them to admit more explicitly that the Mosaic narrative does not represent correctly the history of the universe up to the appearance of humanity. Their harmonizing schemes, for all that they are incompatible with each other, share contempt for the plain-sense meaning of the biblical text. They succeed in eliminating contradiction with science only by draining Genesis of any factual content whatsoever. It is absurd to call this harmony. Goodwin argued that rather than seek to harmonize the Bible and science we should adopt the idea of progressive revelation and accept that God made use of imperfectly informed men as agents for teaching mankind. If we read the Bible as a human utterance that providence has used in a special way for the education of mankind, we shall not be troubled to discover that it contains some errors. Echoing Jowett, Goodwin declared that the value of the Bible is only harmed by striving to prove it scientifically exact at the expense of every sound principle of interpretation and in defiance of common sense. Religion does not belong to, and has no authority over, the sphere of science: 'It would have been well if theologians had made up their minds to accept frankly the principle, that those things for the discovery of which man has faculties specially provided are not fit objects of a divine revelation.'[51]

Essays and Reviews provoked outrage in Britain rivalling that sparked in Germany a generation earlier by Strauss's *Life of Jesus*. The Church press denounced the essayists, classically then biblically, as the 'Seven Against Christ' and 'the seven extinguishers of the seven lamps of the Apocalypse'.[52] Samuel Wilberforce, Bishop of Oxford, spoke for many clergy and laypeople when he blamed the 'scarcely veiled atheism' of the contributors on their adoption of the fallacies of 'German rationalism'.[53] The furore over *Essays and Reviews* indicates how conservative and traditional British churchmen and scholars were when it came to biblical criticism. While Jowett's maxim, 'Interpret the Scripture like any other book', might have been truly radical, the biblical theological notion of progressive revelation, which was the centre of gravity of the volume, entailed acceptance of the general reliability of the history and religion of Israel as presented in the Old Testament.[54] Indeed, over the next three decades the Anglican establishment largely made its peace with the moderate form of higher criticism represented in the volume.

The controversy over *Essays and Reviews* overshadowed for a time a book published four months earlier in which historical-mindedness, in the form of a history of life on Earth, posed questions that ultimately proved at least as troubling to Christians as the biblical criticism of *Essays and Reviews* – Charles Darwin's *Origin of Species*.

Chapter 8

EVOLUTION AND DESIGN

In 1859, the year Darwin's *Origin of Species* appeared, the special creation by God of distinct species as set forth in Genesis was still the prevalent belief in Britain among both the masses and the educated.[1] When the latter thought about the creation of species, the Genesis 'after his kind' sprang to life in Milton's evocation of the sixth day:

> God said,
> 'Let the earth bring forth soul living in her kind,
> Cattle and creeping things and beast of the earth,
> Each in their kind'. The earth obeyed, and straight
> Op'ning her fertile womb teemed at a birth
> Innumerous living creatures, perfect forms,
> Limbed and full grown...[2]

Theologians and laypeople alike considered the creation of species an irrefutable instance of divine action. Geology and palaeontology might have discredited the biblical accounts of the age of the world, the Flood, and so on, but science, they held, cannot explain the creation – or periodic re-creation – of species. Scientists, for their part, were at one with the theologians in accepting the special creation of species. This was not a matter of subservience to religion; even scientists who were devout Christians, such as Charles Lyell and Roderick Murchison, could have accepted the idea that God had brought about the origin of new forms of life indirectly through the intermediary of natural laws had scientific evidence for it been convincing. The problem was the difficulty in imagining that any natural cause could account for the apparent designfulness of organisms.[3] To maintain that the evident matching of form to function in plants and animals had arisen purely by chance was as inconceivable in the first half of the nineteenth century as it had been in the previous century to David Hume (1711–1776). The great Scottish philosopher, in the course of demolishing the philosophical validity of the design argument in *Dialogues Concerning Natural Religion* (1779), had offered several logically possible alternative explanations for the correspondence of form and function. And while in hindsight some of them look like stunning anticipations of Darwin's theory, Hume advanced them as speculations calculated to expose the weakness of the logic of the design argument and not as true explanations for the design manifest in nature.[4]

Fixity of species

Most scientists, then, firmly maintained the doctrine of the fixity of species, which had been powerfully defended in the early nineteenth century by Georges Cuvier's work in comparative anatomy that had established the four major branches of animals (the phyla of modern taxonomy): vertebrates, molluscs, articulates and the lower invertebrates. Cuvier insisted that no meaningful anatomical comparisons may be drawn between the branches, nor may they be ranked in a single developmental scale. Further, subsequent palaeontological work indicated that the four branches of animals were as distinct at the points of their appearances in the fossil record as they are today. Cuvier did, however, allow that comparison and succession are valid within a given branch; thus, within the vertebrate branch, anatomists are correct to point to analogies between fish and reptile forms of organization, and palaeontologists are justified in concluding from the fossil evidence that the fish and reptile forms of organization date back to the early Secondary era whereas mammalian organization emerged only in the late Secondary or early Tertiary era.[5]

The fixity of species was for Cuvier more than simply another conclusion arising from empirical observation. It was linked to the rational principles of the 'subordination of characters' and 'necessary conditions of existence' of organisms on which his synthesis of taxonomy, comparative anatomy and palaeontology was based. These principles assert that organisms possess a functional integrity by which their various organs and parts coexist in a mutually dependent manner. For example, if an animal has teeth appropriate for it to feed on flesh, we can be sure without further examination that its digestive organs are adapted for this kind of food and that the structure of its entire body and its sense organs are formed in such a way as to make it skilful in hunting and killing its prey. A creature with the teeth of a leopard, the stomach of a sheep, and the skeletal framework of an iguana could not survive. Variation is limited to functionally indifferent parts of an animal's body because any major variation in its essential organization would render it unviable. Cuvier concluded that 'species' are real and stable units of the animal kingdom, each grounded in the inescapable necessities of the conditions of existence and each the embodiment of a distinct mode of life.[6] Cuvier, in sum, accepted limited variation within species and a progressive succession of bodily organizations within each of the four branches of the animal kingdom, but adamantly rejected evolution in the sense of either the emergence of new species from changes in existing species or a single, progressive ladder of life linking all living beings. Believing fundamentally that sound biological science was grounded on the concept of the fixity of species, Cuvier implacably opposed any theory advocating the transmutation of species.[7] The principal offending theories in his day were those of Jean-Baptiste Lamarck and Etienne Geoffroy Saint-Hilaire.

Lamarck is best known today for his doctrine of the inheritance of acquired characters. An animal – an ancestral giraffe, let us say – strives day after day for something that it desperately wants, such as leaves high up on a tree; as a result of this continual effort its body changes appropriately – its neck lengthens; finally, the change is inherited by the next generation, in which the process continues, and giraffes' necks continue to lengthen.[8] While creationist tracts often conflate Lamarckian and Darwinian evolution, Lamarckianism also lives on in popular culture. A playful case in point is the movie *Witches of Eastwick*, in which the characters played by Michelle Pheiffer, Cher and Susan Sarandon each have a child by Jack Nicholson's Satan. Blonde Pheiffer has a blond child, brunette Cher has a brunette child, and red-haired Sarandon has a red-haired child. But Sarandon's character started the movie with brown hair and dyed it red part way through – the inheritance of acquired characters! More relevant for our present purposes is Lamarck's claim that species are nothing more than artificial abstractions from the seamless variety of nature. His *Zoological Philosophy* (1809) proposed that organisms are continually in the process of transformation, driven by an internal force that gradually but ceaselessly increases their complexity and perfection of organization. Driven by this impulse, and provoked by external circumstances that force deviations from a linear progressionism, new beings are formed with characters appropriate to the conditions of the world in which they must live. In rejecting the special creation of each species, Lamarck distinguished between God's creative act and the modality by which he acts; God, that is, willed the natural order into being, but it operates by means of secondary causes – including those governing the transmutation of species – under the direction of nature, which is itself an active, demiurge-like power distinct from the material universe and to which God delegated productive authority. Lamarck's defence against charges that his evolutionary system was atheistic depended precisely on his distinction between nature and the material universe.[9] This critical distinction notwithstanding, Lamarck was widely held during the first decades of the nineteenth century to have dispensed with God. Contemporaries perceived the implication of an internal impetus replacing the independent creation of each species: whatever Lamarck's God might be, it was not the God of the Bible. Hence the charges of materialism and atheism brought against him by orthodox creationists.

Lamarck worked out his evolutionary theory in the absence of fossil evidence for the progression of life. Etienne Geoffroy Saint-Hilaire, a colleague of Cuvier's at the Museum of Natural History, developed a theory of evolution in the 1820s that incorporated palaeontological evidence (much of it Cuvier's own work). He argued that living species of crocodiles had 'descended by an uninterrupted path of generation' from extinct species of crocodiles. Like Lamarck, Geoffroy considered animal organization to be indefinitely changeable under environmental influences, but he was able to present his theory as scientifically superior to Lamarck's by attributing the progressive direction of change to the directionally changing history of the Earth established by contemporary geology rather than to Lamarck's mysterious notion of a progressive tendency inherent in life itself. Cuvier nevertheless used the occasion of Geoffroy's crocodile paper to savage him, Lamarck and any other transmutationist who flouted his principle of the functional integrity of organisms. Bringing to bear the full weight of his enormous scientific prestige, Cuvier not only dismissed evolutionists as propagating erroneous theories but, more damagingly, branded them as speculators rather than true scientists. Cuvier's authority in this matter was immense (particularly on the Continent), and as a result evolutionary theories were regarded as dubious science for at least a generation.[10] Even the geological revolutionaries who opposed Cuvier on their home turf concurred with him on the matter of the origin of species. Lyell, for example, could not find sufficient fossil evidence to convince him that species originated in the transmutation of other species. Taxonomic and physiological evidence similarly seemed to support the fixity of species.

In Britain the influence of Cuvier was affirmed and extended by the anatomist and palaeontologist Richard Owen (1804–1892). Owen took over from Cuvier his sense of the designfulness of the adaptation of the structure and function of organisms to their environments, as well as his division of the animal kingdom into four separate and distinct branches. He then, however, under the influence of the transcendental anatomy of German Romantic *Naturphilosophie*, applied within each of the four branches the principle (originally Geoffroy's) of 'unity of composition'. Within the vertebrate branch, for example, Owen recognized the foreleg of a lizard, the wing of a bird, the foreleg of a mammal, and the arm of a human being as the equivalent bone. He called these structural analogies *homologies*. Owen's *On the Archetype and Homologies of the Vertebrate Skeleton* (1848) explained homologies by identifying all the animals within each branch as modifications of a single Ideal Type, or Archetype. All vertebrates, that is, are variations on the vertebrate Archetype; the foreleg of any given mammal, for example, can be recognized and identified in the skeletons of the other classes of vertebrates because all vertebrates correspond to a single Ideal Vertebrate. It is important to realize that Owen's Archetypal Vertebrate was not the common *ancestor* of all vertebrates; in fact, it was not an animal that ever had existed or even could exist. It was a basic pattern that exists only in the divine mind and that has been diversely embodied in actual species, living and extinct, in manners appropriate to the environments in which they live(d). Nevertheless, Owen incorporated development into the relationships among species. The fossil record showed that within each class of vertebrates those with the most generalized body plan (that is, the closest to the Ideal Archetype) came earlier in the history of life than those with more specialized body plans. Human beings fit into this scheme as the culmination of the plan of nature:

> *Nature* ... has advanced with slow and stately steps, guided by the archetypal light amidst the wreck of worlds, from the first embodiment of the vertebrate idea, under its old ichthyic vestment [that is, as fish], until it became arranged in the glorious garb of the human form.[11]

Owen's explanation of the diversity of living organisms as the gradual embodiment through time of pre-existent Ideas located the meaning of the history of life outside that history in the transcendent ideal Archetypes; as in seventeenth-century universal histories there is a meaning *to* history but not *in* history.

Owen himself believed that the history of life follows a preordained, supernaturally guided plan. British natural theologians effortlessly translated his scientific language into creationist idiom: God had originally created a small number of archetypal forms, and over time had gradually introduced an infinite number of variations on them. The palaeontological record of the appearance and vanishing of species then became, in the words of Samuel Wilberforce, bishop of Oxford, 'the transcript in matter of ideas eternally existing in the mind of the Most High'.[12]

Evolution by natural selection

Charles Darwin (1809–1882) did not originate the idea of organic evolution. Lamarck and Geoffroy Saint-Hilaire were only two of the late eighteenth- and early nineteenth-century thinkers who argued for the transmutability of species. What Darwin did in the *Origin of Species* was to provide a wealth of evidence for the fact of evolution and to propose, with his theory of natural selection, a new and scientifically superior mechanism to account for it.

In 1831 Darwin joined the crew of the *HMS Beagle* as the ship's naturalist and as an adherent of the fixity of species. What he observed over the course of the next few years – particularly the biogeographical puzzles of the proliferation of variations of finch and tortoise species on neighbouring islands such as the Galapagos together with the uniformity of animal and bird species over vast areas of the South American continent – converted him to the view that species are not immutable. Darwin returned to England in 1836 convinced of the fact of organic evolution but still at a loss to understand how it came about. Over the next five years he worked out the framework of the theory that he would present to the world in the *Origin of Species*. He had read Lyell's *Principles of Geology* while aboard the *Beagle* and firmly accepted the immensity of deep time and the uniformity of the operations of nature. He was also familiar with Lyell's concept of the 'struggle for existence' among plants, by which Lyell meant only the struggle of organisms against the environment. The decisive insight came late in 1838 when he read Thomas Malthus' *Essay on the Principle of Population* (1795) and realized that an organism must struggle for existence not only against the environment but also against others of its species. Darwin's basic theory quickly took shape as a set of hypotheses that, if true, would explain the apparent 'designfulness' of organisms, or, in Cuvierian language, the correspondence of the form of organisms to their respective modes of life. If individual variations occur from time to time in a given species, and if variant forms are capable of being inherited by subsequent generations, and if certain variations enhance the chances of their possessors surviving and multiplying within a specific environment at the expense of others of their species, then those animals best adapted to their environment will succeed in the struggle for existence. Further, given the immensity of time, on which Darwin would insist time and time again in the *Origin of Species*, the differential effect of the exposure of a population of one species to different environmental and competitive conditions would eventually produce populations so distinct from each other as to constitute separate species. Darwin's synthesis of the double selection of Lyell's struggle against the environment and Malthus' struggle against competitors plus deep time gave Darwin the mechanism of natural selection. His South American observations at last made sense: 'Hence the Galapagos Islands are explained. On distinct Creation, how anomalous that the smallest newest & most wretched island should possess species to themselves.'[13] Natural selection explained how species close in time and space could be so different and how other species widely separated could be so similar.

The elements of his theory were in place by the end of 1839 but, well aware of the opposition any evolutionary theory would encounter, Darwin wanted to amass as much supporting evidence for his theory as possible before publishing (he freely admitted that he could not explain the cause of the individual variations on which natural selection works). Over the next twenty years he patiently built his case for evolution by natural selection. Meanwhile, he wrote an abstract of his theory (1842), and steadily expanded the draft of a book. Then, in 1858 one of his botanical correspondents, Alfred Russel Wallace, wrote Darwin a letter in which he set out his own theory of evolution. In studying the orchids of the Malayan archipelago Wallace had encountered the same combinations of likeness and difference that Darwin had noted in the Galapagos and, unaware of Darwin's theory but having also read Malthus, had independently come up with the idea of 'natural selection' to explain them. Darwin contacted leading naturalists with whom he had discussed his now two-decade-old theory. They arranged that both Darwin and Wallace would present preliminary reports to the Linnaean Society. Darwin immediately wrote a summary of his massive manuscript, publishing it in 1859 as the *Origin of Species, by Means of Natural Selection*.[14]

The theory of descent with modification (Darwin's preferred term for evolution by natural selection) is an alternative, naturalistic explanation for the apparent designfulness of living things that natural theologians explain by the wisdom and foresight of their Creator. Darwin had absorbed Paley at Cambridge, and read Ray's *Wisdom of God Manifested in the Works of Creation* in the late 1830s while working out his theory.[15] Recognizing that design language was descriptively correct – organisms do appear to be designed for their mode of existence – but explanatorily false, Darwin used design language in the *Origin of Species* and elsewhere in order to subvert the design argument by replacing miraculous intervention with a natural process. This was a conscious strategy; in a letter to his publisher he compared his about-to-be-published work on *The Various Contrivances by which Orchids are Fertilized by Insects* (1862) to a work of natural theology: 'Like a Bridgewater treatise, the chief object is to show the perfection of the many contrivances in Orchids.'[16]

There is, nevertheless, a limit to the apparent designfulness of nature. Evolution by natural selection produces not a perfect match between an organism and its environment but a match relative to selectionary pressures. This, Darwin pointed out, explains why the denizens of one region – Australia, say – which on the creationist view are specially designed for that environment, can be overcome and supplanted by imported species. The pressures of competition being much more severe on less isolated regions, adaptation has produced species of a fitter competitiveness than those produced by the relatively low adaptive pressures of Australia.[17] This relativizing of adaptation carried with it tremendous consequences for historical thinking. In theorizing that evolution is driven by adaptation to environmental and competitive challenges, Darwin was asserting that it is a haphazard, branching and open-ended process. Evolution is haphazard because migration and environmental change continually present new and unforeseeable adaptive challenges; branching, because separated populations of a given species continue to diverge and may again redivide; open-ended, because there is neither a predetermined goal nor a fixed sequence of stages guiding the process. Darwin's radically historical theory, in which the form of a given species can be explained only in light of its own particular history, subverts any ideology of progress.[18]

Two notes are warranted here. First, to move from biological evolution to the celebration of progress as a cultural value allegedly endorsed by nature, as so many did in the late nineteenth century, is to move from evolution as a scientific fact and a theory about the mechanism by which it operates to evolution*ism* as an ideology.[19] Second, while evolution by natural selection is a haphazard process, this is not to say that complex biological entities are random or chance products. As Richard Dawkins points out, each step in the evolutionary process arises by chance but the complexity of living things is the result of the accumulation of a long sequence of such steps. It is impossible to believe that the eye – Paley's prime example of designed complexity – randomly appeared in a single step, but that is not what evolution by natural selection asserts. The eye, like all instances of organized complexity, evolved step by step, gradually increasing in complexity over thousands of generations. The eye, in fact, has evolved numerous times in independent lineages.[20]

Just as seventeenth-century opponents of the world-machine model like Burnet and Scilla had reconceptualized fossils, mountains and caves as signs of Earth history, so in Darwin's work rudimentary organs and homologies gained new significance as signs of the history of life. Rudimentary organs, or non-functional things such as nipples on male mammals, which Darwin noted are superfluous to the functioning of the organism and therefore inexplicable on the hypothesis of special creation, and homologous structures across species became evidence of the modification over time of species descended from a common ancestor.[21]

Induction

One of the most frequently repeated nineteenth-century criticisms of Darwin was that his theory was not *inductive*; that is, it was based on assumptions instead of facts. On the face of it, the charge was plausible since Darwin had had to concede not only his inability to explain the origin of variations but also that palaeontological research had uncovered only a tiny fraction of all the intermediate specific forms that must have once existed if his theory was correct. His defence for the former was that there was undoubtedly a scientific explanation but it was as yet unknown, and for the latter that the geological record was imperfect. His opponents, however, accused him on both counts of having deserted the sound scientific tradition of Bacon and Newton in favour of speculative hypothesizing (this charge is still made by creationists today). Such critics were invariably partisans of natural theology. And since they had no need to posit the existence of as-yet-undiscovered natural laws or missing fossil evidence they could claim that the design theory was scientifically superior to evolution by natural selection precisely because it did not require the supposition of hypothetical entities. It is true, of course, that both Darwin's acceptance of the fact of evolution and his mechanism of natural selection were hypothetical. He could provide no experimental evidence to prove either the transmutation of one species into another or descent by modification. What Darwin had done in the *Origin of Species* was to show that resemblances of animals and their historical and geographical distribution could be explained on the assumption that they were related to each other by descent, while at the same time their divergences could be explained on the assumption that the offspring of the same parents vary randomly and that among these variations are some that improve their possessors' chance to survive in the struggle for life.[22]

The lack of direct evidence for Darwin's theory was a genuine scientific stumbling block. But most of those who attacked evolution by natural selection declined to weigh the overall scientific value of the theory, preferring instead to insist that good science abjures the fabrication of hypotheses in favour of ascertaining facts and erecting theories on those facts. Bishop Wilberforce, preaching to the savants of the British Association for the Advancement of Science during their 1847 meeting at Oxford, captured this view in a memorable image compounded of inductive philosophy, moral theology, Cuverian suspicion of speculation, and Victorian gender stereotypes: the hypothesis-wielding speculator, instead of approaching nature reverently like a gentleman and following her guidance, is driven by pride to 'deal boldly' with her by forcibly maintaining his theory despite her evidences to the contrary.[23] While Darwin, for his part, bemoaned such scientific illiteracy, the general public was confident that its view of science was also that of most naturalists and, encouragingly, of the eminent philosopher of science William Whewell (1794–1866). Things were not quite so simple. Whewell, in fact, though a vocal opponent of evolution by natural selection, insisted as firmly as Darwin that scientific enquiry cannot proceed without hypotheses and that Newton's much-touted claim, 'I do not make hypotheses', should not be taken at face value. His objection to Darwin's theory turned instead on the use to which hypotheses were put. The criteria Whewell imposed on the framing of hypotheses were that they should be 'clear and appropriate'. In practice, 'clear' meant that hypotheses should be expressible mathematically and 'appropriate' that they should not contradict knowledge established extra-scientifically. Evolution by natural selection was disqualified on both counts. So while not rejecting the role of hypotheses in science, Whewell did appear to endorse the popular view of science by declaring Darwin's theory of evolution by natural selection to be baselessly hypothetical and not founded on proper induction.[24]

Darwin the empiricist and Whewell the idealist disagreed fundamentally over the nature of science. For empiricists, hypotheses serve as guides to scientific enquiry. Laws of causation are hypothetically postulated, their consequences deductively calculated, and the deductions in turn confronted with the observed facts. While no restriction is placed on the framing of hypotheses other than that they should be capable of being tested by empirical evidence, strict conditions must be satisfied before any hypothesis may be accepted as proven. Scientific explanation, on the empiricist view, deals with the uniformities of nature but never asks *why* there are uniformities in nature to be explained in the first place, as such questions do not belong to the realm of science. Idealists, for their part, refuse to accept that science cannot address the 'why' question; that is, science should not stop at whatever point scientists are unable to explain a sequence of events in terms of secondary causation. Any such breaks in the chain of causation point rather to the origin of the chain in the First Cause. Since, then, a proper explanation of the origin of the organic world must culminate in the First Cause, science leads, in the language of the seventeenth century, to the author of the Book of Nature. Idealists, that is, do not see science as a self-sufficient intellectual activity; it must be reconcilable with knowledge derived from revelation. The idealist position underlay the British Government's practice earlier in the nineteenth century of denying copyright to scientific books that contradicted biblical truths. On a less philosophical level, controversialists endlessly repeated the Evangelical Thomas Rawson Birks' charge in *The Scriptural Doctrine of Creation* (1872) that Darwin had violated the laws of induction by neglecting the 'direct evidence' of the Bible on the origin of species. We may now recognize that the charge that Darwin's science is not inductive actually meant that his theory disregarded revelation. Whewell and the other Victorian scientific idealists rarely used the language of the Book of Nature but their concept of science permitted, indeed demanded, a natural theology.[25]

The choice between empiricist and idealist understandings of science could not be decided by logic or evidence. Empiricists realized that they could not prove that their understanding of science is right and the idealist understanding wrong, but pointed out that only the empirical approach makes scientific enquiry and scientific progress possible. In contrast, the idealist understanding constantly threatens to cut off scientific explanation in favour of demonstrating the wisdom and benevolence of the Creator. (Darwin himself protested against idealists' refusal to offer a scientific explanation of speciation.) Indeed, inasmuch as inductive philosophy of science attempted to preserve a theological interpretation of nature, it was (and is) a protective strategy designed to substitute a religious explanation of natural phenomena for possible scientific ones.[26]

A devil's chaplain

Darwin set down a history of his religious views in an autobiographical sketch written in 1876. This history features two principal branching points. The first was his loss of faith in the biblical Christianity of his conventionally pious youth in the years following his return to England after the *Beagle* voyage. Darwin recalled that he gave considerable thought to religion in these years, with the consequence that he came to see the Bible as a historical, human document rather than divine revelation. Aided by biblical criticism and Humean sceptical arguments, Darwin concluded that miracles are unbelievable in the light of the fixed laws of nature, the Gospels are not eyewitness accounts of the events they describe, and the writers and original audience of the biblical books were ignorant and credulous by modern standards. By 1839 he had come to regard the books of the Bible as no more trustworthy than the books claimed as sacred by other peoples.[27]

The years in which Darwin's faith in biblical Christianity fell away were precisely those in which he worked out the essentials of his theory of evolution by natural selection. His notebooks for the years 1837 and 1838 show that he questioned the special creationist position for religious reasons as much as scientific ones. In a representative entry he remarked that the idea of evolution by natural causes is far grander than the 'cramped imagination' that since the Silurian epoch God has occupied himself in making a long succession of vile molluscous animals.[28] Darwin here, in thinking of evolution as the secondary cause through which God carries out his creative will, was articulating the natural-law theism that figured so prominently in contemporary geology and biology. He considered its conception of the Creator to be superior, both theologically and scientifically, to the miracle-making personal God of the Bible.[29] Darwin wrote the *Origin of Species* as a believer in natural-law theism, and it is this belief that is enshrined in its concluding pages:

> Authors of the highest eminence seem to be fully satisfied with the view that each species has been independently created. To my mind it accords better with what we know of the laws impressed on matter by the Creator, that the production and extinction of the past and present inhabitants of the world should have been due to secondary causes.[30]

That Darwin was unable to persevere in natural-law theism in the years after the publication of the *Origin of Species* marks the second branching point in his religious history. It was brought about by reflection, spurred by orchids and Asa Gray – both of which preoccupied Darwin in the early 1860s – on the religious implications of evolution by natural selection. His work on the co-adaptation of the nectaries of various species of orchid and insects' proboscises, published as *The Various Contrivances by which Orchids are Fertilized by Insects*, confirmed for him the explanatory power of the theory of evolution by natural selection. Gray, an eminent Harvard botanist and Evangelical Christian, cross-examined him about design in nature in an exchange of letters that crested between 1860 and 1862.[31]

Darwin's difficulties with natural-law theism centred on theodicy and providence. In the *Origin* itself Darwin had rewritten Paley's 'It's a happy world, after all' in more sombre tones:

> We behold the face of nature bright with gladness, we often see superabundance of food; we do not see, or we forget, that the birds which are idly singing around us mostly live on insects or seeds, and are thus constantly destroying life; or we forget how largely these songsters, or their eggs, or their nestlings, are destroyed by birds and beasts of prey; we do not always bear in mind, that though food may now be superabundant, it is not so at all seasons of each recurring year.[32]

Three years before he had commented to his friend, the botanist Joseph Hooker: 'What a book a devil's chaplain might write on the clumsy, wasteful, blundering, low, and horribly cruel works of nature!'[33] In the years following the publication of the *Origin of Species* his sense of the suffering inherent in the natural order deepened. Writing to Asa Gray in 1860 Darwin linked theodicy and design:

> I own that I cannot see as plainly as others do, and as I should wish to do, evidence of design and beneficence on all sides of us. There seems to me too much misery in the world. I cannot persuade myself that a beneficent and omnipotent God would have designedly created the Ichneumonidae with the express intention of their feeding within the living bodies of Caterpillars, or that a cat should play with mice. Not believing this, I see no necessity in the belief that the eye was expressly designed.[34]

Providence had become equally problematic:

> I cannot look at the universe as the result of blind chance, yet I can see no evidence of beneficent design, or indeed of design of any kind, in the details. As for each variation that has ever occurred having been preordained for a special end, I can no more believe in it than that the spot on which each drop of rain falls has been specially ordained.[35]

This statement from the end of the decade sums up numerous letters Darwin wrote in the 1860s addressing the possibility, hopefully put forward by Asa Gray and Charles Lyell, among others, that variation is guided by a higher power. Again and again Darwin patiently replied that such a view not only makes natural selection superfluous but removes the question of the appearance of new species from the realm of science. He suggests that those who argue that each variation has been providentially arranged are misusing the *Origin*'s analogy with artificial selection. Variations in domestic and wild conditions arise from unknown (but natural) causes and are without purpose. Artificial selection becomes purposeful when human beings select variations for some end of their own, but natural selection operates without conscious purpose.[36] Darwin makes this same point in a long passage at the end of *The Variations of Animals and Plants under Domestication* (1868), to which he referred several correspondents who wished to maintain that evolution has been led along beneficial lines.[37]

Darwin's autobiography records his stark conclusion: 'The old argument from design in Nature, as given by Paley, which formerly seemed to me so conclusive, fails, now that the law of natural selection has been discovered.'[38] Natural-law theism, including natural theology, had become as unbelievable as biblical revelation. A single sentence from a letter to Gray summed up his double loss of faith: 'I cannot admit that man's rudimentary mammae … were designed. If I was to say I believed this, I should believe it in the same incredible manner as the orthodox believe in the Trinity in Unity.'[39] Darwin suggested, in a passage suppressed in the version of his autobiography eventually published in 1887, that religious belief is little more than an inherited instinct, like a monkey's fear of snakes.[40]

Evolution as development

The fact of evolution became widely accepted among both naturalists and Christians in the years following the publication of the *Origin of Species*. Richard

Owen, for his part, had for some time accepted the fact of evolution within each of the four taxonomic branches (although he was coy about this until after the appearance of the *Origin of Species*), but doggedly opposed Darwin's mechanism of natural selection. Louis Agassiz, now famous for establishing an ice age as the source of Buckland's 'diluvial deposits' and as the leading authority on fossil fishes, seconded Owen's idealist alternative to natural selection by opposing both the transmutation of species across the boundaries of the four branches of animals and any non-teleological account of the progressive development of life. Agassiz, in whom Cuvierian empiricism supplemented German idealist *Naturphilosophie*, had taken Darwin's first step away from biblical Christianity in moving from the Calvinism of his Swiss upbringing to the American Unitarianism he embraced when, as a professor at Harvard, he married into a Boston Brahmin family; but there he rested, his faith in natural theology ever undiminished. Correspondingly, he accepted evolution within each branch of the animal kingdom in place of special creation of each and every species, but insisted both that the original species of each of the four branches had been specially created by God and that the purpose of divine creation was the ultimate emergence of human beings.[41]

As Owen and Agassiz illustrate, it is not the transmutation of species or deep time itself that opposes design and providence, but Darwin's mechanism of natural selection. Very quickly after 1859 theologians and pious naturalists therefore attempted to reconcile the transmutability of species with Christianity, or at least theism, by affirming that the operation of evolution is providentially guided. The result was a proliferation of non-Darwinian models of evolution that replaced natural selection as the mechanism of evolution with an external guide or designer.

Two scientifically prominent practitioners of the strategy of reconciling natural theology with Darwin's generally convincing case for the fact of evolution by retaining a place for design in the mechanism by which it operates were the statesman and accomplished amateur naturalist the Duke of Argyll (George Douglas Campell) and Asa Gray. Argyll, in the *Reign of Law* (1867) and other popular books, argued that natural selection cannot explain the modification of species because it merely selects among variations that originate by some other 'law'. Argyll recognized that Darwin could not explain the origin of variation, and then leapt to the conclusion that variations do not come into being by natural processes. Rather than consider the possibility that variation is caused by some yet-to-be-discovered natural law, Argyll simply proclaimed that variation is designed by God and therefore the entire evolutionary process is providentially guided. His assertion that Darwin needed a 'principle of design' became a standard argument among the general public against the theory of evolution by natural selection.[42]

Asa Gray, who described himself as being 'scientifically, and in his own fashion a Darwinian, philosophically a convinced theist, and religiously a [Nicene Christian]',[43] was unusual among theistic evolutionists for his acceptance of the mechanism of natural selection, but he attempted to draw its sting by insisting that 'at least while the physical cause of variation is utterly unknown and mysterious, we should advise Mr. Darwin to assume, in the philosophy of his hypothesis, that variation has been led along certain beneficial lines'.[44] It was only after having thereby returned natural selection to the direction of providence that Gray defended it against its theological opponents in his pamphlet *Natural Selection Not Inconsistent with Natural Theology* (1861). Darwin recognized that Gray's providentialism and teleology destroyed the value of natural selection as a scientific explanation, and yet he was grateful both for Gray's recognition of the role of hypothesis in science in general and for his defence of the hypothesis of natural selection in particular. He praised Gray's pamphlet as the best theistic essay on evolution he had read and arranged and paid for its publication in England.[45]

The various pre-Darwinian theories of evolution had featured inexorable progressivism and often a providentially directed teleology. In their day these theories had been tarred with the odium associated with materialist philosophies, to which were attributed, and nowhere more than in early nineteenth-century England, the social and moral catastrophe of the French Revolution. But once the fact of evolution had become widely accepted these theories were taken up, often without attribution, by those seeking a non-Darwinian mechanism for its operation.[46] Non-Darwinian versions of evolution coalesced, especially in America, into what came to be known as Neo-Lamarckism. Lamarck had explained the transmutation of species by the dual mechanism of an inherently progressive life force that pushes living things up the chain of being and toward increased biological complexity and the inheritance of acquired characters, which adapts them to ever-changing environments. Neo-Lamarckians seized on the inheritance of acquired characters and the idea that variation is not random, but otherwise drew on post-Lamarckian biology, including some aspects of Darwinism itself.[47]

Neo-Lamarckism above all applied to evolution the pre-Darwinian developmental model of growth. Idealists, from the German *Naturphilosophen* through Owen to Agassiz, understood growth as a process of recapitulation. On this theory a human embryo, in the course of its growth in the womb, passes through the chain of being; that is, it is successively a fish, a reptile and a mammal, before culminating as a human being. Agassiz added another series to the parallelism by integrating the history of life as revealed in the fossil record with embryonic growth and the fixed hierarchy of living species. The growth of an embryo additionally recapitulates the successive appearance in deep time of fish, reptiles, mammals and finally human beings. And yet, as a creationist of the idealist type, Agassiz adamantly denied that his integration of growth with the history of life implied evolution. Recapitulation is the discontinuous succession of special creations according to the divine plan for reaching creation's predetermined goal.[48]

Agassiz's American students, notably the invertebrate palaeontologist Alpheus Hyatt (1838–1902) and the zoologist Alpheus Packard (1839–1905), along with similarly minded naturalists such as the palaeontologist Edward Drinker Cope (1840–1897), could not accept the master's rejection of the fact of evolution. But they realized that Agassiz's recapitulation model could be adapted to an

evolutionary interpretation simply by inverting his argument. If, instead of re-
garding the history of life as a divinely established independent parallel to
embryonic growth and the hierarchy of living species, one were to accept the
fossil record as the actual history of physical descent, then the history of life
would explain the other two sequences. In this way the Neo-Lamarckian analogy
between growth and evolution yielded a developmental model of evolution as
progressive and teleological: just as an embryo grows inevitably toward its mature
form, so the history of life evolves through a fixed and preordained hierarchy of
stages toward its goal. Neo-Lamarckian recapitulation thereby substituted for
Darwin's haphazard, branching, open-ended process of evolution an orderly,
goal-directed, and preordained process that cannot be affected by environmental
conditions.[49] The Neo-Lamarckian developmental model of evolution offered a
similar solution as the universal histories of an early century had to a similar
problem. Where the universal histories had attempted to reintegrate the historical
records of the Gentile nations into sacred history, Neo-Lamarckism attempted to
reintegrate the history of life into a providential order.

The Neo-Lamarckians, however, were not the first to promote a developmental model of organic evolution. Such a model had been at the heart of the
notorious 1844 work *Vestiges of the Natural History of Creation*. Reaction to this
anonymous book had recapitulated the charges of blasphemy and bad science
that had greeted Lamarck himself.[50] Aside from its scientific deficiencies, the
difference in the reception accorded to *Vestiges* and to Neo-Lamarckism may be
explained by chronology. Compared to special creation, developmental evolution
had seemed materialist and blasphemous; but once the fact of evolution had been
accepted and the relevant comparison was to the random, non-teleological mechanism of natural selection, developmentalism positively exuded piety.

And, in fact, the Neo-Lamarckians themselves understood developmental
evolutionism as permitting a reformulation of the design argument. Building on
Owen and Agassiz, who had argued that the orderly relationships among species
based on a common Archetype are better evidence of design than any number of
individual cases of specific adaptation and better in keeping with the scientific
emphasis on secondary causes, Neo-Lamarckians saw in teleological development evidence that the benevolent deity had delegated to life the power of
designing itself in accordance with a transcendental pattern. Contributors to the
American Naturalist, founded by Hyatt and Packer as the organ of American
Neo-Lamarckism, were encouraged to present their work as illustrating the
wisdom and goodness of the Creator. The party line received popular expression
from the pen of the Unitarian (originally Quaker) Cope in his *Theology of
Evolution* (1887). Consciousness, Cope argued, is not a product of evolution but
instead governs the evolutionary process by directing animals' efforts toward
new goals and so shaping the successive forms of species. Further, consciousness
itself derives from the divine mind immanent in the universe, a mind that expresses its will in the progressive advance of life toward higher levels.[51] Neo-
Lamarckism was both a scientific and a metaphysical programme; its adherents
affirmed Paley's conviction that the world is a temple and life itself one continued act of adoration even as they discarded his mode of natural theology.

Modern commentators, recognizing the non-teleological, non-purposive nature of Darwin's theory of evolution by natural selection, use metaphors to convey his revolutionary insight. Daniel Dennett attributes life on Earth in all its complexity and beauty to a mechanical, mindless algorithmic process; Richard Dawkins, subverting Paley, speaks of the unconscious, automatic process of natural selection as a blind watchmaker.[52] The Darwinism mechanism for evolution opens the door to a truly historical study of the history of life in place of the teleological, pre-programmed pattern of the developmental analogy with growth. And yet, Darwin's revolutionary insight was largely lost on his contemporaries. Darwin himself assumed that reproduction and growth are essential aspects of the evolutionary process. Self-proclaimed Darwinians such as Ernst Haeckel invoked the growth analogy, with its teleological implications, and championed a progressivist view of evolution incompatible with Darwin's branching model. In fact, Haeckel's 'biogenetic law' that ontogeny recapitulates phylogeny epitomized the developmentalist belief that the evolutionary history of a species (phylogeny) is recapitulated in the embryonic growth of each individual (ontogeny) of that species.[53]

If Haeckel, along with 'Darwin's bulldog', the equally progressivist Thomas Henry Huxley, were thought to be the most prominent biological Darwinians of the late nineteenth century, then far and away the most famous social Darwinist was the philosopher Herbert Spencer (1820–1903). Spencer, in fact, was primarily responsible for popularizing the term 'evolution' itself, and yet his conception of evolution was thoroughly Neo-Lamarckian: characters contributing to fitness which are acquired through the struggle for existence are passed down and shape the development of future generations. Further complicating matters, Spencer's abstract formulation of evolution – 'a change from an indefinite, incoherent homogeneity, to a definite, coherent heterogeneity' – was borrowed directly from an opponent of both the recapitulation thesis and organic evolution, the embryologist Karl Ernst von Baer. Spencer integrated von Baer's principle that growth is not a progressive ascent but a process of successive differentiation with the evolutionism he had already embraced as a result of reading Lyell's attempted refutation of Lamarck in *Principles of Geology*. The resulting ideology was first announced in an 1857 article, 'Progress: Its Law and Cause', and then made the basis of Spencer's systematization of all knowledge in the multiple volumes of his *System of Synthetic Philosophy* (1862–96): all natural and human phenomena, from the differentiation of stars and planets from an incoherent gassy nebula to the rise of the division of labour in industrial society from agricultural uniformity, follow a progressive pattern from lesser to greater complexity.[54] Spencer's philosophy of progress, like the socially and politically progressive editorial programme of the *Westminster Review*, to which he contributed, represented a secularized version of liberal Protestant theology in which nature rather than God guarantees the ongoing social and moral improvement of humanity. At the same time it assured Victorians that the struggle and suffering inherent in capitalism and imperialism were meaningful.[55]

Neo-Lamarckism drew on religious discontent with Darwinism, but it also exploited legitimate scientific objections to Darwin's theory of evolution by natural selection. Darwin himself had acknowledged the imperfection of the fossil record in substantiating the gradual transmutation of species and had confessed his inability to explain the origin of variation. Other objections, such as William Thomson's (later Lord Kelvin) argument from the principles of physics that the Earth was not old enough to permit the immense time needed for the operation of natural selection, or the argument from blending heredity that any advantageous mutation would be swamped by the mass of unmutated individuals, were powerful until they were dispelled in the early twentieth century by, respectively, the discovery of radioactivity and Mendelian genetics. Neo-Lamarckism for a time seemed to answer many of these objections although, ominously, attempts to prove experimentally the inheritance of acquired characters repeatedly failed.[56]

Neo-Lamarckians, as we have seen, reformulated the design argument by internalizing God's power in the creative adaptability of life. But the immanentist strategy had its risks; just as Vico's immanent providence could be read as a secular theory of civil history, so Neo-Lamarckism could be secularized into a purely naturalistic model of development. This is precisely what the concept of orthogenesis effected. Orthogenesis, or linear evolution driven inexorably and independently of environmental influences toward non-adaptive goals, denied that variation was random, but whereas Neo-Lamarckism held that the pattern of growth unfolds according to a divine plan, orthogenesis maintained that laws of growth are built into the fundamental character of nature. In detaching the belief that nature is a system of orderly, directed development from natural theology, orthogenesis reflected the general trend in late nineteenth-century science away from recourse to the supernatural and toward the conviction that natural phenomena were to be explained in naturalistic terms.[57]

That Darwinism was in eclipse, to use Julian Huxley's image, in the decades either side of 1900 is undeniable. Neo-Lamarckism and orthogenesis were for a time plausible and influential alternatives. Another apparent enemy, however, would turn out to be a powerful friend. Mendelian genetics arose as an attempt to supersede both teleological models of evolution and Darwinism by means of laboratory research into the processes of heredity and variation. Geneticists severed the study of heredity from the embryological model of ontogeny by demonstrating that new genetical characters are produced by mutation and that mutation is governed by events taking place within the genetical material itself rather than by any sort of growth process. Because Mendelian genetics, rather than Darwin, eliminated teleology from biological development by destroying the analogy between evolution and growth, the revolution in historical-mindedness in biology, the first shot of which was the *Origin of Species,* triumphed only with the Modern Synthesis of genetics and evolution by natural selection achieved between the 1920s and the early 1940s.[58]

Evolution and theology

Liberal-minded Christians in the nineteenth century found little difficulty in assimilating a theistic model of evolution into their faith. The immediate response of the liberal clergyman Charles Kingsley on reading the *Origin of Species* was characteristic:

> I have gradually learnt to see that it is just as noble a conception of Deity, to believe that he created primal forms capable of self-development into all forms needful *pro tempore* and *pro loco*, as to believe that He required a fresh act of intervention to supply the *lacunas* which He Himself had made. I question whether the former be not the loftier thought.[59]

Echoing Jowett on the higher criticism a generation earlier, theistic evolutionists argued that not only could Christians embrace evolution but those who attacked it in the name of religion risked driving thinking people into unbelief. Frederick Temple, contributor to *Essays and Reviews* and future Archbishop of Canterbury, who as Bishop of Exeter wrote and spoke extensively on the question of the relation of science to religion, epitomized the clerical assimilation of evolution. His message in the 1884 Bampton Lectures on 'The Relations between Religion and Science' and elsewhere was that Christians ought to replace Paley's sort of natural theology with a new natural theology based on evolution. Darwin, he assured Victorian England, had not overthrown but updated and strengthened the argument from design. Rather than constantly intervening to create individually the perfect adaptations of living forms to their environment, God had instead, theists argued, foreseen in advance all the various changes that would occur both in the organic and inorganic world and infused into the first created germ of life an internal 'law of development' that would carry its descendants infallibly in the direction beneficial to each.[60] Liberal Christians, like Neo-Lamarckian scientists (of course, the categories overlap), embraced progressive development as a fundamental natural law. As such, the evolutionary process attested not only to purpose but also to divine intelligence and benevolence.

As so often, Tennyson spoke for the liberal position. *In Memoriam* had enshrined a developmentalist model of evolution: the doubts posed by geology and palaeontology were overcome in section 118 in a celebration of recapitulation: 'move upward, working out the beast', and the Epilogue similarly expressed its concluding vision of cosmic optimism in images of ongoing evolutionary ascent.[61] When Tennyson read the *Origin of Species* soon after its publication he could not find in Darwin's bleak account of the cruelty, suffering and pointless fecundity of nature the God of love in whom *In Memoriam* had trusted. Tennyson and Darwin met once during summer holidays on the Isle of Wight in 1868. A house guest reported that after Darwin's visit Tennyson had paced the garden declaring: 'What I want is an assurance of immortality.' He never did accept the full implications of natural selection; evolution, he trusted, would continue in the afterlife, bringing progressively greater happiness and spiritual development of the human race.[62]

The Darwinian mechanism of natural selection explains the organic world without recourse to an intelligent designer and doubts the benevolence of the evolutionary process. For all their praise of Darwin, Temple and other liberal theologians ignored these implications of natural selection. For them, Darwin stood simply for the fact of evolution. On the other hand, even a teleological and developmentalist model of evolution contradicts a plain-sense interpretation of

Genesis. This, however, caused barely a ripple in liberal consciences because they had already abandoned biblical literalism under the impact of the historical criticism of the Bible (in fact, it was their rejection of biblical literalism that had made them liberal Christians in the first place). Those who regarded the Bible as a historical document saw no need to contort Scripture so as to reconcile its words with the findings of science. The deeply religious Richard Owen may stand here for an attitude toward the Bible widely shared by liberal Christians. Speaking before a YMCA audience in 1862, Owen linked his vision of scientists as God's servants and ministers of truth to a version of the theory of progressive revelation. The Bible, he said, represents an early phase in divine self-revelation; its understanding of the physical world in general and the Genesis accounts of creation and the Flood in particular are crude fables characteristic of ignorant and semi-barbarous ages. In today's world scientists have replaced the prophets of old as the illuminated vessels of divine revelation; their discoveries represent nothing less than ongoing revelation. The truths contained in the Bible, Owen concluded, are moral and spiritual; its heart is the Sermon on the Mount. Clergymen and theologians who set against modern science an insistence on the historical accuracy and inspired nature of the Bible betray their calling by subverting God's ongoing revelation in the name of its obsolete forms. Owen's attack on conservative biblicism, which was part of his campaign to diminish the authority of the Church over science, closely corresponds to the position of the biblical theologians. The kernel of truth in the Genesis creation narrative was that God had created the universe and human beings, but its account of how he had done so was an ancient Hebrew myth. These liberal Christians synthesized biblical theology and theistic evolution into a single, mutually reinforcing developmentalist ideology: the recognition of the Bible as a historical document soothed concerns that evolution contradicted a literal reading of Genesis, while the obvious incompatibility of Genesis with the findings of science lent support to the higher critics' historical analysis of the Bible.[63]

Conservative Christians, naturally enough, were more hostile than liberal ones to the whole idea of the transmutation of species, but even some conservative theologians accepted a version of theistic evolution. One who emphatically did not was Charles Hodge (1797–1878), professor of systematic theology at Princeton Theological Seminary. Drawing on his reading of Agassiz, whose observation that facts are revelations from God whereas theories are the mere speculations of fallen humanity he often quoted, Hodge rejected evolution in any form and especially evolution by natural selection. In *What is Darwinism?* (1874), he answered, 'it is atheism, because it leaves the soul entirely without God, without a Father, Helper, or Ruler'. Hodge, reading *Origin of Species* more carefully than the liberal Christians, understood that natural selection excluded design and purpose. He recognized that Asa Gray was not a true Darwinian, and that Darwinism conflicted not only with biblical Christianity but also with natural-law theism. And yet, Hodge was not a biblical literalist; he accepted the geologists' demonstration that the Earth is very old, and therefore recognized that the biblical creation narrative required interpretation (he himself favoured the day/age theory over the gap theory) and cannot be used as a scientific authority. His position was that science itself (represented by Agassiz) has shown that Darwinism is *scientifically* untenable, and therefore one may accept the design and providentialism of the biblical account as consistent with sound science.[64]

Hodge's rejection of Darwinism as bad science rather than as unbiblical permitted other Princeton men to accept a form of evolution that retained design and providence (since these were the core issues and not special creation). James McCosh, president of the College of New Jersey (as Princeton University was then called) from 1868 to 1888, was as appalled by Darwin's radical naturalism as was Hodge, but rather than reject evolution outright he championed a teleological model of evolution according to which God guides organic progress along a predetermined path. McCosh thought that Hodge's Paleyan concept of design was to blame for his hostility toward evolution. Even before he had come to accept the fact of evolution McCosh had criticized Paley's analogy between the natural world and a mechanical contrivance as simplistic. He set about providing a demonstration of design more adequate to the nineteenth-century understanding of the natural order in a book written in collaboration with George Dickie, a professor of morphology at Queen's College, Belfast. In *Typical Forms and Special Ends in Creation* (1855) they spoke of the 'collocation' of natural forces, or the idea that the operations of nature are the result of the coordinated interaction of forces that are in themselves essentially blind or indifferent to the others. McCosh and Dickie pointed to the pollination of plants by bees as an example of collocation: neither the plant nor the insect knows anything of the needs of the other, but the harmony of their separate functions perpetuates both species. The interplay of gravitational and centripetal forces in the solar system exemplifies collocation on a cosmic scale, since the precarious balance between these forces that permits life on Earth would be destroyed by only a slight alteration in either of them. Arguing that these 'mutual adaptations of different and independent powers' cannot proceed from chance, McCosh offered collocation as evidence of design in nature superior to Paley's mechanical model.[65]

Typical Forms was non-evolutionary, and in fact predated the *Origin of Species* by four years. As its Owenesque title suggests, McCosh at this time was a partisan of idealist morphology. He took a particular interest in homologies, noting, for example, that the fivefold division in the structure of a whale's fin corresponds to the five fingers of the human hand, even though the fin, unlike the hand, functions as an inflexible paddle. This homology posed a problem for the Paleyan model of design since the subdivisions in the structure of the fin are irrelevant to its function. But McCosh, like all idealist morphologists, read the apparent design flaw as a sign that all vertebrates are part of a single plan culminating in human beings. The fivefold division of the fin, while irrelevant to the way of life of the whale itself, exists because it is an anticipation of and preparation for the highly functional fingers of the human hand. For McCosh, as for Owen, such evidence proves that the idea of humanity existed before the appearance of human beings, and that nature is ordered in relation to its preordained end in us. For these men, no less than for Kepler and Newton in the seventeenth century, the task of science is to uncover the divine blueprint of creation. But they considered the old mechanical model of natural theology to have now been superseded by their idealist model of natural theology, which displayed the unity underlying creation.[66]

It was a short step from the idealist concept of the order of nature to a developmental version of evolution, a step McCosh had taken by the early 1870s in response to mounting evidence for the fact of evolution. The passage was as emotionally smooth as it was short because McCosh was able to retain collocation and final cause. After all, what is the history of life as the development of one species from another but collocation on a vast scale? McCosh's *The Religious Aspect of Evolution* (1888) enshrined the developmental model of evolution within natural theology: 'the union and conspiracy of forces involved in Evolution furnish new proof, as it certainly supplies new illustrations, of purpose and ends'.[67] McCosh's position explains the surprising presence of a defence of evolution in *The Fundamentals* (1910–15), the series of pamphlets from which Fundamentalism takes its name. In 'Science and the Christian Faith' James Orr, a Scottish Presbyterian professor of church history, insisted that the theory of evolution ought not to be equated with Darwinism. Here, and in *The Faith of a Modern Christian* (1910), he allowed that the 'genetic derivation of one order or species from another' had occurred, although with the double qualification that the entire process was providentially guided and that the human species had originated in a special act of creation.[68]

It was yet another Princeton Theological Seminary scholar, Benjamin Breckinridge Warfield, who set out the theory of biblical interpretation that allowed these American Presbyterians to regard their acceptance of evolution and an ancient Earth as compatible with orthodox Calvinism. Writing on 'Calvin's Doctrine of the Creation' (1915) in the *Princeton Theological Review*, Warfield argued that Calvin's general interpretive practice of accommodation trumps his specific interpretation of the six days of creation as literal, 24-hour days. The Bible is indeed errorless, but the defence of inerrancy does not demand a literal reading of the Genesis narratives. In understanding the six days as six ages, twentieth-century Christians may accept the testimony of geology while remaining true to Calvin's interpretive principle of accommodation. Similarly, Calvin had taught that 'creation' proper designated only the initial creative act, when God had called primeval matter into existence from nothingness. Subsequent creations, except for each and every human soul, were modifications of the primeval matter by means of the interaction of its intrinsic forces. Warfield concluded that because Calvinist orthodoxy permits an explanation of the natural world, including human bodies, in terms of secondary causes operating under the guiding hand of divine providence, nothing forbids modern Presbyterians from accepting a teleological model of evolution.[69] Warfield's accommodationist hermeneutic exemplifies the strategy used to reconcile the Bible with science by conservative Christians who rejected the higher criticism and regarded the entirety of the Bible as directly inspired by God. Whereas the creation narrative in Genesis was originally given to a scientifically ignorant audience, nevertheless the words of the

Bible, when rightly interpreted, correspond to the findings of modern science. A more aggressive version of this strategy cited the parallels between the successive creations of the Genesis narrative and the stages in the history of life disclosed by science as evidence for the divine inspiration of the Bible.[70]

In 1887 Darwin's nephew, Francis Darwin, published a collection of his uncle's papers, under the title of *Life and Letters of Charles Darwin*, that included the autobiographical sketch describing his two-stage loss of faith. Darwin's lapse from biblical Christianity had been widely known but not his subsequent rejection of natural-law theism. Warfield, among others, pounced on the revelation of Darwin's ultimate agnosticism as evidence of the terrible spiritual consequences necessarily entailed by his theory of evolution by natural selection. Nevertheless, the compatibility of theistic, developmental evolution and biblical Christianity was repeatedly affirmed in the pages of the *Princeton Theological Review* throughout the late nineteenth century.[71]

Chapter 9

PREHISTORIC HUMANS

In June 1845 the biblical scholar John William Burgon (1813–1888) recited before an Oxford audience his prize-winning poem on the ruins of the 3,000-year-old city of Petra, discovered 32 years before in a spectacular red-rock chasm in present-day Jordan. Burgon's *Petra* is a meditation on the vanity of splendour, a biblically inspired *Ozymandias*, though lacking both the brilliance and brevity of Shelley's poem. Burgon identifies Petra with ancient Edom, and reads its present-day desolation as the fulfilment of the biblical prophecies concerning Israel's ancient enemy. The poem ends with an evocation of the 'awful contrast' between the extinction of Edom and the glorious promise in store for the posterity of Jacob. Of course, by 'posterity of Jacob' he means the Christian Church; allusions to Christ and the sacraments appear throughout the poem thanks to a typological reading of Old Testament passages, and the final lines celebrate the awakening of Israel as the Heavenly Jerusalem of the book of Revelation. The line for which Burgon's poem is remembered today hails Petra as 'A rose-red city – half as old as Time!' Burgon meant it literally; given the biblical chronology of 6,000 years for the age of the world, which he accepted unquestioningly, 3,000-year-old Petra was precisely half as old as time itself.

Burgon's poem seamlessly joins a non-critical approach to the Bible with the rejection of deep time. In 1845 the higher criticism of the Bible had scarcely begun to infiltrate English minds, and while an immense age for the pre-human Earth was increasingly granted, most among the educated classes would have agreed that humanity, if not time itself, was no more than roughly six thousand years old. And yet, in retrospect, Burgon wrote his poem almost exactly midway in the three decades during which the understanding of humanity's past was transformed. Between 1830 and 1859 humanity itself was firmly placed in deep time and soon after made subject to radical change. The concept of 'prehistory' and the new historical sciences of archaeology and anthropology are the intellectual signs of this extension of deep time and historical-mindedness to yet another aspect of the world. In 1830, however, archaeology and anthropology were sciences of the future. The first steps toward the recognition of human prehistory were taken by geologists and palaeontologists, who encountered human remains – either actual bodily remains or, more commonly, tools and other artefacts – in the course of their fieldwork.

Human prehistory

The work of Georges Cuvier had offered the early nineteenth century scientific confirmation of the biblical chronology of roughly six thousand years of human history. Humans, he ruled, had not appeared until the Earth had attained its modern form both geologically and zoologically; that is, after the deposition of the superficial gravels and the extinction of the great mammals, both caused by the most recent catastrophe, which had reshaped the Earth a few thousand years ago. Cuvier's authority gave wide credence to the conviction that humanity was doubly recent: in the absolute sense of the years of the biblical chronology and in the relative sense of postdating the appearance of the modern Earth.[1] In England clerical naturalists took the further step of integrating Cuvier's science with the content of the Bible, and not only its chronology. William Buckland, as we have seen in an earlier chapter, identified Cuvier's most recent catastrophe with the biblical Flood. His *Relics of the Flood* (1823) plausibly argued that all extant human remains postdate the Flood. Those cases in which human remains had been found in close proximity to the bones of extinct mammals – hitherto exclusively from caves – Buckland dismissed as instances of the haphazard mixing of strata in the complex geological environment of caves. Of course, the remains of humans slightly predating the superficial gravels and other diluvial deposits ought to exist since people had lived before the Flood. Buckland explained the absence of antediluvian human remains by assuring his readers that they were to be found in Asia rather than Europe.[2]

Within a few years of Buckland's *Relics of the Flood* geologists reached a consensus that the diluvial deposits in various parts of Europe were not of exactly the same age and therefore could not be attributed to a single event. This, and other geological evidence, meant that by the early 1830s scientists no longer identified the biblical Flood as the geological agency that had deposited the diluvium (although the term continued to be used). Two principal consequences followed from dissociating the diluvium from the Flood. First, one need no longer puzzle over the lack of human remains in or just beneath the diluvial layer, since its deposition predated the Flood. But second, the direct link between science and the Bible was lost and with it an absolute empirical time-marker for the appearance of humanity on the Earth. Naturalists continued to think of the age of humanity as measurable in a few millennia, but after about 1830 they became leery of both offering an absolute age for humanity and discussing the biblical chronology because neither could now be addressed empirically. For the biblically minded (especially in Britain), the increased age of the diluvium and its extinct mammals raised the stakes should human remains one day be found in association with them. Any such association would now contradict the biblical chronology.[3]

The geologists who established the reality of deep time and detached the diluvium from the Flood were only indirectly interested in human artefacts. Another group of investigators, however, had busily been gathering evidence that would bear directly on the question of the age of humanity. Antiquarians of the sort maligned by Isaac Newton as dilettantes and mere collectors had long been interested in the artefacts made by early humans. Farmers had been finding flaked flint arrowheads in their fields, but just as it had taken a particular mindset to recognize one class of figured stones as the remains of once-living animals, so people did not immediately recognize these other figured stones as tools. They were long explained as petrified thunderbolts, elfshot (fairy arrows), or the exhalations of clouds. The turning point came after the discovery of the New World. Europeans recognized their petrified thunderbolts as stone tools similar to those still in use in the Americas and gradually acknowledged that at one time the use of metal had been unknown in Europe. While this European Stone Age was clearly far in the past, virtually no one suggested that it might be of such antiquity as to explode the biblical chronology. The one notable exception was an English squire, John Frere, who in 1797 discovered in a gravel pit at Hoxne, Suffolk a cache of stone axes in close proximity to the bones of extinct mammals. Frere's announcement of his discovery, as well as his speculation that the axes might be significantly older than six thousand years, was ignored for two generations.[4]

Frere had run up against the overwhelming conviction of the recentness of humanity and the unimpeachableness of the biblical chronology. Until geologists established beyond reasonable doubt the reality of deep time in the first decades of the next century, no one – aside from the notorious Isaac La Peyrère – made a serious case for an ancient humanity. The fourth chapter of Genesis, which lists the founders of culture, credits Tubal-Cain with the invention of metal-working, thus establishing that metal tools were in use before both the Flood and the dispersion of peoples after the debacle of the Tower of Babel. Before 1800 the challenge was to account for both the use of stone tools in Europe and the lack of metal ones among some modern non-Europeans without contradicting the Genesis account of early humanity. It was triumphantly met by invoking the Flood itself; metal tools had indeed been in use in antediluvian times but the trauma of the Flood had caused a cultural degeneration in which knowledge of metal-working was lost. The Bible itself confirmed this account inasmuch as at Exodus 4:25 and elsewhere it describes the use of stone tools well after the Flood. In this way, and paralleling the geologists' identification of Cuvier's most recent catastrophe with the Flood, seventeenth- and eighteenth-century antiquarians reconciled the discovery of stone tools with the biblical narrative.[5]

The question of the 'antiquity of man' was revolutionized between 1830 and 1859. The shifting reputation of Jacques Boucher de Crêvecœur de Perthes (1788–1868) may serve as index of the progress of this revolution. Beginning in the late 1830s Boucher de Perthes, a customs official and amateur antiquarian, became fascinated with the chipped flints found, sometimes in association with the remains of extinct animals, in the gravels of the Somme river valley near his home at Abbeville in northern France. In 1838 he exhibited some of the flints, which he called 'diluvian axes', and in 1839 began publication of a multipart work on the Somme flints entitled *On Creation: An Essay on the Progression of Beings*. Boucher de Perthes continued his researches over the next decade, and in

1847 published *Celtic and Antediluvian Antiquities*. Note that he now claimed that the people who had chipped the flints had lived before the Flood. More had changed than his realization that the association of stone axes with extinct mammals pushed their age well into antediluvian times. Boucher de Perthes was no longer an amateur on the margins of science, and the new book placed his evidence in a far more convincing theoretical framework than the speculations of his earlier work.[6] Nevertheless, the reception of his new book by the experts was much the same as that of his first: indifference leavened with ridicule. Part of the problem was that much of the key evidence had not been reproduced in the new volume. More decisively, the professional naturalists – those in the position to grant official recognition to a prehistoric humanity – were those most in thrall to the posthumous authority of Cuvier. Convinced that human beings had not coexisted with extinct animals, they both rejected outright any claims to the contrary and saw no point in carrying out research designed to legitimate such claims.[7]

Boucher de Perthes persevered, yet his ultimate vindication was not the result of the French scientific establishment finally listening to him, but of the willingness of elite naturalists in Britain to give him a fair hearing owing to English developments in the study of human antiquity. In the late 1850s excavations in several south Devon caves turned up flint tools and other artefacts in association with extinct animals. The most famous of these sites was the Windmill Hill Cave at Brixham, where a local schoolmaster and geologist named William Pengelly discovered flint tools amid the bones of extinct species of elephant, rhinoceros, cave bear and hyena. Even more impressive, the cache of tools and bones lay beneath a sheet of rock several inches thick that itself enclosed the remains of extinct mammals, which indicated that they were very old indeed. Pengelly's report on his findings to the 1858 meeting of the British Association for the Advancement of Science attracted immense interest. Leading British geologists, including Hugh Falconer, John Evans, Joseph Prestwich and Charles Lyell, reviewed the Brixham evidence. While they found it highly suggestive, the fact remained that it came from a cave, and as such was subject to the scepticism inherently accompanying data from geologically complex sites. The British luminaries' next step was to cross the Channel, in ones and twos, to talk with Boucher de Perthes and examine his collections and, crucially, his sites. The relatively simple stratigraphy of the Somme river valley terraces permitted artefacts to be correlated, and therefore dated, not only with the faunal content of the beds (as in caves) but also, and confidently, with geological strata. The Somme evidence convinced the British visitors that ancient human beings had indeed coexisted with extinct mammals, and they in turn at long last admitted Boucher de Perthes' evidence into received science.[8]

The British experts announced their new conviction in a series of papers read to the principal British scientific associations between May and September 1859. One by one, Pengelly, Prestwich, Evans, Falconer and Lyell informed their scientific colleagues of the overwhelming evidence that the human lineage was very old, both absolutely and relatively: human beings had lived on the Earth for thousands of years beyond the limits of the biblical chronology and at a time when neither the Earth nor its fauna had yet attained their modern form. Because of who its author was and who he had been, the most epoch-making of these reports was Lyell's. As President of the geology section of the British Association for the Advancement of Science, Lyell spoke from a position of prestige and authority; further, in edition after edition of his *Principles of Geology* through 1855 he had upheld the recency of human beings and categorically denied their coexistence with extinct animals. His report marked the capitulation of a long-time opponent. Collectively, the 1859 reports constitute another landmark in historical-mindedness. The majority of naturalists, not just in Britain but all over western Europe, now accepted that humanity was both ancient and had coexisted with extinct animals.[9] Two widely read books by illustrious scholars published in the 1860s placed the new knowledge before the general reading public: Lyell's *Geological Evidences of the Antiquity of Man* (1863) and the archaeologist John Lubbock's (later Lord Avebury) *Prehistoric Times* (1865). Neither author soft-pedalled the message; they reviewed site after site, hammering home the inescapable implication of the stratigraphical evidence: humanity is ancient and had coexisted with extinct animals on a geologically pre-modern Earth.

Once the ancientness of humanity was generally accepted, Genesis yielded its place as the authoritative account of humanity's early past to the new discipline (and word) of prehistory. In the process, antiquarians were reborn as archaeologists through the midwifery of geology. The rebirth of antiquarians as archaeologists and the establishment of the ancientness of humanity are two sides of the same coin.[10] And just as Cuvier's revelation of extinct monsters had publicized the then-new science of palaeontology, so the revelation of extinct civilizations fired public interest in the new science of archaeology. Heinrich Schliemann spectacularly inaugurated the process by unearthing the remains of Troy in 1871. Within a decade modern scientific techniques were being developed by German archaeologists at Olympia and by Flinders Petrie in Egypt. In the decades after 1900 the recovery of a number of lost or previously unknown civilizations – paralleling the avalanche of new dinosaur species unearthed after Cuvier – began to map the continent of prehistory: the Minoans at Crete, the tells of the Near East, the cities of the Akkadians and the Sumerians, Yang Shao Tsun and other Chinese prehistoric sites, and Harappa and Mohenjo-Daro in the Indus Valley.[11]

Almost as soon as the reality of prehistory was accepted archaeologists began to subdivide it in an effort to classify ancient artefacts. Their efforts at cultural stratigraphy replayed in a new discipline the construction of the geological column almost a century earlier. Lubbock modified the stone–bronze–iron sequence already used to systematize Scandinavian archaeological collections in recognition that the significant technological advance represented by polished stone tools over chipped stone tools warranted the division of the Stone Age. While his framework of Palaeolithic, Neolithic, Bronze and Iron Ages set out in *Prehistoric Times* became standard, archaeologists quickly realized that the Palaeolithic was by far the longest of the prehistoric eras, and began to subdivide it. Much of the foundational archaeological work was carried out in the limestone caves and rock-shelters of western France. The French palaeontologist Edouard Lartet and the English banker Henry Christy distinguished among the artefacts they dug up in various sites in the region on the basis of technique and style. Lartet named the periods to which they assigned each group of artefacts after the animal bones characteristically found with them, announcing a Cave Bear period, a Mammoth period and a Reindeer period. Archaeologists embraced the underlying concept of using technological and stylistic differences as chronological markers, but objected to a nomenclature derived from palaeontology. They replaced it with a system that named distinctive methods and styles for the site at which they were first found or best exemplified. The leader in this effort was the eminent French archaeologist Gabriel de Mortillet. The successive editions of his *The Prehistoric Age* (first published in 1883) divided the Palaeolithic into (from oldest to most recent), the Chellean (later Abbevillian), Acheulean, Mousterian, Aurignacian, Solutrean and Magdalenian periods. This classification, modified and further sub-divided, still provides the basis for modern palaeolithic archaeology.[12]

Developmentalist anthropology

Once evidence of human prehistory was accepted and archaeologists began to classify its ages and periods, the question of its meaning came to the fore. Archae-ology, and increasingly its newly emerged sister discipline of anthropology (often embodied in the same individual), answered that the key to understanding human prehistory was the same developmentalist conception of evolution that was so powerful in contemporary biology. The British school of evolutionary anthropology, in such works as Lubbock's *Origin of Civilization* (1870) and Edward Burnett Tylor's *Primitive Culture* (1871), identified the ages and periods of the archaeological record as a hierarchy of cultural stages through which each race must pass in the course of its development. As in biology, the developmental analogy with growth excludes random change; each race, regardless of, in Tylor's words, 'date in history or place on the map', passes through the same invariant sequence of stages toward the fixed goal of civilization. Tylor could ignore the historical and environmental context of peoples because his teleological faith in development-as-growth trumped a true historical-mindedness.[13] In applying the analogy between growth and evolution to human prehistory, the evolutionary anthropologists posited a version of an ideal, eternal history in order to explain the distant human past – the reality of which Vico had created his theory to deny.

The archaeological record, like the geological record, was imperfect. Archae-ologists were able to provide an outline of technological development and, increas-ingly late in the century, morphological change, but none of this told them about the origin of fundamental human qualities such as social institutions, language, art and religion. Their response was to supplement the archaeological record with another category of evidence. Various scholars noted the similarities between stone tools recovered at European archaeological sites and those still in use in the savage regions of the world over which European colonialism had recently established dominion. This, and other perceived parallels between Stone Age peoples and modern primitives, irresistibly suggested that the latter might be used as proxies for the former. After all, as Lubbock pointed out, in so doing anthropologists were only adopting the method of palaeontologists who study living species of animals in distant lands to learn about extinct European species of the same animals: 'the Van Diemaner [Tasmanian] and the South American are to the antiquarian what the opossum and the sloth are to the geologist'.[14] The ease with which anthropologists identified modern savages with Stone Age peoples directly reflects their developmental paradigm, which in turn provided the justification for the designations 'primitive' and 'savage'. Since all races pass through the same stages of development regardless of historical or environmental location, races at the same stage of development must be more or less equivalent. The result was a single evolutionary framework into which all races and peoples, past and present, could be placed. The American anthropologist Thomas Henry Morgan defined the major stages of this framework as savagery, barbarism and civilization. As a final step, the developmentalists extended the growth analogy to a third class. Stone Age peoples and modern savages are equivalent to the children of civilized races. Just as a human foetus in its growth was thought to pass successively through the phylogenetic stages of fish, reptile and mammal, so an infant Victorian must pass through the stages of savagery and barbarism before reaching civilized maturity. Development no longer merely works out the beast, but the savage too.[15]

The evolutionary anthropologists offered their readers grand evolutionary epics in which the rise of humanity to civilization was as stirring and as inevitable as Rome's rise to greatness in the *Aeneid*. Moreover, these epics were consciously secularizing, if still teleological, offered as alternatives to the biblical drama in which human beings are spiritual beings fallen from a higher estate. We are descended from savages, the anthropologists unanimously affirmed; and yet, they argued, this fact is grounds for optimism. Having progressed so far from our benighted origins, we may confidently look forward to continued progress; indeed, Lubbock hailed the law of evolution as guaranteeing the realization of a terrestrial paradise: 'Utopia, which we have long looked upon as synonymous with an evident impossibility, which we have ungratefully regarded as "too good to be true", turns out, on the contrary, to be the necessary consequence of natural laws.'[16]

The evolutionary anthropology of the late nineteenth century was obviously non-Darwinian; its model of evolution was the developmentalist analogy with growth shared by Neo-Lamarckism and orthogenesis.[17] This was the environment into which Darwin's own account of human prehistory appeared in 1871. Darwin had barely mentioned human beings in the *Origin of Species*, limiting himself to an oblique comment worthy of David Hume: 'Light will be thrown on the origin of man and his history.'[18] He had nevertheless avidly followed the unveiling of human prehistory, remarking to Lyell in 1860, 'What a grand fact about the extinct stag's horn worked by man!'[19] By the time he took up the subject in the *Descent of Man* (1871) Darwin could take for granted the widespread acknowledgement that humanity was ancient. Early in the work he refers his readers on this point to the books of Lyell and Lubbock, among others. In fact, references to

Lubbock, Tylor and other evolutionary anthropologists abound in *Descent of Man*, with the result that many readers concluded that Darwin was endorsing not only their evidence for human prehistory but also their developmentalist model of human evolution. And indeed, in response to critics Darwin himself had in the years since 1859 incorporated the growth model into his own evolutionary thought as a supplement to natural selection.[20]

Darwin almost entirely ignored fossil and archaeological records in the *Descent of Man*. His case for our descent from 'some less highly organised form' was the biological argument that the numerous anatomical and embryological similarities shared by humans and apes (already established in the popular mind by T. H. Huxley's *Man's Place in Nature* (1863)) are to be explained by shared descent from a common ancestor more generalized than any of its living descendants. Darwin specified that this ancestor was most likely a 'hairy, tailed quadruped, probably arboreal in its habits, and an inhabitant of the Old World'.[21] This ancestor, in turn, had descended from a long line of diversified forms that Darwin traced back to a simple animal resembling present-day molluscs. Darwin noted that the homologies and rudimentary structures linking humans and lower animals had long been known but until recently had told us nothing with respect to human origins. Now, viewed in light of the theory of evolution by natural selection, their meaning is unmistakable. Darwin equated those who continue to promote the special creation of humanity with savages because, in refusing to accept the key to our history offered by evolutionary theory, they, like the savage, look at the phenomena of nature as disconnected.[22]

If human bodies bear the indelible stamp of a lowly origin, what about our minds? Darwin recognized that the most important differences between human beings and animals are our intellectual and moral powers, but denied that this recognition warrants the conclusion that we are not descended from animals after all because, he insisted, these powers have arisen from animal instincts over a long period of time. In summarizing his chapters on mental and moral powers Darwin declared that 'the difference in mind between man and the higher animals, great as it is, certainly is one of degree and not of kind'. Our intellectual powers are the inheritance of natural selection working on faculties possessed by lower animals, and our moral powers and spiritual beliefs are the inevitable consequences of advanced intellectual development in a social animal.[23]

Soul and mind

The naturalization of humanity within an organic evolutionary process posed two separate, though intertwined, problems for Western culture. First, it contradicted the biblical account of humanity, thereby calling into question the theological content of sacred history. Earlier theories of deep time had left human history untouched, since the geological evidence was consistent with the recent appearance of humanity. Theologians had accommodated an immense age for the Earth in part by the dual claim that what was important in Genesis was not its account of the Earth's creation but of human history, and that the history of the Earth told the story of its providentially guided development into a fit habitat for human beings as the crown of creation. Second, the naturalization of humanity denied the traditional view that our mental and moral faculties derive from the soul, or a spiritual agency added to the physical body, and therefore seemed to deny our spiritual status.[24] Indeed, Tylor had argued in *Primitive Culture* that the ideas of the soul, immortality and even God had arisen in the remote past as the result of the inevitable operations of the primitive human mind when faced with the phenomena of death and dreams.[25]

These ideas were far more dangerous to Christianity than the mere fact of deep time because they offered an alternative history of humanity to that of the Bible. The biblical narratives that set out humanity's relationship to God in history express (believers would say reveal) the central Christian doctrines of our creation in the image of God, the Fall, sin, atonement in Christ and redemption. Almost all Christians in the late nineteenth century regarded the idea of the descent of the human species from other animals as an attack on the truth of Christianity. If humans had not been created in God's image, then our moral and mental attributes do not truly distinguish us from the animals, there is no basis for God's special redemptive relationship with the human species, no grounds for the hope of each person for eternal life, and no justification for the anthropocentric interpretation of the history of the Earth and life as subordinate to the spiritual drama of human redemption.[26] Worst of all, making humanity continuous with the animals instead of set in dominion over them eliminates the need for Christ the Saviour. Hugh Miller's response to *Vestiges of the Natural History of Creation* had identified the heart of the matter for Evangelicals: if there was no Fall, and Adam merely took the first human step in an ongoing upward march, then there is no need for us to be redeemed from sin and therefore no need for the 'second Adam', Jesus Christ, to die on the cross in atonement for the sins of the world.[27] Miller's warning was repeated time and time again in the years after the *Origin of Species*. The Methodist theologian Miner Raymond's 1877 summary is exemplary: 'if the origin of the race be found anywhere else than in the special creation of a single pair, from whom all others have descended, then is the whole Bible a misleading and unintelligible book'.[28]

An evolutionary descent for humanity was similarly thought to threaten morality by subverting belief in a divinely sanctioned moral law.[29] Here Miller's argument that if human beings had come into being by an evolutionary process then they could not be held morally responsible for their actions and the whole fabric of society would collapse was seconded by the decidedly non-Evangelical *Edinburgh Review*. The review of the *Descent of Man* in this liberal quarterly began with the warning that

> If our humanity be merely the natural product of the modified faculties of the brutes, most earnest-minded men will be compelled to give up those motives by which they have attempted to live noble and virtuous lives, as founded on a mistake.[30]

Broadly speaking, theological responses to the mounting evidence for human evolution followed one of three strategies: deny it and identify cavemen and modern savages as degenerate descendants of Adam; isolate our soul and mind from our physical frame; or radically reinterpret the traditional doctrines. The third option was open only to extremely liberal Christians. A rare example of its exercise in the late nineteenth century was the American Congregationalist Lyman Abbott's argument, in *The Evolution of Christianity* (1892) and *The Theology of an Evolutionist* (1897), that the Fall should not be understood as the historical origin of a burden of sin that can only be relieved by the atonement of Christ but rather as an allegory of every individual's experience. 'Every broken resolve, every high purpose lowered, every sacrifice of reverence to sensual desire, of conscience to passion, of love to greed or ambition or wealth', he declared, 'is a fall.' Here again, liberalism and evolution reinforced each other: evolutionary theories of human origins cannot contradict the biblical account because the Bible's truth is moral and not historical.[31]

At the other, much more populous, extreme, the Evangelical strategy interpreted the history of humanity not as a story of evolutionary ascent but of degradation. For the Duke of Argyll and Hugh Miller, cavemen and savages represent not earlier stages of our evolution but graphic evidence of the degeneration of humanity from its original high state because of the Fall and the Flood. The most eminent naturalist to defend this position was the Canadian geologist and devout Calvinist John William Dawson (1820–1899). In *The Story of the Earth and Man* (1873) and elsewhere, Dawson maintained that after the glaciers, 'the ploughshares of the Lord', had readied the Earth for human habitation God created humans in his image and placed them in a geologically prepared Eden. The spiritual sin of the Fall tarnished the divine image and reduced a physically transformed humanity to savagery. The human species has not evolved everupwards, but has only partially and unevenly recovered from the loss of its original state in the Fall. The evolutionists' depiction of the first humans as brutish savages inverts the true order of things; modern savages are not survivals of our earliest state but signs of the Fall.[32]

The third strategy granted deep time and even conceded that evolution explains the structure of our bodies but drew the line at the idea that our souls and minds can be so explained. None other than Alfred Russel Wallace thought this way. He had at first shared Darwin's non-teleological understanding of evolution by natural selection, and even applied it to human origins in an 1864 article in the *Journal of the Anthropological Society of London*. But he soon found it impossible to accept that human beings, and the human mind in particular, could have resulted from random natural events. His palinode was a long article in the *Quarterly Review* (1868) in which he depicted humanity as the purpose of the divinely guided evolutionary process. Distinguishing between human bodies, which evolved by natural selection, and human minds, Wallace maintained that our physical evolution had come to a halt some time in the distant past while we continued (and continue) to evolve culturally and morally as the result of an immaterial spirit infused in us by a higher power that, independently of natural selection, guides mental and cultural development ever upwards. Darwin was appalled, although to Wallace he merely voiced the hope that 'you have not murdered too completely your own & my child'. Wallace responded by telling Darwin that his experiences at Spiritualist séances had convinced him of the reality of spirit forces; he now believed that there was more to the universe than mere matter and that God or spirit must play an important role in human evolution. Science, he informed Darwin, would one day demonstrate the existence of the immaterial forces channelled by Spiritualist mediums.[33]

Wallace's spiritualism aside, many orthodox Christians seized on the idea that one could accept that Adam's body had been formed by evolution but that humanity properly speaking was created only at the moment, roughly six thousand years ago, when God infused into his animal frame a rational soul. Frederick Temple, for example, assured the audience of his prestigious Bamford Lectures that religion has nothing to fear from evolutionary theories because science will never be able to deny that our moral and spiritual faculties were given to us by 'a direct creative act as soon as the body which was to be the seat and the instrument of the spiritual faculty had been sufficiently developed to receive it'.[34] The most influential advocate of this view in Britain was the Catholic convert St George Jackson Mivart (1827–1900). In *On the Genesis of Species* (1871) and numerous subsequent books Mivart doubly subverted Darwin. First, he argued that our bodies had evolved through a process in which natural selection was subordinated to 'special powers and tendencies existing in each organism' that God uses to produce those forms he has conceived. And second, each soul, the possession of which makes us ethical and rational beings, is created from nothing by divine will.[35] Mivart offered this theory as evidence that Catholicism was open to science. Regrettably, the last third of the nineteenth century was a period of entrenchment by the Roman Church against the modern world, including science. Mivart eventually fell foul of his ecclesiastical superiors and his biological theories were condemned, although among British and American Protestants his strategy as well as his writings continued to be held in high esteem.[36] (A position on human evolution in some respects very close to Mivart's is now the official teaching of the Roman Catholic Church. John Paul II announced in a 1996 address to the Pontifical Academy of Sciences that in the matter of evolution the essential point is that 'if the human body takes its origin from pre-existent living matter the spiritual soul is immediately created by God'.)[37]

If theologians regarded the threat to Christian doctrine and morality as two sides of the same coin, other, less traditionally minded thinkers who had ceased to fret about the soul were nevertheless deeply troubled by the implications of human evolution for the mind. One possible response would be to follow the lead of the theologians and argue that while the human body had evolved naturally the mind had not. But by the end of the nineteenth century such special pleading was no longer acceptable in science (as opposed to the theological use of science). Those who accepted the fact of human evolution also accepted that the mind too was a product of nature. But here the developmentalist model of evolution came to the rescue. The moral and mental powers of humanity derive from the growth of the brain, but the independence of the mind from the material world could be defended by presenting the growth of the brain as the goal, the *purpose* of evolution. Charles Lyell's *Antiquity of Man* (1863), so influential for the widespread acceptance of human prehistory, is an early example of the defence of the human mind against materialism by means of a progressivist model of evolution:

> It may be said that, so far from having a materialistic tendency, the supposed introduction into the earth at successive geological periods of life, – sensation, – instinct, – the intelligence of the higher mammalia bordering on reason, – and, lastly, the improvable reason of Man himself, presents us with a picture of the ever-increasing dominion of mind over matter.[38]

'Mind over matter' became the rallying-cry of those developmentalists who argued for an evolutionary origin of humanity while at the same time maintaining the uniqueness and special value of humanity by means of a version of the traditional body/soul dualism.[39]

For some researchers the distinction between mind and body was a defensive strategy that allowed them to study human anatomy and physiology without getting caught up in theological or metaphysical quarrels.[40] But many other scientists genuinely believed that evolutionary theory must separate itself from any taint of materialism. Neo-Lamarckism and orthogenesis showed them the way. A good, if somewhat late, example is the American palaeontologist Henry Fairfield Osborn (1857–1935). A former student and then associate of McCosh at Princeton, Osborn had embodied the turn in American science from Neo-Lamarckism to orthogenesis. Then, in the 1920s, by which time he was president of the American Museum of Natural History in New York City, he renounced his previously held view that human beings had descended from ape-like creatures in favour of a theory that explained the similarities between ape and human evolution as the result of parallel lines of development. Consistent with, and indebted to, his orthogenetic understanding of evolution as the gradual actualization over time of a non-material potential inherent in organisms, Osborn argued that apes and humans have developed independently but in parallel thanks to an internal force that drives them onward towards a common goal. He wrote a popular survey of human evolution, *Man Rises to Parnassus* (1927), expressly to refute the belief, widespread since Huxley's *Man's Place in Nature*, that human beings had descended from apes. Osborn recognized that many people found the theory of ape descent deeply disturbing. He hoped to make the idea of evolution more palatable to the general public by distancing human origins from the apes.[41] Osborn's belief in multiple evolutionary lines advancing in parallel over vast periods toward a common goal extended to humanity itself. *Man Rises to Parnassus* divides modern human beings into three primary stocks, each subdivided into numerous species. While on the one hand this diversity indicates the great antiquity of the human race, it also has implications for present-day society. Osborn's leadership role within the American eugenics movement is only one indicator of the complicity of developmentalist biologists and anthropologists with eugenics and scientific racism in the late nineteenth and early twentieth century.[42]

Developmentalist approaches to human prehistory were eventually driven from the field by attacks from cultural anthropology, and then, independently, from a truly Darwinian palaeoanthropology. The model of the geological column that had given conceptual order to the idea of prehistory began to be called into question near the end of the nineteenth century. The problem was that archaeologists every so often were uncovering artefacts assigned to one period at the same site and in the same deposit as artefacts belonging to some other period. No one denied the basic chronological sequence of Palaeolithic, Neolithic, Bronze and Iron, but it was becoming apparent that some of the subdivisions of each era were contemporary with each other and therefore could no longer be thought of as distinct chronological periods. This realization marks the beginning of the independence of prehistoric archaeology from geology. In reconceptualizing their discipline, archaeologists seized on an idea circulating among social scientists: human groupings could be thought of as cultures. Subdivisions now marked distinct cultural assemblages as often as they marked successive periods.[43]

E. B. Tylor, the arch-evolutionary anthropologist, had famously defined culture on the first page of *Primitive Culture* as 'that complex whole which includes knowledge, belief, art, morals, law, custom, and any other capabilities and habits acquired by man as a member of society'. Tylor's concept of culture was part and parcel of his developmentalist evolutionary worldview; culture was the general, cumulative accomplishment of humanity through the ages. Tylor could speak of 'primitive culture' precisely because he conceptualized it as an early stage in a single hierarchy. This evolutionary idea of culture was overthrown within anthropology through the efforts of a loosely affiliated group of German, American and British scholars who insisted that societies possess an integral unity and therefore must be studied specifically and contextually. Given their new definition of culture (which would dominate twentieth-century anthropology) as the totality of a particular way of life, the goal of the anthropologist was no longer to assign each culture to its proper niche in the grand evolutionary sequence from savagery to civilization, but to interpret its specific and unique meaning.[44] In the work of the German-American anthropologist Franz Boas (1858–1942) and his many American students, for example, a pluralist and relativist view of culture replaced the unitary and evolutionary view of the late nineteenth-century founders of anthropology. And yet, the repudiation of a developmentalist hierarchy of races and cultures did not lead to a truly Darwinian approach to anthropology. The model of cultural development was now branching rather than linear, but, convinced that evolutionism was both intellectually false and fatally implicated in racist theories, cultural anthropologists on both sides of the Atlantic – and later functionalists and structuralists – insulated anthropology from biology. In recent years attempts by the new disciplines of sociobiology and cognitive science to introduce a genuinely Darwinian form of biology into the social sciences have been vigorously resisted by most anthropologists, who see them (wrongly) as a return to the biological determinism of late nineteenth-century evolutionary anthropology.[45]

Palaeoanthropology

Palaeoanthropology, naturally enough, has been more receptive than anthropology to Darwinism (though it took time). Darwin himself in the *Descent of Man* denied that the human race is the inevitable goal of evolution. Years earlier, in a notebook entry, he had chastised the theological claim that the universe is adapted to human needs as an 'instance of arrogance'.[46] But Darwin's attempt to sever human prehistory from teleology was swamped by developmentalist theories according to which humanity was the predetermined goal of evolutionary progress. Theologians and most scientists could not accept that we are the accidental products of an undirected, and hence possibly amoral, historical process. Neo-Lamarckism and orthogenesis, according to which we are the culmination and purpose of the preprogrammed and progressive order of creation, allowed early twentieth-century palaeontologists to maintain instead that evolution has striven to create the human form and mind.[47]

Debates over human evolution heated up from the last decade of the nineteenth century in response to the proliferation of fossil evidence for radical human change. While both Lubbock and Lyell had recognized that radical geological and faunal change is an index of the immense age of humanity, and despite Lyell's daring reference to humanity as 'part of the fauna of the northern hemisphere',[48] neither had suggested that human beings themselves have changed radically in the course of their history. Darwin, for his part, had largely ignored the fossil record in the *Descent of Man*. It was not until Neanderthal skulls were recognized in the mid-1880s as the remains of a species of humans distinct from modern humans and, even more critically, the accumulation in the 1890s of more complete specimens of Neanderthals together with the discovery of the even earlier Java Man (*Pithecanthropus erectus*) that there was solid fossil evidence that ancient humans were morphologically distinct from modern humans.[49]

And yet Neo-Lamarckian and orthogenetic interpretations of human evolution could not be overthrown merely by accumulating fossil evidence. What was required was a revolution in theory, or, more precisely, the extension of the Modern Synthesis of genetics and Darwinian evolution into the field of palaeontology. Special pleading for our species delayed this extension, but eventually, and with George Gaylord Simpson's *Tempo and Mode in Evolution* (1944) as the turning point, palaeontology joined the other branches of biology in accepting the new model. Neo-Lamarckism and orthogenesis were finally debunked as scientists showed time and time again that wherever sufficient fossils were available to reconstruct a detailed phylogeny, the course of evolution turned out to be a haphazard branching process rather than a linear ascent toward a fixed goal. The modern synthesis of genetics and natural selection finally made it impossible to accept the teleological character of the progressionist theory of brain development, and therefore to believe that nature had been striving throughout evolution to create the human form. The way was now open for a genuinely historical account of human evolution in which the contingency of opportunistic adaptation replaces the necessary unfolding of a preprogrammed, progressive teleology.[50]

The Darwinian model of evolution, as we recall from Chapter 8, posits a haphazard, branching and open-ended process. Applying it to humanity yields a branching genealogy in place of a linear ascent and requires specific adaptive scenarios to explain the cause of each branching, since there is no prepro-grammed sequence moving the entire evolutionary process toward a predetermined telos. The evolutionary sequence from ape-like creatures to modern humans does indeed form a branching tree in which the Neanderthals and the later Australo-pithecines, whose discovery drove late nineteenth- and early twentieth-century discussions of human evolution, have proven to be side branches of hominid evolution leading to extinction. The early Australopithecines and early *Homo* species who are our actual ancestors were only discovered in subsequent dec-ades. Turning from genealogy to adaptive scenarios, present-day palaeoanthro-pologists agree that the growth of the brain has been critical to human evolution. But whereas the older developmentalist school made brain growth the driver of evolution, Darwinian palaeoanthropologists attempt to explain brain growth itself as an adaptation to changed environmental conditions. The dominant scenario today proposes that the loss of or migration from forest habitat to the open grasslands of the African savannas on the part of one or more population of the common ancestor of apes and humans led to the acquisition of an upright posture, or bipedalism. A bipedal way of life in which the hands may be put to other uses than locomotion, in turn, led to the enlargement of the brain in crea-tures thereby classified as belonging to the genus *Homo*. The earliest stone tools are associated with these archaic humans (*Homo habilus, Homo ergaster*). Con-tinued growth of the brain, accelerated by the manipulation of tools, created further branches of *Homo*, including *Homo erectus, Homo neanderthalensis* and, eventually, *Homo sapiens*.[51]

Throughout the nineteenth century and into the twentieth palaeontology and geology lacked an absolute chronology. Age was relative; this extinct species was older than that extinct species because its remains had been found in older geological strata. Palaeontologists had great confidence in their relative chronolo-gies of prehistoric life, but – analogous to the problem faced by seventeenth-century compilers of civil chronologies – they could not assign actual dates to them.[52] Moreover, Lord Kelvin's calculation of the age of the Earth had forced palaeontologists to reduce Darwin's own estimates of the duration of the geologi-cal epochs. They allowed, for example, the Pleistocene (which together with the Holocene comprises the Quaternary Era) a duration of between two and four hundred thousand years. Only in the twentieth century did the development of radiometric techniques shatter these modest estimates of the geological and palaeontological time-scale and provide absolute dates for human prehistory, dates that pushed human history much farther back than even Darwin had imag-ined.[53] The following dates may serve as representative highlights. The first anatomically and culturally modern people in Europe (and those responsible for cave paintings), the Aurignacians of the Palaeolithic, flourished between 40,000 and 28,000 years ago. Neanderthals, to whom Mousterian culture is attributed (hominid species attain their anatomical form long before producing their char-acteristic cultural achievements), came into being between about 200,000 and 150,000 years ago. Their cultural achievements peaked around 40,000 years ago, and they disappeared from Europe (exterminated by the Aurignacians) about

10,000 years later. Neanderthal and human lineages diverged no later than half a million years ago. *Homo ergaster*, responsible for Achulean stone tools, lived around 1.5 million years ago. Specimens of *Homo habilis*, first discovered by the Leakeys in Olduvai Gorge, date to between 2 and 1.6 million years ago. The oldest *Homo* species are 2.4 million years old. *Homo* species evolved from a species of *Australopithecus*; the famous Lucy, an unusually complete skeleton of a female hominid discovered in Ethiopia, is classified as *Australopithecus afarensis* and dated to 3.2 million years. Finally, the ancestors of gorillas and chimpanzees diverged from the ancestors of humans between ten and six million years ago.[54]

These absolute dates are made possible by various radiometric techniques that exploit the decay of radioactive atoms into stable atoms at constant rates and independently of environmental conditions. The first such method of dating to be introduced was the radiocarbon (carbon-14) technique, invented in 1950. The half-life of radiocarbon is only 5,730 years, which means that this technique is effective for dating organic samples no older than about forty to fifty thousand years, or to the latest part of the Pleistocene. In the 1960s the potassium–argon (K/Ar) method was developed, which, owing to the extremely long half-life of potassium-40, is used to date rocks (and indirectly the organic remains found in them) that are millions of years old. A number of new technologies introduced since the 1980s, among them electron spin resonance (ESR), thermolumines-cence (TL), uranium-series (U-series) and the molecular clock (based on known rates of genetic mutation), have provided absolute dates for the period between the effective ranges of potassium-argon and radiocarbon – a period critical to human evolution.[55]

Chapter 10

THE BIBLE IN AMERICA

By the first years of the twentieth century the cumulative effect of the various historical disciplines posed a formidable challenge to the status of the Bible. Civil history, geology, palaeontology, biblical criticism, evolutionary biology and anthropology offered powerful alternatives to sacred history in understanding the world and humanity's place in it. The three possible responses – to abandon the Bible altogether as an authoritative source for knowledge about the world, to attempt to reconcile science and scholarship with the Bible, or to reject anything that seemed to compromise the authority of the Bible – correspond to modernism, liberal Protestantism, and reactionary biblicism.

Edmund Gosse's (1849–1928) memoir, *Father and Son*, records how the state of play looked to an educated Englishman in 1907. Gosse's father was the naturalist Philip Gosse (1810–1888), the leading authority on the marine biology of Britain, author of a definitive *History of British Sea-Anemonies and Corals* and a dozen other, more popular works on natural history, and inventor of the aquarium.[1] Philip Gosse was also a devout Calvinist; his wife, Emily, a noted author in her own right, was if anything more devout. They believed in the absolute truth, historical veracity and continued relevance of every statement in the Bible. The Gosses deferred every decision, no matter how small, to the will of God, which they discovered by prayer and reading their Bible; they refused to belong to any church that did not share their rigorous biblicism. Their thoroughly pre-critical approach to the Bible was exemplified in their favourite activity, the interpretation of prophecy. They regarded every statement in the prophetic books, and especially Revelation, as a factual statement of things that had happened or would happen and sought to discern in contemporary events the fulfilment of the veiled but literal prophecies. Like Isaac Newton and the other seventeenth-century interpreters of prophecy whose books they read as aids to their own efforts, Gosse's parents lived in the hope of witnessing the Second Coming.[2] Later, after Emily's early death, Philip led a group of Plymouth Brethren, a loose fellowship of similarly minded separatist and millennial biblicists in the west of England.

Edmund Gosse offered the narrative of his break from his parents' religion in *Father and Son* to his contemporaries as an index of religious change. The historical sciences play a key role in the story. Philip Gosse was one of a number of respected naturalists who had been informed of Darwin's theory of evolution by natural selection shortly before the publication of *Origin of Species*. According to Edmund, his father's immediate response had been positive; he greatly respected

Darwin as a naturalist and the evidence for the gradual modification of organic structures seemed overwhelming. But then doubts had swarmed in: how could the theory be true, since Genesis clearly states that everything in the world was created in six days of twenty-four hours? Philip's solution to the dilemma was *Omphalos: An Attempt to Untie the Geological Knot* (1857).[3] In fact, Edmund telescoped Philip's reaction to *Origin of Species* into his more general and long-standing opposition to the deep time of the geologists, which is the true target of *Omphalos*. The book is one long argument against the necessity of accepting the evidence for deep time, whereas it simply dismissed the possibility of organic evolution out of hand.

Omphalos opens with an extensive and fair-minded summary of the fossil and geological evidence for deep time (the entire book is structured as a courtroom trial of the case for an ancient Earth). The rest of the book is Gosse's brief as opposing counsel. His opening statement noted that the defence cannot produce any eyewitness testimony in support of the vast antiquity of the Earth and life. In the absence of direct testimony, the case for deep time becomes one of inference, which opens the door to an alternative explanation of the fossil evidence. Gosse next proposed a law that he claimed will explain the evidence without requiring the inference that fossils once formed parts of living creatures which lived in the remote past. This is the 'law of creation', but before stating it Gosse demanded that his readers grant him two postulates: the creation of matter (that is, the universe is not eternal) and the persistence of species (here he simply rejects the possibility of organic evolution). He then proceeded to the law. Echoing Hutton on the cyclic world-machine, Gosse cited the life-cycle of various organisms as proof that all of organic nature runs in an endless circle: the scarlet runner bean displays a cycle of seed, shoot, stem, bud, flower, legume, seed; the hawkmoth of moth, egg, larva, pupa, moth; cattle of cow, ovum, embryo, foetus, calf, heifer, cow. It is impossible simply on the basis of observation, he wrote, to identify any one point in the history of a creature as the beginning of its existence: the cow follows as inevitably from the embryo as the embryo from the cow. Gosse invoked the law of creation in order to break this empirical stalemate: the sovereign fiat of Almighty God irrupts into the circle at an arbitrary moment and thereby brings an organism into being. If the world is not eternal (assent to which Gosse demanded as one of his postulates), then organisms must have had an origin, and the only imaginable origin in a steady-state universe is divine creation.

Gosse next pointed out that a newly created being will display signs of age:

> But the whole organisation of the creature thus newly called into existence, looks back to the course of an endless circle in the past. Its whole structure displays an endless series of developments, which as distinctly witness to former conditions as do those which are presented in the cow, the butterfly, and the fern, of the present day. But what former conditions? The conditions thus witnessed unto, as being necessarily implied in the present organisation, were non-existent; the history was a perfect blank till the moment of creation. The past conditions or stages of existence in question, can indeed be as triumphantly inferred by legitimate deduction from the present, as can those of our cow or butterfly; they rest on the very same evidences; they are identical in every respect, except in this one, that they were *unreal*. They exist only in their results; they are effects which never had causes.[4]

The law of creation excludes previous history. Gosse called the unreal history falsely implied by the organization of newly created organisms 'prochronic' because time did not yet exist. Gosse's prochronic time is analogous to Scaliger's proleptic time; both are desperate attempts to save the biblical chronology in the face of contrary evidence from outside the Bible.

His argument set out, Gosse then surveyed the organic world in chapter after chapter in order to drive home the point that an organism created five minutes ago would display evidence of age to an investigating naturalist because it was created at a certain point in a cycle with the appearance of having passed through the other points in its cycle. Whether the evidence is tree rings, rattlesnake rattles, the human navel from which the book derives its title, or any of his many, many other examples implying a past existence, Gosse triumphantly drew from them the conclusion that, given his postulates, every one of them can be as plausibly explained as evidence of prochronic development as of actual, lived history. The massive repetition of a single argument gives *Omphalos* the same structure as Paley's *Natural Theology* or a Bridgewater Treatise.

Gosse made the key transition from living species to the age of the world by drawing on the idea that before the creation of the world an ideal conception of its whole life-history 'lay like a map before [God's] infinite mind'.[5] Creation occurred at a specific point in this ideal life-history when God so willed it; all history previous to that point is prochronic because it existed only in the mind of God and not in time. The bones of extinct animals in Devon caves, fossil ichthyosaurs, Old Red Sandstone, and the rest of the phenomena interpreted by geologists and palaeontologists as evidence of deep time exist because they are part of the ideal, unlived history of the world at the moment God chose to bring it into actual being. Had God chosen to create the world millions of years ago instead of a few thousand, ichthyosaurs would have had real rather than only prochronic or ideal existence.

Logically, then, we know that organisms were created at a specific point in their life cycle, but there is no way to infer from the natural order what that point was. On the basis of the phenomena alone (the law of nature) we would conclude that organic life is eternal (again, compare Hutton's argument that geology discovers 'no vestige of a beginning, – no prospect of an end'), but as this has been ruled out of court we must look elsewhere in order to determine the age of species and of the Earth itself. In declaring our only other source of data to be the testimony of witnesses, Gosse wonderfully exemplified William Whewell's rules of inductive science: science is a matter of the direct observation of facts, and where direct observation runs out one is free to draw on extra-scientific testimony. In Gosse's phrase, 'the law of creation supersedes the law of nature'.[6] Naturalists who base their conclusions on natural phenomena alone are liable to err because they reject the biblical account of creation even though they were not there to witness the moment of creation and therefore cannot be certain that the biblical account is not true. *Omphalos* is not a scientific proof of a young Earth, but a lawyer's brief arguing for the conceivability of a young Earth and then leaving the jurors to choose between trusting human reason or God's revealed Word. Its concluding sentence sent the jury off to the deliberation room with the testimony of the one Witness to creation ringing in their ears: 'In six days Jehovah made Heaven and Earth, the sea, and all that in them is.'[7]

Gosse's case rests on the assumption that proper science is based on direct observation. Since no human witnessed creation, our unaided reason can only generate inferences about it rather than give us sound knowledge. This being so, we are free to consider alternatives to the inference of deep time. It seemed obvious to him that we should trust the testimony of the Bible and accept that the Earth was created in six days roughly six thousand years ago. Inasmuch as the opposing, impious option was not organic evolution but the eternity of matter, Gosse seems to inhabit the intellectual world of the seventeenth century rather than the nineteenth; just as his interpretations of biblical prophecy paralleled Newton's, so he seems to have been arguing against the eternal world-machine of the Mechanick Atheists rather than against Darwin.

Edmund Gosse summarized the reception of the book that his father had hoped would once and for all reconcile science with religion: 'atheists and Christians alike looked at it, and laughed, and threw it away.'[8] Edmund regarded his father's hope as a delusion that fell apart when he had to renounce the testimony of things as deceptive. This is the modernist position: science and revelation are incompatible, and revelation is false. *Father and Son*, in fact, which Edmund presented as 'the diagnosis of a dying Puritanism', as 'a record of educational and religious conditions which, having passed away, will never return',[9] is a monument to the apparent triumph of modernism. But Edmund was wrong in his diagnosis. As we know, the views on the Bible, deep time and evolution held by Philip Gosse, far from expiring with the nineteenth century, have flourished in the century since the publication of *Father and Son*. In fairness to Edmund, though, the causes of this turn of events are not to be found in England or Europe, but in America. We therefore direct our attention across the Atlantic, and first of all to the status of the Bible in the early Republic.

A democratic Bible

The Bible was the one traditional authority to emerge from the revolutionary period even stronger than before. This was so because of a uniquely American synthesis of Evangelical Protestantism, political republicanism, and common-sense moral philosophy.[10] Whereas colonial-era wars against the French and then the Revolution brought together Protestantism and republicanism in American minds, the third element in the synthesis – the philosophy of common sense – derived from the Scottish Enlightenment, particularly the works of Francis Hutcheson (1694–1747) and, to a lesser extent, Thomas Reid (1710–1796). The Scottish common-sense philosophy, in attempting to answer Hume's scepticism, taught that all normal people possess various faculties that produce beliefs on which they must rely in everyday life. Our physical senses are such faculties, but so too is our moral sense. And just as Bacon defined science as the collecting of data derived from the physical senses and then drawing general laws from them by inductive reasoning, so Hutcheson taught that moral science was a matter of examining one's own conscience and drawing from this data the natural laws governing virtue and vice. Morality thus becomes the natural, almost instinctive consequence of our God-given moral sense, just as perceiving the external world is the natural consequence of our innate faculty of sight. Two normal people would no more differ as to moral perception any more than they would differ as to visual perception. Hutcheson regarded common-sense beliefs as innate, universal and not culturally specific; only philosophers or fools would doubt them.[11]

The common-sense philosophy was influential as a philosophical school within Scotland, but elsewhere was judged an inadequate answer to Hume (Kant despised it and set about constructing his critical philosophy as an alternative response to Hume). Its most significant influence was as a public ideology for Americans of the Revolutionary period. Hutcheson's thought provided a means for republicans and Protestants alike both to justify rebellion against the legal authority of Britain and to produce a new basis for social order once the old institutions had been overthrown. Common-sense philosophy justified anti-colonial resistance by placing the innate moral truths of justice and the right of individuals to be governed by the dictates of their consciences rather than external authorities above the traditional authority of King and Parliament. The evocations of 'self-evident truths' and 'inalienable rights' in the Declaration of Independence are translations into political rhetoric of the principles of Hutcheson's moral philosophy. Similarly, once the Revolution had been won, common sense provided a foundation for social order by upholding traditional values without seeming to rely on external religious authorities. The natural operation of the innate moral sense replicated Christian moral teaching, but dispensed with a state church or a privileged class of religious specialists. Even external revelation could be eliminated from the foundations of public order because belief in God arises inevitably as an inference from the interior authority of conscience. Despite the warnings of traditionalist Anglicans and Calvinists that the common-sense philosophy compromised orthodoxy by severing the Christian life from the operations of grace, American Protestants could reject traditional forms of Christian authority secure in the knowledge that their own moral sense bound them closer than ever to God and his moral order.[12]

The American synthesis of Evangelicalism, republicanism and common-sense philosophy took place during, and interacted with, waves of revivalism that reshaped the landscape of American Protestantism. Revivalism is part of the cycle of falling away and revival characteristic of American Puritanism. From the moment they landed on Plymouth Rock the New England Puritans saw themselves as building a holy commonwealth in the New World. This is summed up in the Puritan conception of America as a covenanted nation called into being by a divine providence, guided by God, and fulfilling God's plan for the world. As the decades went by, however, every now and then it was realized that New England society was not the communion of saints it was supposed to be. This realization brought about furious attempts to renew the original Puritan fervour and conviction. Such bouts of renewed conviction were called revivals or 'awakenings'.

The Great Awakening was one such revival. Its beginnings date from the preaching of the Congregationalist pastor Jonathan Edwards (1703–1758) in Massachusetts in 1734. Edwards' sermons dwelt in graphic detail on God's anger toward sinners and the desperate urgency of the need for repentance. Other preachers, including George Whitefield, spread the Great Awakening throughout New England. People wept in repentance for their sins, some shouted for joy at having been pardoned, and a few were so overwhelmed that they fainted. Such reactions led opponents of the Great Awakening to accuse its leaders of undermining the solemnity of worship, and of substituting emotion for study and devotion. It must be said, however, that its leaders did not wish to provoke continual shows of emotion, but rather a single experience of conversion that would lead each believer to greater devotion and more conscientious study of Scripture. This may be seen in Jonathan Edwards' writings; they are not emotional harangues, but careful theological expositions.[13]

Although the colonial revivalists were doctrinally conservative, the revivals of the eighteenth century encouraged ordinary men and women to treat their own religious experience as on a par with the teachings of traditional Church authorities.[14] This process greatly accelerated in the early decades of the Republic, particularly when westward migration removed people from the social and religious constraints of the established state churches of the eastern seaboard. In this context, the Second Great Awakening was a critical transition in the religious history of America. It began among the educated elites of New England around 1800 but soon spread to people of less education and lesser means, many of whom were moving west. Out on the frontier away from the structures of New England town life the Second Great Awakening became more emotional and less intellectual. The Cane Ridge Revival of 1801 in Kentucky marked a significant step in that process. It was a camp meeting organized by a local Presbyterian pastor for the promotion of a deeper faith. Thousands gathered to hear the preachers, Baptist and Methodist as well as Presbyterian. Many went to Cane Ridge for religious reasons, although others made it an opportunity to socialize, gamble and carouse. A critic of camp meetings later declared that at Cane Ridge as many souls were conceived as were saved. In any case, the response to the call to repentance was overwhelming: some people wept, some laughed uncontrollably, some trembled, some ran about and some even barked. The meeting lasted a week, and many drew the conclusion that camp meetings were the best way to proclaim the gospel on the American frontier.[15]

Although the Cane Ridge camp meeting had been organized by a Presbyterian, that denomination did not favour the unbridled emotionalism that was becoming an integral part of frontier revivalism. Neither did the like-minded Congregationalists. Soon Presbyterians and Congregationalists began to discipline ministers who participated in camp meetings. Episcopalians, of course, had never participated in them. But Methodists and Baptists, for whom emotion was a primary religious category, took to camp meetings like fish to water. And since such revivals were becoming an important part of social life on the frontier, both Methodists and Baptists achieved rapid growth. Further, they were willing to present their message as simply as possible, and to use preachers with little or no education to do so. This was a major advantage as the older denominations were hampered by the lack of educated personnel on the frontier. On the intellectual level, revivalism devalued doctrinal rigour and emphasized personal experience in its place. The net result was that by the middle of the nineteenth century Methodists and Baptists had become the largest Protestant denominations in the country.[16]

Revivalism in the churches augmented the distrust of traditional authority encouraged by political republicanism. The Revolution and revivalism together had undermined the authority of state churches. Historic creeds and confessions were no longer binding on individuals, ordained ministers could no longer expect deference merely on the basis of their office, and all manner of traditional beliefs and practices had been put to the test of personal experience and found wanting. Just as common-sense moral philosophy offered a substitute for traditional political authority, so too it offered a substitute for the traditional theological authority. The Constitution, a written document approved by the people on the basis of their intuitive sense of justice, replaced traditional authorities in politics; similarly, the Bible, a written document approved by the people on the basis of their intuitive sense of truth, displaced all other traditional authorities in religion. But while the Bible emerged with its status intact and even exalted, Revolution and revivalism together forged an alliance between common-sense philosophy and populist readings of the Bible that transformed the nature of religious knowledge.[17] Populist preachers urged the people to throw off servile dependence on religious authorities and learn to prove things for themselves. Echoing Hutcheson's warning that education can damage common sense, they considered the common sense of ordinary citizens more reliable than the judgement of university-educated and seminary-trained clergymen. The old theological categories and values were attacked as by-products of elite, and therefore suspect, education that undemocratically oppressed common people's religious experience.[18] The massive success of the revivalist preacher Charles G. Finney epitomizes this revolution in what passed for religious knowledge. Finney made a national reputation for himself in the 1830s by scorning traditional theological study and homiletics in favour of what he called the 'language of common life'.[19] Successful preachers in nineteenth-century America were increasingly those whose language, appearance and life-experiences were one with those of the common people whom they addressed. This feedback loop between preaching and republican common sense became characteristic of American Evangelical Protestantism. Because Evangelicals appealed to 'the Bible alone' and were deeply suspicious of central Church authorities and elite scholarship, they had no mechanism for settling theological or exegetical disputes and so relied by default on the court of public opinion. Authority in Evangelical Protestantism became synonymous with winning and retaining popular support.[20]

Populism in religion is one aspect of a broader rejection of elite authority in early nineteenth-century America. The monopolies of educated elites over law, medicine and other professions were similarly broken in the decades following the Revolution in the name of democratic populism. State laws permitted almost anyone to practise law, while Congressional refusal to regulate healing permitted a golden age of patent medicines. Lawyers and doctors gradually reasserted their professional status, eventually establishing qualifications and standards that must be met and enforcing them by educational and licensing requirements. In the course of the struggle they created the category of 'quackery' for what they excluded from their officially authorized knowledge. Even today, however, the American Bar Association and the American Medical Association are not absolute monopolies. This is particularly true in medicine, where manufacturers of herbal supplements draw heavily on populist rhetoric in their legal challenges to regulatory legislation.[21] In religion, however, the theological monopoly of the established churches was permanently destroyed. There is, and can be, no theological equivalent of the AMA and therefore, whatever one's intuitive sense, no category of religious quackery. The constitutional separation of Church and state, augmented by Evangelical suspicion of any authority other than the Bible, ensures that the religious views of Americans are not subject to regulative oversight.[22]

This free market in religion, aided by demographic, economic and social upheavals, created an environment in which sectarianism flourished. Nineteenth-century America witnessed the emergence of Adventist churches, Universalist churches, the Church of Jesus Christ of Latter-Day Saints, Restorationist churches and Holiness churches, to name only a few, plus numerous groups split off from mainstream denominations over this or that point of doctrine or practice. Each of these sects was distinctive in terms of its teaching, and yet underlying and giving order to the sectarian profusion was a remarkably uniform approach to the Bible. William Miller the Adventist, Hosea Ballou the Universalist, Joseph Smith the Mormon, Alexander Campbell the Restorationist and Lorenzo Dow the unruly Methodist shared with many other preachers the faith that the Bible is the only valid religious authority for Christians and that the meaning of the Bible is so clearly set out in its pages that it requires no special education to understand but only common sense. There was, in short, a distinctive populist hermeneutic of the Bible underlying the surface diversity of nineteenth-century American Protestantism.[23] Mark Noll, in an important study, has identified this hermeneutic as 'a Reformed, literal hermeneutic of the Bible'. It was Reformed because its threefold understanding of the scope of biblical authority derived from historical Calvinism: the Bible is the sole religious authority; the Bible is the highest moral authority; and only those ways of living positively enjoined in the Bible are permissible. It was literal because if the Bible is to be understood by ordinary Christians then its meaning must be easily grasped without specialized historical, linguistic or theological training; Scripture means simply and exactly what it says.[24]

A further consequence of the American populist hermeneutic was a turn toward Baconian induction in theology. Hutcheson had already described his moral philosophy in terms of Baconian science. American Evangelicals now promoted an empirical theology based on facts of consciousness and facts from the Bible: through careful reading one determined what the words of the Bible meant; these scriptural facts could then be known as surely and as clearly as the facts discovered by the naturalist. As the Restorationist James S. Lamar said in his *Organon of Scripture; or, The Inductive Method of Biblical Interpretation* (1859),

> The Scriptures admit of being studied and expounded upon the principles of the
> inductive method; and…when thus interpreted they speak to us in a voice as certain
> and unmistakable as the language of nature heard in the experiments and observations
> of science.[25]

Miller and Campbell both urged Christians to renounce speculation and draw principles inductively from the 'facts of the Bible'. Every one of the new sects justified itself as the restoration or inauguration of a true, pristine Christianity on the basis of the facts of the Bible.[26] Miller hazarded specific predictions of the date of the Second Coming precisely because he considered the interpretation of prophecy to be a rational, democratic discipline analogous to the study of nature.[27] Similarly, Campbell's boast that 'I have endeavored to read the scriptures as though no one had read them before me' should be understood as a declaration of Baconian induction in theology.[28]

The closest analogue in Christian history to the American post-Revolutionary hermeneutical situation is England during the Civil War of the seventeenth century. And here, too, the critical element was the proliferation of populist readings of the Bible, and therefore of sects, in the absence (in this case temporary) of official control over biblical interpretation during the Puritan rebellion against Church and state. The Restoration era poet John Dryden (1631–1700) magnificently captured elite disdain for the Puritans' claim to be able to read the Bible for themselves:

> The Book thus put in every vulgar hand,
> Which each presumed he best could understand,
> The common rule was made the common prey;
> And at the mercy of the rabble lay.
> The tender Page with horny fists was galled;
> And he was gifted most that loudest bawled:
> The Spirit gave the doctoral degree:
> …
> No measure ta'en from knowledge, all from grace.
> Study and pains were now no more their care;
> Texts were explained by fasting and by prayer:
> This was the fruit the private Spirit brought;
> Occasioned by great zeal, and little thought.[29]

Dryden might have been speaking for the American theologians and ministers of the old state churches whose erudition and exegetical caution were so contemptuously treated by populist preachers. Moreover, and critically important for our purposes, the development of the higher criticism occurred after most Americans outside the elites had cut themselves off from all but a Reformed, literal hermeneutic of the Bible.

Liberal Protestantism

The Civil War caused a theological crisis in American Protestantism. Common-sense moral philosophy was supposed to produce universally accepted moral positions and common-sense theology was supposed to produce universally accepted interpretations of the Bible. But, in fact, both North and South used the Reformed, literal hermeneutic of the Bible in their condemnation and defence, respectively, of black chattel slavery.[30] If the 'facts of the Bible' could be contrarily interpreted by similar-minded exegetes on such a fundamental issue, could the Bible truly be an infallible authority? For some Americans, the answer was firmly negative. These people, few in number but increasing among the intellectual elites as the century advanced, abandoned the Bible as the authoritative guide to life. This is the modernist position. A more acceptable alternative to modernism for many educated Americans was a liberal Protestantism in which the Bible retained its central place but the Reformed, literal hermeneutic was rejected in favour of some version of biblical theology.[31] (The terms 'modernist' and 'liberal' are both used within theology, with modernist signifying ultra-liberal positions. I am using 'modernist' as it is used more generally in cultural history to indicate a secularist position, as, for example, the literary modernism of Virginia Woolf. I therefore use 'modernist' as an alternative to, not a subset of, liberal Protestantism.)

Modernity explains humanity and the universe through the secular disciplines of science, history, psychology, sociology and so on, rather than by the Christian three-act drama of creation, the Fall and redemption in Christ. American liberal Protestants, like their British counterparts, tried to meet the challenge of defining the relationship of Christianity to modernity by accommodating as much as possible of the intellectual revolutions of the nineteenth century. Its programme was encapsulated by Shailer Mathews (1863–1941) of the University of Chicago Divinity School: 'the use of scientific, historical, and social methods in understanding and applying evangelical Christianity to the needs of living persons'.[32] The higher criticism and organic evolution were particularly prominent in this intellectual programme. Liberal Protestants built on what Chapter 7 identified as an epochal moment in the intellectual history of the West: the hermeneutical reversal by which biblical interpretation became a matter of fitting the biblical story into the world established by science and scholarship. Biblical theologians such as William Newton Clarke understood the Bible as a historical document in which one might trace the development of religious consciousness from a child-like externalism involving miracles and ritual to the universal ethical monotheism of Jesus' teaching. These liberal Christians honoured the Bible because they could find in it modern spiritual and ethical values, but they dismissed as obsolete other elements of the Bible that were incompatible with these values. Similarly, we have seen in Chapter 8 how liberal Christians assimilated organic evolution into Protestantism by substituting various providentially guided mechanisms for Darwin's mechanism of natural selection.

The tendency of liberal Protestantism to slight traditional doctrines has led to its being described as 'morality tinged with emotion' and 'the Ten Suggestions'. But most liberal Protestants were committed Christians whose very commitment drove them to respond to the intellectual challenges of their time in the hope of making the faith credible for modern people. Herbert Willett of the Disciples of Christ spoke for many when in 1905 he described his mission in words closely echoing Jowett: 'I am only trying to save the Bible for the parents and teachers of this generation.'[33] And yet, the cost of saving the Bible was high; rethinking Christianity in terms of biblical criticism, organic evolution, and other modern ways of understanding the world transformed the traditional faith. Liberal Protestants understood sin, for example, not as essential depravity marking a fallen creature but rather as corrigible error or limitation. Correspondingly, education and moral reform replaced Christ's atoning death as the means of redeeming humanity from sin and Jesus himself became a fully human moral teacher rather than the divine Saviour, the God who has taken on flesh. Liberal Protestants valued the Bible for its moral teaching; they interpreted revelation, creeds and dogmas as progressive human constructions whose ongoing relevance depends on their consonance with modern ethical values. They minimized ritual and rationalized what they retained of it: the sacraments of baptism and the Eucharist became, respectively, communal and memorial acts rather than channels of grace. Finally, they historicized messianism; the glorious destiny of humanity will be achieved within history through education and social improvement. Liberal Protestants, in short, thoroughly naturalized Christianity, although their use of traditional formulas and pious language obscured the full extent of their naturalism. They spoke, for example, of Jesus as divine, but what they meant was that his message – his moral teaching – was divine. Their faith did not conflict with biblical criticism or organic evolution because almost all supernatural elements had been evicted from it.[34]

Liberal Protestantism was not a separate denomination but a tendency within most mainline denominations. Its vanguard was comprised of biblical theologians like William Newton Clarke and biblical scholars such as Charles Augustus Briggs at Union Theological Seminary in New York and William Rainey Harper at Yale and later the University of Chicago. Harper did more than anyone else to introduce laypeople to biblical criticism through his journal, *The Hebrew Student*, extensive lecturing on the Chautauqua circuit, and above all the correspondence courses and subsidiary local study groups of the American Institute of Sacred Literature.[35] By the late nineteenth century liberal Protestantism had become widespread among educated Americans in New England and parts of the Midwest. Congregationalists, Methodists (especially Northern Methodists) and Episcopalians were particularly receptive to liberalism, as were to only a slightly lesser degree Northern Presbyterians, Northern Baptists, and the Disciples of Christ. It had come to dominate many seminaries, especially those in the northeast associated with great universities – Harvard Divinity School, Yale Divinity School, Union Theological Seminary – plus the University of Chicago Divinity School.[36]

Reactionary biblicism

Conservative Protestants regarded liberal Protestantism in general and its capitulation to the higher criticism in particular as a catastrophic betrayal of true Christianity. The conservative position received influential intellectual support from a group of Princeton theologians. Princeton Theological Seminary, conspicuously absent from the list given above of seminaries that had come under the influence of liberal Protestantism, was the citadel of Calvinist orthodoxy in nineteenth-century America. Its theologians drew on common-sense philosophy and a Baconian approach to science in constructing a defence of biblical inerrancy.

Charles Hodge, whose *What Is Darwinism?* we encountered in Chapter 8, was the first standard-bearer. Hodge asserted in his *Systematic Theology* (1873) that

> the Bible is to the theologian what nature is to the man of science. It is his store-house of facts; and his method of ascertaining what the Bible teaches is the same as that which the natural philosopher adopts to ascertain what nature teaches.[37]

He then argued that anyone who makes a careful, inductive and open-minded examination of the Bible will arrive at a set of facts; that is, the meaning of the words of the Bible. One such fact of the Bible for Hodge was the fact that it is an inspired text. The Bible itself asserts this and no examination of the biblical text will produce contradictory evidence. This being so, the inerrant nature of the Bible necessarily follows from the proper application of common-sense epistemology and Baconian science. Moreover, since common sense tells us that the Bible means what it says, there is no need to look behind the words themselves for some other meaning not directly stated. The words of the Bible, therefore, are not hostages to history but transparently express the true and changeless will of God. Christians may ignore the higher criticism and biblical theology because in denying an inerrant Bible they transgress both common sense and proper Baconian science.[38]

The Princeton men who took up the standard of biblical inerrancy after Hodge – his son Archibald Alexander Hodge and Benjamin Breckinridge Warfield – could not simply dismiss the higher criticism and biblical theology, given the inroads liberal Protestantism had begun to make into the churches. In their 1881 article on 'Inspiration' for the *Princeton Theological Review* and elsewhere, Hodge and Warfield defended by means of a double strategy the inerrantist position that the words of the Bible not merely contain, but *are*, the Word of God. First, they repeated the common-sense position that an inductive examination of the Bible will endorse the claims made in the Bible itself. This circular argument (essentially, the Bible's claim to be true and inspired may be trusted because we trust its claim that it is inspired) represented no advance on the elder Hodge. But then, second, they challenged the higher critics to disprove the inerrancy position. Specifically, they insisted that in order to *prove* that the Bible contained errors a critic would have to fulfil three conditions. First, he would have to show that the passage in question was in the original text of the Bible, which Hodge and Warfield referred to as the 'original autographs'. Obviously, since no such original autograph remains extant they could always claim that any passage that did truly seem to be in error had not belonged to the original revelation but had been introduced by human copiers. Second, a critic would have to show that the passage really does mean what a critic claims it means. Third, the critic would have to show that the passage truly was in conflict with science. The second and third conditions could be combated by disputing interpretation or arguing that the 'scientific fact' it was allegedly in conflict with was wrong, but in practice it was their recourse to the 'original autographs' argument that gave heart to conservative Protestants.[39]

These theologically conservative scholars did not think of themselves as enemies of science or reason. The Hodges and Warfield insisted that it was the higher criticism that was not truly scientific because it played fast and loose with empirical evidence (the 'facts of the Bible') and manipulated that evidence to support their philosophical predisposition against the possibility of revelation (it was deductive, not inductive). Further, and closely paralleling their critique of Darwinism as deductive speculation rather than inductive science, the conservatives pointed to disagreements among the higher critics themselves as proof that biblical criticism was human speculation rather than true science.[40] The Princeton theologians' defence of biblical inerrancy, however, was designed not to persuade liberal Christians but to rally conservatives. And indeed its net result was to separate conservative Evangelicals further from mainstream American intellectual life because almost all American scientists and philosophers rejected the common-sense and Baconian foundations of the Princetonians' reasoning and therefore dismissed their theology as philosophically unintelligible.[41] Even within the Presbyterian Church itself the Princeton inerrancy theology encountered opposition. In the 1880s Charles Briggs, teaching at the Presbyterians' Union Seminary, challenged the Princetonians in the name of a very mild version of the higher criticism. For his pains Briggs was convicted of heresy by a church court, but the victory of the conservatives divided Presbyterians and many liberals followed Briggs out of the Church. In the end his seminary itself severed its connection with the Presbyterian Church.[42]

The defection of Union Theological Seminary showed that the Princeton theologians would not succeed in recalling all educated Presbyterians to the inerrancy doctrine. But there were many, many others in America for whom the Princeton teaching came as a blessed rain on parched fields. That the Hodges and Warfield possessed in full the Presbyterian distrust of emotionalism in religious matters was no obstacle to their theology being taken up by revivalists who merged their arguments for inerrancy with their own emotional piety. Although for the most part these Baptists, Southern Baptists, Methodists and members of innumerable Bible churches could not have named its authors or its domicile, the Princeton theology gave a kind of intellectual authority for what revivalists knew in their hearts to be true but had hitherto been unable to articulate.[43]

Revivalism itself had evolved since the camp meetings of frontier days. In particular, its base was now the cities and its audience the newly urbanized masses. The economic and moral circumstances of the late nineteenth-century city provided both a pool of men and women receptive to the revivalist message and a panorama of sinfulness – drink, exploitation, vast wealth and grinding poverty, Catholicism, woman's suffrage – to frame it. Leading revivalists – above all Finney, Dwight Moody and Billy Sunday – developed an organizational structure in which touring preachers were sponsored by coalitions of conservative-minded

Protestant denominations and individual congregations. A second institutional framework for conservative Protestantism that emerged in the last decades of the nineteenth century and that interacted with the Princeton theology was the network of Bible and prophecy conferences. Bible conferences offered the opportunity for in-depth study of the Bible with like-minded conservative Protestants. At the Niagara Bible Conferences, for example, laypeople read and discussed the Bible with prominent preachers and teachers at one- and two-week summer retreats. Since the conferences were built on the common-sense hermeneutic and an absolute faith in an inerrant text, participants could be sure that no higher critic or biblical theologian would cast his shadow over the sacred page. While Bible conferences catered to laypeople with the time and money for summer retreats, Bible institutes and colleges provided a similar diet for Christians who felt a call to evangelize their neighbours. The Moody Bible Institute became the first of these new institutions in 1880 when Dwight Moody lent his name to a Chicago Bible training school, and by the end of the century several more Bible Institutes had opened their doors. The rise of Bible institutes was directly related to the increasing influence of the higher criticism in the seminaries of mainstream Protestant denominations. Conservative individuals and congregations, no longer trusting the seminaries, looked elsewhere for sound theological instruction. Bible institutes and Bible colleges met this need by founding Christian education on the rock of the inerrant Bible and its facts.[44]

Parallel to and overlapping with Bible conferences were prophecy conferences, at which participants attempted to decode the facts of the prophetic books in order to interpret current events in light of their hope that the Second Coming of Jesus was imminent. The dominant interpretation to emerge was that of dispensational premillennialism. Traditionally, Christians affirm two dispensations, or phases in God's dealings with humanity: the Old Testament and the New Testament. Various other divisions of history have been worked out from time to time (such as Joachim of Fiori's three-stage theory in the thirteenth century) but the modern idea of multiple dispensations seems to date from the work of John Nelson Darby (1800–1882), the Irish Protestant leader of the Plymouth Brethren. Darby's extensive lecturing in Britain and America popularized both his scheme of dispensations and his peculiar interpretation of Paul's discussion of the end-times in 1 Thessalonians 4:16–17. Darby taught that true Christians would be caught up to heaven (the Rapture) *before* the period of suffering ruled by the Antichrist (the Tribulation), which itself would end when Christ returned with his saints to battle the Antichrist at Armageddon, after which he would reign for one thousand years (the Millennium), to be followed by Satan's final rebellion and defeat, the resurrection of the dead, and the Last Judgement. Millennialists in the modern period had added to the traditional Christian eschatological teaching that at the Parousia, or the Second Coming of Christ in glory, the Christian dead would be resurrected the belief that it would immediately be followed by the Rapture of living Christians. What was unusual about Darby's interpretation is that most millennialists expected the Rapture to occur after the Tribulation.[45] Darby's reading was therefore a 'premillennial' interpretation.

While Darby's dispensational premillennialism was taken up in America by the Moody Bible Institute and many of the Bible and prophecy conferences, its most effective exponent was Cyrus Ingerson Scofield (1848–1921), a Congregationalist minister and regular contributor to the Niagara Bible Conferences. Scofield's reading of the Bible convinced him that human history is divided into seven dispensations. We are now living in the seventh and last age, in which humanity awaits amid increasing corruption and infidelity for God to bring history to a close. There is no continuity or progressive development from age to age: 'These periods are marked off in Scripture by some change in God's method of dealing with mankind ... and each ends in judgement – marking utter [human] failure in every dispensation.'[46] A more pointed denial of the developmentalist assumptions of biblical theology cannot be imagined. Further, dispensationalist premillennialism was (and is) not only a scheme for interpreting the inerrant Bible; it also provides an explanation for the success of liberal Protestantism and secular ideologies. Modernity and its attendant ambiguities, provisional truths and historical-mindedness are only to be expected in this seventh age of corruption and infidelity; they are signs of the increasing ascendancy of the Antichrist as the Last Days draw near.[47]

Scofield's interpretive schema massively influenced conservative Protestantism through the Scofield Reference Bible (1909). This work, which has sold millions of copies, presents itself as an edition of the King James Version. And yet, because Scofield surrounded the biblical text with dogmatically asserted annotations, footnotes, cross-references and divisions of the text all designed to persuade the reader that dispensationalism and many other conservative readings are inherent in the biblical text itself, the Scofield Reference Bible is actually a commentary on the Bible disguised as an edition of the KJV.[48] In fact, the Scofield Reference Bible structurally resembles nothing so much as the medieval *glossa ordinaria* in which the biblical text was surrounded with the commentaries and annotations of the Church Fathers.

Not all inerrantists, it is true, were dispensationalists, and by no means all those who attended Bible and prophecy conferences and Bible institutes could have named the Princeton theologians, but all three groups carried into the twentieth century the double heritage of the Reformed, literal hermeneutic of the Bible and the common-sense, Baconian approach to theology.[49] And the interpreters of prophecy were right that a great battle would soon be joined. It would not be Armageddon, but it would be a battle for the soul of Protestant America.

Chapter 11

FUNDAMENTALISM

Reactionary biblicism crystallized into Fundamentalism early in the twentieth century. Conservative Christians who regarded liberal Protestant attempts to reinterpret Christianity in light of modern ideas and values as a betrayal of the faith of their fathers identified five core doctrines that all true Christians must affirm: the verbal inerrancy of Scripture, the divinity of Christ, the virgin birth, a substitutionary theory of the atonement, and the physical resurrection and bodily return of Christ. The Niagara Bible Conferences in 1895 declared these to be 'five points of fundamentalism' or 'The Fundamentals', and other conservative Protestant assemblies issued similar statements over the next few years. *The Fundamentals: A Testimony of Truth* is also the title of a series of 94 tracts, designed to combat the corruption of Christianity by modern ideas and values, published between 1910 and 1915 in twelve booklets and sent free of charge to Protestant pastors, teachers and other religious leaders. Defence of the 'fundamentals' became the rallying-cry for those who opposed liberal Protestantism, and the tendency – more a loose coalition of like-minded groups than a single movement – became known as 'Fundamentalism'.[1]

By 1920 Fundamentalists formed a militant faction in various mainstream Protestant denominations, above all the Presbyterians and the Baptists, and these denominational factions were linked together by extra-denominational conferences and associations. Their common goal was to expose liberal Protestants as false Christians whose sceptical questioning of traditional beliefs and doctrines destroys what they claim to believe in. Fundamentalists cited as damning evidence from their own mouths the remark by a popular liberal Presbyterian writer that the coat of arms of this age of doubt 'is an interrogation point rampant, above three bishops dormant, and its motto is Query?'.[2] And yet, while Fundamentalists claimed to be defending age-old Christian tradition, the means by which they did so were specific to late nineteenth-century America: biblical inerrancy, common-sense realism, and premillennial dispensationalism. Some Fundamentalists, it is true, were neither dispensational or premillennialism, but most, whether they realized it or not, operated with a common-sense epistemology and all championed an inerrant Bible.[3]

An inerrant Bible

Twenty-seven of the 94 tracts comprising *The Fundamentals* attack the higher criticism of the Bible; no other topic (including evolution) is treated more than four times. The urgent need to combat the higher criticism arose from Fundamentalists' conviction that to admit the Bible contains any error whatsoever initiates a chain of questions that ultimately throws into doubt its testimony to the redemptive work of Christ. If the Bible contains any errors at all, then how can it be divinely revealed? If the higher critics are right in their reconstruction of the real meaning of the Old Testament as distinct from its plain-sense meaning, then Jesus and/or the apostles erred because the New Testament reports Jesus endorsing its plain-sense meaning. And if Jesus or the apostles erred, how can we trust the New Testament's witness to the saving truths? From another quarter, inerrancy necessarily followed from the widespread Fundamentalist conviction that interpretation of prophecy indicates that we are living in the Last Days, because if the Bible is wrong about the history contained in the early chapters of Genesis then how can its prophecies be trusted? Finally, and underlying all these specific anxieties, to admit that the Bible contains errors is to place a human standard above the Word of God.[4]

Fundamentalists saved themselves from these doubts by applying the Reformed, literal hermeneutic to the matter of biblical authority. The Bible itself asserts that it is inerrant – 'The scripture cannot be broken [annulled]' (John 10:35) and 'All Scripture is inspired by God' (2 Timothy 3:16); therefore it is inerrant. William Bell Riley, a Baptist from Minneapolis and a national Evangelical leader, spoke for all Fundamentalists when he affirmed that 'If one runs through the Old Testament he will find God everywhere assuming the Authorship of the Sacred Scriptures.'[5] Of course, this line of argument is convincing only if you already believe that the Bible is God's errorless Word. For secular-minded people, its claims are no more authoritative than those of an Aztec tradition asserting that continuation of the cosmos requires periodic sacrifice of human beings. Biblical theologians, we recall, had saved the Bible from such a demotion to the status of just another human book by means of the concept of progressive revelation; the biblical claims as a whole represent the progressive attainment of knowledge of God through the mediation of human minds, but no specific claims – except Jesus' moral teachings – are considered absolute truths (Chapter 7). Fundamentalists rejected the higher criticism outright precisely in order to avoid facing the problem of biblical authority posed as a result of it. In this way the higher criticism itself gave rise, reactively, to the emphasis on biblical inerrancy among conservative Protestants. Fundamentalists proudly called (and call) themselves 'Bible believers'. They mean by this that anyone who does not accept the total inerrancy of the Bible does not really believe in the Bible but in some human standard that he or she has substituted for God's revealed Word. Inerrancy, we might say, is the levee Fundamentalists built to protect the city of God against the toxic floodwaters of theological liberalism.[6] This militant opposition to biblical criticism and liberal theology distinguishes Fundamentalists' commitment to biblical inerrancy from the unquestioned assumption of most Christians before the late nineteenth century that the Bible was factually and historically reliable.[7]

The historical consciousness of the higher critics had destroyed the surface unity of the Bible, to which the biblical theologians responded by reunifying the

Bible around the reconstructed history they claimed it contained of humanity's spiritual development (see Chapter 7). In repudiating the higher criticism Fundamentalist inerrantists reasserted the surface unity of the Bible. No passage can contradict another and every word is as true and as relevant to the believer today as when it was first revealed. Any problem facing a present-day Christian, Fundamentalists therefore believe, has an answer in the Bible; it is just a matter of searching out the applicable verse or phrase. This practice is called proof-texting. The original intention of the biblical author is irrelevant here, as is usually the theological or other content of the chapter or book in which the verse or phrase is found. Nancy Ammerman has provided a telling example of Fundamentalist application of proof-texting to the problems of everyday life. A man testified to his fellow Bible believers that he had wanted to buy a new camping tent but was troubled over where to buy it because he had bought his last tent at Sears Roebuck and it had leaked. Knowing that the Bible contains the answer to all questions, the man opened his Bible and began to search for guidance. He found it in Deuteronomy 14:5, where, among the names of the animals Yahweh declares to be pure, he located the word 'roebuck'. Clearly, it was the will of God that he should indeed buy his new tent from the Sears Roebuck Company.[8] Trivial as this incident may seem, it makes crystal-clear Fundamentalists' underlying conviction that the words of the inerrant Bible transcend history.

It is important to distinguish the Fundamentalist insistence on the inerrancy of the Bible from literalism. Fundamentalists defend not the literal truth of the entire Bible but the claim that from cover to cover it is errorless. When possible, of course, they read their Bibles literally, but sometimes the literal meaning of a passage would endorse what they consider to be a scientific or historical error or a practice they judge to be immoral such as polygamy or slavery. In such cases Fundamentalists sacrifice literalism in order to save inerrancy.[9] William Bell Riley, for example, interpreted the days of creation as ages in order to reconcile the Genesis narrative with geological evidence of an ancient Earth, while the Scofield Reference Bible's annotations achieve the same end by means of the gap interpretation.[10] In these and many other instances Fundamentalists must decide what to read literally and what to read figuratively in order to protect the Bible from error. The ever-present need to make such interpretive decisions in part explains why, despite their faith in *sola scriptura*, ordinary Fundamentalists seek out guides to direct their reading of the Bible.

Biblical inerrancy, as in the matter of the age of the Earth, applies to scientific knowledge. Fundamentalists not only believe that any assertions the Bible makes about the natural world are both intended as scientific statements and absolutely true, but, further, that whatever they accept as scientific knowledge may be found in the Bible. Logically, there is no reason why the Bible has to contain modern scientific knowledge as well as saving knowledge, but Fundamentalists are committed to a strong theory of the Bible as containing *all* important truths and since they value science, as they understand it, they are sure that all true scientific knowledge can be found in its pages. For any given piece of scientific knowledge, therefore, Fundamentalists find a biblical passage that could be read as corresponding to it. Riley once again speaks for his fellow Bible believers in declaring that William Harvey's discovery of the circulation of the blood and its relation to life was known to Moses: 'The life [of the flesh] is in the blood'; that the Psalmist knew that the Earth is round: 'the circle of the earth'; that Job, not Newton, first announced the law of gravitation: 'He hangeth the earth upon nothing'; and that Job again, not Galileo, first understood that the atmosphere has weight: 'He maketh a weight for the wind'.[11]

A particularly striking example of the Fundamentalist conviction that all scientific discoveries are already anticipated in the Bible is Riley's attribution of the theory behind high explosives to the book of Job:

> But the most remarkable instance of Scripture [sic] anticipation of science was the late discovery of T.N.A., the highest explosive ever known or conceived. It was conceded from the beginning of the late world war, that the alliance discovering the highest explosive would win. Two young Americans – chemists – set themselves to that task. Knowing that snow and hail were contractions formed at 32 degrees above zero, while ice formed at thirty above and became an expansion, they took the explosive chemicals in liquid state and crystallized them by the temperature of hail and snow and lo, the result was a terror and Germany surrendered. Then for the first time men knew what Job meant when he wrote 3500 years ago, saying, 'Hast thou entered into the treasures of the snow, or hast thou seen the treasures of the hail, which I have reserved against the time of trouble, against the day of battle and war?' Job 38:22.[12]

There are two important points to note here. The first is that the meaning of this verse within the book of Job itself is irrelevant. It has been taken out of its historical and literary context in order to prove that a specific discovery of modern science may be found in the Bible. The second point to note is Riley's assumption that the book of Job was written by Job himself 3,500 years ago. Modern biblical scholars consider Job a difficult text because of obscure words, lack of historical references, and corruptions and additions to the text. Consensus, however, exists on the following points. The framework for the book is an ancient folktale about a man named Job who was proverbial for his endurance in the face of suffering. A philosophically minded anonymous poet, sometime shortly before, or during, or shortly after the Exile, used the folktale as the setting for reflection on the meaning of suffering and the nature of piety. A later editor may have rearranged and added to the work.[13] In contrast, Riley – like other Fundamentalists then and now – while agreeing that Job contains literary and philosophical reflection, read the book of Job as a true record of the events and dialogues of a real person named Job who lived in the land of Uz (Edom, or northern Arabia) during the period of the semi-nomadic patriarchs of the early chapters of Genesis. This is what the opening (folkloric) verses of the book assert, and therefore – if biblical inerrancy is to be upheld – they must be taken at face value. The twofold error into which the commitment to an inerrant Bible leads Riley and Fundamentalists generally is analogous to treating *Hamlet* as a factual document from medieval Denmark rather than as a piece of dramatic literature from Elizabethan England: it mistakes a literary composition for a factual record and it errs chronologically in dating the work by its setting rather than by its authorship.

The most basic thing one can say about Fundamentalism is that it was and is an anti-historical ideology. Fundamentalists repudiated historical-mindedness in order to defend the inerrancy of the Bible; conversely, faith in the inerrancy of the Bible became their greatest weapon against biblical criticism, biological evolution and all other historical sciences. Biblical inerrancy locates the words of the Bible beyond historical processes; the biblical text is a divine revelation that may have been transmitted through human messengers but transcends history and therefore the complexities and uncertainties of historical existence.[14] Fundamentalists not only lacked (and lack) a modern sense of history, but defined (and define) themselves by this lack.

The higher criticism and evolution

William Bell Riley was the first Fundamentalist leader to link the higher criticism with biological evolution. His 1909 book, *The Finality of the Higher Criticism; or, The Theory of Evolution and False Theology*, argued that the liberal theology built on the higher criticism is itself a consequence of accepting an evolutionary philosophy.[15] Riley accused both higher critics and evolutionary scientists of practicing 'a sinister method', by which he meant that their science did not proceed on properly Baconian principles. Riley made no attempt to understand the methods of working scientists; his anti-theoretical definition of science came straight from the dictionary: science is 'Knowledge gained and verified by exact observation and correct thinking'.[16] So armed, Riley denounced both theories of organic evolution and the higher criticism as unsubstantiated speculations that assert hypothetical historical reconstructions of life and of the Bible in place of God's plain Word.[17] Note that there is nothing particularly Darwinian here; Riley simply opposes any sort of historical consciousness, and therefore all forms of evolutionary philosophy, because it is incompatible with biblical inerrancy.

Riley levelled two further criticisms against evolution: it is unscriptural and anti-Christian. It is unscriptural because Genesis declares over and over again that God created each species 'after its own kind' – that is, as fixed and immutable. It is anti-Christian because those who accept some form of evolutionary theory substitute a divine *force* in place of a personal heavenly Father and reduce Christ to merely a remarkable man.[18] Riley identified these – and many further – errors, and the dire social and moral consequences that accompany them, as signs, for those who can read them, that the higher criticism and evolution are satanically inspired ideologies designed to lure people into denying their divine origin and the duties that follow from that origin. He had no doubt as to the ultimate origin of both the higher criticism and evolution:

> If we were asked what was the basal factor in the world's skepticism, we should answer in one word – '*sin*!' If we were asked who was the chief author of the world's infidelity, we should answer in one word – 'Satan!'[19]

Anti-evolutionary views similar to Riley's appear in two tracts from *The Fundamentals*. Whereas James Orr's contribution, 'Science and the Christian Faith',

defended a version of theistic evolution (see Chapter 8), 'Decadence of Darwinism', by a Colorado pastor, and the anonymous 'Evolution in the Pulpit'
dismissed Darwinism and evolution generally as bad science and luridly
denounced the immoral and anti-Christian consequences of accepting any form
of evolutionary theory. They, not Orr, were the voice of emerging Fundamentalism. Even the *Princeton Theological Review*, which in the late nineteenth century
had endorsed theistic evolution as the expression of God's providential concern
for creation, abandoned this position in the first decades of the twentieth century
in favour of total anti-evolutionism.[20]

There are two principal explanations for the repudiation of even theistic models
of evolution by Fundamentalists. First, nineteenth-century conservative Evangelical Christians such as the Princeton theologians had been primarily concerned
to defend the principle of design from Darwin's mechanism of natural selection.
Theistic models of evolution accomplished this function admirably, but all forms
of evolution had to be rejected once biblical inerrancy, not design, came to be
the central focus as a result of the reassertion of reactionary biblicism by
Fundamentalists. Warfield and the other Princeton theologians, inasmuch as
they promoted biblical inerrancy, contributed to this climate despite their own
acceptance of theistic evolution.[21] Second, by 1920 there were many fewer
Christian scientists of high professional standing actively promoting theistic
models of evolution than there had been a generation earlier. The gulf between
science and theology would only widen in the coming decades as the explanatory
power of the Modern Synthesis eliminated Neo-Lamarckism and orthogenesis
and re-established natural selection as the primary mechanism of biological
evolution.[22]

The Fundamentalist repudiation of all models of evolution should be recognized as an epochal moment in American religious history. It marks the first time
that American Evangelicals, many of them heirs of the Calvinist learned ministry, separated themselves from the established science of their day. Fundamentalists did not abandon the old conviction that the discoveries of science and the
claims of theology are in harmony, but they refused to recognize evolutionary
theories – and therefore mainstream biology and related disciplines – as true
science.[23] The Fundamentalists' isolation from modern science was an early and
enduring consequence of their commitment to an inerrant Bible.

The battle for Christian America

Riley's *The Finality of the Higher Criticism* summoned conservative Protestants
to unite against the higher criticism, evolution and liberal theology. World War I
brought home to many Americans the urgency of Riley's call. Surely, the German
militarism that threatened Christian and civilized values alike was simply the
inevitable consequence of a nation accepting the 'survival of the fittest' as its
ethical standard. Similarly, the pestilence of the higher criticism had been incu-
bated in German universities. Billy Sunday, a former professional baseball player
turned revivalist preacher, caught the fears of conservative Protestant America

when he declared that if hell were turned upside down, the phrase 'made in Germany' would be seen stamped across the bottom.[24]

In this atmosphere, and under Riley's leadership, the World's Christian Fundamentals Association (WCFA) was founded in 1918 to combat modern forms of infidelity. Over the next few years Fundamentalists attacked their opponents in the Protestant denominations in confrontations that ranged from skirmishes designed to test the strength of the opponent to all-out trench warfare. Theological liberalism had been so thoroughly assimilated into Congregationalism, Episcopalianism, Northern Methodism and the Disciples of Christ that these churches easily repulsed Fundamentalist advances. Conversely, the Southern Baptist, Southern Presbyterian and Southern Methodist churches were so thoroughly conservative that the Fundamentalist push met with little resistance, and indeed there was little for them to push against. The Somme of this campaign was the Northern Baptist and the Northern Presbyterian churches, where Fundamentalists and their opponents were almost evenly matched. Between 1920 and 1925 Baptist Fundamentalists, led by national figures such as Riley of Minneapolis, John Roach Stratton of New York, and T. T. Shields of Toronto, repeatedly stormed the structures of the Northern Baptist Convention. Among the Presbyterians the Fundamentalists' most prominent general was J. Gresham Machen, Warfield's successor at Princeton Theological Seminary. Machen argued, in *Christianity and Liberalism* (1923) and elsewhere, that theological liberalism has so compromised traditional Christianity that it is essentially a new, humanistic religion. He urged liberals to admit that they were no longer Christians in any meaningful historic sense and withdraw from the churches. By the mid-1920s, however, moderates in both the Northern Baptist and Northern Presbyterian churches had successfully fought off Fundamentalist attempts to seize control. While hardly endorsing extreme liberal positions, these bodies settled on a broader interpretation of Christianity in the modern world than that permitted by Fundamentalism.[25]

Meanwhile, recognizing that they would not be able to eliminate theological liberalism from all the established denominations, the WCFA had opened a second front. Beginning in 1922 it organized state-by-state political campaigns for legislation banning the teaching of evolution in public schools. Evolutionary concepts had been fully integrated into American high school biology textbooks as early as 1900, reflecting the near-universal acceptance of some form of evolutionism among American scientists. Evolution had been taught without incident as long as high school education was largely reserved for children of the social elites. The rapid and massive expansion, especially in the South, of secondary education in the early twentieth century placed evolutionary ideas before students – and their parents and often their teachers – who believed in their bones that evolution was unbiblical and anti-Christian. The WCFA's anti-evolution campaign responded to this expansion of high school science education in regions of the United States where Fundamentalism was strong.[26]

Fundamentalists were able to broaden support for their efforts to ban the teaching of evolution in schools because they supplemented their biblical arguments with a more general appeal to the contemporary revaluation of adolescence as a critical period in a young person's moral and spiritual development. They presented their anti-evolution measures as further protection against moral and spiritual danger for vulnerable adolescents alongside other Progressive Era legislation – including compulsory school attendance, secondary education, child-labour laws and juvenile-justice systems – designed to protect children and teenagers.[27]

Progressivists and Evangelical Christians had, in fact, worked together in the struggle against many of the economic, political and social injustices produced by America's rapid industrial expansion in the late nineteenth century. Massive economic disparities, low wages and negligible rights for workers, child labour, corrupt political machines, farmers foreclosed by banks, government collusion with industrial trusts, and alcoholism all called forth grassroots campaigns, particularly strong in the South and West, for economic and social justice. The alliance between Evangelical Protestantism and Progressivism was personified in William Jennings Bryan (1860–1925), whose populist political campaigns against economic and political injustices earned him the Democratic Party's nomination for the presidency of the United States in 1896, 1900 and again in 1908. The 'Great Commoner', though defeated each time, achieved concrete results through the ultimately successful Progressivist campaigns to redistribute wealth through a tax on inheritances, to regulate commerce and industry, and to extend democracy through the popular election of Senators and women's suffrage, to name only a few instances. When, late in his life, Bryan was drawn into the anti-evolution campaign, he understood it in the same populist terms that had governed his political life. Just as capitalist plutocrats have no right to monopolize economic wealth at the expense of ordinary citizens, so a 'scientific soviet' has no right to monopolize scientific knowledge at the expense of ordinary Christians or to dictate what is taught in public schools.[28] Bryan further shared the Fundamentalists' conviction that evolution is a morally dangerous doctrine. Were not German militarism, the eugenics movement and laissez-faire capitalism all concrete results of 'Darwin's dreadful law of hate' replacing 'the Bible's divine law of love'? It was no coincidence to Bryan that ruthless monopoly capitalists like Andrew Carnegie had seized on 'the survival of the fittest' in order to justify their abhorrent economic practices.[29]

Anti-evolutionism in the 1920s cannot be understood without recognizing how intimately militarism, eugenics and unregulated capitalism were connected with evolution in the minds not just of Bryan, or even Fundamentalists, but Americans generally. We must equally understand, however, that what was primarily at issue here was not biological evolution but Social Darwinism (Herbert Spencer was far more popular in America than in Britain). Bryan himself furnishes an interesting perspective on the matter inasmuch as he did not object to theories of biological evolution as long they were not applied to humanity. He declined, however, to reveal this opinion publicly on the grounds that it would encourage those promoting evolutionary explanations of human origins.[30]

In the early 1920s Bryan made a point of talking with high school and college students, their parents and pastors as he travelled about the country on speaking tours. What he learned appalled him: the teaching of evolution had unleashed an epidemic of unbelief that was killing off young people's faith in the Bible. He concluded that 'the teaching of Evolution as a fact instead of a theory caused the students to lose faith in the Bible, first, in the story of creation, and later in other doctrines, which underlie the Christian religion'.[31] This is precisely the slippage from questioning particular biblical statements to doubting the saving truths that had made Fundamentalists attribute the higher criticism to Satan himself. A shared commitment to defending biblical inerrancy sealed the alliance between Bryan and the WCFA.

The Scopes trial

Thirty-seven anti-evolution bills were introduced into twenty state legislatures between 1921 and 1929. One of the first to become law was Tennessee's Butler Act of 1925, which made it unlawful for state-supported schools 'to teach any theory that denies the story of the Divine Creation of man as taught in the Bible, and to teach instead that man has descended from a lower order of animals'. The WCFA commended the governor and legislature of Tennessee for 'prohibiting the teaching of the unscientific, anti-Christian, atheistic, anarchistic, pagan rationalistic evolutionary theory'.[32] On the other hand, the American Civil Liberties Union (ACLU), then in its early years, immediately identified the Tennessee statute as a violation of the Fourteenth Amendment of the United States Constitution, barring the states from making or enforcing 'any law which shall abridge the privileges or immunities of citizens of the United States', and advertised for volunteers for a test case. Encouraged by civic leaders in the small town of Dayton, John Thomas Scopes, a young high school science teacher and part-time football coach, agreed to be the defendant in a case in which local prosecutors and the ACLU would cooperate in testing the constitutionality of the Butler Act. Scopes spent no time in jail and was not the object of local anger. At the trial itself, which began on 10 July 1925 and lasted eight days, the local prosecutors were assisted by William Jennings Bryan, while the defence team consisted of ACLU attorneys from New York City, local Tennessee legal counsel and the celebrated Chicago attorney Clarence Darrow. Darrow's famous cross-examination of Bryan notwithstanding, a guilty verdict was never in doubt, not only because the jury was wholly composed of Bible believers, but because the defence conceded that Scopes had taught the outlawed theory. Indeed, the whole point of the exercise was to produce a conviction that could then be appealed to higher courts in order to test the statute's constitutionality. This plan was foiled, however, by the justices of the Tennessee Supreme Court, who feared that further appeals would bring ongoing ridicule to their state. In January 1927 they upheld the constitutionality of the Butler Act but overturned Scopes' conviction on the technicality that the jury and not the judge should have imposed the fine, thereby denying the ACLU opportunity for further appeal.[33]

More important for our purposes than the legal outcome of the trial are the positionings and strategies of the two sides. The prosecution combined the

Fundamentalists' charges that evolutionary theories are bad science and morally dangerous with Byran's majoritarian political argument that public school teachers are obliged to teach whatever the taxpayers who fund their salaries wish to be taught.[34] The defence argued that majoritarian control over what is taught in the classroom infringes on the individual rights of both teachers and students. They were prepared to support this defence of academic freedom with testimony from a slate of eminent scientists to the effect that the centrality of the theory of evolution in the biological sciences cannot be annulled by legislative decree, but the judge blocked the appeal to scientific authority by ruling that expert witnesses would not be heard. The ACLU attorneys and the local counsel supplemented the argument for academic freedom with the subsidiary claim that the theory of evolution is compatible with the biblical creation narrative and therefore the teaching of evolution does not violate the statute. This latter belief was the sincere conviction of everyone at the defence table except Darrow, although once again their expert witnesses on this point – this time, eminent biblical theologians – were not permitted to testify.[35]

Darrow's place on the defence team was the result of the ACLU's understanding of the academic freedom of schoolteachers in terms of the rights of organized labour. Darrow had built a national reputation as a defender of radical labour before turning, with brilliant success, to criminal law in the decade before Scopes. While Darrow's star status and his commitment to labour meant that the ACLU could not decline his offer of assistance, it was clear right from the start that his agenda did not fully coincide with that of the rest of the defence. Darrow was an agnostic and a militant secularist who believed that Christianity was both intellectually false and socially dangerous.[36] In the courtroom Darrow took up the ACLU position that the Tennessee statute infringed on individual freedom, but with the twist unique to him that the root of the threat against individual liberties – personified by Bryan – was religion (and not just Fundamentalism). This is particularly interesting because Bryan himself and the Christian churches in general had been the ACLU's allies in previous campaigns to protect the rights of individuals (Darrow himself had voted for Bryan in the 1896 presidential election). Darrow's cross-examination of Bryan (without the jury present) was both an expression of his contempt for Fundamentalist biblicism and a strategic attempt to show that Bryan interpreted the Bible (as with his day/age interpretation of the creation narrative) and therefore that he was advocating a *particular* religious view.[37] This latter point – which Darrow considered key to the legal issue of establishing a particular religious viewpoint – is overlooked when contemporaries and later commentators alike focus on Darrow's own gleeful boast that he had forced Bryan to admit that he interpreted the Bible. Bryan, of course, was simply doing what Fundamentalists always do – sacrificing literalism here and there in order to defend the inerrancy of the whole. His 'concession', moreover, passed unremarked among Fundamentalists of the time because his day/age interpretation of the creation narrative was widely held among them.

Darrow's individual-rights arguments anticipated the direction of judicial interpretation of the disestablishment clauses of the United States Constitution in subsequent decades. Indeed, his closing argument's portrayal of religion as a matter of private belief and science as public knowledge, in opposition to the prosecution's endorsement of the Fundamentalist depiction of the Bible as truth and science as opinion, laid out a view of science and religion that would become the dominant one after mid-century.[38] In 1925, however, few people distinguished between Darrow's interpretation of Constitutional law and his anti-religious views. Even opponents of anti-evolutionism vilified Darrow for his attacks on religion at Dayton.

For their part, the rest of the defence team truly believed that evolution was compatible with Christianity, a conviction that liberal Protestants from a variety of mainline denominations before, during, and after the trial echoed in and out of the pulpit. This response reminds us that the Scopes trial took place at the height of the battle for control of the Protestant denominations. And as with the wider battle, those who opposed the Fundamentalists were those whose theological liberalism was based on an understanding of the Bible as a historical document. At Dayton itself Tennessee's few indigenous liberal Christians (mostly huddled together in Nashville under the protection of Vanderbilt University, then a liberal Methodist school) were reinforced by visiting northerners, including those invited as expert witnesses for the defence. Prominent among the latter was Shailer Mathews, now Dean of the University of Chicago Divinity School. Mathews, like all biblical theologians, regarded the Bible as the record of the progressive development of humanity's understanding of God: 'The writers of the Bible used the language, conceptions, and science of the times in which they lived. We trust and follow their religious insights with no need of accepting their views on nature.' The religious insight Mathews recognized in the creation narrative is that 'God is in the processes which have produced and sustain mankind'.[39] Even more theologically liberal than Mathews was the New York Unitarian minister Charles Francis Potter, who spoke extensively in and around Dayton during the trial. Potter regarded every part of the Bible as obsolete except Jesus' moral teaching.

The common ground between liberal Protestants and the ACLU team was epitomized in the issue of the prayers that opened each day of courtroom proceedings during the trial. The first few days' prayers were offered by one local Fundamentalist pastor after another. When Potter and other visiting liberal ministers asked the judge to permit non-Fundamentalists to offer the prayer, the ACLU attorney formally moved that 'we have the opportunity to hear prayers by men who think that God has shown His divinity in the wonders of nature, in the book of nature quite as much as in the revealed word'. Only Darrow opposed the whole idea of courtroom prayers, for which he was berated by Fundamentalist and liberal Christians alike.[40]

The argument that evolution was compatible with religion was seconded by scientists who maintained an orthogenetic understanding of the evolutionary process, notably Henry Fairfield Osborn of the American Museum of Natural History. The Scopes trial provoked Osborn, who for years had been using his scientific and institutional status to denounce Fundamentalist attacks on evolution, to intensify his efforts to persuade the American public that orthogenesis, according to which evolution is a slow, gradual process of development toward a predetermined goal, is – unlike Darwinism – entirely compatible with biblical teaching and natural theology.[41] Osborn wrote *Evolution and Religion in Education* (1926) in the months after the trial expressly in order to assure Americans that evolutionism, properly understood, is a spiritual doctrine that defends the uniqueness of humanity. This is the context for his attempts, noted in Chapter 9, to dissociate evolution from 'the myth and bogey of ape-man ancestry'. Osborn's enemy was discontinuous change, whether in science or in society. Natural selection and the newly ascendant Mendelian genetics threatened established order in science, just as social order was under attack from the unnatural discontinuities embodied in the Russian Revolution, income tax and women's suffrage. If Osborn embodied the East Coast establishment on these points, he deferred to no Fundamentalist in linking communism, militarism, materialism and any number of other social and moral ills to the dire effects of allowing Darwinism to be taught in schools.[42]

In sum, the Scopes trial did not pit science against religion. The only person in Dayton who saw the trial in those terms was Clarence Darrow. Everyone else, on both sides, recognized the trial as an outlying skirmish in the battle for Christian America between Fundamentalists and their theologically liberal and moderate opponents. Scopes' supporters, Darrow alone dissenting, accepted some sort of theistic model of evolutionism – Darwinism, strictly defined, was emphatically not on trial at Dayton – and their Fundamentalist opponents directed their anger not against secularists but against liberal Protestants whose embrace of biblical criticism and theistic evolution betrayed the inerrant Bible and the true faith. Bryan himself memorably denounced theistic evolution as 'an anaesthetic that deadens the Christian's pain while his religion is being removed'.[43] The trial's consequences for the teaching of evolution in public schools similarly paralleled the outcome of the battle for the churches. Evolution continued to be taught in those regions where liberals and moderates had beaten back the Fundamentalist assault, while it was restricted or banned in states and school districts where Fundamentalists controlled the churches.

Outside the latter areas, it is true, many people regarded the Scopes trial as a crushing defeat of Fundamentalism by the forces of reason and modernity, a view seemingly confirmed by a marked decline in Fundamentalist anti-evolution activity in the 1930s. This interpretation of the Scopes trial – first voiced in the journalist Frederick Lewis Allen's *Only Yesterday: An Informal History of the Nineteen-Twenties* (1931) – came to be widely embraced by educated Americans. And yet, in the immediate aftermath of the trial no one – and certainly not the ACLU – saw it as a decisive defeat for Fundamentalism. Moreover, anti-evolution activity continued unabated in many areas of the country and publishers fell over each other in their rush to dilute or eliminate the sections on evolution in their high school biology textbooks. Anti-evolutionary political and legal activities truly did diminish from the early 1930s, but the cause was not the extinction of Fundamentalism but a change of strategy on the part of Bible believers.[44]

Fundamentalist separatism

Early Fundamentalists understood themselves within the logic of revivalism: true America is Christian America; if liberalism and secularism now haunt it like the bad dreams of a sleeping believer, there will be an Awakening in which America will rouse itself, throw off the night terrors, and once again dedicate itself to the will of God as set out in the inerrant Bible. But this self-understanding was shattered by their failure to drive biblical criticism and liberal theology out of the churches and the widespread support for theistic evolution among non-Fundamentalist Christians revealed in the Scopes trial. Forced by these events to acknowledge that their values were not those of mainstream America, Fundamentalists drew the logical conclusion: America is not asleep but apostate; the churches, no less than the secular world, bow down to an anti-biblical ideology that Fundamentalists eventually came to call 'secular humanism'.[45] Under this new dispensation Fundamentalists regretfully renounced the understanding of themselves in terms of revivalism that had sustained American Protestants since Plymouth Rock, and fell back on alternative Christian self-understandings. America was no longer the city on the hill, but Vanity Fair, from which, like the hero of the Puritan handbook, *Pilgrim's Progress*, they resolved to flee for the sake of their souls. Inasmuch, however, as Fundamentalism was a matter of institutions as well as individual souls, flight was less like the lonely journey of Bunyan's Christian and more like the communal withdrawal of the early Christians in Rome who sought refuge from persecution in the catacombs beneath the city. Mainstream America having become a hostile and alien world from which they could expect only contempt and opposition, Bible believers fled underground. Not to literal catacombs, of course, but from the late 1920s Fundamentalists withdrew from mainstream denominations and secular institutions and set to work building a separate network of churches and schools beyond the control of the apostate churches and secular educational establishment. As with the ancient catacomb churches, this work was largely hidden from the surrounding society.

The foundation on which Fundamentalists (together with Holiness and Pentecostal churches) built their separatist world was the network of Bible and prophecy conferences that had been so important to the emergence of Fundamentalism in the first place. The spread of dispensationalist premillennialism coincided with and in part propelled the shift to separatism. Premillennialist historical pessimism discouraged belief in America as the new Zion and prophecy writers began to identify the newly apostate nation with the Babylon of Revelation.[46] With prophecy affirming that the only possible result of national apostasy would be divine wrath, Bible believers expanded the existing conference framework into a network of independent but linked churches, Evangelical organizations, schools and colleges, mission boards, publishing houses, syndicated radio programmes and summer camps. Bible colleges and institutes were particularly important to Fundamentalist separatism. Conservative Protestants had watched in dismay as all over America institutions of higher learning had come under liberal or secular control and denominational seminaries had fallen to the higher criticism and liberal theology. Even Princeton Theological Seminary was lost in 1929 when J. Gresham Machen conceded defeat and departed with a remnant of conservatives to found Westminster Theological Seminary. A few schools, it is true, remained true to the faith – notably Wheaton College in Illinois and the dispensationalist Dallas Theological Seminary. These, together with existing Bible schools like the Moody Bible Institute in Chicago and the Bible Institute of Los Angeles (now Biola University), became the models for a massive expansion of educational institutions whose curriculum centred on the inerrant Bible. Bible colleges, then as now, offered a facsimile of a liberal arts education, the crucial difference being that the Bible is the supreme authority in all matters and nothing is taught that challenges its inerrancy. Bible institutes, for their part, were more specialist institutions devoted to training pastors, evangelists and missionaries in biblical interpretation, preaching, theology and related skills. Bible institutes required little to no academic qualifications for admission; they were not houses of scholarship but training grounds for the rough and ready business of winning souls by and to the words of the inerrant Bible.[47] Bible colleges and schools, in short, were as far from mainstream intellectual life as Fundamentalist anti-evolutionism was from mainstream biology.

If, as Diogenes Teufelsdrock once suggested, ideas were clothes, Fundamentalists would be as recognizable as the Amish; both, after all, repudiate the modern world because it is incompatible with their interpretation of the Bible. Evolution was no more accepted within the separate world Fundamentalists were building for themselves than the higher criticism of the Bible. And yet, because Fundamentalists were building their own schools in which nothing incompatible with an inerrant Bible would be taught, instead of actively campaigning to ban the teaching of evolution in public schools, outside observers correctly noted a decline in the legal and political activities of anti-evolutionists. Above the catacombs, that is, mainstream America went about its business unaware of the ongoing anti-evolution movement just out of sight, and assumed that it had been decisively defeated in Dayton.[48] This comforting assumption may be seen in the revival of interest in the Scopes trial as a metaphor for McCarthyism. While Darrow's defence of individual rights against Bryan's majoritarianism made Scopes an obvious analogue for those defending civil liberties against McCarthy's demagoguery, historical fidelity was willingly sacrificed in the effort to convert Scopes into a cautionary tale for the 1950s – and nowhere more influentially than in *Inherit the Wind*, the 1955 play by Jerome Lawrence and Robert E. Lee that became the 1960 movie starring Spencer Tracy and Fredric March. But the critical point here is that Fundamentalist anti-evolutionism could serve as a metaphor for McCarthyism only because it was no longer considered to be a danger in itself. This, in turn, testifies to how thoroughly and effectively Fundamentalists had separated themselves from mainstream American society by the 1950s. Anti-evolutionism was alive and flourishing in every Bible college and institute, in every Fundamentalist church and mission, and yet to mainstream America it seemed as historically remote as the Salem witchcraft trials that served a parallel symbolic function in Arthur Miller's *The Crucible* (1953).[49]

Chapter 12

Young-Earth Creationism

Anti-evolutionism refused to retire into allegorical status. Even as *Inherit the Wind* was playing in theatres across America, an Old Testament professor at an Indiana Fundamentalist seminary named John C. Whitcomb (b. 1924) and a hydraulic engineer at Virginia Polytechnic Institute named Henry M. Morris (b. 1918) were putting the finishing touches on *The Genesis Flood: The Biblical Record and its Scientific Implications* (1961), the book that opened a new phase in Bible believers' opposition to evolution.

Whitcomb and Morris wrote against Evangelical Christians who interpreted Scripture in such a way as to reconcile it with mainstream geological science and even a limited version of evolution. First among the offenders was the Baptist theologian Bernard Ramm, who, in works such as *The Christian View of Science and Scripture* (1955), combined 'progressive creationism' with a pictorial theory of the days of Genesis. His idea was that the creation narrative is a true record of Earth history but, as for Hugh Miller a century earlier, the days of Genesis should be understood not as six literal days of creation or even as six geological ages but as the six literal days over which Moses received visions revealing the divine work of creation. Since the days of Genesis thus refer to the revelation, not the work, of creation, Ramm argued that Christians should accept the millions of years of Earth history adduced by geologists as the setting for a progressive creationism whereby God intervenes in the natural order from time to time – as marked by gaps in the geological record – in order to create new 'root-species'.[1] Ramm's reconciliation model, according to which the profusion of species extant today is the result of evolution operating on the divinely created root-species, was welcomed by many science-minded Evangelicals. To Whitcomb and Morris, however, it was nothing more than a convoluted attempt to elude the plain-sense meaning of the Bible. For Whitcomb this was the beginning and end of discussion. Morris, however, was unwilling to concede that proper science could ever contradict the plain sense of Scripture; he therefore sought to oppose Ramm's science as well as his interpretation of the creation narrative. Morris turned first to the writings of the Presbyterian pastor and self-styled scientific authority Harry Rimmer (1890–1952), whose books had previously convinced the young Morris that evolution was false. Rimmer, though extremely popular among Fundamentalists, accepted an ancient Earth and taught the gap interpretation of the creation narrative. Morris, however, soon abandoned an ancient Earth – and therefore the need for any non-literal reading of Genesis – as a result of his life-changing encounter with a writer whom he discovered through Rimmer: George McCready Price.[2]

Price (1870–1963) was a Seventh-Day Adventist from the Canadian Maritimes whose 'Flood Geology' eventually became the principal expression of Adventist opposition to any scientific theory that demanded a non-literal interpretation of the days of creation. While early Fundamentalists had accepted non-literal readings of the creation narrative, Seventh-Day Adventists from the beginning were compelled to reject the day/age, gap, or any other interpretation allowing an ancient Earth because they read Genesis in light of visions received by their prophet, Ellen Gould White (1827–1915), of God creating the universe in six 24-hour days and resting on the seventh. Other visions had revealed to her the catastrophic nature of Noah's Flood, which had transformed the surface of the Earth and buried fossils.[3] Price, self-taught in geology, wrestled with geological evidence that seemed to argue so powerfully for an ancient Earth. In the end he remained faithful to Adventist teaching because he was able to convince himself that it was the uniformitarian and evolutionary *theories* of the geologists and not the *facts* of geology that opposed a literal reading of Genesis. His alternative Earth history, or Flood geology, remained true to White's visions by identifying the Flood as the principal geological agent responsible for the current appearance of the Earth. He called it the 'new catastrophism' in order to distinguish his single, universal Flood from the old catastrophism of Cuvier and Agassiz, according to which a series of revolutions had successively reshaped the Earth over millions of years. In the central matter of fossils, Price at first argued that their stratigraphy signified not an actual history of life but simply the differential settling of suddenly deceased life-forms according to their specific gravity during the Flood. Soon, however, he dispensed with the geological column altogether, and therefore with even the appearance of a history of life, on the basis of his (erroneous) interpretation of the geology of overthrust regions in the Rockies. Price's *The Fundamentals of Geology* (1913) announced his Law of Conformable Stratigraphical Sequence, which henceforth became the bedrock of his arguments: 'Any kind of fossiliferous rock may occur conformably on any other kind of fossiliferous rock, old or young.'[4]

Professional geologists ridiculed Flood geology. Price, however, kept the faith throughout his long life, sustained by his conviction that both the hostile reception of his work and his ultimate vindication were in fulfilment of biblical prophecy. The passage in question – 2 Peter 3:3–7 – is the same as that which Thomas Burnet had seized on in the seventeenth century. But whereas Burnet had used Peter's words in the latter two verses of the passage about the world that then perished in the Flood in order to justify the then-revolutionary idea that the present Earth has undergone radical change from its original state, Price pointed to Peter's warning in the first two verses that

> there shall come in the last days scoffers, walking after their own lusts, And saying, Where is the promise of his [Christ's second] coming? For since the fathers fell asleep, all things continue as they were from the beginning of the creation.

In his reading the verses that follow about scoffers being ignorant of how the world of old perished in a great Flood testify not to radical change of the Earth itself (which no one now doubted) but to the illegitimacy of uniformitarian geology and therefore of claims for an ancient Earth. The modern scientists who wilfully refuse to recognize the merits of Flood geology are none other than the scoffers of the Last Days foretold by Peter.[5]

Price's new catastrophism, with its young Earth, special creation in six literal days and fossil-forming Flood, at first made little headway among Fundamentalists, both because combating the higher criticism seemed more urgent than intramural debates over the correct interpretation of Genesis and because Fundamentalists were leery of Adventism in general and White's visions in particular. Nevertheless, by the early 1920s, as opposition to evolution rose to the top of their agenda, Fundamentalists began to give Flood geology a hearing and increasingly cited Price as a reliable scientific authority. William Jennings Bryan invited him to Dayton as an expert witness for the Scopes prosecution, although he had to decline since he was lecturing in England that summer. In retrospect, it is clear that in the 1920s Fundamentalist leaders like Bryan and William Bell Riley failed to recognize that Price's system was incompatible with their non-literal interpretations of the creation narrative; they thought of his Flood geology not as a rival interpretation of Genesis but simply as another weapon against evolutionists to be added to their armoury.[6]

The Genesis Flood

In converting to young-Earth creationism Henry Morris largely adopted Price's Flood geology. But while Price himself had not wanted to alienate his only supporters by pointing out the incompatibility of his system with the gap and day/age interpretations of Genesis favoured by Fundamentalists, the authors of *The Genesis Flood* revelled in polemic. Scorning the efforts of Evangelical thinkers such as Orr, Warfield and Ramm to reconcile the Bible with modern science as a 'chronicle of ... pervasive theological apostasy',[7] Whitcomb and Morris set a stark alternative before Bible-believing Christians: 'either the Biblical record of the Flood is false and must be rejected or else the system of historical geology which has seemed to discredit it is wrong and must be changed'.[8]

In their preface to *The Genesis Flood* the authors affirmed that the divinely inspired Bible has a clearly discernible meaning, and that there is an absolute correlation between the meaning of the Bible and Truth.[9] The inerrantist conviction that the Bible as God's inspired Word is authoritative on all subjects with which it deals underlies the authors' entire programme:

> Our main concern, as honest exegetes of the Word of God, must not be to find ways of making the Biblical narratives conform to modern scientific theories. Instead, our concern must be to discover exactly what God has said in the Scriptures, being fully aware of the fact that modern scientists, laboring under the handicap of non-Biblical philosophical presuppositions (such as materialism, organic evolution, and uniformitarianism), are in no position to give us an accurate reconstruction of the early history of the earth and its inhabitants.[10]

They did not wish to suggest, however, that Christians must reject all the accumulated data of geology and related sciences. Echoing Price, they distinguished facts from interpretation: 'It is not the facts of geology, but only certain interpretations of those facts, that are at variance with Scripture.'[11] Christians, therefore, require a means of interpreting the facts of geology independently of the unbiblical principles of uniformity and evolution. This is the task Whitcomb and Morris carried out in the rest of their book. (Morris, who was the senior of the two collaborators, wrote most of the sections dealing with scientific data and interpretations, while Whitcomb was responsible for presenting the biblical framework for creation and Earth history.)[12] They first demonstrated to their satisfaction the unbiblical and fallacious nature of the methods and conclusions of historical geology in light of the Bible's teaching, then offered young-Earth creationism as an alternative geological scheme that is both biblical and more truly scientific (in the Fundamentalists' peculiar understanding of science).

Young-Earth creationism interprets scientific data within a biblical framework that attributes geological agency to three primary events – creation, the Fall and the Flood – although it accepts that geological forces were at work in a relatively minor way in the period between the Fall and the Flood and in the centuries since the Flood. In their exposition of the biblical framework Whitcomb and Morris began with a plain-sense reading of the Genesis creation narrative, according to which in six 24-hour days, using methods unknown to us, God brought the universe and everything within it into being. Soil, plants, fish, birds, terrestrial animals and mankind were created from nothing and placed in an environment already perfectly adapted to them. Further – and here *The Genesis Flood* reproduced Philip Gosse's notion of mature creation, even though Gosse is not mentioned by name – they were created with the appearance of age. The first fruit trees, that is, were mature, fruit-bearing trees, not seeds; the land had fertile topsoil covering it; rocks possessed a variety of isotopes and elements, and so on. Given that God created the world with the appearance of age, the authors remarked, it is impossible for us to deduce the age or manner of creation by studying the laws of nature now in operation. The only way to learn about creation is through revelation from God.[13] It is fascinating to see a line of reasoning that met with devastating ridicule in 1857 Britain reappear in America in 1961.

Continuing with the biblical framework, the catastrophic events of the Fall and the Flood transformed the original form of the Earth. Adam and Eve's act of disobedience against God shattered the original harmony of creation and introduced sin, decay and death into the world. Not only humanity but all of creation henceforth must labour under the 'bondage of decay' and has ever since been 'groaning and travailing together in pain'.[14] Physical death, in this view, is a consequence of sin; the plain sense of the Bible is that there was no death in the world before the forbidden fruit was eaten. This is a critical point for young-Earth creationism because it establishes that Bible believers may be certain that all fossils, as the remains of once-living creatures, postdate the Fall. The fossil record therefore testifies to sin and death, not to the evolution of life. Morris and

Whitcomb made no attempt to refute scientifically palaeontological and palaeoanthropological evidence of the evolution and immense duration of the history of life; they simply dismissed it 'on the basis of overwhelming Biblical evidence'.[15] At other times, however, they endorsed science when they thought it supports biblical evidence for the effects of the Fall. *The Genesis Flood* and many subsequent works by Morris point to the First and Second Laws of Thermodynamics as the scientific reflections, respectively, of divine creation and of God's curse on the world because of sin. Morris's Museum of Creation and Earth History illustrates the principle of universal disorder, or the principle that all processes tend to go in the direction of increasing entropy, by means of a display case containing various objects in a state of decay, including a tarnished silver spoon, melted glass, photos of the sunken *Titanic* and a melted 45 rpm record ('Bad Luck' by Dale and Grace).

In sketching the world as it was between creation and the Flood, Morris and Whitcomb introduced the idea of a vapour canopy that had once surrounded the Earth. While this idea in part follows from the reference to 'the waters above the firmament' of Genesis 1:7, Whitcomb and Morris used it to provide a source for the waters of the Flood and to argue that it would have produced a benign and even climate on the antediluvian Earth through a greenhouse effect, which in turn, by protecting the early descendants of Adam from the harmful effects of cosmic radiation, would account for the longevity of the antediluvian patriarchs. Their use of science here directly parallels seventeenth-century sacred physics: as for Thomas Burnet and his contemporaries, their goal is to explicate scientifically the biblical narrative. Burnet, of course, lived before the birth of deep time; Morris and Whitcomb, in contrast, must not only explicate the biblical narrative but also elude scientific evidence for an ancient Earth. And here the idea of a vapour canopy served them magnificently by allowing them to contest the great ages produced by radiocarbon dating techniques. The canopy, they claimed, would have shielded the Earth from cosmic radiation and therefore reduced the amount of radiocarbon formed in the high atmosphere, which in turn would falsify radiometric techniques, which assume a constant ratio over time of radiocarbon to ordinary carbon.[16]

In the matter of the third great geological event, the Flood, Morris and Whitcomb made no attempt to convince scientists on geological grounds of the reality of a universal, catastrophic Flood roughly five to seven thousand years ago, but instead cited selectively chosen scientific data that seem to support an event whose reality is firmly established extra-scientifically by the evidence of the sixth and seventh chapters of Genesis and 2 Peter 3:6. They summarized the implications of the overwhelming biblical evidence for the Flood in two terse and polemical sentences:

> There is no escaping the conclusion that, if the Bible is true and if the Lord Jesus Christ possessed divine omniscience, the Deluge was the most significant event, geologically speaking, that has ever occurred on the earth since its creation. *Any true science of historical geology must necessarily give a prominent place in its system to this event.*[17]

The Genesis Flood proclaimed that the evidence of the Bible conclusively shows that the Earth is young, that sin predates death, and that the great Flood was a worldwide cataclysm. Since all true science must conform to these facts, historical geology and evolutionary biology must be false. And not only are they scientifically false, they are spiritually lethal. Throughout his creationist career Morris has preached the catastrophic spiritual consequences of not accepting young-Earth creationism, consequences he summed up in a 2000 tract entitled 'The Vital Importance of Believing in Recent Creation'. Without special creation and a young Earth, God cannot be the personal, loving, omniscient, omnipotent, holy, righteous God depicted in the Bible because a God of grace and mercy would never have created the groaning, suffering, dying world implied in the millions of years required for evolution. Similarly, if the Bible is wrong on matters of science and history, how can we trust it in matters of salvation, heaven and everlasting life? Further, the Gospel of Mark tells us that Jesus Christ taught that God 'from the beginning of the creation made them male and female' (Mark 10:6) and elsewhere the Bible reveals that before becoming our Saviour Christ was our Creator (John 1:1–3; Colossians 1:16). Now, if human beings came into existence only millions of years after the beginning of the creation, how can we possibly believe that Christ, who was ignorant of this, was our Creator? And finally, if death is not the wages of sin, then Christ's death on the cross was unnecessary. If the Bible is wrong about creation and about the meaning of Christ's death, how can we trust its prophecies and promises concerning future salvation or its claim that Christ is our Saviour? The tract concludes:

> If suffering and death in the world – especially the suffering and death of Christ – are not the result of God's judgment on sin in the world, then the most reasonable inference is that the God of the Bible does not exist. The slippery slope of compromise finally ends in the dark chasm of atheism, at least for those who travel to its logical termination.[18]

It was these theological difficulties within a biblical inerrantist worldview that years earlier had made Morris a young-Earth creationist; scientific evidence had nothing to do with it.[19] His faith in the literal truth of the New Testament claims for Jesus and about the end-times explains his insistence on a literal interpretation of the first chapters of Genesis. In *The Genesis Flood* Whitcomb and Morris confronted Christians with biblical citations demonstrating that Jesus repeatedly upheld the historical accuracy of the Old Testament in general and of Genesis in particular.[20] Throughout his subsequent career Morris has linked trust in the historical veracity of the creation narrative to faith in the historical reality of the prophecy of the end-times in Revelation. The truthfulness and accuracy of the cosmological and human history narrated in Genesis and other books of the Old Testament guarantees that Revelation is a true and accurate prophecy of things to come. In his books, videos and lectures Morris frequently alludes to his faith that the Second Coming of Christ will occur very soon.[21]

A science of the catacombs

The Genesis Flood became a best-seller in the Fundamentalist world and polarized Evangelical opinion. While university scientists and liberal Christians ignored it completely, Evangelical thinkers with some knowledge of mainstream geology, such as Ramm and J. R. van de Fliert of the Free University of Amsterdam, denounced it as a pseudo-scientific travesty.[22] On the other side of the ledger, however, young-Earth creationism was enormously successful at the grassroots level in Fundamentalist churches and schools. The key question posed by the phenomenon of *The Genesis Flood* is why young-Earth creationism became dominant among Bible believers only after 1960 when biblical inerrancy had been basic to Fundamentalism from the beginning. There are two elements to the answer. The first is that young-Earth creationism better defended a plain-sense reading of the inerrant Bible than did the old-Earth creationism of Ramm and the earlier Fundamentalists, whose reconciliation schemes appealed to the authority of science as well as of Scripture. The great advantage, within the Fundamentalist world, held by young-Earth creationists is that they appeal only to the plain-sense meaning of the Bible, and hence can always present themselves as truer to the Bible than the reconcilers.[23] Legions of Bible believers responded gratefully to Whitcomb and Morris because their system eliminated once and for all the need for interpretative contortions that twist and bend the words of the Bible in order to reconcile them with the findings of modern science. The second element is that three decades of separatism had produced a generation of Fundamentalists almost entirely ignorant of modern-day historical geology and evolutionary science. Even the increase among Fundamentalists of scientific and technological credentials as a result of the national expansion of physical science and technology education in the 1960s produced very few Fundamentalists trained in geology or the life sciences.[24] Morris himself, though assumed by Fundamentalists to be a respected scientist, holds no credentials in geology, evolutionary biology or any related historical science; his training was in hydrology.

These two elements reveal young-Earth creationism to be a science of the catacombs. I mean by this that its origin and success are explicable only in light of the separatism that from the late 1920s protected the inerrant Bible by isolating Fundamentalists from intellectual modernity, including the historical sciences. Just as Fundamentalism itself is a reactive movement and not simply traditionalist, so young-Earth creationism, while no doubt believed unreflectively by most Christians prior to the nineteenth century, arose as a self-conscious movement in the twentieth century from the reaction of defenders of the inerrancy and perspicuity of the Bible against modernity. In Morris' words:

> Those of us who still believe not only that the Bible is the inerrant Word of God, but also that God intended it to be understood by ordinary people (not just by scholarly specialists in science or theology) have been labeled 'young-earth creationists'.[25]

Philip Gosse had similarly defended a plain-sense reading of an infallible Bible, and the young-Earth creationism of *The Genesis Flood* strongly resembles that of *Omphalos*. Gosse faced ridicule because the audience of educated Christians for whom he was writing no longer accepted his rigorous biblicism and therefore found laughable his attempt to explain away the scientific evidence of deep time. Whitcomb and Morris shared Gosse's biblicism because as a consequence of the flourishing of reactionary biblicism in America during the intervening century the Fundamentalist plain-sense reading of an inerrant Bible closely resembles the interpretative practice of Gosse's Plymouth Brethren. Unlike Gosse, however, Whitcomb and Morris were not writing for a general educated audience but for fellow Bible believers. Fundamentalist separatism had created in mid-twentieth-century America a mass audience receptive to young-Earth creationism such as had not existed in mid-nineteenth-century Britain.

One further element, this time external to Fundamentalism, contributing to the success of *The Genesis Flood* was another twist in the tortuous relationship between evolution and American textbook publishers. In the decades since the Scopes trial high school biology textbooks had progressively diluted and even deleted altogether their treatment of evolution so that by the early 1950s some of the most widely used high school biology textbooks made no mention of Darwin or evolution whatsoever. The situation changed suddenly and dramatically as America awakened to the Soviet challenge to its scientific leadership. Even as Sputnik, the first artificial satellite, circled the Earth, the American government took steps to improve scientific education. One concrete result was the commissioning of the prestigious Biological Science Curriculum Study (BSCS) in 1959 with a mandate to produce high school biology textbooks that placed evolution at the centre of the biological sciences. BSCS textbooks were soon in wide use all over America, including those in regions of the country where Fundamentalists dominated. The Cold War, short, terminated the unofficial post-Scopes truce and evolution, including human evolution, once again confronted high school students, their parents and their pastors. Whitcomb and Morris produced their book independently of these events, but it appeared at precisely the right moment to capitalize on Fundamentalist outrage over the BSCS textbooks.[26]

This explanation in terms of biblicism and separatism was not, of course, how Whitcomb and Morris understood either the success of their work among Fundamentalists or opposition to it among non-Bible believers. They offered instead a biblical explanation: whereas true believers humbly accept the evidence of the Bible and therefore freely accept young-Earth creationism, the biblical teaching of a divine judgement on human sin and rebellion profoundly offends the intellectual and moral pride of modern men and women, who then grasp hold of the unbiblical doctrine of evolution in order to try to escape from personal responsibility toward their Creator and from the 'way of the Cross'.[27] The underlying assumption here is that modern men and women still think in terms of the biblical framework, only they reject the Bible's teaching, rather than that they have ceased to think biblically altogether. Whitcomb and Morris, as inerrantists, equate the meaning of the Bible with truth. Evangelical Christians like Ramm agree that the meaning of the Bible corresponds to truth, but quarrel with young-Earth creationists over whether the meaning of Genesis is its plain sense or some figurative one. The non-biblicist alternative is to agree with the Fundamentalists on the plain-sense meaning of Genesis but to deny that it corresponds to the truth, thus making the Bible irrelevant to science. This, of course, has been the modern view ever since the rise of the higher criticism. Whitcomb and Morris, however, seem unable even to conceive of the non-biblicist alternative. They elude this unthinkable thought by providing a biblical explanation for those who refuse to think biblically. In their scenario, which exemplifies the characteristic 'us versus them' mentality of Fundamentalism, humanity throughout history has been divided between two basic philosophies or religions. One, biblical Christianity, is oriented toward God and teaches the fundamental truths of creation, the Fall, the Flood, the Incarnation, and salvation through the atoning death and resurrection of Jesus Christ. The other, oriented toward humanity, appears in an almost infinite variety of forms but always supposes that human beings are spiritually, intellectually and morally self-sufficient. Even where the idea of divinity is accommodated in the system, it is somehow subordinate to the system as a whole, perhaps as pantheism or as the highest development of humanity itself. Common to all forms of the second basic religious and philosophic system, from ancient idolatries and primitive animism to modern existentialism and atheistic communism, is the idea of development, of growth, of progress, of improvement – of, in short, evolution.[28] Seen in this perspective, the modern historical sciences of geology and evolutionary biology are properly understood as late varieties of the human-centred ideology that has been the rival of biblical religion since earliest days. God, of course, is the author of biblical religion, whereas the human-centred religions and philosophies and the idea of evolution that sustains them have their source in the pride and selfishness of human beings and ultimately in the pride and deception of Satan himself.[29]

Morris further developed this scenario, in which evolution is understood in terms of the age-old warfare between God and Satan, in various subsequent works, notably *The Troubled Waters of Evolution* (1974) and *The Long War Against God* (1989), and it features prominently at the Museum of Creation and Earth History. In these works Morris provides a very different context for Darwin's *Origin of Species* than the one sketched in Chapter 8 of this book. In Darwin's day, Morris begins, Satan was particularly active, as evidenced by the widespread revival of ancient demonism known to his contemporaries as Spiritualism. Darwin himself was not a Spiritualist, but Alfred Russel Wallace was. Further, Morris continues, Wallace was extensively influenced by the beliefs of the animistic tribes among whom he pursued his botanical researches. The theory of evolution by natural selection that Darwin had hitherto been unable to formulate even after twenty years and with all the advantages of living at the centre of the scientific establishment of the day came to Wallace in the Malaysian jungle as he lay in his hammock in the grip of a fever-induced fit. Wallace's letter to Darwin announcing his discovery pushed him into publishing the *Origin of Species*. Wallace's Spiritualism, animistic contacts, and the trance in which he hit upon the theory all point, in Morris's view, to its true source and nature: Satan communicated the theory of evolution to Wallace through demonic spirits in order to cause Darwin to publish the book that loosed upon the world Satan's greatest weapon in his long war against God.[30]

And yet, Morris does not consider Darwin and Wallace's theory of evolution to be anything new. There were many evolutionists before them, including Lamarck and Darwin's grandfather Erasmus Darwin (to whom Morris wrongly attributes evolution *by natural selection*).[31] These earlier evolutionists, in turn, had simply temporalized the Great Chain of Being, which itself derived, via the Middle Ages and certain Church Fathers, from Neoplatonism and the evolutionist philosophies of ancient Greece and Rome.[32] From there, Morris traces the true origin of the evolutionary idea to the poetry of Homer and Hesiod (which, he notes, is remarkably similar to the cosmologies of other ancient peoples), and then to the source of the Greeks themselves: the myths of the Babylonians. At this point Morris pauses to note that we do not have much evidence about Babylon – except from the Bible! Genesis 10–11 tells us that the Babylon of Nimrod, who was the first great emperor of the world after the Flood, was the radiating centre of error. All the non-biblical cosmologies of the world derive from the Babylonian idea, enshrined in the *Enuma elish*, that the world itself is ultimate reality and that all things developed from a watery chaos.[33]

In this manner Morris traces evolutionism – or, the denial of a transcendent personal God as Creator of all things – back to an ancient Sumerian ideology according to which spirits – associated with the stars, personified as gods and goddesses, and worshipped at the Tower of Babel – controlled the various forces of nature and had 'evolved' all things into their present form. Morris's term for this system of evolutionary pantheism, which subsumes polytheism, astrology, spiritism and idolatry, is 'animism', which he defines as the very widespread worshipful belief in spirits that inhabit objects and natural phenomena. In Morris's use, however, the term has a negative rather than a positive content – it simply signifies 'non-biblical'. Morris identifies animism as the foundation of all religions and philosophies except for biblical religion: it is at the core of the religions of uncivilized tribes, of the mythologies of ancient civilizations, of Aztec and Inca religion, of Buddhism, Hinduism, Confucianism, and Shinto, of modern atheistic philosophies, and, of course, of Darwinian evolution.[34] Moreover, all these religions and philosophies belong to a single historical lineage. When post-diluvial humanity was scattered over the world following God's destruction of the Tower of Babel, the various groups of humans carried with them to their new homes the Babylonian religion and from it developed all subsequent forms of evolutionary pantheism.

The Babylonian cosmogony therefore underlies the human-centred religions and philosophies that constitute the second of the two mutually exclusive worldviews between which humanity is divided. But is Babylon the ultimate source of the idea of evolution? Was Nimrod its originator? Morris's answer to both questions is 'No'; Nimrod learned about evolution from the same source as Alfred Russel Wallace: Satan. Morris's final explanation of evolution shows that the idea of evolution is intimately connected with the circumstances of Satan's rebellion against God (and as such is the first non-biblical idea ever conceived). Once Satan's pride had driven him to rebel against God in order that he might usurp his place he had to refute the depiction in the Word of God itself of God as the Creator of all things or else his rebellion could not be justified. So, needing an alternative creation narrative (or philosophy of origins), Satan constructed one from his own experience (Satan the empiricist!). When he had first come into existence he had found himself in a watery chaos. God's spirit began to move over the face of the waters and an ordered creation soon came into being. Satan concluded that all things, including himself, God's spirit, and God, had simply emerged from the watery chaos and evolved into the profusion of life. The idea of evolution, the original lie, was the necessary self-deception by which the Father of Lies eluded the true history contained in the Word of God.[35]

Morris's purpose in constructing this genealogy of deceit is to provide a biblical explanation for those who refuse to think biblically. But two further points are worthy of notice. The first is that Morris dismisses evidence from the modern disciplines of ancient history, archaeology, comparative religion, linguistics and so on. He insists (echoing Isaac Newton's seventeenth-century view) that the only *real* history is that documented by written sources and therefore it only covers the past few thousand years; all evidence for earlier human history is based on the unprovable assumptions of the evolutionists. There is, however, one historical source that does predate the earliest human writings and is absolutely reliable: the written Word of God himself in Genesis.[36] Just as true science for creationists is that which is compatible with the biblical evidence of the early cosmological chapters of Genesis, so true ancient history is that which is compatible with the biblical evidence of chapters 10 and 11 of Genesis. Creationists oppose the historical human sciences as unbiblical in precisely the same way that they oppose historical geology and evolutionary biology. The second point is that while Darwin's theory of evolution by natural selection was revolutionary because it overthrew teleological models of development, Morris assimilates Darwinian evolution to any and all developmentalisms simply on the grounds that they are all unbiblical. The fact that this common element is so critical for Morris that it overrules distinctions among versions of evolutionism explains why creationist tracts often conflate Darwinian evolution with Lamarckism, Social Darwinism, Haeckel's biogenetic law, New Age ameliorism and other developmentalist ideologies.

Creation evangelism

Young-Earth creationism is for Henry Morris a version of natural theology. This is the basis for the creationist ministry to which he has devoted himself since the publication of *The Genesis Flood*. Creation evangelism, as he calls his version of natural theology, testifies to God the Creator through the study of his works as a means of reaching people who do not accept the testimony of the Bible. Its biblical warrant is Paul's appeal in Acts 17:23–28 to the Athenians' instinctive and traditional knowledge of the Creator in order to prepare them to receive the gospel. In the past, Morris says, natural theology served to convert the ancient pagans and modern tribal peoples; today, it brings knowledge of the true God to university campuses.[37]

Having decided that the most effective means of creation evangelism would be research and education rather than traditional preaching, Morris, along with nine other science-minded conservative Evangelical Christians, founded the

Creation Research Society in 1963. Membership in the CRS was limited to individuals holding post-graduate degrees in the natural sciences, medicine and engineering (in fact, virtually none of its members held degrees in the historical sciences). The CRS protected itself against the infiltration of evolutionary ideas that had corrupted other Evangelical science bodies (notably, the American Scientific Affiliation) by requiring members to sign a 'statement of faith' affirming belief in the historical truth of the plain-sense meaning of Genesis, the fixity of species, and the universality of the Flood. Acknowledging that 'creation research' strictly speaking is impossible because nobody was there to observe the divine act of creation, Society members instead devoted themselves to researching evidence of God's creative activity. At first their research consisted primarily of library work in which they scanned scientific journals for anything that might be used to cast doubt on the findings of historical geology and evolutionary biology; later, as finances improved, they carried out field studies designed to produce evidence supporting a catastrophic universal Flood or in some other way fitting scientific data into the biblical framework of creation, the Fall and the Flood. The CRS publicized members' research through its journal, the *Creation Science Research Quarterly*, books and tracts, and textbooks, notably *Biology: A Search for Order in Complexity* (1971) for high schools.[38]

In 1970 Morris decided that he was called to devote himself full-time to creation evangelism. He resigned his position at Virginia Tech and moved to California in order to establish a centre for creation research as part of Christian Heritage College, a Bible college near San Diego recently founded by the Baptist pastor and prominent Fundamentalist Tim LaHaye (later famous as the theological framer of the 'Left Behind' series of Rapture novels). Morris set up the Creation Science Research Center in partnership with the mother-and-son team of Nell and Kelly Segraves. Morris and his allies very soon came to distrust the Segraves' tactics and their competence to speak for creation science. In the resulting schism the Segraves faction, who retained the right to the name Creation Science Research Center, set up on its own but soon became marginal within creation science. Morris, for his part, reorganized those loyal to him as the research division of Christian Heritage College under the name of the Institute for Creation Research. The ICR, which became autonomous in 1981 and moved to its own quarters in Santee, California, quickly became the leading voice of young-Earth creationism and a powerful force within Fundamentalism.[39] The mission of the ICR 'is to bring the field of education – and then our whole world insofar as possible – back to the foundational truth of special creation and primeval history as revealed first in Genesis and further emphasized throughout the Bible', or, in the pithy formulation printed as a footer to the main text of the tracts in the ICR's 'Back to Genesis' series: 'We believe God has raised up ICR to spearhead Biblical Christianity's defense against the godless dogma of evolutionary humanism.'[40] The ICR carries out this mission through a threefold ministry of research, writing and speaking, funded by donations, staff honoraria and royalties from institute publications.[41]

Like the CRS, the ICR at first engaged primarily in literature reviews, and then increasingly in field studies as finances permitted. Representative ICR research projects include: exploration of Mount St Helens and Spirit Lake in Washington State for evidence of rapid sediment layering and canyon erosion, rapid formation of 'fossil forests', and rapid formation of future coal seams; exploration of the Grand Canyon for evidence of rapid formation of its component formations and rapid cutting of the Canyon itself; determination of anomalous and fallacious radiometric 'ages' of Grand Canyon formations; search for remains of Noah's Ark on Mount Ararat; study of anomalous fossils, especially the allegedly contemporaneous human and dinosaur footprints near Glen Rose, Texas; exploration of alleged fault thrusts; and computer modelling of the antediluvian vapour canopy.[42] The ICR's writing ministry began with its monthly newsletter, *Acts & Facts*, and quickly expanded. A recent publications catalogue lists over two hundred books and monographs by ICR staff and allied authors, plus children's books, textbooks, tracts, videotapes and DVDs, and software reference databases. ICR staff members follow an active speaking schedule. They give public lectures, offer seminars such as the enormously successful 'Back to Genesis' series that the ICR publishes as tracts in print and online, run summer institutes, and participate in debates with evolutionists on university campuses.[43] Duane Gish, one of Morris's early recruits to the ICR, specializes in such debates, a form of evangelization dear to creationists because the format fits their either/or model of the world and allows them to attack evolutionary accounts for alleged scientific weaknesses before scientifically ill-informed audiences while leaving their evolutionist opponent insufficient time to take the audience through the steps needed to respond with a scientifically adequate answer.[44]

The ICR does not participate in the culture of mainstream science (that is, of godless evolutionary humanism). Its staff members do not submit their work to peer review journals, they do not seek funding from the National Science Foundation or other standard granting bodies, and they do not participate in collaborative research with non-Fundamentalist scientists. While these practices, of course, guarantee their isolation from mainstream science, the mission of the ICR is not to convert scientists to young-Earth creationism but to recall Christians to the plain sense of the inerrant Bible. The work of the ICR – research, writing, speaking – is directed at the general public.

The Museum of Creation and Earth History, located next door to the ICR's offices in Santee, exemplifies the creation evangelism to which the ICR is dedicated. Biblical proof-texts anchor the Museum's professional-looking science and history exhibits to the framework of creation, the Fall and the Flood. The point is continually driven home that failure to accept the plain-sense meaning of the biblical testimony on creation and Earth history means renouncing hope in the Bible's promise of salvation through Christ. The corridor devoted to the Ice Age may serve as a sample of the Museum's approach. The corridor is painted light blue, moulded sheets of ice creep up the wall, and ice stalactites hang down from the ceiling; the sound of whistling wind from an audio speaker adds to the sense of bleakness. Several 'Notes' placed at intervals along the corridor interpret the scene for visitors: for hundreds of years after the Flood the world continued to be shaken by massive volcanic eruptions and earthquakes, causing severe and erratic weather patterns; in some regions this worldwide instability resulted in cold temperatures and constant snowfall – in short, an ice age (Morris thinks that most likely the Earth has endured only one period of glaciation). *The Genesis Flood* had described the evidence for one recent ice age and attributed it to the catastrophe of the Flood.[45] In the years following its publication, and apparently stung by criticism from fellow Evangelicals that in accepting a period of glaciation he was going beyond the biblical evidence,[46] Morris worked up a biblical warrant for an ice age from the book of Job. As a Fundamentalist, Morris, like William Bell Riley before him, considers Job to be both a true record of a real person who lived in northern Arabia soon after the Flood and a reliable textbook of scientific knowledge. More specifically, noting that there are more references to cold, snow and ice in Job than in any other book of the Bible, Morris identifies Job as an eyewitness to the environmental conditions during the Ice Age and the book as legitimating the incorporation of an ice age into the biblical framework of Earth history.[47] At the Museum citations from Job serve as proof-texts for the Ice Age exhibit.

The next display presents the consequences of the Ice Age for the Earth and for human life. Its intent is to undermine geological and palaeontological evidence for an ancient Earth and ancient hominids. Brief 'Notes' point out that glaciation on a scale unknown today may well have disrupted natural processes – from the formation of tree rings to the production and decay of carbon-14 – cited by evolutionists as evidence for an immense age of the Earth. Visitors are similarly informed that the Ice Age provided the environmental context for the scattering of human groups after the Flood and particularly after the Tower of Babel as recounted in Genesis 11. On the one hand, the lower water levels caused by imprisonment of large amounts of ocean water in massive glaciers assisted the spread of human beings across the globe. On the other, some of the migrating groups found themselves living in extremely harsh conditions. Morris suggests that some such groups – among them the Neanderthals – adapted to the cold and physically resembled modern Inuit (obviously, by 'adapted' he does not mean evolved). Other groups, faring poorly in the struggle for scarce resources, retreated into caves, where, malnourished and having lost the use of technology, they degenerated both physically and culturally into 'cave men' (Morris is probably thinking of the Cro-Magnons). Far from representing extinct lines of hominid evolution, these cave men, who were still alive in Job's day (Morris's proof-text is Job 30:1–8), were, like Vico's *bestioni*, degenerate human beings descended from Adam and Eve whose dismal existence is to be explained within and by the Earth history set out in Genesis.

The ICR is the flagship of young-Earth creation evangelism, but it hardly sails alone. In 1989 Morris himself estimated that worldwide there were at least one hundred creationist associations,[48] and since then the creationist armada of organizations, institutes, magazines, museums, radio and cable television programmes, summer camps, science fairs, and, above all, websites, has only swelled in size. A separatist creation-science world parallels mainstream science and science education, just as a separatist world of Fundamentalist churches and schools parallels mainstream worship and education.[49]

Chapter 13

CREATION SCIENCE

Henry Morris and his fellow labourers in the creationist vineyard regard creation evangelism as something other than biblical testimony – something they came to call scientific creationism or creation science. Whether or not creation science truly is something other than biblical testimony is the subject of this chapter.

The classic statement of creation science is a volume prepared by Morris with contributions from other Insitute for Creation Research staff members, *Scientific Creationism* (1974, 2nd edn 1985). We shall turn to this work in a moment, but it is worth noting that the framework for creation science was set out in the prefaces to *The Genesis Flood* itself. There Whitcomb and Morris made four points: the historical sciences are not true science and evolution is an assumption about origins that is not susceptible of genuine scientific proof because extrapolation of present processes into the unobservable prehistoric past is not really science; creationism is another assumption about origins, based on the Bible; true science shows overwhelming support for the creationist viewpoint, thereby supporting the creationist assumption about origins; and the real issue, in any case, is not the correctness of the interpretation of various details of the geological data but simply what God has revealed in his Word concerning the origin of humanity and the universe.[1]

The two-model strategy

The Genesis Flood simply presented young-Earth creationism; in *Scientific Creationism* Morris and his colleagues distinguish between 'scientific creationism', or the evaluation of the physical evidence relating to creation without referring to the Bible or other religious authorities, and 'biblical creationism', or the framework of creation, the Fall and the Flood set out in Genesis 1–11. The two versions of *Scientific Creationism* correspond to this distinction: the Public School Edition purports to show how scientific evidence supports creationism rather than evolution, while the General Edition adds a concluding chapter laying out the biblical model as the context for understanding the scientific evidence.[2] Morris formally introduces the two-model strategy in Chapter 1 of both editions. It is impossible, he says, to prove scientifically any particular concept of origins because the scientific method is experimental observation and repeatability and a scientific investigator can neither observe nor repeat origins. This being so, a better approach would be to think in terms of conceptual frameworks within which one tries to correlate and predict observable data. The *evolution model* and the *creation model* are alternative models of origins that can be compared as to their respective capacities for correlating scientific data.[3] The following six chapters of *Scientific Creationism* (comprising the balance of the Public School Edition) attack the evolution model as not truly scientific and as riddled with guesses, errors and inconsistencies, while showing how selected scientific data align with the creation model. Science, Morris declares, means 'knowledge', and knowledge is restricted to what we have observed. Since written records date back at most to four to six thousand years ago, and since 'no one can *know* what happened before there were people to observe and record what happened', there can be no scientific knowledge of events prior to the first human records.[4] In attempting to demonstrate the guesses, errors and inconsistencies of the evolution model Morris repeatedly returns to four basic claims already made in *The Genesis Flood*: the radiometric and other dating techniques that give an immense age to the universe, the Earth and life are mere guesses since nobody was around to confirm that the assumptions on which they are built held true in the prehistoric past; the basic laws of physics, and particularly the First and Second Laws of thermodynamics, flatly contradict the evolution model, while the principles of mathematical probability demonstrate its astronomical unlikeliness; and evolutionists frequently disagree with each other, thereby proving that what they have to offer is not science but opinion. The creation model, for its part, while necessarily a model of origins rather than true science, is shown to be more compatible with scientific data than the evolution model. Creationism, in short, is not science but it is scientifically acceptable and indeed scientifically superior to the evolution model of origins.

Morris's assertion in the General Edition that 'the real factual record is in the Bible, and that is the subject of our final chapter' signals the transition from scientific creationism to biblical creationism. Here we are told that the early chapters of Genesis are the true record (written by patriarchal eyewitnesses and by God himself) of the facts of the primeval history of the universe and of humanity, which science is unable to determine, and at the same time an intellectually satisfying framework within which to interpret the facts which science can determine. Inasmuch as the historical accuracy and divine inspiration of Genesis is affirmed in other books of the Bible and accepted by all the writers of the New Testament and by Jesus Christ himself, Morris concludes, 'man should bow before its Author in believing obedience, acknowledging that He has clearly spoken, in words that are easy to be understood, concerning those things which man could never discover for himself'.[5]

Sleight of hand

The arguments contained in *Scientific Creationism* concerning radiometric dating techniques, the laws of thermodynamics, evidence from mathematical probability, and many, many others are, as has been shown repeatedly by scientists and philosophers of science, either misinterpretations or simply false. The specific scientific claims of creation science are in fact techniques of distraction, akin to a magician's coloured handkerchiefs, puffs of smoke and the attractions of his beautiful assistant; they are designed to direct attention away from the sleight of hand by which creationists substitute biblicism for science. Bluntly, creation science is a travesty of genuine science. It would take many books to demonstrate this statement; happily, many have been written.[6] Rather than repeat in detail the refutations of creation science by scientists and philosophers of science (important as they are), I wish instead to examine the sleight-of-hand by which creation science gives the illusion that it is something other than biblical testimony. The first step is to examine the creationists' understanding of the nature of the historical sciences.

Morris's insistence that true science is limited to what we have directly observed perpetuates the Baconian claims of early Fundamentalists. William Bell Riley, we recall from Chapter 11, defined science as knowledge gained and verified by exact observation and correct thinking. He excluded evolutionary theories from the rolls of true science on the grounds that they were nothing more than unverified – and unverifiable – speculations about the past. All historical so-called sciences fail to meet the inductive test because, in the absence of direct observation of what happened in the past, they are necessarily hypothetical. Fundamentalists' insistence that true science is inductive locates their understanding of science as an artefact of the mid-nineteenth century. Darwin's contemporaries, as we saw in Chapter 8, invoked Bacon in their criticism of the theory of evolution by natural selection as not inductive because it is based on speculative assumptions instead of facts. William Whewell, the idealist philosopher of science, offered a more sophisticated argument that conceded the appropriateness of hypothesis in science but demanded that permissible hypotheses not conflict with knowledge established extra-scientifically. In practice, this meant that science must not contradict truths revealed in the Bible and must point to God as the final cause of all natural phenomena. Twenty-first-century Fundamentalists perpetuate Whewell's idealist model of science, even to the point of allowing some carefully restricted hypothesizing, but have narrowed the scope of true science even further by insisting that it is the plain-sense meaning of the inerrant Bible that must not be contradicted, whereas mid-nineteenth-century idealists commonly interpreted the Genesis cosmological narratives figuratively as permitting an ancient Earth. In the hands of Fundamentalists, then, the insistence that true science is inductive has become a protective strategy designed to safeguard not just the Bible but the plain-sense meaning of an inerrant Bible. The nineteenth-century figure closest to the Fundamentalists in this sense is Philip Gosse – and this is as we would expect, given that Gosse shared their commitment to biblical inerrancy and the plain-sense meaning of Scripture.

Darwin opposed to Whewell's idealist understanding of science his own empiricist understanding in which hypotheses guide science and the only restriction placed on them is that they be capable of being tested by empirical evidence. Science, in this view, is a self-sufficient intellectual endeavour in that empirical evidence alone can disprove a hypothesis. Philosophically, the empirical understanding of science cannot be proven to be true and the idealist one false, but Darwin recognized that questions which cannot be resolved empirically must be left (perhaps temporarily) unresolved; appealing to a supernatural final cause stops science in its tracks. Specifically, while he could not prove experimentally either the transformation of one species into another or descent by modification, and while he conceded that he could not explain the origin of the variations on which natural selection works (although he was confident that there was undoubtedly a scientific explanation for it), his theory of evolution by natural selection made sense of a great deal of evidence about the resemblances and differences among animals and their historical and geographical distribution. As such, it deserved consideration as science.

Modern science endorses Darwin's position, both the general empiricist understanding of science and the particular claim for the scientific status of his theory of evolution by natural selection. 'Theories' or hypotheses are not mere guesses and do not stand in opposition to 'facts'. Scientific theories are intellectual structures that explain facts, while 'facts' are data about the world acquired through empirical observation (even facts about the world, as opposed to logical facts, are not absolutely certain, but rather overwhelmingly likely). Theories are never proven in an absolute sense; they are tested by means of available evidence and either confirmed or disconfirmed to varying degrees of confidence. To say that a scientific theory is true is to say that it is thoroughly confirmed by all available empirical evidence. That scientists as scientists never speak of absolute Truth but only of truths that may at some later date be overturned is not philosophical relativism, but rather the consequence of the empirical nature of science.[7] Similarly, no theory – and certainly no scientist – is treated as inerrant. Theories are tested by being confronted with new data or with alternative explanations for existing data. What makes science science is not this or that conclusion about the world but the method used to reach the conclusion. Morris's remark in a videotape lecture that science used to say that the Earth has been proved to be two billion years old but now we are told that it has been proved to be 4.6 billion years old is meant to show that science is unreliable because it contradicts itself.[8] But this view (aside from its confusion over the nature of proof in science) mistakes science for a fixed body of statements about the world rather than a method of investigation.

The modern understanding of the nature of science has important consequences for the creationist claim that no one has observed evolution occur. As the National Academy of Sciences points out in their booklet on *Science and Creationism*, this claim

> misses the point about how science tests hypotheses. We don't see the Earth going around the sun or the atoms that make up matter. We 'see' their consequences. Scientists infer that atoms exist and the Earth revolves because they have tested predictions derived from these concepts by extensive observation and experimentation.[9]

Rational inference, that is, is part of science (and note that it is part of physics as much as of evolutionary science). When Henry Morris says that 'though it is important to have a philosophy of origins, it can only be achieved by faith, not by sight' because scientific proof of either model is impossible since no one was there to observe the origin of the universe and life,[10] his either/or contrast between faith and direct observation suppresses the third option of rational inference and does so because rational inference has been pre-emptively ruled out by the Fundamentalists' Baconian definition of science.

Scientists operating with the empiricist understanding of science have been deeply engaged with Darwin's theory of evolution by natural selection. They do not, of course, regard either the man or the theory as inerrant. From the synthesis with genetics in the 1930s to recent research in molecular biology, new developments in the biological sciences have advanced evolutionary theory well beyond the place where Darwin left it in the *Origin of Species* (and in the process vastly expanded the scope of its explanatory and unifying power). On the other hand, scientists have not ceased to challenge the efficacy of the mechanism of natural selection by testing it against alternative or supplementary mechanisms. Meanwhile, neo-Darwinism continues to unify new areas of science and to generate research programmes. Contrary to the claims of Fundamentalists who interpret these challenges as proof that evolutionary theory is guesswork riddled with inconsistencies, all life scientists accept the fact of evolution as one of the most firmly established facts of biology, and arguments among them over the mechanism, timing or rates by which it operates are the normal activities of men and women engaged in the empirical exploration of the natural world.

Creation science, on the other hand, neither meets the standard of science nor is scientifically acceptable. First of all, since creation science does not commit itself to any hypothesis about how creation occurred (indeed it forbids any such hypotheses since the means of creation is unknowable), it offers no theories to test against empirical data and therefore no research programmes. Second, creation science claims that the evidence provided by true science supports the Genesis account. We have already noted that creationists' understanding of science is hopelessly flawed and that their scientific arguments are nonsense. The point to be added here is that creationists reverse the direction of proof. Whereas science begins with a problem and works toward a rational explanation by means of hypotheses and empirical testing, creation science begins with the Truth and looks for empirical evidence confirming what believers already know. Because creation science rests on the inerrant authority of the Bible rather than on the conditional, corrigible, empirically tested authority of science, what will count as true science is predetermined: true science will be that which can be made to support the cosmogonic framework of creation in six days, the Fall and a worldwide Flood. *Dirk Gently's Holistic Detective Agency*, the novel by Douglas Adams, provides an analogy to the creationists' logic. A character in the novel, Gordon Way, recognizes that computer programs designed to help decision-making by organizing and analysing relevant facts are seriously flawed in that the conclusion to which the programs direct one is often not the conclusion one wants to reach. Way becomes extremely wealthy by inventing a back-to-front program in which one specifies in advance the conclusion one wishes to reach and the program then constructs a plausible series of logical-sounding steps to connect the facts of the case with the desired conclusion. Any number of creation sciences could be constructed on this back-to-front model simply by substituting for the biblical creation narrative other cosmogonic myths – Hindu, Ojibwa, Aztec, Raëlian, etc., etc. – as the predetermined creation scenario one wishes to confirm. Indeed, a number of satiric websites have exposed the back-to-front logic of creation science by using creationist arguments to defend their own deliberately ridiculous 'alternative' theories of creation.[11]

Creation evangelism is predicated on accepting creation science as genuine scientific study of the universe independent of biblical revelation. While ICR members and other creation scientists truly believe that they are practising science, creation science cannot be considered to be an independent study of the universe because its authority is not empirical evidence but the biblical revelation. Fundamentalist creation science, because it exists not to explain the natural world but to defend the Bible, is not science but apologetics.[12] And because it is apologetics not for just any supernatural creation model or even just any biblical creation model but for the particular model derived from a plain-sense reading of an inerrant Bible, it advocates a particular religious viewpoint. Even when creationists appear to use standard scientific language they ground their usage not on scientific method but on the Bible. A good example is 'peer review'. Many creationist sites and publications announce that their content has passed peer review. This does not mean, of course, that it has been submitted to the standard scientific review process, but only that it has been approved by other creation scientists. But what is more revealing is their justification for peer review in the first place. Creationists find a biblical warrant for those aspects of scientific method that they appropriate, just as they do for acceptable scientific data. The proof-text for peer review is Proverbs 27:17: 'Iron sharpens iron; so a man sharpens the countenance of his friend.'[13]

Imagine the following scenario. A group of people affirm that a certain man was at a certain place at a certain time. No one actually saw him there, but some heard his voice inside, others recognized his car parked outside, his footprints were found leading to and departing from the place, his fingerprints were on the doorknob. But the man himself denies that he was there; he dismisses the forensic evidence and accuses those who advance it of being habitual liars and of malice toward him. While the man's behaviour seems markedly peculiar, it starts to make sense if we are told that the man is the defendant in a criminal trial. However weak and unconvincing his charges against the witnesses, we at least understand them as a desperate attempt to save himself from conviction. Creationists' attacks on evolutionists (particularly virulent against Richard Dawkins and, curiously, Charles Lyell) should be understood analogously. It is their motivation for denying the evidence and impugning the witnesses, and not the strength of their arguments against the evidence and witnesses, that is of interest. Creationists attack both science and the character of evolutionists in a desperate attempt to save biblical inerrancy.

As an interpretive activity designed to defend biblical inerrancy by correlating biblical claims with a body of external data, creation science is close kin to millennialist interpretation of prophecy. From Isaac Newton through Philip Gosse and William Miller to modern-day premillennialists, these interpreters begin with the conviction that the biblical prophecies are true and then look for evidence – in this case, historical – to correlate with them. It is unthinkable that the evidence should prove the Bible wrong. Any error in correlation – Jesus does not return on a specified date, a world leader identified as the Antichrist fails to fulfil his role, etc. – demands an interpretive adjustment in order to maintain the fit between the words of the Bible and historical reality.[14] Scientific creationists too are constantly tinkering with their correlations in order to maintain the fit with the Bible. New bits of scientific data that seem compatible with the creation model are added (even to the point of accepting 'microevolution', or change within existing species), and other claims are quietly dropped if they prove embarrassing. But scientific data can never falsify creation science any more than historical data can ever falsify a prophecy because in each case the inerrant authority of the Bible is above suspicion and therefore in cases of conflict the data are either thrown out as false science or as an erroneous historical correlate, respectively, or reinterpreted.

Creation science exists only to confirm Fundamentalists in their faith in an inerrant Bible, *whether or not* it explicitly acknowledges biblical authority. This is why its claim to be something other than biblical testimony is an illusion. Henry Morris's demand that both evolution and creationism should be taught in public schools assumed that creation science is genuine science.[15] Recognizing that creation science is not science at all but biblical testimony is the key to understanding the legal difficulties creationists have faced in attempting to introduce creationism into public schools.

Schools and law courts

At the Scopes trial neither side invoked the Establishment Clause of the United States Constitution because it was considered irrelevant to anti-evolution statutes passed by individual states. By the 1960s, however, a number of federal Supreme Court decisions had extended the rights held by individuals against the federal government as stated in the Constitution and its Amendments to apply against state interference as well. In the 1940s the clauses guaranteeing the free exercise of religion and forbidding an established church were so extended, thereby transforming the legal environment in which the struggle between those opposing and those promoting the teaching of evolution in public schools would play out. In 1963, finally, the Court's decision in *Abington School District v. Schempp*, which prohibited required prayers and Bible reading in public schools, established the legal test that statutes pertaining to education must be religiously neutral; that is, they must have 'a secular legislative purpose and primary effect that neither advances nor prohibits religion'.[16]

Evolution in public schools first came before the Supreme Court in 1968 as a result of events in Arkansas. Schools in that state had adopted the new BCSC biology textbooks that restored evolution to a central place and so offended

Fundamentalists at the time of *The Genesis Flood*. And yet a 1929 law passed by plebiscite in the aftermath of Scopes made it illegal to teach evolutionary theory in Arkansas. The state teachers' association together with the ACLU challenged the constitutionality of the existing (albeit unenforced) anti-evolution law, with a young biology teacher named Susan Epperson playing John Scopes' role as nominal plaintiff. The trial judge in Little Rock swiftly overturned the statute on the constitutional grounds that the state has no right to forbid the teaching of evolution. The case reached the United States Supreme Court because the Arkansas Supreme Court, sensitive to the Fundamentalist views of its electorate, reversed the trial judge's decision in a terse opinion that simply ignored the relevant constitutional arguments. The federal Supreme Court upheld the original decision on the grounds that the statute had a clear religious purpose.[17]

The Schempp and Epperson cases marked the end of Scopes-era anti-evolution legislation, but rather than terminate the battle over evolution in public schools they inaugurated a new phase of anti-evolution activism in which the critical element became the court-imposed standard of religious neutrality. Conservative Christians identified certain scientific theories as being directly opposed to their religious beliefs and argued that teaching them in public schools amounted to state-sponsored attacks on religion. They construed the teaching of evolution in particular as hostility toward religion and demanded relief from this clear violation of the principle of religious neutrality. The first action embodying this reasoning was brought in 1966 when Nell Segraves and Jean Sumrall petitioned the California State Board of Education to protect their children from attacks on their religion by incorporating creationism into biology class and requiring textbooks to designate evolution as a theory. By the end of the decade California had rewritten its framework for teaching science in public schools to incorporate creationism and demanded that textbook publishers follow suit.[18]

Relief under the neutrality test was one prong of the Fundamentalist response to the new legal environment. The other was to insist that the creationist alternative to evolution was not religion at all, but sound science. This, of course, is the position of Henry Morris; and, in fact, Morris developed creation science specifically in response to the new legal and educational environment. Morris, we recall, moved to California in 1970 in order to set up the Creation Science Research Center in partnership with none other than Nell Segraves and her now-grown son, Kelly. Morris had come to realize, despite Whitcomb's objection that creation science betrayed biblical theology – he complained that 'One might just as well be a Jewish or even a Muslim creation scientist as far as this model is concerned' – that appealing to the authority of the Bible, in the manner of *The Genesis Flood*, had no hope of meeting the test of religious neutrality but that if creationism could be made scientifically respectable then the schoolhouse door would be wide open to it.[19]

In 1975 a young lawyer named Wendell Bird (b. 1954) joined the ICR and set about crafting a legal strategy for Fundamentalists to use in persuading school boards to incorporate creationism into their curriculum. Bird's strategy depended crucially on accepting the non-religious nature of creation science. He argued that, first, because scientific creationism is science and not religion, teaching it in public schools does not constitute state support for religion, and, second, teaching evolution without also providing the creationist alternative is an act of hostility against conservative Christians' religious beliefs and therefore prohibited by the test of religious neutrality. The remedy, Bird announced, was to provide equal time in public schools for evolution and creationism. Bird's equal-time strategy, which was a legal version of Morris's two-model approach in *Scientific Creationism*, was first brought to bear against local school boards, as its creator had intended. But events soon carried it beyond the local level when conservative Christians adopted Bird's framework in drafting a new generation of anti-evolution legislation. Bills requiring 'balanced treatment' for creation science and evolution science were debated in numerous state legislatures, and became law in Arkansas and Louisiana in 1981.[20]

The ACLU immediately challenged the Arkansas law on behalf of a coalition of non-Fundamentalist churches and the National Association of Biology Teachers. At the trial in Little Rock in December 1981 each side, as in Dayton, assembled slates of expert witnesses but, even aside from the fact that this time the judge allowed expert testimony, the trial was hardly a replay of Scopes because the changes in the legal environment since 1925 focused the new trial narrowly on the constitutionality of teaching creationism. The ACLU's strategy was simple and devastating: demonstrate that creationism is not science but an apologetic for a particular religious viewpoint. The plaintiffs' religious experts – two non-Fundamentalist clerics, a theologian, a church historian and a sociologist – testified that the young-Earth creationism specified in the Arkansas statute is inseparable from the Fundamentalist faith in an inerrant Bible and therefore it is not only a religious movement but a particular religious movement because it depends on an interpretive approach to the Bible not shared by the majority of Christian churches. Next, the plaintiffs' scientific witnesses explained how creationism fails to qualify as science owing to its total lack of empirical evidence, the complete absence of creationist papers in scientific journals, and its failure to conform to scientific method. The Arkansas Attorney General's defence of the balanced-treatment law followed the Morris–Bird strategy of claiming creationism to be a scientific, non-religious theory of origins. But the bottom fell out of the strategy when the state attempted to substantiate the claim with testimony from reputable scientists. The one scientist with an international reputation whom the state produced was a British astrophysicist who testified that he doubted the evolutionary explanation for the origin of life from non-life but who went on to deny absolutely that creation science was genuine science. Retreating from the debacle of expert testimony, the Attorney General fell back on the populist argument that the citizens of Arkansas overwhelmingly support incorporating creationism into the classroom as a way of balancing – achieving neutrality in – teaching about origins.[21]

The trial judge, in delivering his decision overturning the balanced-treatment law, endorsed the plaintiffs' argument that creationism is not science, that it is a particular interpretation of biblical teaching, and therefore that by introducing creationism into public schools the purpose of the Act is to advance religion. He further noted that what the majority of the citizens of Arkansas may or may not believe on this matter is irrelevant. The American Constitution forbids the use of organs of government, including public schools, to promote religion, no matter how popular such an action might be at the given time and place.[22] The Supreme Court struck down the Louisiana law a few years later on similar grounds in *Edwards v. Aguillard* (1987).

As at Scopes, the creationist trials of the 1980s were not matters of science versus religion, but of alliances of elite science and elite religion versus populist science and populist religion. Creationist legal and legislative initiatives flourish in milieux where reactionary biblicism is dominant, but as soon as creation science rises above the local level and moves out of the world of Fundamentalism its violations of both scientific method and constitutional law are exposed and attempts to introduce creationism into public schools are defeated. Some Fundamentalists responded to the court decisions of the 1980s by withdrawing their children from public schools in favour of private Christian schools or home schooling; other creationists, however, believing retreat to the separatist option premature, turned instead to refining their strategies to get creationism into public schools.

Intelligent Design

The Arkansas and Louisiana balanced-treatment laws were overturned because the courts determined the creationism they advocated to be religion rather than science. The Intelligent Design movement arose as a response to these defeats. Its goal is to elude constitutional objections to introducing creationism into public schools and other areas of public life by eliminating overt references to the biblical framework of creation science in writings and talks intended for mainstream audiences. The Intelligent Design movement is the work of a tightly linked group of lawyers, philosophers of science and scientists whose institutional home is the Center for Science and Culture at the Discovery Institute, a conservative think-tank funded by foundations firmly aligned with the Religious Right.[23] Under the leadership of the Berkeley law professor emeritus Phillip E. Johnson, the philosopher of science Stephen Meyer, and the non-practising biologist and Unification Church theologian Jonathan Wells, the Center for Science and Culture coordinates strategy for the Intelligent Design movement and promotes the work of scientists that challenges Darwinism or supports intelligent design. Its most visible allies are the Lehigh University biochemist Michael Behe and the itinerant mathematician (and senior CSC Fellow) William Dembski.

The Center for Science and Culture is dedicated to the renewal of biblical religion as the foundation of American culture. Indeed, its name on its founding in 1996 was the Center for the Renewal of Science and Culture. It seems, however, that the religious implications of 'renewal' were thought to subvert their strategic efforts to distance the Intelligent Design movement from biblical creationism and so the new name was adopted in 2002.[24] The National Center for Science Education has monitored a parallel evolution in the banner placed at the head of the Center for Science and Culture's website. The original banner, in place from November 1996 to April 1999, featured Michelangelo's Sistine Chapel image of God's hand touching Adam's hand; between October 1999 and August 2001 a double helix replaced Adam but Michelangelo's God remained. Only since October 2001 has the Sistine theme been dropped entirely and replaced by a photograph taken by the Hubble Space Telescope of a planetary nebula that bears a marked resemblance to that favourite of natural theologians over the centuries, the eye.[25] Changes in name and banner notwithstanding, the Center for Science and Culture has been as relentlessly monomaniacal in pursuing its mission of combating scientific and cultural naturalism as Henry Morris and the ICR. The Intelligent Design movement, however, does not insist on the plain-sense meaning of Genesis 1–11: its leading proponents do not publicly defend the claims that universe was created in six 24-hour days, that the world is no more than ten thousand years old, or that a universal Flood has been the principal geological agent of Earth history; nor do they publicly attribute evolutionary theory to Satan or inscribe it in the Last Days scenario from Revelation. Nevertheless, the Intelligent Design movement shares with ICR-style creation science and Scopes-era anti-evolutionism the conviction that evolutionary theory is one of the principal causes of modern society's catastrophic abandonment of biblical values and the corresponding goal of reintroducing supernatural explanations into science as the remedy.[26] Moreover, one must not confuse strategy with underlying beliefs. Despite Johnson's broad definition of a creationist as 'a person who believes that the world (and especially mankind) was *designed*, and exists for a *purpose*',[27] the leaders of the Intelligent Design movement and the Center for Science and Culture are, as we shall see below, personally committed to conservative Christian biblicism.

The principal scientific authority of the Intelligent Design movement is Behe, who in *Darwin's Black Box: The Biochemical Challenge to Evolution* (1996) and other writings has revived Paley's argument from design and tricked it out with flashy new exempla drawn from recent work in molecular biology. Behe argues that it has become apparent over the last few decades that cells are vastly more complex than biologists had previously realized. So far, this is uncontroversial. But Behe further argues that Darwinian evolution is unable to account for the massive complexity of cells – what he calls their 'irreducible complexity' because the arrangement of proteins in a cell is such that any change to one of them destroys the functionality of the entire mechanism – and therefore biochemical complexity points to the existence of an intelligent designer of organic life.[28]

Behe's version of the design argument has failed to convince scientists, and for two reasons. First, Behe is attempting to exploit the fact that while scientists can explain in Darwinian terms Paley's examples of apparent design such as the eye, biochemists do not yet understand all the pathways involved in cellular evolution. But to leap – in the manner of the Duke of Argyll – from this lack of understanding to a supernatural conclusion is unwarranted, just as it would have been unwarranted in the nineteenth century to conclude that the complexity of the eye will always be inexplicable in Darwinian terms. Behe also overstates the difficulties in providing Darwinian explanations for cellular complexity.[29] Second, Intelligent Design has failed as a positive research programme. Neither Behe nor any other Intelligent Design theorist has published peer-reviewed research in a scientific journal, nor have they offered hypotheses to be tested, generated experimental programmes, or in any way added to the sum of scientific knowledge.[30]

William Dembski's contribution to Intelligent Design, which he presents as 'a scientific theory having empirical consequences and devoid of religious commitments', is threefold: he has recast the design argument in terms of information theory; he has constructed what he calls an explanatory filter to assist in detecting design; and more recently he has used a set of mathematical theorems known as No Free Lunch theorems to argue that Darwinian evolution cannot produce the informational complexity displayed in the DNA of living things.[31] Though celebrated by creationists, none of Dembski's arguments convince knowledgeable non-creationists. His recourse to the intimidating mathematics of information theory adds nothing to the classical design argument other than a novel way of expressing the idea that the complexity manifest in the natural world seems very unlikely to have arisen by chance. Similarly, his vaunted explanatory filter (even ignoring the severe shortcomings noted by qualified critics) does not so much detect design as detect the *appearance* of design. Darwin himself, of course, accepted the appearance of design but then explained it in terms of naturalistic processes. Dembski, however, insists that natural causes are in principle incapable of explaining the appearance of design, or what he calls complex, specified information. Dembski has enshrined (Herbert Spencer-like) his contention that natural causes can transmit but not originate complex, specified information in his Law of the Conservation of Information. He claims that his law gives definite scientific content to the inference of design from organic complexity, and his recourse to No Free Lunch theorems is meant to support this claim by demonstrating that the blind algorithms comprising Darwinian evolution cannot generate complex organisms. The problem here, as many critics have pointed out, is that Dembski has neglected to take into account the way biologists understand biological processes actually to work and therefore what degree of complexity evolutionary processes may reasonably be expected to bring about. His misuse of No Free Lunch theorems directly parallels Morris's misuse of the laws of thermodynamics. Further, the very applicability of No Free Lunch theorems to biology is contentious, and one of the original authors of the theorems, the physicist David H. Wolpert, has denounced Dembski's use of them as 'fatally informal and imprecise'. Dembski's version of intelligent design no more stands up to scientific scrutiny than does Behe's.[32]

In responding to his critics Dembski has argued that evolutionists refuse to accept intelligent design not because of its faulty reasoning and total lack of supporting evidence but because they unfairly demand that science adhere to methodological naturalism. Moreover, according to Dembski, methodological naturalism, the procedure by which scientists seek natural explanations for natural phenomena, is functionally equivalent to metaphysical naturalism, or the dogmatic assertion that nothing exists outside of material nature.[33] Dembski is here draw-ing on an argument originated by Phillip Johnson in an essay first published in 1990, 'Evolution as Dogma: The Establishment of Naturalism', and further developed in *Darwinism on Trial* (1991). Johnson argued, as part of the ongoing creationist effort to equate evolution with creationism as alternative philosophies of origins, that evolutionary theory 'is not based upon any incontrovertible evi-dence, but upon a highly controversial philosophical presupposition'.[34] Evolu-tionary theory, that is, is not science but an ideological construct supported by the dogmatic authority of the established scientific priesthood. Johnson's term for this dogmatically asserted secular religion is *scientism*.

Johnson's rehearsal of the familiar creationist claim that there is no incontro-vertible empirical evidence for evolution need not be addressed again. We have seen that there is massive empirical evidence from multiple scientific disciplines for the fact of evolution and that disagreements over the mechanism, timing and rates of evolution are part of the normal operation of science. I shall take up instead his claim that scientific naturalism is a philosophical ideology that amounts to an established secular religion. It is, of course, uncontroversial to point out that scientists, as human beings, possess epistemic and other values that influence their work in various ways, including the area of science they enter or the kinds of scientific questions they ask. But Johnson's claim is the much more far-reaching assertion that science itself has been illegitimately constrained by the ideology of naturalism. Johnson has here conflated two senses of naturalism: metaphysical and methodological. Metaphysical naturalism asserts that no non-material forces or entities exist. Methodological naturalism abstains from making assertions about the nature of reality and instead lays down rules for discovering reliable knowledge about the universe. The critical point is that these rules give pride of place to empirical evidence. No hypothesis about the universe is ruled out in advance (contrary to what would be the case with metaphysical natural-ism), but equally every hypothesis must be tested by empirical evidence and revised, abandoned or affirmed in light of such evidence. Methodological natu-ralists, contrary to Johnson and Dembski, do not reject out of hand hypotheses that point to supernatural causes owing to ideological bias, but demand to exam-ine the empirical evidence and the methods by which it was obtained before endorsing such a hypothesis, just as they demand to examine the evidence for non-supernatural hypotheses such as cold fusion or that the Egyptian pyramids were built by extra-terrestrials. Nor, to complete this line of thought, is the demand to test hypotheses by empirical evidence itself dogmatic. On the contrary, methodological naturalism is essential to science because empirical testing rests on the lawful regularities of nature, which in turn are the bases for controlled, repeatable experimentation, fertile research programmes, inductive inference and prediction, which are the hallmarks of science. Supernatural forces or entities violate or circumvent natural law, thus stopping scientific explanation in its tracks and transforming the explanation of the natural world from a public and transparent activity into a private and untestable one. Evolutionists do not reject intelligent design because they are the bigoted devotees of a materialist secular religion, but because the available empirical evidence does not support favouring a supernatural explanation for the origin and history of life over a naturalistic one. Methodological naturalism does not pass judgement on the existence of supernatural forces or entities, but it does define what counts as science. Intelligent Design theorists possess academic credentials that are the envy of young-Earth creationists, but their work *as Intelligent Design theorists* is junk science because of the failure of their claims to stand up to empirical and methodological scrutiny.[35]

Johnson is not a scientist; he is a lawyer, and he is leading a counter-revolution designed to undo the nineteenth-century evidentiary revolution in which scientific expertise overthrew legal proceduralism in substantiating claims about the natural world. Two nineteenth-century naturalists already familiar to us – Philip Gosse and Robert Owen – represented the traditional and the modern views of what constitutes reliable evidence. At issue were alleged sightings of enormous sea-serpents by the crews of ocean-going ships. Gosse accepted the existence of giant sea-serpents because certain claims to have seen them were backed up by sworn oaths and affidavits from witnesses of 'fair and unblemished character'. He was here following the judicial method of deciding claims about nature by gathering sworn testimony from witnesses and gauging their credibility. The important thing was the moral character and sober reputation of the witnesses, not their scientific qualifications. Owen, however, refused to accept the judicial model in scientific enquiry and insisted that only those people with the requisite scientific training and empirical expertise were qualified to arbitrate claims about the natural world. Accordingly, he denied the reality of giant sea-serpents because scientifically trained anatomists and zoologists could find no empirical evidence for the existence of such creatures. In the matter of sea-serpents, and in natural history generally, Owen's method triumphed over the older practice: the study of nature would proceed by professional scientific expertise rather than judicially authenticated evidence from non-scientists.[36]

Johnson seems to be arguing that non-scientists should once again have a voice in deciding what constitutes science. The key terms, which appear frequently in the writings of Johnson and his colleagues from the Center for Science and Culture, are 'fairness' and 'democracy'. This is a refinement of the populist tactic of early anti-evolutionists, and it turns on the refusal of many Americans to accept that science is not fair or democratic: empirical evidence, not majority rule, decides matters of science.

Johnson constructed his argument that Darwinian evolution is a polemical ideological position rather than science not as an insight into the nature of science but as the foundation for yet another round of creationist legal challenges to the exclusion of creationism from public schools. Johnson laid out his strategy in two books from the second half of the 1990s, *Reason in the Balance* (1995) and *Defeating Darwinism by Opening Minds* (1997). The key to his strategy is the neutrality test. Johnson accepts that governments may not establish or support one religion or religious teaching over others, but argues that the evolutionary account of life violates the test of neutrality because it is a metaphysical worldview. This being so, state support for evolution over creationism amounts to state support for one religious view over another, or what Johnson calls 'viewpoint discrimination'. Since Johnson believes that Intelligent Design creationism is at least as rational a theory of origins as Darwinian evolution, it follows that public schools must admit creationism into science class or be in violation of the neutrality test. The balanced-treatment statutes of the 1980s failed, in Johnson's opinion, because they incorporated elements of the Genesis creation narrative into their definition of creationism. He proposes that the next generation of legislation follow the Intelligent Design movement itself in defining creationism as the minimal claim that an intelligent designer was necessary for the origin of the universe and of life and leaving aside all details of the nature, methods and time-scale of the designer.[37]

Johnson's strategy has become the model for a new wave of Fundamentalist agitation against school boards, most visibly in Kansas and Ohio, although proposals to encourage teaching Intelligent Design creationism have been advanced in 37 states since 2001. The Center for Science and Culture has actively assisted local campaigns in numerous states to rewrite science standards in favour of creationism, and has established state-wide organizations, such as the Intelligent Design Network in Kansas, to continue the struggle and build popular support.[38] The weak point in the latest round of creationist challenges – and the grounds on which they have so far been turned back in Kansas and Ohio – is that Intelligent Design is not science. Whatever its grassroots supporters may have come to believe, Intelligent Design creationism has not established any testable scientific claims.[39] It is therefore legitimately excluded from public school science curricula and the appeal to the neutrality test fails. So far, that is, the idea that scientific questions are not decided by the will of the people has survived.

On the other hand, if we pretend for a moment that Intelligent Design is science, then it would lend support not only to the young-Earth creationism of Fundamentalists but to any and all theories of origins from Hindu cosmogonies to Ojibwa and Aztec cosmogonies to Raëlian extra-terrestrial cosmogonies. But of course Johnson and his colleagues have no intention of encouraging such promiscuous creationism. Their legal strategy is merely one aspect of the Center of Science and Culture's master plan, or what they call the Wedge strategy. The Wedge is a coordinated programme designed to re-establish biblical religion as the foundation of American life by means of (1) establishing the scientific status of intelligent design; (2) achieving a presence in higher education by means of credentialled advocates in research universities; (3) influencing popular opinion and policy-makers through extensive writing and speaking; and (4) opening public school science classrooms to Intelligent Design theory.[40] It might seem that failure to establish the scientific status of Intelligent Design means that the other elements of the programme must also fail. But this would be to mistake Intelligent Design creationism for a scientific movement. In fact, the Center for Science and Culture has pushed on with the other elements of the Wedge strategy despite the total failure of Behe, Dembski and others to establish a scientific basis for intelligent design. The true function of Intelligent Design creationism is to lend credibility among the general public and policy-makers to the rest of the Wedge programme. The prize they seek is not the acclaim of scientists but access to the status and resources of academia in order to further their religious goals behind the façade of science. For the Wedge to succeed, Intelligent Design need not be science, but only be *perceived* as science by non-scientists. The ability and willingness of the Center for Science and Culture to continue with its other aims despite the failure of Intelligent Design as science reveals clearly the religious nature of both the Wedge strategy and of Intelligent Design creationism itself.[41]

In recent years, moreover, the leaders of the Center for Science and Culture have begun to speak openly of their religious commitments. Johnson himself, addressing the Reclaiming America for Christ conference in 1999, candidly acknowledged that the purpose of the Wedge in splitting apart scientific naturalism is to lead people to Christ:

> The objective, he [told the attendees], is to convince people that Darwinism is inherently atheistic, thus shifting the debate from creationism vs. evolution to the existence of God vs. the non-existence of God. From there people are introduced to 'the truth' of the Bible and then 'the question of sin' and finally 'introduced to Jesus'.[42]

The next year, in *The Wedge of Truth*, Johnson publicly placed the Wedge strategy under the biblical authority of the Christian gospel.[43] The two key biblical passages are the opening lines of the Gospel of John and Romans 1:20–23. After quoting the first three verses of John, Johnson lays out his theological alternative to naturalism:

> These simple words make a fundamental statement that is directly contradictory to the corresponding starting point of scientific materialism. Using the Greek word *logos*, the passage declares that in the beginning there was intelligence, wisdom, and communication. Moreover, this Word is not merely a thing or a concept but a *personal being*. This is important because only persons have purposes. If a personal entity is at the foundation of reality, then we have a secure basis for discussion what the world is *for* rather than merely the material means by which it works.[44]

Johnson's reinsertion of teleology back into science depends on the biblical revelation that God is a person (note the difference from religious cosmologies that identify the ultimate power in the universe as an impersonal force). Of course, modern science does not accept the Gospel of John as a methodological authority, but rather than acknowledging the scientific reasons for this Johnson instead turns to the Romans passage, in which Paul presents natural theology as an aspect of divine self-revelation. Every human being in the world, Johnson glosses, therefore knows in the core of his or her being the reality of God, but modern scientists perversely deny this interior knowledge out of a sinful rebelliousness that prevents them from submitting their wills to God. Instead, they set up idols – scientific theories that make no reference to God, evolution first among them – and worship the work of their own hands instead of the true God.[45] Johnson's biblical explanation of modern science in terms of sin and idolatry is more sophisticated than Henry Morris's (Johnson would not dream of publicly attributing modern science to Satan), but in essence the same. Finally, and again paralleling Morris, Johnson's programme for a teleological, supernatural science is not simply a Christian one rather than generally theistic; that it depends on a particular interpretation of the Bible may be seen from Johnson's attack on theologians from liberal or mainstream denominations whose interpretations of the Bible allow them to accept some sort of theistic model of evolution. Just as the early Fundamentalists condemned biblical theologians for their accommodation of the higher criticism and biological evolution, so Johnson condemns the likes of Ian Barbour, Howard Van Till and John F. Haught as having abandoned the biblical God for an idol fashioned by science.[46]

Dembski, for his part, is similarly biblically motivated:

> If we take seriously the Word-flesh Christology of Chalcedon (i.e., the doctrine that Christ is fully human and fully divine) and view Christ as the *telos* toward which God is drawing the whole of creation, then any view of the sciences that leaves Christ out of the picture must be seen as fundamentally deficient.[47]

Here, too, faith in the biblical revelation and its theological codifications replaces empirical investigation as the criterion of science. As with Johnson, Dembski's views hark back to earlier generations of Evangelicals and Fundamentalists. While a student at Princeton Theological Seminary in the mid-1990s Dembski, already a member of the Wedge, immersed himself in the works of the Princeton inerrantists of an earlier day. His explicitly apologetic writings denouncing mainstream Protestant theological seminaries for having betrayed biblical Christianity through accommodation to modern ideas, especially biblical criticism and evolution, take as their model J. Gresham Machen's stalwart defence of biblical inerrancy and his refusal to recognize churches that compromised with modern ideas as truly Christian.[48]

Like the early Fundamentalists, the Intelligent Design movement is driven by the conviction that the only acceptable model for human life is that given by an inerrant reading of the Bible. Not just sound scientific knowledge, but also morality and social well-being, depend on subordinating human reason, moral intuitions and imagination to the authority of the inerrant Word. The alternative, they say, is despair arising from meaninglessness.[49] In Johnson's words:

> What we need is for God himself to speak, to give us a secure foundation on which we can build. If God has not spoken, then we have no alternative to despair. If God has spoken, then we need to build on that foundation rather than try to fit what God has done into some framework that comes from human philosophy.[50]

The biblical commitments of the leaders of the Center for Science and Culture show us why the scientific failure of Intelligent Design does not matter to them: Intelligent Design is a strategy to bring people back to the Bible rather than a genuine attempt to advance scientific knowledge.

Looking back at almost a century of legal battles over creationism one feels something akin to watching episode after episode of *Road Runner* cartoons. Wile E. Coyote's endlessly ingenious schemes never succeed in catching Road Runner, but he always returns to the drawing board full of faith that the next design will be the one to succeed. I do not know what drives the coyote; creationists, however, are driven by faith in the inerrant Bible and an overwhelming desire to subject the modern world to its authority. Creationist legal challenges to teaching evolution in public schools will continue as long as millions of Americans continue to operate within the worldview of reactionary biblicism. And, of course, the ground rules may change – the animators may allow Wile E. Coyote to catch the Road Runner or a Supreme Court dominated by Bush appointees may decide that creationism is science after all.

The evolutionary anthropologist James Frazer discussed in *The Golden Bough* (1890–1915) the widespread belief in an external soul, or the idea that someone's soul could be hidden in an object such as a tree, an egg or a distant castle, thereby rendering the person invulnerable and immortal unless the object containing the soul was found and destroyed. The literary critic Pierre Macherey has offered a modern variation on this theme: 'an ideology is made of what it does not mention; it exists because there are things which must not be spoken of'.[1] Just as a sorcerer is invulnerable as long as his soul is hidden away, so an ideology is invincible as long as it is allowed to set the terms of discussion. Creationism presents itself as a matter of true science as opposed to speculation, as a scientifically respectable philosophy of origins, as a matter of fairness or of majority rights. The purpose of this book has been to take creationism out of the frame of reference in which it understands itself (and wishes others to understand it) and to locate its essential nature in a repudiation of historical-mindedness that serves to defend biblical inerrancy. Creationism opposes not only biological evolution but all historical sciences in order to protect the inerrancy of the Bible by locating its words beyond the complexities and uncertainties of historical existence.

Attacking creationism for its scientific errors is like attacking the body of a sorcerer whose soul is safely hidden away. The attack must instead be directed against its unspoken conviction that the Bible transcends history. Scholars of religion, who have been far less vocal in opposing creationism than have scientists and philosophers of science, have much to contribute here. The modern, critical study of religion, which exists in an intellectual and civil space created by the displacement of the Bible as the supreme authority in Western culture, demonstrates that the various revealed texts of the world's religions are historical documents and contests claims that human beings have access to any infallible source of knowledge and law that transcends historical existence and before which we must bow down. Religions do not belong to a realm of truth and authority separate from that of human knowledge and authority; religions are part of the single reality of human existence and as such their claims are subject to the same standards of empirical evidence and reasoned judgement as any other area of human knowledge.[2]

The critical study of religion, like modern science, shares in the linked intellectual, social and political values that are the heritage of the Enlightenment. Enlightenment thinkers laid the foundation of the modern world by opposing to the authority of revelation and tradition the standard of empirical evidence and reasoned judgement. These epistemic values (as opposed to some of the actual practices of men and women of the Enlightenment, or, indeed, some scientists and scholars today) are both provisional and public. Claims for knowledge, and the authority that follows from them, must be conditional, corrigible, open to public scrutiny and testing, and are never absolute.[3] Creationism attempts to destroy these intellectual, social and political values by reimposing biblical authority, and the intellectual, social and moral views of those who control its interpretation, onto modern society as a whole.[4] As such, it has much in common with other anti-modernist religious movements. Indeed, Islamicist opponents of Turkey's secular government have adapted anti-evolutionist publications of the Institute for Creation Research to their programme of resubmitting Turkey to the authority of the Qur'an.[5]

The critical division in the world today is not between the West and Islam or between believers and secularists, but between those who recognize that human beings are historical beings who, in the absence of transhistorical authorities, must decide for themselves how best to live their lives as individuals and as societies, and those who hold to some kind of transhistorical standard (usually revelation) to which individuals and societies must submit. Creationism and its opposition to evolutionary science will not die until citizens accept that the Bible is a historical document and therefore that it offers no escape by means of a recourse to transhistorical values from the difficult negotiations that historical beings must engage in with each other over truth and law.

Prologue

1. Personal communication from former Royal Tyrrell staff members Jalene Lumb and Brad Tucker, Halifax, Nova Scotia, Sept. 2005.

2. Survey on scientific literacy cited in Ruse, *The Creation–Evolution Debate*, 249.

Chapter 1

1. Lubac, 1–2, 227–28, 249.

2. Harrison, *The Bible*, 30, 32, 264.

3. Ibid., 38, 44–45.

4. Bono, *The Word of God*, 29, 82–83.

5. Ibid., 55, 76–77.

6. Ibid., 35–36.

7. Ibid., 130–38.

8. Ashworth, 303, 308, 312.

9. Quoted in ibid., 316.

10. Bono, *The Word of God*, 65–66; Harrison, *The Bible*, 113.

11. Harrison, *The Bible*, 93.

12. Ibid., 113; Preus, 'The Bible and Religion', 16.

13. Harrison, *The Bible*, 111.

14. Ibid., 122, 126.

15. Mandelbrote, 151; Harrison, *The Bible*, 133–34.

16. Quoted in Manuel, *The Changing of the Gods*, 5.

17. Bono, *The Word of God*, 83, 193, 198; Harrison, *The Bible*, 168–69, 264; Katz, 100.

18. Bono, 'From Paracelsus to Newton', 73; Harrison, *The Bible*, 4.

19. Galileo, *The Assayer*, quoted in Bono, *The Word of God*, 194.

20. Ibid., 194–98.

21. Scholder, 59; Mandelbrote, 152.

22. Manuel, *The Changing of the Gods*, 8–9, 12–13.

23. Harrison, *The Bible*, 136–40.

24. Rossi, *Francis Bacon*, 162–63; Bacon, *Advancement of Learning,* quoted in ibid., 148–49.

25. Bono, *The Word of God*, 215–16, 227, 235.

26. Bacon, *The Great Instauration*, quoted in ibid., 199.

27. Rossi, *Francis Bacon*, 138, 222.

28. Westfall, 299–307; Markley, 135.

29. Manuel, *The Changing of the Gods*, 14.

30. Westfall, 314–15.

31. Manuel, *Isaac Newton*, 156; Westfall, 313–15.

32. Westfall, 315.

33. Ibid., 327–28.

34. Newton MSS, King's College, Cambridge, quoted in Katz, 114.

35. Hutton, 46–49; Kochavi, 106–08; quotation from Newton MSS, King's College, Cambridge, quoted in Katz, 112.

36. Manuel, *Isaac Newton*, 144–45.
37. Daniel 12:9–11.
38. Kochavi, 116–17.
39. Manuel, *Isaac Newton*, 145–46.
40. Quoted ibid., 146. Newton's *Observations upon the Prophecies of Daniel and the Apocalypse of St. John*, published in 1730 three years after his death, was constructed by cobbling together two of his private manuscripts.
41. Coudert, 39; Bono, 'From Paracelsus to Newton', 75.

Chapter 2

1. Harrison, *The Bible*, 203; Boyle, 'A Disquisition about the Final Causes of Natural Things' (1688), quoted in Ruse, *Darwin and Design*, 39.
2. Ruse, *Darwin and Design*, 36.
3. Harrison, *The Bible*, 172.
4. Greene 3–4.
5. Ibid., 5; Haber, 105.
6. Ray, 65–66.
7. Ibid., 156.
8. James, 536–37.
9. Greene, 6; Rudwick, *The Meaning of Fossils*, 64; on the great chain of being, see Lovejoy.
10. Descartes, *Principles of Philosophy*, Principle 28, quoted in Ruse, *Darwin and Design*, 25.
11. Greene, 8–10; Haber, 103.
12. Bono, *The Word of God*, 184–85; Rudwick, *The Meaning of Fossils*, 21.
13. Rudwick, *The Meaning of Fossils*, 24–25, 34–35.
14. Rossi, *The Dark Abyss of Time*, 3–4; Rudwick, *The Meaning of Fossils*, 54–56.
15. Rudwick, *The Meaning of Fossils*, 56.
16. Rossi, *The Dark Abyss of Time*, 3; Rudwick, *The Meaning of Fossils*, 61–64.
17. Rudwick, *The Meaning of Fossils*, 65–68, 73–75.
18. Hooke, *Posthumous Works*, quoted in Greene, 46.
19. Rossi, *The Dark Abyss of Time*, 15–18.
20. Scheuchzer, *Sacred Physics* (1731), quoted in Rudwick, *Scenes From Deep Time*, 14; ibid., 14–16; Rudwick, *The Meaning of Fossils*, 87.
21. Rudwick, *Scenes From Deep Time*, 4; Rudwick, *The Meaning of Fossils*, 87.
22. Scilla, *Vain Speculation Undeceived by Sense: Answering Letter Concerning the Marine Bodies that are Found Petrified in Various Terrestrial Locations* (1670), quoted in Rossi, *The Dark Abyss of Time*, 20.
23. Burnet, 110.
24. Ibid., 121.
25. Ibid., 15.
26. Ibid., 65–66.
27. Ibid., 91.
28. See Nicolson.
29. Donne, 'An Anatomy of the World: The First Anniversary' (1663), ll. 285–94, 300–04.
30. Harrison, *The Bible*, 128.
31. Rudwick, *The Meaning of Fossils*, 80–82; Mandelbrote, 157–58.
32. Burnet, 216.
33. Ibid., 16.
34. Ibid., 61.
35. Ibid., 77.
36. Ibid., 193–94.
37. Ibid., 105.
38. Ibid., 89.
39. Ibid., 224–26.

40. Ibid., 90.
41. Ibid., 118.
42. Ibid., 228.
43. Ibid., 124.

Chapter 3

1. Preus, 'The Bible and Religion', 15–17; Preus, *Spinoza*, 105.
2. Popkin, *The History of Scepticism*, 218–19.
3. Grafton, *Joseph Scaliger*, 5–6; Mungello, 42–43.
4. Verbrugghe and Wickersham, 13–34, 95–120.
5. Grafton, *Joseph Scaliger*, 133.
6. Grafton, *Defenders of the Text*, 129–31.
7. Grafton, *Joseph Scaliger*, 262–98; Grafton, *Defenders of the Text*, 104–44.
8. Wilcox, 197–99.
9. Grafton, *Joseph Scaliger*, 715–18; Wilcox, 201–02.
10. Trevor-Roper, 132–33, 158–60.
11. Grafton, *Defenders of the Text*, 23–46.
12. Haber, 69.
13. Preus, 'The Bible and Religion', 16–18; on Buxtorf see Burnett, 203–39.
14. Champion, 87–91.
15. Ibid., 90; Suelzer and Kselman, 1115.
16. Preus, *Spinoza*, 97.
17. Popkin, *Isaac La Peyrère*, 46, 50–51, 54.
18. Ibid., 43–47; Scholder, 83.
19. Quoted in Popkin, *Isaac La Peyrère*, 43.
20. Fitzmyer, 845–46.
21. Popkin, *Isaac La Peyrère*, 43–44.
22. Ibid., 53, 69–71.
23. Ibid., 49, 52.
24. Grafton, *Defenders of the Text*, 210–11.
25. Popkin, *The History of Scepticism*, 221–23; Popkin, *Isaac La Peyrère*, 15–16.
26. Preus, 'The Bible and Religion', 22; Preus, *Spinoza*, 27n; Popkin, *Isaac La Peyrère*, 73, 76.
27. Paine, 91.

Chapter 4

1. Rossi, *The Dark Abyss of Time*, 139.
2. Walker, 1–21.
3. Harrison, 'Religion', 136–37.
4. Mungello, 103, 125–28.
5. Rossi, *The Dark Abyss of Time*, 124, 140–43.
6. Ibid., 152.
7. Ibid., 145–48.
8. Bietenholz, 232–35.
9. Rossi, *The Dark Abyss of Time*, 153–54.
10. Manuel, *Isaac Newton*, 65; Westfall, 353.
11. Manuel, *Isaac Newton*, 101–02.
12. Force, 253–55; Markley, 135–37.
13. Force, 254–55; Westfall, 355–56; Markley, 138.
14. Rossi, *The Dark Abyss of Time*, 149, 158–62.
15. Vico, ¶ 374.
16. Ibid., ¶ 330.
17. Ibid., ¶ 34.
18. Ibid., ¶ 331.

19. Ibid., ¶ 377.
20. Ibid., ¶ 340.
21. Ibid., ¶ 427.
22. Ibid., ¶¶ 44, 50.
23. Ibid., ¶ 81.
24. Ibid., ¶¶ 916–18.
25. Ibid., ¶ 349.
26. Ibid., ¶¶ 238–40.
27. Ibid., ¶ 342.
28. Ibid., ¶ 1108.
29. Ibid., ¶ 313.
30. Ibid., ¶133; Pompa, 57.
31. Manuel, *Isaac Newton*, 103.
32. Force, 249–50; Feldman and Richardson, 124–25.
33. Markley, 126–27.
34. Rossi, *The Dark Abyss of Time*, 152–53; Manuel, *The Eighteenth Century*.
35. See Markley, 123.
36. Buchwald, 25–30.
37. Aveni, 1–7.
38. Buchwald, 30–31; Dupuis, 432.

Chapter 5

1. McPhee, 87–89.
2. Haber, 6, 106, 159.
3. Toulmin and Goodfield, 143–46; Grayson, 31–33. See also Roger.
4. Toulmin and Goodfield, 146; Grayson, 33–35.
5. Gould, *Time's Arrow*, 61–97; Toulmin and Goodfield, 157–58.
6. Gould, *Time's Arrow*, 84–85; Toulmin and Goodfield, 156–57.
7. Hutton, *Theory of the Earth*, quoted in Gould, *Time's Arrow*, 86.
8. Rudwick, *Scenes from Deep Time*, 27–28; Toulmin and Goodfield, 151–52.
9. Toulmin and Goodfield, 151–52.
10. Grayson, 22–25.
11. Rudwick, *Scenes from Deep Time*, 104.
12. Ibid., 101.
13. Ibid., 124–25.
14. Rudwick, *Georges Cuvier*, 174; Rudwick, 'Minerals, Strata, and Fossils', 281.
15. Toulmin and Goodfield, 165–66; Rudwick, *Georges Cuvier*, 44, 175; Rudwick, *Scenes from Deep Time*, 130, 149.
16. Rudwick, *Scenes from Deep Time*, 143–45; Rudwick, *Georges Cuvier*, 80.
17. Rudwick, *Scenes from Deep Time*, 134; Rudwick, *Georges Cuvier*, 36n, 90, 174, 180.
18. Gillispie, 98–120.
19. Rudwick, *Scenes from Deep Time*, 134–36; Rudwick, 'Minerals, Strata, and Fossils', 283.
20. Haber, 214; Rudwick, *The Great Devonian Controversy*, 42–43.
21. Rudwick, *Scenes from Deep Time*, 168, 180.
22. Lyell, 25, 27–28.
23. Alvarez, 139.
24. Lyell, 437.
25. Rudwick, *Scenes from Deep Time*, 191–94, 197–99.
26. Ibid., 199–200.

Chapter 6

1. Byron, *Cain*, II, i, 174–75.
2. Ibid., II, ii, 44–61.

3. Marchand, 87; Byron, letter to Thomas Moore, 19 September 1821, in Marchand (ed.), 216.

4. Byron, *Cain*, II, ii, 80–84.

5. Ibid., II, ii, 120–25.

6. Ibid., II, ii, 133–146.

7. Paley, 32.

8. Ibid., 54–55.

9. Ibid., 84.

10. Buckland, 8–33, 103.

11. Ibid., 44–70, 99.

12. Ibid., 139–40, 223.

13. Ibid., 164.

14. Ibid., 572–74, 586.

15. Rudwick, *Scenes from Deep Time*, 76; see figs 22, 26 and 27 for examples of pastoral scenes of deep time.

16. Ibid., 21, 83, 85; for examples of Martin's work, see figs 36, 37.

17. Ibid., 80, 95–96.

18. Ibid., 140–49, 259.

19. Tennyson, *In Memoriam*, 33, 1–4.

20. Ibid., 34, 1–4, 9, 13–16.

21. Ibid., 35, 8–16.

22. Ibid., 35, 13–16.

23. Ibid., 50, 7–8.

24. Ruskin, letter to Henry Acland, 24 May 1851, quoted in Cook and Wedderburn, 115.

25. Tennyson, *In Memoriam*, 54, 1–20.

26. Ibid., 55, 1–20.

27. Ibid., 56, 1–4.

28. Ibid., 56, 13–20.

29. Ibid., 56, 21–28.

30. Ibid., 95, 33–44.

31. Ibid., 96, 5–24.

32. Ibid., 118, 1–28.

33. Ibid., 124, 1–24.

34. See Welch.

Chapter 7

1. Allison, 80–1.

2. See Reventlow.

3. Talbert, 2–14; Howard, 82.

4. Allison, 82–83, 95–96.

5. Ibid., 100; Talbert, 31–32.

6. Frei, *The Eclipse of the Biblical Narrative*, 118, 195.

7. Allison, 134.

8. Rogerson, 16–17; Howard, 35–36.

9. Bietenholz, 285–86.

10. Shaffer, 125–27; Howard, 36–37.

11. Clements, 111–12.

12. Ibid., 113–14; Suelzer and Kselman, 1115.

13. Clements, 116–17; Rogerson, 29.

14. Howard, 8, 34, 39–42.

15. Ibid., 62, 65, 98.

16. See Frei, 'David Friedrich Strauss', 222–23.

17. Strauss, 692–93.

18. Frei, 'David Friedrich Strauss', 222, 235; Frei, *The Eclipse of the Biblical Narrative*, 234.

19. Rogerson, 265–66, 271; Suelzer and Kselman, 1119.

20. Friedman, 162–73, 207–216.

21. Dever, 102.

22. Frei, *The Eclipse of the Biblical Narrative*, 131–33.

23. Rogerson, 79, 82, 87.

24. Barr, 91–93, 173–74; Frei, *The Eclipse of the Biblical Narrative*, 63–64, 91–92.

25. Neil, 300–01; Barr, 91–92.

26. Clarke, 183–84.

27. Ibid., 189–90.

28. Frei, *The Eclipse of the Biblical Narrative*, 118.

29. Clarke, 73–74.

30. Frei, *The Eclipse of the Biblical Narrative*, 130.

31. Neil, 269–70; Rogerson, 175–76, 250–52.

32. Ellis, 31.

33. Altholz, 4–5; Rogerson, 188, 192.

34. Willey, 156.

35. Jowett, letter to Dean Eliot, 8 Feb. 1861, quoted in Willey, 141.

36. Shea and Whitla, 50–51.

37. Temple, 'The Education of the World', 139–40.

38. Ibid., 162.

39. Rogerson, 212.

40. Jowett, 504.

41. Ibid., 499.

42. Ibid., 483; Willey, 154–56.

43. Hinchliff, 65.

44. Ibid., 73–76; Shea and Whitla, 118; Jowett, 503.

45. Jowett, 420, 425, quotations at 348, 373.

46. Hinchliff, 48, 230–31.

47. Shea and Whitla, 84–85.

48. Goodwin, 359.

49. Haber, 236–38.

50. Goodwin, 367.

51. Ibid., 347, 354, 368–69; final quotation 346.

52. Willey, 137.

53. Wilberforce's review of *Essays and Reviews* in the *Westminster Review*, Oct. 1860, quoted in Katz, 244. On the reception of *Essays and Reviews*, see Shea and Whitla, 636–873.

54. Rogerson, 218–19.

Chapter 8

1. Ellegård, 95.

2. Milton, *Paradise Lost*, vii, 450–56.

3. Rudwick, *The Meaning of Fossils*, 201–02.

4. Hume, 67–71, 78–83; Dennett, 31–32.

5. Rudwick, *The Meaning of Fossils*, 142–43, 149–50, 203.

6. Ibid., 103–04.

7. Ibid., 17.

8. Dawkins, *The Blind Watchmaker*, 291.

9. Jacob, 147–49; Barthélemy-Madaule, 25, 31–40.

10. Rudwick, *The Meaning of Fossils*, 124, 152–53.

11. Rupke, 195–200; Rudwick, *The Meaning of Fossils*, 208–12; Bowler, *Life's Splendid Drama*, 48; Owen, *On the Nature of Limbs* (1849), quoted in Rudwick, *The Meaning of Fossils*, 212.

12. Ellegård, 120.

13. Darwin, *Charles Darwin's Notebooks*, 640.

14. Toulmin and Goodfield, 200–05 (for the last three paragraphs in the text).

15. See Notebook C in Darwin, *Charles Darwin's Notebooks*, 270, 275.

16. Darwin, letter to John Murray, 21 Sept. 1861, in Darwin, *Life and Letters*, ii, 441; Ruse, *Darwin and Design*, 112.

17. Darwin, *Origin of Species*, 445.

18. Bowler, *The Non-Darwinian Revolution*, 7–9, 51.

19. Ruse, *The Creation–Evolution Struggle*, 78–80, 213.

20. Dawkins, *The Blind Watchmaker*, 43; on the step-by-step evolution of the eye, see 77–86.

21. Darwin, *Origin of Species*, 452; Darwin, *Charles Darwin's Notebooks*, 192.

22. Ellegård, 121, 174–75.

23. Wilberforce, cited in Secord, 436.

24. Ellegård, 183–85.

25. Ellegård, 175–76, 193, 243; Moore, *The Post-Darwinian Controversies*, 201; Beer, 20.

26. Ellegård, 154, 183; on protective strategies, see Proudfoot, 220–21.

27. Darwin, *Life and Letters*, i, 277–78.

28. Darwin, *Charles Darwin's Notebooks*, 343.

29. Ruse, *Darwin and Design*, 124–25.

30. Darwin, *Origin of Species*, 458.

31. Browne, 174–78.

32. Darwin, *Origin of Species*, 116.

33. Darwin, letter to Hooker, 13 July 1856, in Darwin, *More Letters of Charles Darwin*, i, 94.

34. Darwin, letter to Gray, 22 May 1860, in Darwin, *Life and Letters*, ii, 105.

35. Darwin, letter to Hooker, 12 July 1870, in Darwin, *More Letters of Charles Darwin*, i, 321.

36. Darwin, letter to Lyell, 2 Aug. 1861, ibid., i, 190–92.

37. Darwin, *The Variation of Animals and Plants*, ii, 524–26; see Darwin, letter to Hooker, 8 Feb. 1867, in Darwin, *Life and Letters*, ii, 245.

38. Darwin, *Life and Letters*, i, 278–79.

39. Darwin, letter to Gray, 11 Dec. 1863, ibid., ii, 174–75.

40. Browne, 433–34.

41. Ruse, *The Evolution Wars*, 90–95.

42. Ellegård, 124–26.

43. Gray, 5.

44. Gray, 121–22.

45. Browne, 155–56; for Gray on hypothesis in science, see Gray, 88, 144, 207.

46. Ellegård, 268–69.

47. Bowler, *The Eclipse of Darwinism*, 58.

48. Gould, *Ontogeny and Phylogeny*, 65–68; Bowler, *The Non-Darwinian Revolution*, 58.

49. Gould, *Ontogeny and Phylogeny*, 68–69; Bowler, *The Eclipse of Darwinism*, 120; Bowler, *The Non-Darwinian Revolution*, 10, 51.

50. Bowler, *The Non-Darwinian Revolution*, 11; on *Vestiges of the Natural History of Creation*, see Secord.

51. Rupke, 220; Moore, *The Post-Darwinian Controversies*, 146–50; Bowler, *The Eclipse of Darwinism*, 16, 46, 126.

52. Dennett, 51; Dawkins, *The Blind Watchmaker*, 5.

53. Bowler, *The Non-Darwinian Revolution*, 30, 51, 83.

54. Gould, *Ontogeny and Phylogeny*, 55–56, 112–13,

55. Bowler, *The Non-Darwinian Revolution*, 36; Secord, 486.

56. Bowler, *The Eclipse of Darwinism*, 23–25; Livingstone, 'Science, Region, and Religion', 54.

57. Bowler, *The Eclipse of Darwinism*, 15, 46, 141.

58. Bowler, *The Non-Darwinian Revolution*, 117–20.

59. Kingsley, letter to Darwin, 18 Nov. 1859, in Darwin, *Life and Letters*, ii, 82.

60. Ellegård, 32; Hinchliff, 223.

61. Secord, 530–32.

62. Browne, 188–89, 299–300.
63. Roberts, *Darwinism and the Divine*, 149–56.
64. Livingstone, *Darwin's Forgotten Defenders*, 102; Ruse, *The Evolution Wars*, 108–09.
65. Hoeveler, 190–91.
66. Ibid., 192; Bowler, *Life's Splendid Drama*, 48.
67. Hoeveler, 204–06; McCosh, quoted in ibid., 206.
68. Livingstone, 'Science, Region, and Religion', 19–20.
69. Ibid., 28–29.
70. Roberts, *Darwinism and the Divine*, 147–48.
71. Ibid., 99–100; Livingstone, *Darwin's Forgotten Defenders*, 122.

Chapter 9

1. Grayson, 52.
2. Ibid., 65–68.
3. Ibid., 69–71, 201.
4. Tattersall, 7–8.
5. Grayson, 11–13.
6. Daniel and Renfrew, 34–35; Grayson, 176–79.
7. Grayson, 207.
8. Ibid., 182–85, 206–208.
9. Ibid., 186–95.
10. Ibid., 14.
11. Daniel and Renfrew, 45, 49, 62.
12. Tattersall, 24–26.
13. Bowler, *The Non-Darwinian Revolution*, 133–34; Stocking, 161.
14. Lubbock, 430.
15. Stocking, 153, 172–73; Bowler, *The Non-Darwinian Revolution*, 135–36.
16. Lubbock, 593.
17. Bowler, *The Non-Darwinian Revolution*, 140.
18. Darwin, *Origin of Species*, 458.
19. Darwin, letter to Lyell, 8 May 1860, in Darwin, *Life and Letters*, ii, 100.
20. Stocking, 178–79.
21. Darwin, *Descent of Man*, 930.
22. Ibid., 926–27; see also Tattersall, 29.
23. Darwin, *Descent of Man*, 947, 192–94.
24. Ellegård, 159; Grayson, 41; Bowler, *Theories of Human Evolution*, 1.
25. Stocking, 195.
26. Ellegård, 97; Roberts, *Darwinism and the Divine*, 104–05.
27. Miller, *Footprints of the Creator* (1849), cited in Secord, 282.
28. Raymond, quoted in Roberts, *Darwinism and the Divine*, 212.
29. Ibid., 111.
30. Rudwick, *The Meaning of Fossils*, 207; quotation from the *Edinburgh Review* in Ellegård, 100.
31. Roberts, *Darwinism and the Divine*, 197.
32. Grayson, 218–19.
33. Browne, 317–19.
34. Temple 'Lecture Six', 202.
35. Ellegård, 314–15; Moore, *The Post-Darwinian Controversies*, 117–20.
36. Moore, *The Post-Darwinian Controversies*, 120.
37. John Paul II, 'Message to the Pontifical Academy of Sciences'.
38. Lyell, *Geological Evidences*, 552.
39. Bowler, *Theories of Human Evolution*, 1–2, 150–51; Rudwick, *The Meaning of Fossils*, 243.
40. Rudwick, *The Meaning of Fossils*, 244.

41. Bowler, *Theories of Human Evolution*, 125–28.

42. Ibid., 50–58.

43. Daniel and Renfrew, 73–74.

44. Masuzawa, 79.

45. Bowler, *The Non-Darwinian Revolution*, 133–41; Stocking, 284–329.

46. Darwin, *Charles Darwin's Notebooks*, 347.

47. Bowler, *Theories of Human Evolution*, 14; Bowler, *The Non-Darwinian Revolution*, 151.

48. Lyell, *Geological Evidences*, 412.

49. Grayson, 213; Bowler, *Theories of Human Evolution*, 5. For the accumulating fossil evidence, see Grayson and Tattersall.

50. Bowler, *Theories of Human Evolution*, 129–30, 240–41, 249; Bowler, *The Non-Darwinian Revolution*, 151.

51. Bowler, *Theories of Human Evolution*, 246–48. For details see the later chapters of Tattersall.

52. Tattersall, 98.

53. Bowler, *Theories of Human Evolution*, 24, 245.

54. Tattersall, 229–46.

55. Tattersall, 98–99, 110–11, 122. For a refutation of young-Earth creationists' attempts to undermine the validity of radiometric techniques, see Miller, 63–80.

Chapter 10

1. *Dictionary of National Biography*, viii, 258–60.

2. E. Gosse, 77–78.

3. For the entire episode, see ibid., 99–113.

4. P. Gosse, 124.

5. Ibid., 352.

6. Ibid., 337.

7. Ibid., 372.

8. E. Gosse, 105.

9. Ibid., 33.

10. Noll, 9.

11. Ibid., 94–110; Marsden, 'Everyone One's Own Interpreter?', 83.

12. Noll, 109–11.

13. Ahlstrom, 280–87.

14. Noll, 106, 145.

15. Ahlstrom, 432–35.

16. Ibid., 435–45.

17. Noll, 371.

18. Hatch, 36.

19. Noll, 191.

20. Hatch, 134; Marsden, *Reforming Fundamentalism*, 291.

21. See Specter.

22. Hatch, 16.

23. Noll, 375; Hatch, 134–35.

24. Noll, 376–77, 381.

25. Ibid., 235 [Lamar, quoted in ibid., 383]; Marsden 'Everyone One's Own Interpreter?', 83.

26. Hatch, 179.

27. Boyer, 83.

28. Campbell, quoted in Hatch, 179.

29. Dryden, *Religio Laici* (1682), ll. 400–06, 412–16.

30. Noll, 384–85.

31. Ibid., 397–98.

32. Mathews, quoted in Larson, *Summer for the Gods*, 34.

33. Willett, quoted in Marty, 32.

34. Ahlstrom, 779–81.
35. Wacker, 123–24.
36. Ahlstrom, 775.
37. Hodge, quoted in Weber, 106.
38. Weber, 105–06; Ammerman, 'North American Protestant Fundamentalism', 15.
39. Ammerman, 'North American Protestant Fundamentalism', 15–16; Marty, 234.
40. Roberts, *Darwinism and the Divine*, 219.
41. Marty, 235.
42. Marsden, *Reforming Fundamentalism*, 112.
43. Marty, 232–35.
44. Ammerman, 'North American Protestant Fundamentalism', 18–21.
45. Marty, 222–23; Ammerman, 'North American Protestant Fundamentalism', 16–17.
46. Scofield Reference Bible, quoted in Marty, 220.
47. Ammerman, 'North American Protestant Fundamentalism', 17.
48. Ahlstrom, 810.
49. Marty, 221–22.

Chapter 11

1. See Ammerman, 'North American Protestant Fundamentalism', for an overview of Fundamentalism.
2. Henry Van Dyke, quoted in Riley, *The Finality of the Higher Criticism*, 54.
3. Moore, 'The Creationist Cosmos', 45; Marty, 237.
4. Marsden, *Reforming Fundamentalism*, 213–14; Numbers, *The Creationists*, 86–87.
5. Riley, *The Finality of the Higher Criticism*, 97.
6. Marsden, *Reforming Fundamentalism*, 214.
7. Ammerman, 'North American Protestant Fundamentalism', 14.
8. Ammerman, *Bible Believers*, 53–54.
9. Barr, 168–69.
10. Numbers, *The Creationists*, 45–46.
11. Ammerman, *Bible Believers*, 55; Riley, *The Finality of the Higher Criticism*, 108–10. Riley's references are to Leviticus 17:11, Isaiah 40:22 (not 'the Psalmist'), Job 26:7 and 28:25.
12. Riley, 'The Scientific Accuracy of the Sacred Scriptures' (1920), in Riley, *Antievolution Pamphlets*, 134.
13. Kee *et al.*, 252–57; MacKenzie and Murphy, 466–68.
14. Wacker, 127.
15. Trollinger, n.p.
16. Riley, *The Finality of the Higher Criticism*, 76.
17. Ibid., 30–31, 74–82.
18. Ibid., 86, 88–91.
19. Ibid., 175.
20. Livingstone, *Darwin's Forgotten Defenders*, 152–54.
21. Ibid., 165–66.
22. Larson, *Summer for the Gods*, 25.
23. Roberts, *Darwinism and the Divine*, 230.
24. Trollinger, n.p.; Sunday, quoted in Albanese, 303.
25. Ammerman, 'North American Protestant Fundamentalism', 24–25.
26. Larson, *Trial and Error*, 36–37, 39.
27. Ibid., 36–37.
28. Livingstone, *Darwin's Forgotten Defenders*, 160; Numbers, *The Creationists*, 44.
29. Larson, *Summer for the Gods*, 26–29; Bryan, quoted in ibid., 29.
30. Numbers, *The Creationists*, 43–44.
31. Bryan, quoted in ibid., 42.
32. Larson, *Trial and Error*, 60–61.

33. Numbers, *Darwinism Comes to America*, 77–78; Larson, S*ummer for the Gods*, 88–92. Of the vast literature on the Scopes trial, Larson's book is particularly good.

34. Larson, S*ummer for the Gods*, 44.

35. Ibid., 95, 107.

36. Ibid., 69–73.

37. Ibid., 187–190.

38. Ibid., 218.

39. Mathews, quoted in ibid., 118.

40. Ibid., 116–19, 167.

41. Rainger, 131–32.

42. Ibid., 141, 144, 233; Bowler, *Theories of Human Evolution*, 128.

43. Bryan, quoted in Larson, S*ummer for the Gods*, 121.

44. Ibid., 206, 225–33.

45. Ammerman, 'North American Protestant Fundamentalism', 27–28.

46. Boyer, 226, 231.

47. Ammerman, 'North American Protestant Fundamentalism', 31–33; Hatch, 216.

48. Larson, S*ummer for the Gods*, 232–34.

49. Ibid., 238–40. The distortions of the play/movie are documented in ibid., 240–43. For an updating of *Inherit the Wind*'s revisionist version of Scopes, in which dancing replaces courtroom drama, see *Footloose* (1984).

Chapter 12

1. Moore, 'The Creationist Cosmos', 47; Numbers, *The Creationists*, 186–87.

2. Numbers, *The Creationists*, 194; on Rimmer, see ibid., 60–71.

3. Ibid., 74.

4. Ibid., 76–82.

5. Ibid., 87.

6. Ibid., 97–99.

7. Whitcomb and Morris, quoted in Livingstone, *Darwin's Forgotten Defenders*, 172.

8. Whitcomb and Morris, 118.

9. Ibid., xx.

10. Ibid., 62.

11. Ibid., 118.

12. Numbers, *The Creationists*, 200.

13. Whitcomb and Morris, 233, 238.

14. Ibid., 239, quoting Romans 8:21, 22.

15. Ibid., 457.

16. Ibid., 240–41, 375; Numbers, *The Creationists*, 203–04.

17. Whitcomb and Morris, 216.

18. Morris, 'The Vital Importance'.

19. See Morris's account of how he became a young-Earth creationist in Morris, 'Naïve Literalism'.

20. Matthew 5:18; Luke 16:17, 18:31, 24:25; John 10:35; and for Genesis, Matthew 19:4, 23:35, 24:37–39; Luke 17:29, 32.

21. See Morris, *The Revelation Record*.

22. Numbers, *The Creationists*, 204–08.

23. Ibid., 338.

24. Moore, 'The Creationist Cosmos', 48.

25. Morris, 'The Vital Importance'.

26. Larson, *Trial and Error*, 87–91; Numbers, *The Creationists*, 238–39.

27. Whitcomb and Morris, pp. xxii, 328.

28. Ibid., 440–41.

29. Ibid., 447.

30. Morris, *The Long War Against God*, 168–75.

31. Ibid., 157.

32. Ibid., 175–95, 200–08.

33. Ibid., 233–55.

34. Ibid., 218–27.

35. Ibid., 255–60.

36. Ibid., 25, 248–49.

37. Ibid., 300–01, 316–17; see also Morris, *The God Who Is Real*.

38. Moore, 'The Creationist Cosmos', 49; Numbers, *The Creationists*, 251–52; see also <www.creationresearch.org/about_crs.htm>.

39. Numbers, *The Creationists*, 283–86.

40. Morris, *Reflections*.

41. Numbers, *The Creationists*, 286.

42. Morris, 'ICR – The First Twenty-Five Years'.

43. Moore, 'The Creationist Cosmos', 49.

44. Montagu, 301–03; Pennock, *Tower of Babel*, 164, 182–83; Dawkins, *A Devil's Chaplain*, 218–21.

45. Whitcomb and Morris, 292–311.

46. See Numbers, *The Creationists*, 235.

47. Morris, *The Remarkable Record of Job*.

48. Morris, *The Long War Against God*, 106.

49. For a sampling of creationist organizations, from the large-scale Answers in Genesis to one-man-band operations like Kent Hovind's (aka Dr Dino) Creation Science Evangelism ministry and Dinosaur Adventure Land, see <www.answersingenesis.org>, <www.creationillustrated.com>, <www.creationevidence.org>, <www.creationism.org/sthelens>, and <www.dino.com>.

Chapter 13

1. Whitcomb and Morris, xxi, xxvi–xxvi. The preface to the sixth printing of *The Genesis Flood* reprints Whitcomb and Morris's 'Reply to Reviewers' in *Journal of the American Scientific Affiliation* 16 (June 1964), 59–61.

2. Morris (ed.), *Scientific Creationism*, iv.

3. Ibid., 9.

4. Ibid., 131.

5. Ibid., 203–05; quotations, 202 and 206.

6. Douglas J. Futayama, *Science on Trial* (New York: Pantheon, 1983); Laurie R. Godfrey (ed.), *Scientists Confront Creationism* (New York: W. W. Norton, 1983); Philip Kitcher, *Abusing Science: The Case Against Creationism* (Cambridge, Mass.: MIT Press, 1984); Montagu (ed.), *Science and Creationism*; Langdon Gilkey, *Creationism on Trial: Evolution and God at Little Rock* (San Francisco: Harper & Row, 1985); Dawkins, *The Blind Watchmaker*; Arthur N. Strahler, *Science and Earth History: The Evolution/Creation Controversy* (Buffalo: Prometheus Books, 1987); G. Brent Dalrymple, *The Age of the Earth* (Stanford: Stanford University Press, 1991); Miller, *Finding Darwin's God*; Pennock, *Tower of Babel*; *Science and Creationism*; Niles Eldredge, *The Triumph of Evolution and the Failure of Creationism* (New York: W. H. Freeman, 2000); Ruse, *The Evolution Wars*; Carl Zimmer, *Evolution: The Triumph of an Idea* (New York: HarperCollins, 2001); Shanks, *God, The Devil, and Darwin*; Forrest and Gross, *Creationism's Trojan Horse*; Young and Edis (eds), *Why Intelligent Design Fails*; Ruse, *The Creation–Evolution Struggle*. Anthropologists and linguists have not been nearly so active in countering creationist attacks on their disciplines as geologists, palaeontologists, biologists and philosophers of science. The reason is obvious enough: creationists have not yet demanded equal time for their theories in anthropology and linguistics classrooms. But for discussions that implicitly refute the creationist construction of early humanity, see Jared Diamond, *The Third Chimpanzee* (New York: HarperCollins, 1992); Ian Tattersall, *Becoming Human: Evolution and Human Uniqueness* (New York: Harcourt, Brace, 1998), Luigi Luca Cavalli-Sforza, *Genes, Peoples, and Languages* (New York: North Point, 2000).

7. Gould, 'Evolution as Fact and Theory', 118; *Science and Creationism*, 1–2; Pennock, *Tower of Babel*, 52.

8. Henry M. Morris, 'The Age of the Earth', in Morris, *Basic Creation Series*.

9. *Science and Creationism*, 21.

10. Morris (ed.), *Scientific Creationism*, 4.

11. A particularly good example (accessible as of December 2005), which demands equal classroom time for the belief that the universe was created by 'the Flying Spaghetti Monster', is <www.venganza.org>.

12. Root-Bernstein, 73–79.

13. See <www.answersingenesis.org/docs2002/1011hovind.asp>.

14. Boyer, 295–96.

15. Morris (ed.), *Scientific Creationism*, 14.

16. Larson, *Trial and Error*, 93–95.

17. Larson, *Summer for the Gods*, 250–56.

18. Numbers, *The Creationists*, 243–44.

19. Ibid., 242–46; Whitcomb quoted in ibid., 246.

20. Larson, *Trial and Error*, 149–53; Numbers, *The Creationists*, 319–20.

21. Larson, *Trial and Error*, 156–60.

22. See Overton.

23. On Center for Science and Culture funding, see Forrest and Gross, 148–50, 264–67.

24. See <www.discovery.org/aboutCSC.php>. On the history, goals and strategies of the Center for Science and Culture, see Forrest.

25. See <www.ncseweb.org/resources/articles>.

26. Pennock, *Tower of Babel*, 373–74.

27. Johnson, *Darwinism on Trial*, 113.

28. Behe has summarized his highly Cuvierian argument in Behe, 2001.

29. Kitcher, 262–67; Shanks, 182–90.

30. Forrest, 19–23.

31. See Dembski, *The Design Inference*, 'Intelligent Design as a Theory of Information' and *No Free Lunch*; quotation, Dembski, 'Intelligent Design as a Theory of Information', 553.

32. See Godfrey-Smith; Shanks, 128–34; Fitelson *et al.*; and Orr, 50–51; Wolpert quoted in Orr, 51. For further analyses of Dembski's misappropriation of information theory, see Young and Edis.

33. Dembski, *Intelligent Design*, 119–20.

34. Johnson, 'Evolution as Dogma', 60.

35. Pennock, *Naturalism, Evidence and Creationism*, 83–90; Shanks, 139–45; Orr, 52.

36. Rupke, 324–32; quotation from Gosse's *Romance of Natural History* (1860), in Rupke, 328.

37. Pennock, *Tower of Babel*, 364–66. Johnson's lead has been followed by CSC Fellows David DeWolf, Stephen Meyer and Mark DeForrest in *Intelligent Design in Public School Science Curricula: A Legal Guidebook* (Richardson, Tex.: Foundation for Thought and Ethics, 1999) and more recently an article in the *Utah Law Review* (2000). See Forrest and Gross, 205.

38. Forrest and Gross, 222–23.

39. Ibid., 142.

40. Forrest, 30–38.

41. Ibid., 6.

42. Johnson, quoted in Forrest, 42.

43. Johnson, *The Wedge of Truth*, 16.

44. Ibid., 151–52.

45. Ibid., 152–54.

46. Ibid., 89–93; for other religious creationist positions excluded by Johnson on the basis of his interpretation of the Bible, see Pennock, 'Naturalism, Evidence and Creationism', 86.

47. Dembski, *Intelligent Design*, 206.

48. Forrest and Gross, 156–57, 261–62.

49. Pennock, *Tower of Babel*, 311–13.

50. Johnson, *The Wedge of Truth*, 158.

Epilogue

1. Frazer, 756–84; Macherey, 132.
2. Preus, *Spinoza*, 33.
3. Buchan, 336; Pennock, *Tower of Babel*, 353–56.
4. Shanks, 231.
5. Shanks, 9, citing Shapiro.

BIBLIOGRAPHY

Adams, Douglas. *Dirk Gently's Holistic Detective Agency*. London: Heinemann, 1987.

Ahlstrom, Sydney E. *A Religious History of the American People*. New Haven: Yale University Press, 1972.

Albanese, Catherine. *America, Religions, and Religion*. Belmont, Calif.: Wadsworth, 1981.

Allison, Henry E. *Lessing and the Enlightenment: His Philosophy of Religion and its Relation to Eighteenth-Century Thought*. Ann Arbor: University of Michigan Press, 1966.

Altholz, Josef L. *Anatomy of a Controversy: the Debate over* Essays and Reviews: *1860–1864*. Aldershot: Scolar Press, 1994.

Alvarez, Walter. *T. rex and the Crater of Doom*. Princeton: Princeton University Press, 1997.

Ammerman, Nancy T. *Bible Believers: Fundamentalists in the Modern World*. New Brunswick, NJ: Rutgers University Press, 1987.

—'North American Protestant Fundamentalism', in Martin E. Marty and R. Scott Appleby (eds), *The Fundamentalism Project*, vol. 1: *Fundamentalisms Observed*. Chicago: University of Chicago Press, 1991, pp. 1–65.

Ashworth, William B., Jr. 'Natural History and the Emblematic World View', in David C. Lindberg and Robert S. Westman (eds), *Reappraisals of the Scientific Revolution*. Cambridge: Cambridge University Press, 1990, pp. 303–32.

Aveni, Anthony. *Skywatchers: A Revised and Updated Version of Skywatchers of Ancient Mexico*. Austin: University of Texas Press, 2001.

Barr, James. *The Bible in the Modern World*. New York: Harper & Row, 1973.

Barthélemy-Madaule, Madeleine. *Lamarck the Mythical Precursor*. Trans. M. H. Shank. Cambridge, Mass.: MIT Press, 1982.

Beer, Gavin de. 'Introduction' to Robert Chambers, *Vestiges of the Natural History of Creation*. New York: Humanities Press, 1969, pp. 7–36.

Behe, Michael. 'Molecular Machines: Experimental Support for the Design Inference', in Robert Pennock (ed.), *Intelligent Design Creationism and its Critics: Philosophical, Theological, and Scientific Perspectives*. Cambridge, Mass.: MIT Press, 2001, pp. 241–56.

Bietenholz, Peter G. *Historia and Fabula: Myths and Legends in Historical Thought from Antiquity to the Modern Age*. New York: E. J. Brill, 1994.

Bono, James J. 'From Paracelsus to Newton: The Word of God, the Book of Nature, and the Eclipse of the "Emblematic World View" ', in James E. Force and Richard H. Popkin (eds), *Newton and Religion: Context, Nature, Influence*. Dordrecht: Kluwer Academic Publishers, 1999, pp. 45–76.

—*The Word of God and the Languages of Man: Interpreting Nature in Early Modern Science and Medicine*, vol. 1: *Ficino to Descartes*. Madison, Wisc.: University of Wisconsin Press, 1995.

Bowler, Peter J. *The Eclipse of Darwinism: Anti-Darwinian Evolution Theories in the Decades around 1900*. Baltimore: Johns Hopkins University Press, 1983.

—*Life's Splendid Drama*. Chicago: University of Chicago Press, 1996.

—*The Non-Darwinian Revolution: Reinterpreting a Historical Myth*. Baltimore: Johns Hopkins University Press, 1988.

—*Theories of Human Evolution: A Century of Debate, 1844–1944*. Baltimore: John Hopkins University Press, 1986.

Boyer, Paul. *When Time Shall Be No More: Prophecy Belief in Modern American Culture*. Cambridge, Mass.: Belknap Press, 1992.

Browne, Janet. *Charles Darwin: The Power of Place*. New York: Knopf, 2002.

Buchan, James. *Crowded with Genius. The Scottish Enlightenment: Edinburgh's Moment of the Mind*. New York: HarperCollins, 2003.

Buchwald, Jed Z. 'Egyptian Stars under Paris Skies', *Science & Engineering* 4 (2003), pp. 21–31.

Buckland, William. *Geology and Mineralogy, considered with Reference to Natural Theology* (Bridgewater Treatise VI). Repr. New York: Arno Press, 1980 (1836).

Burgon, John William. *Petra, a Prize Poem Recited in the Theatre, Oxford. June 4, 1845*. Oxford: Frances Macpherson, 1845.

Burnet, Thomas. *The Sacred Theory of the Earth*. Repr. with an introd. by Basil Willey. London: Centaur Press, 1965 (1691).

Burnett, Stephen G. *From Christian Hebraism to Jewish Studies: Johannes Buxtorf (1564–1629) and Hebrew Learning in the Seventeenth Century*. Leiden: E. J. Brill, 1996.

Byron, George Gordon. *Byron: A Critical Edition of the Major Works*. Ed. Jerome McGann. Oxford: Oxford University Press, 1986.

Champion, Justin A. I. ' "Acceptable to Inquisitive Men": Some Simonian Contexts for Newton's Biblical Criticism, 1680–1692', in James E. Force and Richard H. Popkin (eds), *Newton and Religion: Context, Nature, and Influence*. Dordrecht: Kluwer Academic Publishers, 1999, pp. 77–96.

Clarke, William Newton. *Sixty Years with the Bible: A Record of Experience*. New York: Scribner's, 1909.

Clements, R. E. 'The Study of the Old Testament', in Ninian Smart, John Clayton, Patrick Sherry and Steven Katz (eds), *Nineteenth Century Religious Thought in the West*, vol. 3. Cambridge: Cambridge University Press, 1985, pp. 109–41.

Cook, E. T., and Wedderburn, Alexander (eds), *The Letters of John Ruskin. Volume I: 1827–1851*. London: George Allen, 1909.

Coudert, Allison P. 'Newton and the Rosicrucian Enlightenment', in James E. Force and Richard H. Popkin (eds), *Newton and Religion: Context, Nature, Influence*. Dordrecht: Kluwer Academic Publishers, 1999, pp. 17–43.

Daniel, Glyn, and Renfrew, Colin. *The Idea of Prehistory*. Edinburgh: Edinburgh University Press, 1988.

Darwin, Charles. *Charles Darwin's Notebooks, 1836–1844*. Transcribed and ed. Paul H. Barrett, Peter J. Gautry, Sandra Herbert, David Kohn, and Sydney Smith. Ithaca, NY: Cornell University Press, 1987.

—*Descent of Man*. London: John Murray, 1909 (repr. of 2nd edn, 1874).

—*The Life and Letters of Charles Darwin*. 2 vols. Ed. Francis Darwin. New York: Appleton and Co., 1898 (1887).

—*More Letters of Charles Darwin*. 2 vols. Ed. Francis Darwin. New York: Appleton and Co., 1903.

—*Origin of Species*. Harmondsworth: Penguin, 1968 (1859).

—*The Variation of Animals and Plants under Domestication*. 2 vols. London: John Murray, 1905 (1868).

Dawkins, Richard. *The Blind Watchmaker*. Harmondsworth: Penguin. 1988.

—*A Devil's Chaplain: Reflections on Hope, Lies, Science, and Love*. Boston: Houghton Mifflin, 2003.

Dembski, William A. *The Design Inference: Eliminating Chance through Small Probabilities*. Cambridge: Cambridge University Press, 1998.

—'Intelligent Design as a Theory of Information', in Robert Pennock (ed.), *Intelligent Design Creationism and its Critics: Philosophical, Theological, and Scientific Perspectives.* Cambridge, Mass.: MIT Press, 2001, pp. 553–73.

—*Intelligent Design: The Bridge between Science and Theology.* Downers Grove, Ill.: Intervarsity Press, 1999.

—*No Free Lunch: Why Specified Complexity Cannot be Purchased without Intelligence.* Lanham, Md.: Rowman and Littlefield, 2002.

Dennett, Daniel. *Darwin's Dangerous Idea: Evolution and the Meanings of Life.* New York: Simon & Schuster, 1995.

Dever, William G. *What did the Biblical Writers Know and When did they Know it?: What Archaeology can Tell us about the Reality of Ancient Israel.* Grand Rapids: Eerdmans, 2001.

Dictionary of National Biography. Ed. Leslie Stephen and Sydney Lee. New York: Macmillan, 1908.

Donne, John. *The Poems of John Donne*, vol. 1. Ed. Herbert Grierson. Oxford: Oxford University Press, 1912.

Dryden, John. *The Works of John Dryden*, vol. 2: *Poems 1681–1684*, ed. H. T. Swedenberg, Jr. Berkeley and Los Angeles: University of California Press, 1972.

Dupuis, Charles. *The Origin of All Religious Worship, Containing Also a Description of the Zodiac of Dendera.* Repr. New York: Garland, 1984 (1872).

Ellegård, Alvar. *Darwin and the General Reader: The Reception of Darwin's Theory of Evolution in the British Periodical Press, 1859–1872.* Göteborg: Göteborg University Press, 1958.

Ellis, Ieuan. *Seven Against Christ: A Study of* Essays and Reviews. Leiden: E. J. Brill, 1980.

Feldman, Burton, and Richardson, Robert D. *The Rise of Modern Mythology, 1680–1860.* Bloomington, Ind.: Indiana University Press, 1972.

Fitelson, Branden, Stephens, Christopher, and Sober, Elliott. 'How Not To Detect Design – Critical Notice: William A. Dembski, *The Design Inference*', in Robert Pennock (ed.), *Intelligent Design Creationism and its Critics: Philosophical, Theological, and Scientific Perspectives.* Cambridge, Mass.: MIT Press, 2001, pp. 597–615.

Fitzmyer, Joseph A. 'The Letter to the Romans', in Raymond Brown, Joseph Fitzmyer, and Roland Murphy (eds), *The New Jerome Biblical Commentary.* Englewood Cliffs, NJ: Prentice-Hall, 1990, pp. 830–68.

Force, James E. 'Newton, the "Ancients", and the "Moderns" ', in James E. Force and Richard H. Popkin (eds), *Newton and Religion: Context, Nature, and Influence.* Dordrecht: Kluwer Academic Publishers, 1999, pp. 237–57.

Forrest, Barbara. 'The Wedge at Work: How Intelligent Design Creationism is Wedging its Way into the Cultural and Academic Mainstream', in Robert Pennock (ed.), *Intelligent Design Creationism and its Critics: Philosophical, Theological, and Scientific Perspectives.* Cambridge, Mass.: MIT Press, 2001, pp. 5–53.

—and Gross, Paul. *Creationism's Trojan Horse: The Wedge of Intelligent Design.* Oxford: Oxford University Press, 2004.

Frazer, James. *The Golden Bough.* Abridged and ed. Robert Fraser. Oxford: Oxford University Press, 1994.

Frei, Hans. 'David Friedrich Strauss', in Ninian Smart, John Clayton, Patrick Sherry and Steven T. Katz (eds), *Nineteenth Century Religious Thought in the West*, vol. 1. Cambridge: Cambridge University Press, 1985, pp. 215–60.

—*The Eclipse of the Biblical Narrative: A Study in Eighteenth and Nineteenth Century Hermeneutics.* New Haven: Yale University Press, 1974.

Friedman, Richard Elliott. *Who Wrote the Bible?* 2nd edn. San Francisco: HarperSanFrancisco, 1997.

Gillispie, Charles C. *Genesis and Geology: The Impact of Scientific Discoveries upon Religious Beliefs in the Decades before Darwin*. New York: Harper, 1951.

Godfrey-Smith, Peter. 'Information and the Argument from Design', in Robert Pennock (ed.), *Intelligent Design Creationism and its Critics: Philosophical, Theological, and Scientific Perspectives*. Cambridge, Mass.: MIT Press, 2001, pp. 575–96.

Goodwin, Charles Wycliffe. 'On the Mosaic Cosmogony', in Victor Shea and William Whitla (eds), Essays and Reviews: *The 1860 Text and its Reading*. Charlottesville, Va.: University Press of Virginia, 2000, pp. 345–71.

Gosse, Edmund. *Father and Son: A Study of Two Temperaments*. Ed. Peter Abbs. Harmondsworth: Penguin Classics, 1983 (1907).

Gosse, Philip. *Omphalos: An Attempt to Untie the Geological Knot*. London: John Van Voorst, 1857.

Gould, Stephen J. 'Evolution as Fact and Theory', in Ashley Montagu (ed.), *Science and Creationism*. Oxford: Oxford University Press, 1984, pp. 117–25.

—*Ontogeny and Phylogeny*. Cambridge, Mass.: Harvard University Press, 1977.

—*Time's Arrow, Time's Cycle: Myth and Metaphor in the Discovery of Geological Time*. Cambridge, Mass.: Harvard University Press, 1987.

Grafton, Anthony. *Defenders of the Text: The Traditions of Scholarship in an Age of Science, 1450–1800*. Cambridge, Mass.: Harvard University Press, 1991.

—*Joseph Scaliger: A Study in the History of Scholarship*, vol. 2, *Historical Chronology*. Oxford: Clarendon Press, 1993.

Gray, Asa. *Darwiniana: Essays and Reviews Pertaining to Darwinism*. Ed. A. Hunter Dupree. Cambridge, Mass.: Belknap Press, 1963 (1876).

Grayson, Donald K. *The Establishment of Human Antiquity*. New York: Academic Press, 1983.

Greene, John C. *The Death of Adam: Evolution and its Impact on Western Thought*. Ames, Ia: Iowa State University Press, 1959.

Haber, Francis C. *The Age of the World: Moses to Darwin*. Baltimore: Johns Hopkins University Press, 1959.

Harrison, Peter. *The Bible, Protestantism, and the Rise of Natural Science*. Cambridge: Cambridge University Press, 1998.

— *'Religion' and the Religions in the English Enlightenment*. Cambridge: Cambridge University Press, 1990.

Hatch, Nathan. *The Democratization of American Christianity*. New Haven: Yale University Press, 1989.

Hinchliff, Peter. *Benjamin Jowett and the Christian Religion*. Oxford: Clarendon Press, 1987.

Hoeveler, J. David, Jr. *James McCosh and the Scottish Intellectual Tradition: From Glasgow to Princeton*. Princeton: Princeton University Press, 1981.

Hooker, Richard. *Of the Laws of Ecclesiastical Polity*, vol. 1. Ed. George Edelen. Cambridge, Mass.: Harvard University Press, 1977.

Howard, Thomas Albert. *Religion and the Rise of Historicism: W. M. L. de Wette, Jacob Burckhardt, and the Theological Origin of Nineteenth-Century Historical Consciousness*. Cambridge: Cambridge University Press, 2000.

Hume, David. *Principal Writings on Religion*, including *Dialogues concerning Natural Religion* and *The Natural History of Religion*. Ed. J. C. A. Gaskin. Oxford: Oxford University Press, 1993.

Hutton, Sarah. 'More, Newton, and the Language of Biblical Prophecy', in James E. Force and Richard H. Popkin (eds), *The Books of Nature and Scripture*. Dordrecht: Kluwer Academic Publishers, 1994, pp. 39–53.

Jacob, François. *The Logic of Life: A History of Heredity*. Trans. Betty Spillman. Princeton: Princeton University Press, 1973.

James, William. *The Varieties of Religious Experience*. New York: Modern Library, 1994.

John Paul II, 'Message to the Pontifical Academy of Sciences', 22 Oct. 1996. Available at <www.vatican.va/holy_father/john_paul_ii/speeches/2005/february/documents/hf_jp-ii_spe_20050201_p-acad-sciences_en.html>.

Johnson, Phillip E. 'Evolution as Dogma: The Establishment of Naturalism', in Robert T. Pennock (ed.), *Intelligent Design Creationism and its Critics: Philosophical, Theological, and Scientific Perspectives*. Cambridge, Mass.: MIT Press, 2001, pp. 59–76.

—*Darwinism on Trial*. Washington, DC: Regnery, 1991.

—*The Wedge of Truth: Splitting the Foundations of Naturalism*. Downers Grove, Ill.: Intervarsity Press, 2000.

Jowett, Benjamin. 'On the Interpretation of Scripture', in Victor Shea and William Whitla (eds), Essays and Reviews: *The 1860 Text and its Reading*. Charlottesville, Va.: University Press of Virginia, 2000, pp. 477–536.

Katz, David S. *God's Last Words: Reading the English Bible from the Reformation to Fundamentalism*. New Haven: Yale University Press, 2004.

Kee, Howard Clark, Meyers, Eric, Rogerson, John, and Saldarini, Anthony. *The Cambridge Companion to the Bible*. Cambridge: Cambridge University Press, 1997.

Kitcher, Philip. 'Born-Again Creationism', in Robert T. Pennock (ed.), *Intelligent Design Creationism and its Critics: Philosophical, Theological, and Scientific Perspectives*. Cambridge, Mass.: MIT Press, 2001, pp. 257–87.

Kochavi, Matania Z. 'One Prophet Interprets Another: Sir Isaac Newton and Daniel', in James E. Force and Richard H. Popkin (eds), *The Books of Nature and Scripture*. Dordrecht: Kluwer Academic Publishers, 1994, pp. 105–22.

Larson, Edward J. *Summer for the Gods: The Scopes Trial and America's Continuing Debate over Science and Religion*. Cambridge, Mass.: Harvard University Press, 1997.

—*Trial and Error: The American Controversy over Creation and Education*. New York: Oxford University Press, 1985.

Lessing, Gotthold Ephraim. *The Education of the Human Race*. Ed. John Dearling Haney. New York: Teachers' College, Columbia University, 1908.

Livingstone, David. N. *Darwin's Forgotten Defenders: The Encounter between Evangelical Theology and Evolutionary Thought*. Grand Rapids: Eerdmans, 1987.

—'Science, Region, and Religion: The Reception of Darwinism in Princeton, Belfast, and Edinburgh', in Ronald Numbers and John Stenhouse (eds), *Disseminating Darwinism: The Role of Place, Race, Religion, and Gender*. Cambridge: Cambridge University Press, 1999, pp. 7–38.

Lovejoy, Arthur O. *The Great Chain of Being*. Cambridge, Mass.: Harvard University Press, 1936.

Lubac, Henri de. *Medieval Exegesis*, vol. 1: *The Four Senses of Scripture*. Trans. Mark Sebanc. Grand Rapids: Eerdmans, 1998.

Lubbock, John. *Prehistoric Times, as Illustrated by Ancient Remains and the Manners and Customs of Modern Savages*. 7th edn. London: Williams & Norgate, 1913 (1865).

Lyell, Charles. *Geological Evidences of the Antiquity of Man*. 4th revd edn. London: John Murray, 1873 (1863).

—*Principles of Geology*. Ed. James Secord. Harmondsworth: Penguin, 1997 (1830–33).

Macherey, Pierre. *A Theory of Literary Production*. Trans. Geoffrey Wall. London: Routledge & Kegan Paul, 1978.

MacKenzie, R. A. F., and Murphy, Roland. 'Job', in Raymond Brown, Joseph Fitzmyer, and Roland Murphy (eds), *The New Jerome Biblical Commentary*. Englewood Cliffs, NJ: Prentice-Hall, 1990, pp. 466–68.

Mandelbrote, Scott. 'Isaac Newton and Thomas Burnet: Biblical Criticism and the Crisis of Late-Seventeenth-Century England', in James E. Force and Richard H. Popkin (eds), *The Books of Nature and Scripture*. Dordrecht: Kluwer Academic Publishers, 1994, pp. 149–78.

Manuel, Frank E. *The Changing of the Gods*. Hanover, NH and London: University Presses of New England, 1983.

—*The Eighteenth Century Confronts the Gods*. Cambridge, Mass.: Harvard University Press, 1967.

—*Isaac Newton, Historian*. Cambridge, Mass.: Harvard University Press, 1963.

Marchand, Leslie (ed.), *Born for Opposition: Byron's Letters and Journals*, vol. 8. London: John Murray, 1978).

—*Byron's Poetry: A Critical Introduction*. Cambridge, Mass.: Harvard University Press, 1965.

Markley, Robert. 'Newton, Corruption, and the Tradition of Universal History', in James E. Force and Richard H. Popkin (eds), *Newton and Religion: Context, Nature, and Influence*. Dordrecht: Kluwer Academic Publishers, 1999, pp. 121–43.

Marsden, George. 'Everyone One's Own Interpreter? The Bible, Science, and Authority in Mid-Nineteenth-Century America', in Nathan Hatch and Mark Noll (eds), *The Bible in America: Essays in Cultural History*. New York: Oxford University Press, 1982, pp. 79–100.

—*Reforming Fundamentalism: Fuller Seminary and the New Evangelicalism*. Grand Rapids: Eerdmans, 1987.

Marty, Martin E. *Modern American Religion*, vol. 1: *The Irony of It All: 1893–1919*. Chicago: University of Chicago Press, 1986.

Masuzawa, Tomoko. 'Culture', in Mark C. Taylor (ed.), *Critical Terms for Religious Studies*. Chicago: University of Chicago Press, 1998, pp. 70–93.

McPhee, John. *Annals of the Former World*. New York: Farrar, Straus and Giroux, 1998.

Miller, Kenneth R. *Finding Darwin's God*. New York: HarperCollins, 1999.

Milton, John. *Paradise Lost*. Ed. Scott Elledge. New York: Norton, 2nd edn 1993.

Montagu, Ashley (ed.). *Science and Creationism*. Oxford: Oxford University Press, 1984.

Moore, James. 'The Creationist Cosmos of Protestant Fundamentalism', in Martin E. Marty and R. Scott Appleby (eds), *The Fundamentalist Project*, vol. 2: *Fundamentalisms and Society*. Chicago: University of Chicago Press, 1991, pp. 42–72.

—*The Post-Darwinian Controversies: A Study of the Protestant Struggle to Come to Terms with Darwin in Great Britain and America 1870–1900*. Cambridge: Cambridge University Press, 1979.

Morris, Henry M. *Basic Creation Series* (a series of seven videotapes of talks given at Calvary Chapel, Costa Mesa, Calif., introduced by John Morris and Ken Ham), containing 'Scientific Creationism', 'The Troubled Waters of Evolution', 'The Dark History of Evolution', 'The Genesis Flood', 'The Age of the Earth', 'The Remarkable Record of Job', and 'The God Who Is Real'. El Cajon, Calif.: Master Books, n.d. (*c.* 1990).

—*The God Who Is Real: A Creationist Approach to Evangelization and Missions*. Grand Rapids: Baker Book House, 1988.

—'ICR – The First Twenty-Five Years'. Back to Genesis Tract 86a (Feb. 1996). Available at <www.icr.org/pubs/btg-a/btg-086a.htm>.

—*The Long War Against God: The History and Impact of the Creation/Evolution Conflict*. Grand Rapids: Baker Book House, 1989.

—'Naïve Literalism'. Back to Genesis Tract 68a (Aug. 1994). Available at <www.icr.org/pubs/btg-a/btg-068a.htm>.

—'Reflections on Fifty Years in Creation Evangelism'. Back to Genesis Tract 79a (July 1995). Available at <www.icr.org/pubs/btg-a/btg-079a.htm>.

—*The Remarkable Record of Job*. Grand Rapids: Baker Book House, 1988.

—*The Revelation Record: A Scientific and Devotional Commentary on the Prophetic Book of the End of Times*. Wheaton, Ill.: Tyndale House, 1983.

—*The Troubled Waters of Evolution*. San Diego: Creation-Life Publishers, 1974.

—'The Vital Importance of Believing in Recent Creation'. Back to Genesis Tract 138a (June 2000). Available at <www.icr.org/pubs/btg-a/btg-138a.htm>.

Morris, Henry (ed.). *Scientific Creationism*. General edn. El Cajon, Calif.: Master Books, 2nd edn 1985 (1974).

Mungello, David. *Curious Land: Jesuit Accommodation and the Origins of Sinology*. Honolulu: University of Hawaii Press, 1985.

Neil, William. 'The Criticism and Theological Use of the Bible 1700–1950', in S. L. Greenslade (ed.), *The Cambridge History of the Bible*, vol. 3. Cambridge: Cambridge University Press, 1963, pp. 238–93.

Nicolson, Marjorie. *Mountain Gloom and Mountain Glory: The Development of the Aesthetics of the Infinite*. New York: Norton, 1959.

Noll, Mark. *America's God: From Jonathan Edwards to Abraham Lincoln*. Oxford: Oxford University Press, 2002.

Numbers, Ronald L. *The Creationists: The Evolution of Scientific Creationism*. Berkeley: University of California Press, 1992.

—*Darwinism Comes to America*. Cambridge, Mass.: Harvard University Press, 1998.

Orr, H. Allen. 'Devolution', *The New Yorker*, 30 May 2005, pp. 40–52.

Overton, William R. 'Decision of the Court', in Ashley Montagu (ed.), *Science and Creationism*. Oxford: Oxford University Press, 1984, pp. 365–97.

Paine, Thomas. *The Age of Reason*. Amherst, NY: Prometheus Books, 1984 (1794–95).

Paley, William. *Natural Theology: Selections*. Ed. Frederick Ferré. Indianapolis: Bobbs-Merrill, 1963.

Pennock, Robert T. 'Naturalism, Evidence, and Creationism: The Case of Phillip Johnson', in Robert T. Pennock (ed.), *Intelligent Design Creationism and its Critics: Philosophical, Theological, and Scientific Perspectives*. Cambridge, Mass.: MIT Press, 2001, pp. 77–97.

—*Tower of Babel: The Evidence Against the New Creationism*. Cambridge, Mass.: MIT Press, 1999.

Pennock, Robert T. (ed.). *Intelligent Design Creationism and its Critics: Philosophical, Theological, and Scientific Perspectives*. Cambridge, Mass.: MIT Press, 2001.

Pompa, Leon. *Vico: A Study of the 'New Science'*. 2nd edn. Cambridge: Cambridge University Press, 1990.

Popkin, Richard. *The History of Scepticism from Erasmus to Spinoza*. Berkeley and Los Angeles: University of California Press, 1979.

—*Isaac La Peyrère: His Life, Work, and Influence*. Leiden: E. J. Brill, 1987.

Preus, J. Samuel. 'The Bible and Religion in the Century of Genius. Part II: The Rise and Fall of the Bible', *Religion* 28 (1998), pp. 15–27.

—*Spinoza and the Irrelevance of Biblical Authority*. Cambridge: Cambridge University Press, 2001.

Proudfoot, Wayne. *Religious Experience*. Berkeley and Los Angeles: University of California Press, 1985.

Rainger, Ronald. *An Agenda for Antiquity: Henry Fairfield Osborn and Vertebrate Paleontology at the American Museum of Natural History, 1890–1935*. Tuscaloosa, Ala.: University of Alabama Press, 1991.

Ray, John. *The Wisdom of God Manifested in the Works of the Creation*. Repr. Hildesheim and New York: Georg Olms Verlag, 1974 (1690).

Reventlow, Henning Graf. *The Authority of the Bible and the Rise of the Modern World*. Trans. John Bowden. Philadelphia: Fortress Press, 1985.

Riley, William Bell. *The Antievolution Pamphlets of William Bell Riley*. Ed. William Vance Trollinger, Jr. New York: Garland Publishing, 1995.

—*The Finality of the Higher Criticism, or, The Theory of Evolution and False Theology*. Repr. New York: Garland Publishing, 1988 (1909).

Roberts, Jon H. 'Darwinism, American Protestant Thinkers, and the Puzzle of Motivation', in

Ronald Numbers and John Stenhouse (eds), *Disseminating Darwinism: The Role of Place, Race, Religion, and Gender*. Cambridge: Cambridge University Press, 1999, pp. 145–72.

—*Darwinism and the Divine in America: Protestant Intellectuals and Organic Evolution, 1859–1900*. Madison, Wisc.: University of Wisconsin Press, 1988.

Roger, Jacques. *Buffon: A Life in Natural History*. Trans. S. L. Bonnefoi. Ithaca, NY: Cornell University Press, 1997.

Rogerson, John. *Old Testament Criticism in the Nineteenth Century: England and Germany*. London: SPCK, 1984.

Root-Bernstein, Robert. 'On Defining a Scientific Theory: Creationism Considered', in Ashley Montagu (ed.), *Science and Creationism*. Oxford: Oxford University Press, 1984, pp. 64–94.

Rossi, Paolo. *The Dark Abyss of Time: The History of the Earth and the History of Nations from Hooke to Vico*. Trans. Lydia Cochrane. Chicago: University of Chicago Press, 1984.

—*Francis Bacon: From Magic to Science*. Trans. Sacha Rabinovich. Chicago: University of Chicago Press, 1978.

Rudwick, Martin J. S. *Georges Cuvier, Fossil Bones, and Geological Catastrophes*. Chicago: University of Chicago Press, 1997.

—*The Great Devonian Controversy: The Shaping of Scientific Knowledge among Gentlemanly Specialists*. Chicago: University of Chicago Press, 1985.

—*The Meaning of Fossils: Episodes in the History of Palaeontology*. 2nd edn. Chicago: University of Chicago Press, 1976.

—'Minerals, Strata, and Fossils', in Nick Jardine, James Secord and Emma Spary (eds), *Cultures of Natural History*. Cambridge: Cambridge University Press, 1996, pp. 266–86.

—*Scenes from Deep Time: Early Pictorial Representations of the Prehistoric World*. Chicago: University of Chicago Press, 1992.

Rupke, Nicolaas. *Richard Owen: Victorian Naturalist*. New Haven: Yale University Press, 1994.

Ruse, Michael. *The Creation–Evolution Struggle*. Cambridge, Mass.: Harvard University Press, 2005.

—*Darwin and Design: Does Evolution Have a Purpose?* Cambridge, Mass.: Harvard University Press, 2003.

—*The Evolution Wars: A Guide to the Debates*. Santa Barbara, Calif.: ABC-CLIO, 2000.

Scholder, Klaus. *The Birth of Modern Critical Theology: Origins and Problems of Biblical Criticism in the Seventeenth Century*. Trans. John Bowden. London: SCM Press, 1990.

Science and Creationism: A View from the National Academy of Sciences. 2nd edn. Washington, DC: National Academy Press, 1999.

Secord, James A. *Victorian Sensation: The Extraordinary Publication, Reception, and Secret Authorship of* Vestiges of the Natural History of Creation. Chicago: University of Chicago Press, 2000.

Shaffer, Elinor S. *'Kubla Khan' and* The Fall of Jerusalem: *The Mythological School in Biblical Criticism and Secular Literature, 1770–1880*. Cambridge: Cambridge University Press, 1980.

Shanks, Niall. *God, The Devil, and Darwin: A Critique of Intelligent Design Theory*. Oxford: Oxford University Press, 2004.

Shapiro, Arthur. 'Fundamentalist Bedfellows: Political Creationism in Turkey', *Reports of the National Center for Science Education* 19:6 (Nov. 1999), pp. 15–20.

Shea, Victor, and Whitla, William (eds), Essays and Reviews: *The 1860 Text and its Reading*. Charlottesville, Va.: University Press of Virginia, 2000.

Specter, Michael. 'Miracle in a Bottle', *The New Yorker*, 2 Feb. 2004, pp. 64–75.

Stocking, George W., Jr. *Victorian Anthropology*. New York: Free Press, 1987.

Strauss, David Friedrich. *The Life of Jesus Critically Examined*. Trans. George Eliot, ed. Peter Hodgson. Repr. Ramsey, NJ: Sigler Press, 1994 (1972).

Suelzer, Alexa, and Kselman, John S. 'Modern Old Testament Criticism', in Raymond E. Brown, Joseph A. Fitzmyer and Roland E. Murphy (eds), *The New Jerome Biblical Commentary*. Englewood Cliffs, NJ: Prentice-Hall, 1990, pp. 1113–29.

Talbert, Charles H. 'Introduction' to Ralph Fraser (trans.), *Reimarus: Fragments*, Philadelphia: Fortress Press, 1970, pp. 1–43.

Tattersall, Ian. *The Fossil Trail: How we Know what we Think we Know about Human Evolution*. New York: Oxford University Press, 1995.

Temple, Frederick. 'The Education of the World', in Victor Shea and William Whitla (eds), *Essays and Reviews: The 1860 Text and its Reading*. Charlottesville, Va.: University Press of Virginia, 2000, pp. 137–64.

—'Lecture Six' of *The Relations between Religion and Science* (1884), in Tess Cosslett (ed.), *Science and Religion in the Nineteenth Century*. Cambridge: Cambridge University Press, 1984, pp. 192–204.

Tennyson, Alfred. *In Memoriam, Maud, and Other Poems*. London: J. M. Dent (Everyman), 1974.

Toulmin, Stephen, and Goodfield, June. *The Discovery of Time*. Chicago: University of Chicago Press, 1965.

Trevor-Roper, Hugh. 'James Ussher, Archbishop of Armagh', in *Catholics, Anglicans and Puritans: Seventeenth Century Essays*. Chicago: University of Chicago Press, 1987, pp. 120–65.

Trollinger, William Vance, Jr. 'Introduction' to William Vance Trollinger, Jr. (ed.), *The Antievolution Pamphlets of William Bell Riley*. New York: Garland Publishing, 1995, unpaginated.

Tylor, Edward Burnett. *Primitive Culture*. 2 vols. London: John Murray, 4th edn 1903.

Verbrugghe, Gerald P., and Wickersham, John M. *Berossos and Manetho, Introduced and Translated*. Ann Arbor: University of Michigan Press, 1996.

Verne, Jules. *Voyage to the Centre of the Earth*, in *Works of Jules Verne*, vol. 2. Ed. Charles Horne. New York: Vincent Peake and Co., 1900 (1864).

Vico, Giambattista. *The New Science of Giambattista Vico*. Ed. T. H. Bergin and M. H. Fisch. Ithaca, NY: Cornell University Press, 1984.

Wacker, Grant. 'The Demise of Biblical Civilization', in Nathan Hatch and Mark Noll (eds), *The Bible in America: Essays in Cultural History*. New York: Oxford University Press, 1982, pp. 121–38.

Walker, Daniel Pickering. *The Ancient Theology*. Ithaca, NY: Cornell University Press, 1972.

Weber, Timothy. 'The Two-Edged Sword: The Fundamentalist Use of the Bible', in Nathan Hatch and Mark Noll (eds), *The Bible in America: Essays in Cultural History*. New York: Oxford University Press, 1982, pp. 101–20.

Welch, Claude. *Protestant Thought in the Nineteenth Century*, vol. 1: *1799–1870*. New Haven: Yale University Press, 1972.

Westfall, Richard. *Never at Rest: A Biography of Isaac Newton*. Cambridge: Cambridge University Press, 1980.

Whitcomb, John C., and Morris, Henry M. *The Genesis Flood: The Biblical Record and its Scientific Implications*. Phillipsburg, NJ: Presbyterian and Reformed Publishing Company, 1961.

Wilcox, Donald J. *The Measure of Times Past: Pre-Newtonian Chronologies and the Rhetoric of Relative Time*. Chicago: University of Chicago Press, 1987.

Willey, Basil, 'Septem contra Christus', in *More Nineteenth Century Studies: A Group of Honest Doubters*. New York: Harper & Row, 1956, pp. 137–85.

Young, Matt, and Edis, Taner (eds), *Why Intelligent Design Fails: A Scientific Critique of the New Creationism*. New Brunswick, NJ: Rutgers University Press, 2004.

INDEX

Index